BREAKFAST AT SALLY'S

One Homeless Man's Inspirational Journey

RICHARD LEMIEUX

WITH ILLUSTRATIONS BY MICHAEL GORDON

SKYHORSE PUBLISHING

Note: Some characters' names and other identifying information have been changed to protect their anonymity, and some scenes have been compressed for narrative purposes.

10 9 8 7 6 5 4 3 2 1

Print ISBN: 978-1-63220-346-5
Ebook ISBN: 978-1-62873-205-4
Cover design by Matthew J. Lorenz, TrueSense Marketing

Library of Congress Cataloging-in-Publication Data

LeMieux, Richard.
Breakfast at Sally's : one homeless man's inspirational journey /
Richard LeMieux.
p. cm.
1. LeMieux, Richard. 2. Homeless men—Washington (State)—Bremerton—Biography. 3. Homeless persons—Washington (State)—Bremerton—Biography. 4. Bremerton (Wash.)—Biography. I. Title.
HV4506.B74L46 2008
305.5'69092--dc22
[B]
2008024420

Printed in the United States of America

To "C"

Peace. Be safe,
wherever you may be.

CONTENTS

FOREWORD
TO THE 2015 EDITION

Since the first publication of the book you now hold in your hands, countless street-level, face-to-face *miracles* have happened at the hands of hundreds of volunteers, to help homeless people around the world, one person at a time.

Letters mailed to me and online reviews keep coming in, which overwhelming testify to the change-of-heart wrought by the message of *Breakfast at Sally's*.

On November 18, 2014, I was invited to be a guest on the regional news show *New Day, Northwest* in Seattle, along with Washington State's First Lady, Trudi Inslee, wife of Governor Jay Inslee.

As the host of the news show invited my friend Trudi into the dialogue, she said "It's wonderful what Richard's doing. His book was given to me by a mutual friend. . . . He really puts a face on the homeless. That it could be any one of us. There's a stereotype of homeless people, and people are often afraid of the homeless, because they put on a front—a mask—and act defensive and tough, when they're really not. All they want is to be warm and safe, just like everybody else." (See *http://www.king5.com/story/entertainment/television/programs/new-day-northwest/2014/11/18/richard-lemieux-author-wa-first-lady-trudi-inslee-homelessness-issues/19218783/* for the complete interview.)

Thank you, Trudi, for saying this so clearly, and for working so tirelessly to help alleviate the problems of homelessness, especially among the young people of our country.

I could never have predicted that so many wonderful things would be undertaken by those who have read this book. I hope you, too, will be inspired to use your hands to help those in need around you.

Peace, be safe,

Richard Le Mieux

and the spirit of Willow the Wonder Dog

PREFACE
TO THE 2009 EDITION

There were thirty-three chapters in the first edition of *Breakfast at Sally's*.

Now, I am humbled to write that "angels" across our country are writing the next chapter of the book by reaching out to help the homeless with renewed hope by giving them honor, dignity and respect, and much more. Many people are doing so because they found *Breakfast at Sally's* inspirational and they were moved to help others.

In Dunkirk, New York, Gregg and Judy Cole picked up the book at their local bookstore and after reading it, asked their pastor at Dunkirk First United Methodist Church to read it too. When Pastor Amy FitzGerald finished reading the book, she asked her congregation to do something to help the homeless.

And they have done just that.

They have opened The Willow Mission to provide showers, food, and shelter in their town and have come together with the Salvation Army and other churches and community leaders to lift up men, women, and children out of the hopeless state of homelessness.

The Willow Mission is named after my little dog Willow, "The Wonder Dog," who you will read about in my book.

In Kent, Washington, Sally Goodgion and her friends funded "Willow's Place" to serve a growing homeless population and another new homeless program in Vero Beach, Florida, was named "Willow's Ark." Numerous meal programs have also been started because of the book.

I am hoping that there will be hundreds of Willow Missions in towns and cities across the land providing the homeless with necessities, understanding, and love.

I know people will "write" the next chapters with stories of success until we have a hundred chapters, a thousand, and then a million chapters.

I must thank all the hundreds of readers who have sent me heartfelt letters expressing how they will never look at a homeless person the same way again, and for those who have promised to volunteer time and money to make life better for those who feel lost, frightened, and alone on the streets of America.

And thank you to the organizations, colleges, and groups of people who brought Willow and me to cities to speak for and about the homeless.

In Columbus, Ohio, I was introduced at a speaking event by former astronaut and senator, John Glenn. After another speaking event in San Francisco I was humbled by a man in tears who told me, "I am homeless and I read your book by the light of a flashlight in the back of my car and it gave me hope for the first time in a long, long time."

In my hometown in Washington State, the efforts to help the homeless have increased tenfold as people open their hearts and minds and take action to end homelessness.

Many people not only opened their hearts, they also opened their wallets. The Salvation Army has received over three million dollars in donations from the many people and organizations touched by *Breakfast at Sally's*.

As a writer, I often find myself at a loss for words to describe some of the wonderful, compassionate acts I have seen—as people come together to do small miracles each day to help those in need.

While I may be at a loss for words, a young man named Jeff Brown, who serves as a volunteer for what is called "Teen Feed"—which feeds hundreds of homeless teenagers on the streets of Seattle each day—is just beginning to put down his words on paper.

He told me: "I'm going to write a book like you did about the teenagers on the streets and change the world."

Seven years ago I was a homeless man. I felt I didn't have a friend in the world and wanted to end my life.

I know now that these small miracles can help others.

Today, my life, well, is so unreal. People from all over the country have tracked me down, called me, sent me letters, and even sent Willow bags of dog treats.

Now, this once lonely, homeless man wants to live forever to help others.

Is this heaven?

INTRODUCTION

"What you doin'?" A voice from behind startled me, and I turned from my seat on the picnic bench. "Looks like you're writin' somethin'." A tall, bearded man—maybe thirty, with a round, tan golf cap pulled down over his bushy hair—leaned forward, his hands clasped behind his back, to sneak a peek at the words I had typed on my Underwood Travelwriter typewriter.

"Oh, I'm writing a book," I said. "Just starting, really."

"What's it about?" he asked.

"Well, I'm not really sure." I scratched my head. "Homeless people, I think. People I've met—interesting people. People living, laughing, crying, struggling—people dying."

"You can't beat a good book about people," the man said. "Ever write a book before?"

"No, I haven't," I said.

"I'm Michael," he said, extending a hand stained with automotive grease.

"My name is Richard." I reached out my hand in return. Michael gripped it firmly and shook it as if he were pumping water from a well.

"Always wanted to write a book myself," he said. "Maybe about cars. But it takes a lot of talent and time to write a good book, you know? Not everybody can do it."

He was quiet for a moment. "Well, what do you know?" he finally said. "I was just going for a walk in the park, and I met a man who is going to be a famous author. How about that? Would you give me an autographed copy when you're done?" he asked.

"Sure!" I smiled.

"Well, good luck, man," he said, and walked down a small path until he disappeared into the bushes.

I turned and began writing again. I was on page three.

It was the spring of 2003. I had been homeless for nine months now and living in the back of my van with my little white dog, Willow. I had begged enough money for a four-day stay in the state park campground and gotten a box of food from the local food bank—dried milk, pork and beans, a loaf of white bread, a jar of grape jelly, a box of graham crackers, and a big tub of peanut butter.

I'd had the idea to write a book about the homeless people I'd met, and a kind man at a secondhand store gave me this small typewriter and some paper—free of charge—when I told him my dream. "Nobody wants these old things anymore anyway," he had said, pulling the red five-dollar sticker off the 12-by-15-inch Travelwriter as he handed it to me. It needed some care. Every time I punched the R key, it would stick to the C key, and the J would always stick to the U.

I wrote for four straight days at that picnic table, stopping only to make peanut-butter-and-jelly sandwiches for lunch and dinner and walk my dog in the surrounding forest. Michael would walk past my campsite each day about noon. "How's it goin'?" he would call out, and I would respond with a "Pretty good" and a wave. I went to sleep every night thinking about what I was going to write in the morning.

But then on Saturday morning I woke up to the sound of rain pelting down on the van. I had taken the thirty pages I had written inside the night before, but I realized I had left the Travelwriter out on the table, and it was soaked. *Just as well,* I thought. *I'm not going to write a book anyway.* So on the way out of the campground I tossed the typewriter and those first pages into a big green dumpster.

I spent most of Saturday looking for work, unskilled labor of any sort—as a grocery store bag boy, anything that would earn me gas money. When that failed, because I had no address or phone number to provide on a job application, I went panhandling. I slept that night in the Denny's parking lot just off the freeway, listening to the "jake" brakes of the big trucks as I tried to sleep.

On Sunday I went to a free meal for the poor. It was served in the basement of a church, packed with people. I found a seat in the back. As I was lifting a spoonful of meatball soup to my mouth, I felt a tap on my right shoulder. When I turned, nobody was there. Then there was a tap on my left shoulder. I turned again and spotted someone attempting to duck out of sight.

"Oh, it's you, Michael—from the campground." I smiled at him.

"How's the book coming?" he asked.

"A little slow today," I said.

"Well, I've got something for you in my truck," he said, raising his hand and signaling for me to follow him.

I stood up and followed Michael out the door to his battered blue pickup truck.

Once he got the door open, he reached in and took out a cardboard box and handed it to me. "It's a typewriter," he said. "It looks a lot like the one you have, but it might be a better one. I found it in a dumpster. A couple of keys were sticking, but I fixed them and I oiled it up good," he added, pointing at the box with grease-stained fingers. "Now you have two typewriters—in case one of them breaks." He beamed at me. "I found some paper in the dumpster and tossed it in there, too."

When I looked inside the box, I found the same old Travelwriter I had thrown away, along with the thirty discarded pages. I closed the lid and simply said, "Thanks, Michael."

"We have to take care of each other when we can," he said. Then he turned and walked away.

It was then that I knew I must write this book.

So, write I did—whenever and wherever I could.

Over the days, weeks, and months of writing at picnic tables, I attracted more and more attention from homeless people asking "What're you writing?" "A book about the homeless?" "Am I in it?" Through the homeless grapevine, word spread about my book. It became a topic at the breakfast and lunch tables at the Salvation Army and at church dinner tables at night. I soon gained a fan club of poor and homeless people rooting for me. I felt so honored.

Now I *had* to keep writing.

I kept writing on that old portable typewriter. I wrote at picnic tables in front of the YMCA, in city parks, in the Salvation Army soup kitchen, and in the kitchen of Bremerton First United Methodist Church, where I was allowed to live for nine months.

I finished the book while living in an apartment the people of the church had graciously helped me move into, cosigning the lease and providing financial support.

On days of deep depression, including the final weeks of writing, I came within inches of throwing the manuscript in the dumpster over and over again, feeling that I was worthless and the book was worthless as well.

On some of those days, I would drag myself over to sit with my editor and friend, Sandy Rice. She never failed to encourage me as she painstakingly walked this literary journey with me, helping me make sense of my experience and of myself.

So, the book survived, and now you have it in your hands.

About 98 percent of the events and stories are true. It's "98 proof," as some of my street associates might say. Some names have been changed to "protect the innocent." The time frame of some events has been changed or adapted to make the story more accessible.

But the people are as real as you can find anywhere. I hope you enjoy meeting them.

Chapter 1

SALLY'S

The first time I saw C was at Sally's.

That's what the homeless affectionately call the Salvation Army soup kitchen. It's near the corner of 6th Avenue and Warren Street in Bremerton, Washington.

C looked like he'd just stepped off a seventeenth-century pirate ship as he strode into Sally's and got into the serving line. He wore a navy blue wool coat and thirteen-button wool pants. His head was covered with an expertly folded purple bandana, and he wore a purple sash around his waist. An old duffel bag was thrown over his shoulder, and he was dripping wet from the rain that often falls on this Northwest city.

It was late December—the 26th, actually, the day after Christmas. At 34 degrees, it was just warm enough to keep the rain from changing into snow and just cold enough to chill you to the bone.

C took a serving tray, and the lady behind the counter scooped up a big helping of white rice, a serving of carrots, and a piece of meat, and she then placed two chocolate-covered donuts on his tray. He grabbed a cup of coffee and swaggered to our table. It had the only free seat remaining at Sally's, as 120 or more men, women, and children broke bread together and gave thanks for what was going to be the only meal of the day for many of them.

"Fashionably late again, I see," one of the men said, greeting C.

"Well, if it isn't Gentleman Jake," C responded, placing his tray down on the well-worn round table and settling in on one of the aluminum folding chairs.

C leaned forward, putting his face just inches from his tray of food. "Ahh. It's 'mystery meat' again," he said. "No one seems to know what it is, not even the cook. It's shaped like a pork chop, but it says *chicken* on the box, and it's tasteless," C added, as he stroked his full red beard. "Hmmm . . ."

"Just eat it," Gentleman Jake interrupted. "It fills the stomach."

C pulled a switchblade from his pocket, popped it open, and began cutting up his portion of mystery meat. "It takes a sharp blade to cut this stuff," he said.

C's eyes scanned the table as he ate. "I see we have a new face in the crowd," he said, looking at me. He stood up and extended his hand across the table. "I'm C," he said. "Just C."

"I'm Richard. Glad to meet you," I said.

"I apologize," Jake said, wiping his hand on a napkin and extending it toward me. "I should have introduced myself. I'm Jake. It's a pleasure to meet you, Richard."

"Likewise," I replied.

"Leave it to C to remind us of proper etiquette," Jake said. "Let me introduce Don, Dave, Stephen, and Lenny," Jake continued, pointing out the other men at the table. Three of the four men nodded in response. The fourth just kept eating, his head down.

"Please pass the butter, sir," Lenny asked.

"Jake knows everybody," C said.

"I should by now. I've been coming here for six years. I'm one of Sally's best customers."

I expected the usual battery of questions to follow: "Where're you from?" "Why're you here?" "What's your sad story?" But they didn't ask.

As the men chewed on their mystery meat, a moment of silence fell over the table. Jake broke it. "Richard, right?" he asked. I nodded. "Well, you should have been here yesterday for lunch. Right, C?"

"Damn straight," C said. "We had the full-monty Christmas dinner by Chef Patricia. Turkey, dressing, gravy, cranberry sauce, and all the trimmings."

"All you could eat, too," Jake jumped in, while downing a sip of java.

"*KING 5 News* from Seattle was even here doing a piece on the homeless," said C.

"It was hilarious," Jake said. "You had to be here. The Major announced that the TV crew was going to turn on the cameras. He said, 'Any of you who don't want to be on TV tonight, or have outstanding warrants for your arrest, might want to move to the other side of the room.' And about forty guys ran for cover!"

"Seconds!" Chef Pat yelled, interrupting our laughter. The hungriest—probably half of the folks in the room—grabbed their trays and scurried to get in line again. "Just meat and rice. We're out of carrots," she bellowed.

"You better get up there if you want more. They'll run out today for sure," C said.

I walked to the end of the line for my second helping of Sally's offerings. I was hungry. I had not eaten much in the past three days. I'd never liked white rice and, yes, the meat was mysterious, but it did fill the stomach, as Gentleman Jake had said. And for that I was grateful.

I looked around the big dining hall as the line inched forward. I could hear Jake and C discussing the color of the carrots. C said they were an awfully bright orange to be real. Jake said that was because they were special carrots. "They glow!" C chimed, and Jake laughed. "It's the holidays; what do you expect? Everything glows!"

The soup kitchen had no windows. The walls were painted mustard yellow, and the floor was dark-brown tile, scuffed and stained. Sally's was once the phone company utility building. It was earthquake-proof. A heavy, metal-gray door guarded the entrance. Two signs were duct-taped to the door: NO FIREARMS and NO DOGS TIED TO THE ENTRANCE.

The line moved forward slowly. "I hope they don't run out before we get there," a man behind me said. "I'm still hungry."

The big gray door opened and a man stumbled in, drenched from the rain. He leaned wearily against the wall and took a soiled handkerchief from his back pocket to blow his nose.

"You're a little late, Andy," said the man behind me, greeting the newcomer.

"I've been up by 7-Eleven," replied Andy, slurring his words.

"Let's let Andy go to the front of the line," the man suggested, and the people all waved him by. "He's been panhandling up the street," the man whispered. "And he may have been drinking a bit," he added, laughing. I nodded.

Sally's was like a fortress to many—the only refuge, the last vestige of sanctuary. There were racks of outdated bread lining one wall and two folding tables with boxes of ripe bananas, red peppers, and cucumbers for the taking.

This would be my first of many visits to "Sally's Diner" over the next few years.

I had seen the poor before, of course. I had given to street people many times—a quarter here, a quarter there. As an affluent businessman, I had sent checks to the Salvation Army and the Union Gospel Mission.

I *tried* not to judge the poor as others did. But I had seen them late at night as I came home from a play or a movie, moving across the landscape like nomads, searching for the basics of survival: heat, light, water, and a dry place to sleep. I had also watched them stumbling and mumbling, high on their drug of choice. And I found myself judging as well.

I asked myself the usual questions: "Why don't they just get a job?" "Why do they waste their lives on booze or cocaine?" "Are they just lazy people who don't want to work?"

I was managing thousands of dollars each day at The Source, my publishing company, when it was successful. I used to send money to the poor because it made me feel good—or maybe because I felt I might be able to purchase some good karma for my buck. Besides, I could write it off at tax time.

Just about every age and nationality was represented at Sally's on this day: whites, blacks, Filipinos, Hispanics, and the Indian nations were well represented. All of their faces were etched with the evidence of life's battles. Alcohol and drug abuse had taken their toll.

A man was asleep with his head on the table, his food half eaten. Another man rocked back and forth in his chair, mumbling about the angels coming to take George Bush away. The man before me in line shook when he walked. A woman in the corner was crying, and the Salvation Army's Major was on one knee, trying to console her.

Many had been soldiers, carpenters, cooks, bankers, shipyard welders, salesmen, plumbers, and artists, I supposed. Now, they were the lost. The rejects.

And I was one of them.

How did I get here? I knew I didn't belong here. Who did?

I felt I was shipwrecked, marooned on the rocks off the coast of some foreign land, driven there by a storm. Had the first mate gotten drunk and fallen asleep at the wheel? Had the captain misread his charts? Was this a ship of fools? Was there a way to hoist the sails and take us all to an island of plenty? Or was it every man for himself? Who were my shipmates? Why and how did they get here? Were they castaways like me?

I had always expected a Carnival cruise through life, with an occasional wind-tossed day. But now, I felt like a figure in a Hieronymus Bosch painting, lost in a distorted landscape, a world without credit cards, vacations, or even homes.

I had lost all hope. And I saw no hope in these quarters.

Of all the people in the room, I must be the saddest, I thought, *because I have fallen the farthest.*

As the line moved forward, I could overhear three teenagers talking about their Christmas night.

"Did you go to your mom and dad's?" one sandy-haired boy asked his tablemate.

"Fuck, no!" he said. "You know I never go there! I went to Psycho Betty's Bar and played some pool and then I went to sleep under the Warren Avenue Bridge." He nervously pumped his right leg up and down like he was dancing to some up-tempo beat no one else could hear. "What did you do?" he asked the other boy.

"I went over to Mark's. He gave me a nickel bag for Christmas. I smoked it up and he let me crash there. We watched some TV. He got drunk. You know how he gets mean when he's drunk. I pretended to fall asleep, so he left me alone."

The teenagers were young and strong of body, but they were joyless.

I thought back to when I was their age. On the day after Christmas, I would be dressed in the new jeans, shirt, and tennis shoes my mom and dad had given me. I would be excited about going to the movies with my girlfriend, Bonnie, and necking in the back row of the Gloria Theatre in Urbana, Ohio, near where I grew up. I would wear my Old Spice cologne and slick my hair back.

The teens at Sally's had holes in their shirts. Their jeans were old and dirty, and their shoes were worn and ripped. They had no movie or milkshake money. I counted the children in the room. There were four boys and seven girls. Three of them had to be under two years old. Their mothers were doing what all mothers do: coaxing them to "Sit up straight, Mary," "Don't spill your milk, Johnny," and "Eat your carrots, Billy; they're good for you."

I wanted to cry.

"Rice?" Chef Pat barked, bringing me back to the reason I had come to Sally's. Food. I had reached the front of the line.

"Yes, please," I replied, holding out my tray. Pat slapped a big spoonful of gummy rice onto my plate.

"Chicken?" she asked.

I had to smile. "Sure," I said. "It's delicious."

"And you're a liar!" Pat said, smirking.

Jake and C were discussing the art of dumpster diving when I returned to the table.

"I found these last night in a dumpster off 8th and Veneta," Jake said, pulling some rings out of the pocket of his jeans. "I don't think they're real, but I'm going to check them out." He looked puzzled. "I thought I had four," he said, digging deeper in his pocket. "Oh, yeah, here it is. I'll bet some broad got in a fight with her husband on Christmas Eve and threw them in the trash."

"There's a good one up near the Safeway on 11th," C said. "I've found some good books there."

I took another bite of chicken and began to tune out C's and Jake's conversation and the din in the room. My mind dragged me back to the darkness of the evening before.

It was a rainy Christmas night. Homes were adorned with colored lights, while songs of the season played on the radio. Willow, my dog, was lying in the passenger seat of the Olds Silhouette van with one eye open. We'd been driving around for about three hours with no place to go.

I remembered the warmth and the love that had filled my home on Christmas night just two years earlier, as I cuddled on the couch with my three grandchildren after a full day of excitement, presents, and a full meal of roast beef and Yorkshire pudding.

Now I was driving south, past Gig Harbor on Highway 16 toward Tacoma, tired in body and soul. The hopes and dreams had come and gone. There was nothing left. Depression had robbed me of the defenses that had carried me through many tough times over nearly sixty years. There was no pride, no ego—just pain.

I had begged God many times since last July to take me gently in the night. But He wouldn't do it. So I didn't believe in God anymore.

I remembered what Ernest Hemingway wrote in *A Farewell to Arms*: "The world breaks everyone and afterward many are strong at the broken places. But those that will not break it kills. It kills the very good and the very gentle and the very brave impartially. If you are none of these, you can be sure it will kill you too but there will be no special hurry."

Willow sensed my despair and climbed into my lap as I drove. Tears fell from my cheeks, and she climbed up to lick them off. "It's okay, girl," I said as I pushed her from my lap. "It's okay."

I called her Willow the Wonder Dog, because she was so wonderful. A ten-pound Bichon Frise, she had been my faithful companion for five years and never ceased to amaze me. Willow gave me unconditional love, unlike my former significant other of sixteen years, or my children, or my friends. When I was down, she sensed my despair and snuggled in my lap, or tried to cheer me up by grabbing her ball to play fetch. She asked only for a little food, a trip to the park each day, and a tummy rub.

We had been mostly living in our van since being evicted from our home by the sheriff in July. We slept in state parks if we had money for the camping fees. If we didn't, we tried to find any safe haven: a church parking lot, a Denny's restaurant, or the Suquamish Clearwater Casino, all of which were open twenty-four hours. We would find a safe spot and make a nest among the clothes in the back of the van; then Willow would do her circling ritual a couple of times before snuggling up against me, and we would go to sleep.

It was particularly difficult for me, now fifty-nine years old, because, you see, I had not been merely comfortable—I had been a *rich* man. Just two years before I had been living in a 5,600-square-foot beachfront home in Indianola, with three cars, three boats, a camper, and all the toys any man would want. I was rich not only in material goods, but also in family and friends.

Some called me the man who had everything.

Then The Source, my publishing business, went under, and I lost it all. The rise of the Internet had been my downfall. But even then, like the true believer that I was, I expected an *It's a Wonderful Life* ending to my hardship. Like Jimmy Stewart on Christmas Eve, all the people who said they loved me would rally to save me from despair. Clarence, the angel, would come to earn his wings by rescuing me.

But there was no Clarence in sight this night. No snow. I didn't run into any big oak tree just outside Pottersville. I was headed for the Tacoma Narrows Bridge to end the pain, the agony, the shame, and the disgrace of this lonely, worthless life. The Mr. Potters of the world had won.

I had tried to find Willow a home that morning. I took her to an old friend's house in nearby Poulsbo. I didn't have any money for a gift or a card, so I made a card from a paper bag to give to them. We had been friends for fifteen years, but that was before my financial fall and the accompanying depression and disgrace.

I could hear Christmas music inside when I rang their doorbell. I waited, and rang again. "Who is it?" Bob's wife called out.

"Merry Christmas. It's Richard," I replied.

A curtain was pulled aside and then put back in place.

"Oh. No, I can't let you in. Go away," she said.

"I have a Christmas card for you, and I was hoping to talk to you about Willow," I pleaded.

"Bob says to go away!" she yelled.

So, Willow and I left. We went to the park for a walk and then began driving around with the last of the gas in the car. The gas gauge was nearing empty when we reached the bridge at about midnight. I pulled into the observation area just south of the pedestrian path and took a piece of paper from my old briefcase in the back seat.

With hands shaking, I wrote the note I had been dreading writing all day:

> WHOEVER FINDS THIS VAN, PLEASE TAKE CARE
> OF MY DOG, WILLOW.
> SHE IS 'THE WONDER DOG.'
> PLEASE LOVE HER.

I filled her cup with water and placed it in the cup holder and filled her bowl with food, hoping it would be enough until someone found her. I cracked the windows just a little, put the note on the dash, and left the keys in the ignition. I took a deep breath, reached for the door handle, and pushed. "You guard the car, Willow," I said, stepping out. It was something I'd said to her a thousand times before on our journeys.

I closed the van door and started walking toward the bridge. I told myself not to look back.

But Willow knew something was wrong. She barked and cried like she never had before. I turned to see her frantically scratching with her paws at the window, trying to get out. I hardened myself for what had to be done. *She's just a dog*, I thought; that's what my ex used to say.

I stepped out onto the slippery grate of the bridge and started that last walk. I shook as the cars roared past, but somehow I felt relief knowing the end was in sight. The driving gusts of wind and rain pushed against me, but as I found a place to jump, I realized that ending my life was going to be easier than I thought. A quiet numbness came over me. I could not feel the rain or the wind or hear the cars any longer.

As I put my hands on the rail, I thought I heard Willow's piercing bark. *Not possible*, I said to myself. *I couldn't hear her clear out here.* The silence returned. And I leaned out over the handrail. Swinging my left leg up and over, I straddled it, balanced, and peered at the darkness far below.

I felt warm, yet my hands and clothes were wet. I brought my other leg over.

Now, I said to myself. Jump now . . . now . . . now . . .

Another gust of wind and rain hit my face, pressing me back against the rail, and this time I was sure I heard the barking; my best and only friend was calling.

The sound of a truck roaring past startled me. I climbed back over onto the metal walkway. I felt cold and wet. I had to go back and see if Willow was all right.

I had to go back.

I turned and ran toward the van. The wind was pushing me forward now and I slipped and fell, tearing my jacket and shirt all the way to the skin.

Willow was still barking and clawing at the window when the van came into sight. I opened the door and grabbed her little body and clutched her close. She was panting. Her heart was pounding. Mine was, too.

"You okay?" A voice startled me back to reality. It was C. He was standing behind me with his hand on my shoulder. "You left us for a while," he said.

"I'm okay," I said.

"Well, I'm off," C said, picking up his duffel bag. "It was nice to meet you, Richard. I'll see you later, Jake." Then C held up two fingers and said, "Peace. Be safe."

I took another bite of mystery meat and watched C select three loaves of bread from the rack as he headed out the door. I took another sip of coffee and wondered what I was going to do next. I had no place to go. The van was running on fumes. Sally's was closing in fifteen minutes. I couldn't sleep here.

After leaving the bridge last night, Willow and I had slept in the parking lot of the Department of Social and Health Services. In the morning, a kind social worker had suggested I go to Sally's. She'd searched through her purse to give me her last $1.80, which went straight into my gas tank. I had driven here because I had nowhere else to go. I had no bank account (the bank had closed it due to mounting overdraft fees); no retirement fund; no 401K; no home. I *did* have less than two dollars' worth of gas in my car; my clothes; and a ball for Willow.

I took a last sip of coffee and headed for the door. I was blinded by the bright sunlight as I pushed the old gray door open. The sun had returned! It had been either raining or overcast for twenty-seven straight days.

I had saved a piece of mystery meat for Willow for her lunch. I had cut it up into small bites with great effort, and I gave it to her as soon as we were in the van. She scarfed it down, and I turned the ignition key. We headed out, looking for a miracle, because that was all that was left.

As we turned the corner into the alley by the dumpsters behind Sally's, C was standing in the middle of the road feeding the birds. There were about twenty crows and a dozen pigeons feasting on the day-old bread. The crows were cawing as if in thanks. There was plenty for all. C gave away the last of the bread and then walked up to the van. "Where are you headed?" he asked.

"No place in particular," I said.

"I'll spot you a little gas money if you give me a lift across town," C offered.

"Hop in," I said. I had nothing better to do. I glanced in the rearview mirror as he slid into the van. The sandy-haired young man from Sally's was hanging over the dumpster.

"A tweeter throwing up," C said, shaking his head.

"What's a tweeter?" I asked.

"Heroin user," C replied. "A tweeter knows what he is going to do every day: get up and throw up and go find some more heroin. Welcome to Sally's!"

Willow hopped into C's lap. It surprised me. Willow seldom jumped into the lap of a stranger. "What's this?" C asked, chuckling at Willow.

"This is Willow the Wonder Dog," I said. "She's my best and only friend."

C patted her gently on the head.

"Where are we going?" I said, coasting forward down the alley.

"I'll show you," C said, handing me five dollars for gas.

Chapter 2

A DAY WITH C, CAMPBELL, STEINBECK, AND TWAIN

I guided the van down the alley and then turned onto Park Street and headed for the nearest gas station. The gauge was on "E" and the gas warning light was glowing.

"We're really low on gas. I hope we can make it," I said.

"We will," C said.

Willow hopped back into my lap and assumed her favorite position for a sunny day—head out the window as far as possible, with her ears flying in the breeze.

C reached over and pushed the buttons on the radio. "Do you mind?" he asked.

"Not at all," I replied.

"This is the BBC World News from London on NPR," the announcer said. "U.S. President George Bush warned Saddam Hussein again today that time was running out on his opportunity to adhere to the UN resolution requiring Iraq to destroy all weapons of mass destruction. In London, British Prime Minister Tony Blair echoed Mr. Bush's warning in a special communiqué to the Iraqi leadership."

"It looks like we are going to war," C observed, turning down the volume of the radio. Then, reaching into his duffel bag, he pulled out a book. "Do you read often?" he asked.

"I haven't for quite a while," I said.

"What do you like to read? Novels? Fiction? History?" he asked.

"God, it's been so long since I read a book," I replied. "I think the last was *Eye of the Needle,* by Ken Follett, when I was thirty or so."

"Have you ever read any of Joseph Campbell's work?" he asked.

"No," I said. "I've never heard of him."

C then opened the book he had pulled from his bag and held it up a few inches from his face. He pushed the book forward and looked at me again. "This is from *The Power of Myth,*" he said. "Bill Moyers—you know who Bill Moyers is?" he asked.

I nodded.

"Well, Moyers asks questions of Campbell, and Campbell answers them," said C. "I'm picking up where Campbell has just told Moyers that the depth of the Depression was a great time in his life." He cleared his throat and pulled the book close to his face again, and began to read aloud as I drove.

C tossed off words like "transcendence" and "consciousness" and "bliss" and "rapture." I just drove. Pretty soon he raised his voice about an octave and began to rock back and forth as he read. Then he began to pound his fist on the dash of the van as he concluded with a comment about following your bliss and being refreshed by the life that is within you.

I coasted into the 7-Eleven for gas, just as C snapped the book shut. "I've got to use the restroom," he said.

I put five dollars' worth in the gas tank and waited for C to return.

He climbed in with a paper bag and two paper cups. He then pulled out a big bottle of cheap red wine and poured himself a cup, spilling some on his pants. "Would you like some wine?" he asked.

"It's a little early for me. Thank you, though."

I pulled onto 11th Street and asked, "Which way?"

C pointed north and took a sip of wine as I started driving again. "What do you think of Campbell?" he asked.

"Good. Very good!" I replied.

"He's my hero," said C. "I've learned so much from him." C flipped through the pages of the book. "Here! Here!" he said. "Here's a good part. May I read?"

"Of course."

"Campbell and Moyers are discussing man's relationship to the planet," he said, "and that we, mankind, are part of the earth, not the masters of the earth. Let's jump in here. Campbell is talking."

Again, C read; and again he was soon rocking back and forth, reading louder and louder, accentuating the passages he liked best.

I had been driving for about ten minutes, listening to C read passionately. We were coming to the end of town. "Are we getting close?" I asked, interrupting him.

C squinted as he looked at the street sign. "What's that sign say?" he asked.

"88th Northeast."

"We've gone too far. Turn around and go back," he directed. It was then I realized that C could not see very well. But he was reading the book without missing a comma, like he knew it by heart. He poured himself another cup of wine and asked, "Should I continue?"

"That's great," I said.

"If I get carried away, turn left on 30th Street," he said and then cleared his throat again and read boldly on, this time conveying the beliefs of Chief Seattle: "We *are* brothers, after all."

"Here's 30th," I said, turning left as instructed.

C lowered his book and peered forward. "Go two blocks and take a left," he said, taking a marker and placing it in the book. "Now, pull down that alley," he said, pointing. "It's the green duplex with a bunch of trash cans by the door."

We pulled up in front. The green paint was peeling, and the five dented aluminum trash cans were filled to the brim.

"I'll be just a minute," said C, grabbing his duffel bag and swinging the door open.

I turned on NPR. *Car Talk* was on, and the Tappet brothers were yukking it up, making broken-car sounds and speculating as to why a caller's Mazda was sputtering when it reached forty miles per hour.

C came out of the apartment with a small wad of bills in his hand and climbed back into the van. He counted the money. "Twelve one-dollar bills and seventy-six cents in change," he said, stuffing the money in his pocket. "If you don't mind, could we make another stop? It's nearby."

"I've got no particular place to go," I said, and I backed away from the duplex.

"Turn right," C said.

C reached into his bag and pulled out his bong. Then he retrieved a small plastic bag he had rolled up and stashed in his sock, and took out a marijuana bud. "This is why they call them 'glad bags'!" He reached out and took the cup of water I always keep in the van for Willow and poured some in his tool. Then he put the cup back and set the bud on his knee for a moment as he dug into his pocket for a lighter. Willow, always the curious creature that she is, sniffed at the bud and then promptly ate it.

"Hey!" C yelled. "You ate my stuff!"

"Oh, *no!*" I cried. "Will it hurt her?"

C laughed. "Might make her high, but I don't think it will hurt her. She eats grass like all dogs do, doesn't she?"

C reached for the glad bag again. "Take a right here," he said, as he filled his bong and flicked his lighter on.

As I turned right, we saw two police cars with lights flashing. "Oops! We may just want to keep on going here," he said, sliding down in his seat. When we had passed the police, he straightened up, flicked his Bic again, and inhaled.

"It appears that my friend Randy is having a visit from some of Bremerton's finest," he said.

I checked the rearview mirror for three blocks and then pulled over. "I think I'll take a cup of that wine now," I said. "A big one."

C handed me a cup, unscrewed the top, and poured. "Let's go to the library," he said.

I had not been in a library since I was in college, some thirty-seven years ago. I hadn't had time. I was too busy making enough money to buy cars, homes, and all my dreamed-up creature comforts. I bought food for my body, but I had forgotten to feed my mind.

The grand buffet for the brain was spread out before us as C and I passed through the metal detectors at the Bremerton Public Library. The new chefs of literature had been working overtime, mixing similes, puns, metaphors, and aphorisms to produce their offerings. There was Mitch Albom's *Tuesdays With Morrie,* John Grisham's *The Summons,* and Tom Clancy's *Red Rabbit.* The master chefs were still there, too—John Steinbeck's *Grapes of Wrath* and Mark Twain's *Huckleberry Finn.*

If the hungry mind wanted spice, there were O. Henry and James Joyce; for soul food, there was James Baldwin; for meat and potatoes, Thomas Wolfe; and for dessert, George Bernard Shaw. There was always something fresh and hot, and you could get it to go.

The library was another sanctuary for the homeless. There was always plenty for everyone, rich and poor. Those without a roof over their heads could escape with Wolfe, Kafka, or Robert Louis Stevenson and have shelter from the heat and the cold, the rain and the pain. It was somehow fitting that writers were often poor—sometimes beggars, in fact—until someone discovered their gift.

I cruised through the stacks, pulling a book from its place from time to time and opening to a passage.

Stephen Crane wrote in *War is Kind*:

A man said to the universe: "Sir, I exist!"
"However," replied the universe, "the fact has not created in me a sense of obligation."

John Heywood fashioned:

The loss of wealth is loss of dirt,
As sages in all times assert;
The happy man's without a shirt.

I thought about how much I enjoyed C reading to me in the van, though it may just have been the sound of his voice, since I didn't absorb much of the content. I continued to cruise. I picked up a copy of Mark Twain's *The Adventures of Huckleberry Finn* next and read the first couple of pages, just standing there. Twain started his book with a NOTICE:

Persons attempting to find a motive in this narrative will
be prosecuted; persons attempting to find a moral in it
will be banished; persons attempting to find a plot in it
will be shot.

It had been probably forty-five years since I had read those words. I drifted to a soft chair in the corner and sat down, kicking off my wet shoes.

It was three hours later when C called me back from my trip down the muddy Mississippi with Huck and Jim. "Find a good book?" he asked, standing before me.

"Yeah. Still good after all these years," I said, holding up the well-worn edition.

"Are you hungry?" C asked.

"Yes," I said, "but I'm totally broke."

"Do you like Chinese food?"

"Of course!" said I.

"Well, let's go then. It's on me," said C. "There's a place just four blocks away. The Golden Dragon. It's very good."

With our minds now fed, we headed for the Golden Dragon. We entered and slipped into a booth in the bar, lit delicately with a hanging Chinese lantern.

The waitress recognized C right off and came to serve our table. "Hello, mister," she said, bowing slightly at the waist.

"*Ni hao*, darlin'," C responded in Chinese, as he got up from the booth, bowed at the waist, and gave her a hug. "*Ni hao piaoliang.*"

"*Xiexie*," she said. "*Wo hao gaoxing ni ken lal.*"

C then sat down. "Sandi, *zhe she wo pengyou*, Richard," he said, nodding at me. "Richard, this is Sandi."

Sandi bowed at the waist again and smiled at me, saying, "*Wanan*, Richard."

"Drinks?" Sandi asked, in what sounded like a chirp.

"Two Flaming Mai Tais," C said. "It's my birthday! I'm thirty-three today—the age Christ was when he died. I'm a member of the Thirty-three Club—me and Willie Nelson and Kris Kristofferson.

"You always say it's your birthday when you come in here," Sandi laughed, and then she rushed off to pour and blend.

"I'm impressed you speak Chinese," I said. "What did you say?"

"I said, 'Hello, darlin'. You're looking very attractive.' She said, 'Thank you. I'm delighted you could come.' I said, 'Sandi, this is my friend, Richard.' And she said, 'Good evening, Richard.'

"I know a little of the language," C added. "I respect the Chinese people. It is a shame that they don't use their Chinese names—their *real* names—here in this country. They've changed them to fit in. Chinese people named Al, Mark, David, Bill, or Steve? Come on! Many have such beautiful names, too. Sandi's real name is Yee Wong Chin. Her husband is named Hai. He's the cook. Their son is Jian, who is a junior at Stanford University. I admire the way the Chinese children respect their parents and their grandparents. The lack of respect American children show for their parents may be the worst byproduct of our capitalistic, throwaway society. You won't see Chinese people standing in line to get food at Sally's. The Chinese take care of their own!"

"I was surprised to see so many people at the Salvation Army," I said. "I never knew there were so many poor and homeless people around here."

"Ah, the homeless." C sighed. "They should all just die. But they are too afraid to die. They just keep on living like weeds growing between rocks. You can pull them, you can spray them, and you can walk all over them, but somehow, some way, they keep on coming back," he said.

"And like those weeds growing between the rocks, they can be beautiful for a day, a week, maybe two weeks. I have seen them in Los Angeles, Houston, Detroit, and Seattle. Some places are tougher than others to live in, you know."

Sandi held two flaming concoctions far from her body as she steered her way back toward our table. "Drinks!" she announced as she set them down. "Ready to order?"

C blew out his fire and took a drink. "You choose," he said, motioning to me.

"Oh, let's get some pot stickers and some barbecued pork," I said. "Do you like egg rolls?" I asked, looking at C.

"Sure!" he said.

"Okay then, egg rolls, and—ah—ah—lemon chicken and Mongolian beef."

"Good!" Sandi said.

We sipped our drinks, letting the liquor warm our beings. It felt strange but very good to just be sitting there, anticipating a real meal. It seemed like only moments until Sandi was back; she bustled to our table, pushing a cart of food for our first course of the evening. "Pot stickers, fried egg rolls, and barbecued pork," she said, smiling, as she placed each dish on the table. "Would you like another drink?" she asked.

"Yes, please," C replied, smiling. "I need more fire!" he exclaimed. Sandi giggled and dashed off to get our refills.

We loaded up our plates, savoring samples of one delicious dish after another. C shortly sat back and gave me one of his penetrating looks. His mind was rarely idle for long. "Are you a historian, Richard?" he asked.

"No."

"But you've read *The Grapes of Wrath*, right?"

"Oh yeah, that was quite a book," I said.

"Well, Steinbeck had a great sense of history, and I think he would be appalled to see what's happening here and now. Because once again history is being ignored—ninety percent of the wealth in this country is controlled by ten percent of the people. Steinbeck wrote about it." C reached for his duffel bag and fished around in it, pulling out his own dog-eared copy. "You know, even this great writer had to tiptoe around accusations of being a revolutionary," C said. "He could have been put in jail in a different time and place. Steinbeck believed that people belong together and are part of one another and of a greater whole."

C laid the book down and picked up his drink, aiming the red plastic straw at his mouth, then sucking down the final ounces of his second Mai Tai. He held up his glass, and the ever-vigilant Sandi was quick to acknowledge his call for more.

"People are afraid poverty can happen to them," C said. "And they should be. An illness, a car accident, loss of a job, loss of a business, loss of a loved one—many things can start the process. Weeks, months, then years go by, and the money goes out and none comes in. There are about thirty-one million people living in poverty in the United States.

"It would be so, so, so easy to fix poverty in this country. Just give each of those people a hundred thousand dollars. That's three-point-one trillion dollars. That's how much the IRS estimates is stashed away in offshore accounts by American businesses to avoid taxes. Hello? Hello? Is anybody listening? And at what point, to paraphrase Bob Dylan, does the man stop turning his head and pretend that he just doesn't see?

"But that's too easy an answer. Instead, we have dozens of agencies with thousands of bureaucrats spending billions of dollars slowly portioning out five hundred to eight hundred a month so the poor remain living in substandard housing, driving junker cars with no insurance, until all the pride and dignity, if they ever had any, has been permanently squeezed from every organ and blood vessel of every poor person.

"Then, when the poor are down and out, crawling around the streets, hoping to get enough drugs and alcohol to anaesthetize themselves from their anguish and worry for a few hours, there are many who enjoy pointing their fingers and calling out, 'Nay, nay! Look at these worthless, lazy, drunken, irresponsible people! If they would just be like me, the world would be wonderful!'"

C took a deep breath and shook his head. He took another sip of his Mai Tai. "Dr. Martin Luther King said something like, 'We all have a task and let us do it with a sense of divine dissatisfaction. Let us be dissatisfied as long as we have a wealth of creeds and poverty of deeds.'

"Ah, the wonderful capitalistic system at work," he continued. "It is a great system, indeed, in the hands of men with hearts. But it is a system like all systems, where men can enslave men. That's what slavery is all about: men selling men for capital to do work to produce more capital.

"The Civil War didn't end slavery in the United States. In fact, there is more slavery today in this country than ever before. Each week, containers of Chinese men, women, and children are landing in San Francisco, San Diego, New York, and Seattle. They have been sold into slavery and must pay off their debt by working in sweatshops making clothing, or selling their bodies in prostitution."

C paused briefly and looked at me intently. "Take a deep breath," he said. I put down my drink and did as he said, sucking the air into my lungs. "Do it again," he said. I complied. "Felt good, didn't it?" I nodded. "That is a gift! It was free—a gift from God, if you will, or a gift from the universe. So far, no king, socialist, communist, or capitalist has been able to capture, bottle, or control the air. But you can be assured that if someone could, he would capture it, price it, market it, and sell it. Those who had the money to buy it, would; and those who did not have the money would die."

The rattling of the serving dishes on Sandi's food cart as she steered it our way interrupted C's impassioned monologue. "Mongolian beef," she said, lifting the lid and placing the metal serving dish on the table. "Lemon chicken. It is very good! Very good! And fried rice!" She expertly laid out our culinary experience. She handed C chopsticks and then asked me, "Chopsticks?"

"No, thank you," I replied. "I have not perfected that art form yet."

"Enjoy!" she chimed and was off again.

I was still hungry, so I quickly dished up a plate of food.

"What do you think Jesus would do if he came back to earth tonight in Bremerton?" C asked, as he spooned some rice onto his plate.

"I don't know," I said, savoring a mouthful of Mongolian beef.

"Would he come in a white robe and sandals, or the dress of this time?" C pressed on. I shrugged my shoulders, forking in the fried rice. "Would he be white, black, Asian, or maybe look like Saddam Hussein instead of Kevin Costner or Tom Cruise? What if he didn't fit our image of him? What if he was bald? Or, for God's sake, what if he was *gay?*

"He wouldn't have any cash, no MasterCard, Visa, Discover Card, or portfolio of any kind. If he went to a bank and said, 'Hello. I'm Jesus, the son of God. I need some of those green things that say "In God We Trust" on them to buy some food and get a place to stay,' the bank manager would say, 'I'm sorry, but I looked in my computer and without a social security number, local address, and credit history, I can't do anything for you. Maybe if you show me a miracle or two, I might lend you fifty dollars.'

"Where would he stay? The state park charges sixteen dollars a night. Could he go to a church and ask, 'May I stay here? I am Jesus'? Would they believe him?"

As I took a sip of my drink, I wondered just who this character was sitting across from me. Was he some angel sent to save me? Or was he, as the Rolling Stones warned in their song, Satan himself here to claim me for some sin of this life or a past life of which I had no recollection? Or was he an alien? Or was *he* Jesus, the Christ himself, just "messing" with me? Was I in the presence of a prophet, or just some hopped-up druggie?

"'Ask, and it will be given you; seek, and you will find; knock, and it will be opened to you.' That's what Jesus said. What doors would be opened to him?" he asked.

"The Salvation Army—Sally's?" I guessed.

"That's about all," C said. "Unless he saw Tony Robbins' TV formula to become a millionaire and started selling miracles to the rich at twenty-thousand dollars a pop. He could go on *Regis*, *Oprah*, maybe get an interview with Bill Moyers, or go on *Nightline*. Or joust with the nonbelievers on *Jerry Springer*! Think of the book deals! He could write a book titled *I'm Baaaaack!*

"He could have his own television show: '*Jesus*—I just cured the sick and made the blind see, and now I'm going to Disneyland.' Would he have to live in a bastion surrounded by a large electric fence with round-the-clock security guards to protect him from those who wished to do him harm, or to keep the press and the paparazzi at bay?"

I must have looked a little worried, because C laughed and said, "I'm being facetious." He paused, then interjected, "Would you pass me the egg rolls?"

"Sure," I said. "Everything is so delicious. Thank you."

But C wasn't finished with his Jesus fantasy yet. "You know, it's my guess that he hasn't changed much in two thousand years and would do pretty much the same thing he did last time: minister to the poor, heal the sick, and console the brokenhearted. He would go to the streets to feed the hungry and to clothe the cold.

"He would ask why there are so many with so little, and so few with so much, and why, in such a land of plenty, people are begging in the streets and children are shivering in the cold.

"He would be homeless.

"With no money and with no army to protect him, the same thing that happened two thousand years ago would happen again. Those who wanted control over the people would see him as a threat. They would conspire against him. He would be charged with some crime and put in jail."

C stopped talking. Sandi looked our way to see if C was okay. He was getting tired.

"You know," C said, finally, "there hasn't been a great writer since Steinbeck or Thomas Mann. Steinbeck thought that the writer must set down his time 'as he can understand it' and that he should 'serve as the watchdog of society . . . to satirize its silliness, to attack its injustices, to stigmatize its faults.' If you wrote a book, could you do that?" he asked.

"I don't know," I responded. "I don't think so."

"Today's writers are not even writers!" C was raising his voice again. "They are manipulators! It's been ingrained in them, taught in journalism school: Write what you know they want to read, what they agree with;

run it through Microsoft Word; don't preach to them; try to touch their emotions. Hell! I say witness! Write what you see! *Witness!* And it *will* be read."

Sandi brought a moment of cheer to our table with her smile and the warmth of two more flaming drinks. She also deposited a handful of fortune cookies. "Drinks and good fortune," she said, as she quickly moved on to help other guests.

C stood up. "Hey, let's take these with us," he said, picking up his drink.

"Wait," he said, setting his glass down. "I forgot this." He picked up the dinner tab, pulled it close to his face. and squinted. He reached into his duffel bag and pulled out a roll of bills, peeled off a few, and put them on the table. "While I'm at it, here's a little for running me around today." He handed me two ten-dollar bills.

"Thanks," I said, shocked. "Normally I would not take it, or let you pay for dinner either. But I am so broke. I—well, I'll pay you back—someday," I stammered.

"Just buy someone else dinner some time when they really need it," he said, nonchalantly picking up his glass again and heading for the door.

I wondered where C got his wad of bills. But it was not my business, and I sure needed that twenty.

It seemed bizarre walking out of a bar with drinks in hand, but C was an unusual person, and Sandi didn't seem to care.

"*Pingan,*" she said, and bowed as C headed for the door.

"*Pingan,*" C responded, and bowed to her.

"What does that mean?" I asked C as we climbed into the van.

"*Pingan?*" he asked.

"Yeah," I nodded.

"It means 'peaceful, safe,'" C said, stoking his marijuana pipe. Then he flicked his lighter on and took a hit. "Would you kindly take me home, sir? I'm getting sleepy."

"Which way?" I asked.

"I live in my RV, which I call the Armadillo, just two blocks south of the hospital. Do you know where the hospital is?"

"I do," I said.

It was then that I realized that I, who had not had so much as a parking ticket in some three years, was driving around with two formerly flaming drinks in the cup holders, while C was smoking pot and Willow was still high. I had no insurance, no license for Willow, and I was not wearing my seat belt. If we were stopped by the police, I could go to jail for the rest of my life.

Fortunately, we made it safely to C's RV, and he stumbled out the van door, grabbing his duffel bag of books. "Pick me up at seven thirty if you want," he said, leaning back into the van.

"Okay."

"Peace. Be safe." C held up two fingers, and then swung the van door shut.

Chapter 3

THE LADY IN RED

I had noticed a parking lot at the Episcopal church about three blocks away, so I headed back up the hill to look for a place to crash there for the night. The reality of my current existence hit me once C's larger-than-life presence exited the van.

There were a couple dozen cars in the lot when I arrived. Apparently I wasn't the first person to find this sanctuary. There was one spot left. I pulled in between an old Chevy station wagon and a Pinto and turned off the engine.

It was a cold, clear night, and frost was already forming on the hoods of the cars. A hand wiped away the moisture that had formed inside the windows of the station wagon, and the face of a man appeared to check me out. He must have approved of my presence, or was at least relieved that I wasn't the police, because he seemed to lie back down in the front seat.

I opened the van door and began the process of preparing our bed. It was a routine that had a sense of ritual to it—it had been going on for five months now and would continue for another year. Willow would wait patiently while I shifted the clothes and the few cherished items I still possessed from the back of the van into the front seat. Then I would roll out a sleeping bag and cover the bag with a blanket. Willow and I had downsized from a 5,600-square-foot waterfront house to a 6-by-16-foot-long home on wheels. Every inch counted, and at times the placement of things became critical. Willow had to have her cup of water ready in the cup holder. She had to have a bowl of food on the front seat. The keys had to be placed where they would not get lost in the night; I had lost them once under a pile of clothes and didn't want to go through that again.

There was a slight variation to our ritual this particular night in that we were not alone. As I moved our meager belongings around, I saw a small hand in the back of the station wagon making a circle on the moist window to fashion a peephole. Little eyes peered out.

"Go back to sleep, girls," I heard a muffled voice say from inside the wagon.

Willow, startled by the noise, sprang to the window and barked twice. "Shuuush, Willow!" I whispered urgently. "You'll wake everyone up!"

The little hands made bigger circles on the glass to form a porthole, and the faces of two children pressed forward. "I told you girls to go to sleep!" the voice said, more sternly this time. One little face disappeared. The other girl raised her hand and waved ever so gently. She looked at Willow and smiled. I waved back, and then her face too disappeared as she lay down.

We continued with our ritual. When everything was in place, I would always take Willow for a quick walk before we settled in for the night.

"Come on, girl. Let's find some bushes," I said, and I headed toward a grassy bank beside the church. Willow followed along and then headed for a light on the side of the building, so I followed her. The light shone down on what appeared to be a pile of blankets and clothes piled up under the eaves. Willow headed right for it. Then I saw her. A head of flowing blond hair was sticking out from under the blankets. The woman appeared to be sound asleep as Willow sniffed around her. "Willow. Come here," I said, as quietly as possible. She either didn't hear me or ignored my command, so involved in her sniffing that she didn't care. "Willow, come. Come now," I called out a little louder. She took one last sniff and trotted back to me.

We went around the side of the church and found some bushes, which sufficed for our purposes, and then quickly scurried back up the bank to the van and climbed in the sleeping bag for warmth. It was going to be a cold night, but Willow never let me freeze. Once in the bag, she crawled toward my feet, turned around and came back to put her head on my shoulder. When we were finally settled in, she exhaled a huge sigh from her little ten-pound body and cuddled close to keep us warm. I placed my hand on her side, where I could feel her little heart beating.

Willow was truly a special creature. She never gave up on me—not once. She could be a clown, cheering me up when she knew I was down. She would hunch down on her front legs and bark at me, turning her head from side to side, and then jump up on her back legs as if to say, "Let's play!" Then she would run in some wild, joy-filled fashion, which always made me laugh. I often wished I could inhabit her world.

Tonight, the flaming drinks had left me a little giddy. I had to chuckle as I remembered Willow eating C's marijuana bud and C ducking down in the front seat, out of the cops' sight. I marveled at his ability to quote Steinbeck and Dr. King from memory. I could not even remember the salute to the flag or the Lord's Prayer at the moment. In a little over twenty-four hours, I had gone from nearly ending my life by jumping off a bridge to buying drugs, going to the library, and drinking flaming Mai Tais with a very mysterious person. It felt good to laugh. From my prone position, I could see the cross high atop the steeple of the church.

A hacking cough broke the silence. It was a big cough from a small child, one of the girls next door in the station wagon. On the day after Christmas, in a land so full and rich, why did a family with two small children have to sleep in a car?

I put my arm around Willow and closed my eyes.

It was at night when broken memories came to visit. The daytime hours were too full with trying to survive, and I had learned to slam the door when the past came calling. But tonight C's spirited dinner discourse, or maybe the three flaming drinks, had my mind spinning. "Oh, what the hell," I said to myself, and the door began to open.

I remembered our trip to Italy and France for my fiftieth birthday. Sandra and I had never been to Europe; it was going to be a dream come true for both of us. I called her my wife, even though we weren't married. It just came so naturally to do so. We had been together for seven years when we made the trip. The plan was to land in Rome and work our way to Paris so I could have my picture taken at the top of the Eiffel Tower on my birthday.

We were not used to elegance—at least not the elegance Europe had to offer. Sure, we had stayed at the Westin and the Hyatt, but when we were escorted to our suite on the fourth floor of the Hotel Excelsior in Rome, we were overwhelmed. There were eighteen-foot-high ceilings with floor-to-ceiling curtains and walls filled with tapestries. We ordered a bottle of champagne and chocolate-covered strawberries, drew a bubble bath in the marble tub with gold-plated faucets, and climbed in together.

The next morning we toured the great city. It was Good Friday, and Rome was abuzz. We saw the Vatican, the Sistine Chapel, the Coliseum, Trevi Fountain, and all the wonderful places we could cram into one glorious day. Then it was off to Florence on a train for Easter, then to

Tivoli and Venice, then to Monte Carlo and on to France. We walked through the great fields of flowers in Provence and toured the magnificent castles and gardens of the Dordogne region.

It was all topped off with four days in Paris, meandering through the Louvre in an awestruck stupor, walking along the Seine to Nôtre Dame, people-watching from tables at the outdoor cafés, and sampling the cuisine and nightlife at the Folies Bergère and all that the "City of Lights" had to offer. Leaning against the rail at the top of the Eiffel Tower, overlooking the city as Sandra positioned herself to take a picture, I felt like a prince. "It's his birthday!" Sandra announced to the other tourists. Many smiled and clapped their hands as several burst into song: "Happy birthday to you . . ."

That was nearly ten years ago. Now I was a pauper.

But I had opened the door to my memories, and it would not close easily. My mind was off its leash, and it insisted on wandering awhile.

It went back to last Thanksgiving Day, 2002. That was the day I learned to beg.

I was up in Poulsbo. I had used the last of my change to buy Willow a hamburger at the McDonald's drive-thru. My gas tank was almost empty, and my stomach was growling. Desperate for money just to keep moving and get something to eat, I began to consider the only option I seemed to have left: begging.

My whole life I had been a people person. As a sportswriter for the *Springfield Sun*, I had seen Woody Hayes motivate players at Ohio State and Sparky Anderson put the spark into Pete Rose. As a sales rep, I had sold hundreds of thousands of dollars of advertising, convincing people they needed to invest in the product I was publishing. I wore the right suits and ties and kept my cordovans shined and did the corporate dance for twenty years. But this, this *begging*, was far more difficult.

I had given to others on the street. They had all types of stories: "I need to buy a bus ticket to Spokane so I can go visit my dying mother." "I lost my wallet this morning, and I need five dollars for gas." I had always given, knowing all along that their tales were suspect. So I decided to just straight-up ask for money. No made-up stories. No sick grandmas waiting for my arrival. No lost wallets.

I started at the store I had shopped at for many years—Central Market. It was a glitzy, upscale place with its own Starbucks, $120 bottles of wine, fresh crab, line-caught salmon, and oysters Rockefeller to go. It was a little bit of Palm Springs dropped into Poulsbo. The parking lot was full of high-priced cars: two Cadillac Escalades, three Lincoln Navigators, and a bright yellow Hummer. I had spent at least $200 a week there ($800 a month, $9,600 a year, $192,000 in twenty years), so I rationalized that I could beg there for *one* day—Thanksgiving Day at that.

I was wrong.

After watching forty people walk by, I finally asked a lady for help. "Ma'am, I'm down on my luck. Could you help me with a couple of dollars?" I blurted out.

"Sorry," she said. "All I have is a credit card," and she moved on.

A man in a red Porsche pulled in. I watched him get out of his car, lock the doors from his key-chain remote, and head for the store. "Sir, I hate to bother you. This is the first time I have ever done this, and I'm not very good at it. But I am down on my luck and need help. Could you—"

"Get a goddamned job, you bum!" he interrupted and kept walking.

Stung, I wanted to run to the van and leave, but I knew I couldn't go far; I barely had enough gas to leave the parking lot.

I spent the next twenty minutes trying to recover from the verbal blast I had received and could not approach anyone else. But the exclamation point had not yet been slapped in place on my failure at begging. The young manager of the store, maybe twenty-five years old, came out to do the honors. "Sir, sir," he called out to me as he approached. "We have a . . ." He halted mid-sentence. "Don't I know you?" he asked instead.

"Probably," I replied. "I've been shopping here for twenty years."

"I thought I'd seen you in the store," he said. "Well," he sighed heavily, "a man complained about you begging in front of the store. You're going to have to move on."

I could tell he didn't want to hear about the $192,000 I had spent in his store. He just wanted to hear what I was going to spend today. So I said, "Okay." He didn't offer me a sandwich, a loaf of bread, a soy latte, or even a plain old cup of coffee.

I had no choice. I had to keep trying. I decided to go across the street to Albertsons. As I walked back to the van, tears filled my eyes. I remembered Thanksgivings of the past. By now, I would be pouring wine for our family and friends, rushing to the door to welcome guests, and taking their coats to be hung in the hall closet. My home would be filled with the smells of turkey and sage dressing. At least twenty people would be there. Children would be jumping on the sofa and racing up and down the hallways and stairs. The football game between the Cowboys and the Packers would be blaring in the background. There would be a buzz. A younger, friskier Willow would stay close to the kitchen, hoping for the first bites of the bird from the oven.

But that was yesterday. Today, I drove across the highway to the "down-market" store, nestled in the strip mall between the drugstore and the card shop. I stepped out of the van to try my luck again. It was getting late, and the shoppers were rushing to get home to their festivities. I had little time to succeed.

I saw an old friend of mine pull into the parking lot and get out of her car. She headed for the grocery store. I turned my back to her and hid behind a pillar. I waited for her to enter the store, and then I approached a man as he walked toward the entrance. "Sir, I'm down on my luck. Could you help me with a little money for food?" I asked.

He walked away muttering, "Jesus Christ, now we've got worthless beggars on the streets of *Poulsbo*."

I closed my eyes for a moment against the failure and fatigue, and then I felt a tap on my shoulder. "Sir," a lady was saying. As I opened my eyes and turned around, a lady in a red hat and an old red coat with a big brooch of an angel pinned to her lapel was standing there. She was digging through her purse as she talked.

"I overheard your conversation with that man. I hope you don't mind. I—well, I can help you a little bit," she said, holding out some rolled-up bills. Her presence and the offered gift surprised me. I stood there a moment, looking into her eyes. "Here," she said, reaching her hand out again. "Take it."

I reached out my hand and took the money from her. "Thank you so much," I said softly. "This is very kind of you."

"Thank you. I know what . . ." she began, and then her sentence was interrupted by a cough. She clutched her purse to her chest with one hand and did her best to cover her mouth with the other. She stiffened and then bent her head toward the pavement as the cough from deep in her chest consumed her. She moved her hand from her mouth to her bosom and just held it there. When the cough subsided, she took a deep breath. She looked up at me with watery eyes. "I've had this darned hacking cough for a month or more now," she said after she recovered. "I can't seem to shake this cold. It's going to be the death of me," she added with a smile. "I'm going back to the doctor after the holiday."

"I hope you get better soon," I said.

The lady then moved her purse from her chest and opened it again. "Wait," she said, looking inside her bag and then reaching in. "I might have some change in here too." She dug to the bottom of her purse. She took out a handful of change and handed it to me. I put my hands together and held them out, and she poured the coins into them. "I hope this helps you," she said, gently placing her hand on mine. "Remember me. I'll see you in heaven. Happy Thanksgiving!" She turned and walked away.

I watched her disappear into her car before I counted the money she had given me. It was sixty-four dollars and fifty cents. I was stunned! I walked back to the van, counted the money again, and then counted my blessings.

I sat there in the drizzle, contemplating what had just happened. A sporadic churchgoer my entire life, I had spent recent months asking God to send his angels to me. But no angels came. Maybe *I* had to go looking for *them*.

With the glimmer of faith I still had left on that Thanksgiving Day, I said a prayer, thanking God for the visit from the Lady in Red.

And now, in the church parking lot, it was time to sleep. I closed the doors of my mind, one by one, and snuggled with Willow.

Chapter 4

MR. C'S NEIGHBORHOOD

The morning came, cold and crisp.

I had buried myself inside the sleeping bag, covered by a couple of blankets, and thanks to Willow's cuddling, I'd kept warm during the night.

I popped my head out of the warmth to see that the front window and most of the other windows were covered in frost. It must have been in the twenties. I could see my breath. Willow wasn't moving yet. She had squirreled her way down to my feet.

The village wasn't really moving yet either, but it was beginning to awaken. I could hear the giggling of the girls in the station wagon next door as they played some wake-up game that I could not see. It must have involved tickling. Then one of the girls said, "Mommy, I've got to go potty."

"You'll have to hold it a minute. Can you?" a female voice replied.

"Nuh uh," was the response. There was a brief silence.

"Earl, can you take Melissa out?" the woman asked.

"Okay," he sighed heavily. "Melissa, p-put on your shoes and let's g-go," he said. "It's c-cold, so we've got to go really f-f-fast."

"Can you start the car, honey? To warm it up in here a little?"

"Hmm. Well, m-maybe just for a m-minute or two. We d-don't have m-much gas left," he said. Then the engine of the wagon started up.

"Daddy, I can't find my shoes," Melissa called out.

"You g-gotta find your shoes, Melissa. I c-can't c-carry you!" Earl said.

"Here they are!" she said, triumphantly.

I heard the sound of one door opening and then the other, and the father escorted his daughter down the hill to the bushes. "Number one, or number two?" he asked.

"Number one," she replied.

"Good!" he said.

The engine of another car started. It coughed, belched, and stopped, then the owner turned the key again, this time racing the motor to keep it going. The noise roused the rest of the encampment.

"I've got to go potty, too," announced the other girl's voice from the wagon.

"Katie, you should have gone with Melissa!" the woman said.

"I didn't need to then," Katie replied.

"Then you'll just have to wait till they come back," said her mom.

"Okay."

Willow was now awake, and she crawled toward the opening at the top of the sleeping bag. As she often did, she began licking my face, cleaning my nose and my ears. I smiled in spite of myself. "Let's get going, girl. It's cold!" I maneuvered out of our warm nest. Like Melissa, I could not find my shoes. I looked under the blankets and in the bottom of the sleeping bag, and I finally crawled forward and found them under the front seat. I slipped them on, along with my coat, and started the engine to get some heat going in the van. Then I jumped out to scrape the ice off the front window.

Earl and Melissa were just coming back from their potty trip to the bushes. Earl, a big man, held the little girl's hand as they climbed up the slippery hill to the parking lot.

"G-g-g-good morning," stuttered Earl. "It's a little f-f-frosty out here!"

"Sure is," I said.

"Earl," the lady in the wagon called out. "Katie has to go now."

"I-I knew th-that was going to h-h-happen," he stammered. "Hold on. I-I-I'll take her d-down."

Willow was now whining and scratching on the window to greet the little girls. "Puppy! Puppy!" Katie squealed, as she climbed out of the wagon. I let Willow out, and she jumped up on Katie first and then Melissa, wiggling her tail wildly. She happily followed Earl and Katie to the bushes as I finished scraping the windows. Willow was delighted to have new playmates.

"So, it's okay to sleep here?" I asked Earl when they returned.

"W-we've been here about th-th-three months," he said. Earl walked around to my side of the van as I was finishing up the last of the window scraping.

"R-r-reverend Randy has been l-l-letting a-all of us s-stay here, but—but i-it may not last much l-l-l-longer," he continued. "The w-word on the s-s-street is the neigh-neighbors have been c-complaining, and the h-h-health department is g-g-going to c-c-close it d-down. I d-don't know w-where w-we'll go if they m-m-make us leave. W-w-wal-Mart won't let us st-st-stay in their l-l-lot unless we have a c-c-camper and b-buy something. It's s-safe here. We got to b-be careful, you kn-know, if y-y-you-know-wh-who sees us. The wife's af-f-fraid they'll take the kids aw-w-way if they, if they, ah, see us."

Earl stopped talking and took his arm and wiped it across his runny nose. His moustache glistened with the moisture. I thought he looked just like a little boy, wiping his nose with his sleeve that way. His hair stuck out from underneath an Oakland Raiders ski cap. He wore an olive-green jacket with one of the pockets torn and hanging off the side. I noticed a hand-carved round wooden peace symbol hanging around his neck.

"You a Raiders fan?" I asked, pointing to his hat.

"No. I-I-I got, I got this free d-d-down at the Army," he replied.

"The lady sleeping under the eaves . . . is she okay?" I asked, nodding in that direction.

"Th-that's Ba-barbara," Earl said. "Well, s-she's kinda o-okay," he continued. "She's kinda . . ." He moved his hand in a circular motion around his head. "She was a n-n-nurse at the ho-ho-hospital up on the h-hill a few years ago. Then she got h-h-hit in the h-head in an ac-ac-accident on the way to w-work one day and just about d-d-d-died. B-b-barbara spent th-three months in the h-h-hospital and was n-never the s-s-same, you know? H-her h-husband left her. S-she l-l-lost her j-job and her h-house. She, she's been here for s-s-six months."

My eyes surveyed the parking lot, and Earl said, "Th-that's R-robert, in the big n-n-noisy white v-van. He's an-n-other f-fucked up N-nam vet. He's a n-n-nice guy. He just got s-s-screwed over at the plant s-s-so many times that he, he c-couldn't take it anymore and h-h-he punched h-h-his boss. He e-ended up in j-jail. He's a g-g-good c-c-carpenter, but he can't f-f-find w-w-work. He's a g-g-good guy, b-b-but be c-c-careful around his van. He's g-g-got two big wh-white Sh-shepherds in there.

"B-bob and Mary live in th-that gray B-b-b-uick with the flat tire." Earl pointed to the next car in line. "Th-they're still cu-cuddling right now. They are tw-tw-tweeters—you know, c-c-crack users—won't be up till n-noon. They ah-ah fight a-a-a lot."

The cold air was beginning to chill me, and my body was calling out for a cup of coffee and a bush of my own, not necessarily in that order. "I've got to get going," I said. "I'm headed down to the Salvation Army for breakfast." As I started to get into the van, Earl moved closer to me.

"Mister, I-I was w-w-wondering if you might be able to l-l-loan me a c-c-couple of bucks for gas?" he asked. "I hate to a-a-ask, but . . ." his voice trailed off.

I dipped into my pocket and pulled out the two tens C had given me the night before. I handed Earl one of them. "Just keep it. Don't worry about paying me back, okay?"

"Th-th-thanks," Earl stuttered, and then he smiled at me. "M-my name is Earl," he said extending his hand. "Th-that's Betty, my w-wife," he added, turning and nodding toward his car. "A-and those are our d-d-daughters, K-katie and Melissa."

"And I'm Richard," I smiled in return. "C'mon Willow," I called. We both hopped in the van, and I closed the door.

Earl stepped up to the window. "W-we'll probably see you d-d-down there, now th-that we h-h-have gas money."

"I'll probably be back tonight," I said.

"G-get here e-e-early," he said. "Th-this place f-f-fills up fast. Y-you were l-lucky to get th-this spot last night."

As I looked over my shoulder and began to back the van out of the parking spot, I could hear Betty telling the girls, "Brush your hair real good. We're going to get some breakfast." I cracked the window and Willow stuck her nose out into the morning air. We were headed to pick up C.

The Armadillo was strategically located next to Allen's Mini-Mart. There was a dumpster right beside Allen's where C could get a day-old paper each morning. In fact, he could even get the paper from Hong Kong that Allen, who was Chinese, tossed away.

The location was also within easy walking distance of The Maple Leaf Tavern, a run-down bar that leaned toward the road but somehow had a perfectly level pool table. That was the only really level spot in the room. You felt like you were in one of those oblique fun houses with a moving floor if you had to navigate to the bathroom. The sideways angle of the tavern appeared to be about 20 degrees before the first beer; after two beers, maybe 10 degrees; and after four beers, everything seemed perfectly level. The Maple Leaf also had a beer garden, horseshoes, friendly folks, and draft beer for a buck. Popcorn was free.

The Leaf didn't serve a microbrew. It had Bud and Bud Light on tap. Milwaukee's Best in a can was the most popular. And for the connoisseur, there was Chablis or white Zin from a box. It wasn't like Bill Gates was going to pop in on his way home from the office.

The Leaf was a slate-gray building stained by multiple layers of mildew, with a pretty pink front door just four feet from the street. The men's bathroom was adorned with pre-breast-implant Playboy centerfolds dating back to 1969.

The patrons of the Leaf were obsessed with bodily functions. At almost any time of day a belching or farting contest could break out. Statements like "I don't give a shit!" or "Up your ass!" accentuated most conversations that could be heard over the roar of country songs about Texan women with big tits and butts. When C pleaded, "Please, no more flatulence," the patrons thought he was talking about a French beer.

The Leaf had its regulars, who cherished their stools at the bar. There was camaraderie and caring. When one of The Leaf's soldiers was late for sentinel duty on his stool, there were worried glances toward the door.

Disagreements over politics, religion, and whether Dolly Parton's breasts were real, fake, or weapons of mass destruction became heated on occasion, but always ended peacefully.

The harshest of insults were forgiven. They all knew they would be back on the same bar stools again tomorrow—God willing—and might need a friend. No grudges were carried home from The Leaf. The patrons would not have liked the comparison, but it was almost Parisian. Hemingway would have lingered there. Norman Rockwell would have painted there.

Sharon was the daytime bartender, and Charlotte ran the place at night. Sharon was a virtuoso at handling the bar, often doing so with a Salem Menthol Long hanging from her lips. She was a big-hipped lady, maybe forty, with black hair held in a ponytail with a rubber band. She glided behind the bar, watching each patron for some signal that they were "dry" and needed a refill, or for a flash of greenbacks laid on the bar to play the assortment of pull-tabs stapled to the wall. It was as if she could read the minds of her customers as she swiped a ten-spot off the bar, saying, "You want ten on 'Lucky 8s'?" When there was a brief lull in the action, she would retreat to the end of the bar and work on Sunday's *New York Times* crossword puzzle. But no one ever felt neglected on Sharon's watch.

Sharon wasn't much up on current affairs—she didn't know that Dick Cheney was the vice president, that Dennis Hastert was speaker of the House, that William Rehnquist was the chief justice, or that the Pope's name was John Paul II. But she knew the important things in her world, like the names of the last six people voted off the island in *Survivor* and who won on *American Idol*.

Sharon also knew everyone's birthday and that Harold had his gall bladder removed on St. Patrick's Day in 1995, that Helen's husband died the day before Halloween in 1990 and she still misses him, that Jean wears a colostomy bag, and that Steve's wife was running around on him while he was off to the Gulf War (Steve didn't know it, and she wasn't going to tell him). She also knew that Old Bill had a DWI last year, so she had established a three-highball limit for him. She would coyly flash three fingers when she served him his last drink of the day, rather than announcing to all in attendance.

In a voice like Rosie O'Donnell's, Sharon would welcome each patron with the proper greeting. When C arrived, she would usually call out, "Here comes trouble!"

C did his best to bring culture to The Leaf, one day by standing on the bar and reading a poem called "Casualty" by the Irish poet Seamus Heaney. He held the book high as he read. He was belched and farted down and carried out the door, but he kept reading nonetheless, raising his voice.

I found out later that C had been "asked to leave" (and in some cases removed by force) from just about every tavern in town, for a variety of offenses. He and Robert Frost were booted out of Brewskis, and W. Somerset Maugham and C were unceremoniously tossed from The Blue Goose.

Allen's Mini-Mart was open from seven in the morning to ten at night, seven days a week, except from six to seven in the evening when Allen went home for dinner. Allen's was staffed by Allen, and nobody else.

Allen was a man of few words. He would sit on a stool at the end of the counter in his store with his arms folded. A sign posted by the cash register stated: PLEASE RING BELL FOR SERVICE. When a customer would come in, Allen would wait with arms folded while the customer picked out the items for purchase and then rang the bell at the counter. Allen would then quickly hop off his stool, make the transaction, and then return to his stool and fold his arms across his chest once again.

That's the way he treated everyone, except C.

Allen talked to C. He liked him.

I asked C one day why Allen talked to him.

"He's my neighbor," C replied. "You know, like Mr. Rogers' neighborhood." Then he sang: "Would you be mine? Could you be mine? Won't you be my neighbor?"

"He's very intelligent," C said of Allen. "He's like Buddha. When he has something to say, it's profound. Allen just skips all the small talk."

This morning, I parked the van next to the Armadillo and walked into Allen's. I rang the bell and Allen leaped off the stool.

"Do you have any Tums?" I asked.

Allen handed me a package, took my ten, gave me change, and returned to his perch. He didn't say a word.

I went out and knocked on the door of the Armadillo. There was no answer.

I waited a few minutes and then knocked again.

I could hear clunking around inside . . . and then the door opened. Two cats came pouncing out to greet me, followed by C, who appeared a little frazzled and was rubbing his eyes.

"Good morning," he said, his voice creaking. "I stayed up last night reading *Horatio Hornblower*. I started out with the idea of reading just a few pages to fall asleep and the next thing I knew, it was five o'clock."

Purring and meowing, each of the cats rubbed against one of my legs. "Meet MyLynx and Calico," C said, introducing his fuzzy friends. "They keep me warm at night."

"Come in and take a look around," C invited.

I stepped on the metal fold-down step and peeked inside C's home. Martha Stewart would have had a heart attack on the spot. Pots and pans and dirty dishes were piled in the small sink. Heads of lettuce and bunches of carrots and loaves of bread were piled in a corner on top of a mountain of dirty clothes. There must have been three hundred books, many sprouting makeshift bookmarks, and piles of handwritten notes lying on the bed.

A crow had landed on the roof, and its call captured C's attention. "The crows are hungry," he said, grabbing a loaf of bread and pulling the plastic tie from the end as he headed outside. He broke the bread into pieces and tossed them to the birds as he talked. "I've been here since August or September," he said. "I've just been waiting for you."

I didn't know what to say.

"Are you ready to go to Sally's?" I asked.

"You'll have to excuse me this morning," C said, his gravelly voice breaking. "I stayed up too late with Hornblower and Captain Morgan to go anywhere except back to bed."

"Well, I'd better get going," I said, heading for the van.

"I think they're having gruel this morning," C said, laughing. "Overcooked oatmeal in a big pot! Hey, would you do me a favor, though? Take something down to Jake for me."

"Sure."

C retrieved a wrinkled paper bag from the Armadillo and handed it to me. "Here," he said, reaching in his pocket. "Here's ten bucks for delivering it. It saves me some time."

So I took the bag and headed for Sally's.

I wanted to look inside the bag but chose not to. I wondered if I was carrying pot, needles, contraband, or some illicit drug. Sally's was only ten minutes away, and I drove carefully. I breathed a sigh of relief when I got there and handed Jake the rumpled bag, saying, "C asked me to give this to you."

"How is the old boy this morning? Still his birthday? Still thirty-three, is he?" Jake asked, taking the bag from my hand. He opened the bag, looked, and then reached inside. "Great," he said, pulling out a paperback book. "*Rita Hayworth and the Shawshank Redemption*," Jake said, holding up the novella. "Have you read it?" he asked.

"No," I answered.

"I've seen the movie," Jake continued. "I like Morgan Freeman!

'There are places not made of stone . . . Yet, let me tell you something, my friend: Hope is a dangerous thing.'" Then he motioned to the serving line, saying, "Let's go get some gruel."

As we headed up to collect our bowls, I heard a voice. "R-Richard!" It was Earl, Betty, and the girls, sitting at a table at the back of the room. Earl raised his hand and smiled as he waved. I waved back.

I ate three bowls of oatmeal and then decided to take the money C had given me last night and this morning and go out into the world. With my stomach full and warm and a few bucks in my pocket, there seemed to be the faintest rebirth of hope, or at least a willingness to not give in to despair.

Perhaps it was time for an adventure. Perhaps I needed to go searching for angels in Bremerton, Washington. What harm could it do?

Chapter 5

GOING LOOKING FOR ANGELS

A fog had settled over the city.

As I pulled out of the alley beside Sally's, I had no idea where I was going or what I was going to do. I was just going for a ride, with no destination. In a few blocks I came to a T junction; most of the cars turned left, so I turned right. Big white letters spelling out PUGET SOUND NAVAL SHIPYARD were painted on the side of a looming old brick building on my left, set behind the high fence that ran the length of the street.

On my right was a string of little houses, block after block of them, built side by side. I thought of that song Pete Seeger used to sing:

> Little boxes on the hillside.
> Little boxes, all the same.

I kept on driving and came to another T in the road. This time, most of the people turned right, so I turned left.

As I rounded the corner, I could see the tall towers of a line of old aircraft carriers in the distance. I slowed down as I got closer. They were mammoth World War II–era ships. They sat in the harbor side by side—gray ghosts from another time and place. The traffic just whizzed past them, drivers changing lanes as if they were in the final lap of the Daytona 500.

It was a dumping ground for the old ships.

Stray thoughts continued to rattle around in my brain. I wondered if I was alive. Perhaps I had succeeded in my leap from the bridge and this was just some dream in the final stage of dying. Perhaps I was a ghost.

The sound of a horn directly behind me verified that I was still among the living. Looking in my rearview mirror, I saw the face of a young man. I could see his eyes as he brought his Ford truck within inches of my bumper, yelling obscenities and flicking his cigarette ash out the window. He pulled out to pass me, the blaring music from his stereo jarring my fragile nerves.

Three other vehicles passed by me, including the ice-cream wagon, bellowing its *doodilly, doodilly* tune. The driver gave me the finger.

The road I was on branched up ahead into two freeway entrances, one heading north (but I didn't have enough gas to go far that way) and the other heading south toward the Tacoma Narrows Bridge (and I couldn't face seeing that again today). I pulled off to the side of the road, rolled down my window, and turned off the engine.

I stared out at the ships. I remembered one of my friends telling me about them a few years ago when we were on our way for a round of golf. This was a graveyard, all right. Like those old iron hulks, I seemed to be trapped in not-quite-life.

We had driven past Bremerton a number of times, my affluent golf buddies and I, on the way to a well-manicured course called Gold Mountain. With my polished Ping Zing golf clubs in the back of the van, Mark, Ted, Steve, and I would cruise along.

We were an odd foursome: Mark and I were staunch Republicans, and Steve and Ted were dedicated Democrats. We would jab at each other in political swordplay, but we also knew when to stop—just before drawing blood. We were linked together in our worship of the god of golf at least once a week.

One morning we exited at the cloverleaf just on the edge of the city and drove to a local restaurant for breakfast before hitting the links. We swung into a parking place right near the door. As we got out, I locked the doors with my key-chain remote. "The van still running pretty good?" Ted asked.

"Sure is," I replied.

"What did Danny DeVito call that type of van in *Get Shorty*?" Ted asked.

"The Cadillac of minivans," I replied. We went into the bar adjoining the dining area and sat down.

The waitress stepped up right behind us, menus in hand. She knew good tippers when she saw them; she could tell by our attire. I was sporting my tan $250 Mephisto loafers and a $125 Cutter and Buck polo shirt. Steve, a tall, sandy-haired attorney, was pure Johnston and Murphy, and Mark, an insurance salesman, wore his Dockers golf ensemble—shirt, pants, and belt. Ted, a contractor, was a Calloway man, with the logo stitched on the breast pocket of his shirt, on the wallet pocket of his blue pants, and even on his socks. All together, we could have stepped right off the pages of *Golf Magazine*.

I scooted into a seat of the booth that faced out to the busy street and glanced at my Rolex. "What's our tee time?" I asked.

"We're up at 12:05," answered Steve. "We've got plenty of time."

"Then I'll have a Bloody Mary to get me rolling," I said to the waitress.

She nodded in response to my order. "You headed for the golf course?" she asked, handing each of us a menu.

"How did you guess?" Mark smiled. "I think I'll have a Bloody Mary, too."

"And you two gentlemen?" the waitress asked Ted and Steve.

"Just coffee for me," Steve said.

"Coffee for me, too," Ted replied, opening his menu.

"I recommend the Eggs Benedict here," Ted said.

"You've eaten here before?" I asked.

"Yeah, I've been in a few times when I've been down here bidding on some projects," he said.

"Did you land any of those bids?" Steve asked.

"No," Ted said. "Actually, good jobs are few and far between down here. When they built the mall up the highway, the city began a slow death. First the Sears and then the Penney's closed. It's like a ghost town now." He nodded toward the downtown area. "There's lots of bums wandering around town during the day. Some call it 'Bummertown.' And at night you really don't want to go down there. Lots of homeless people begging for money to buy booze; lots of druggies, too. There's meth everywhere, and it's pretty rough. You could get killed."

"Well, it's obvious you're not working for the Bremerton Chamber of Commerce," I laughed.

Two waitresses rounded the corner with laden trays. "It's breakfast time, gentlemen," one of them said as she served us our feast.

As I dug into my Eggs Benedict I asked, "So, is there anything good about this town?"

"The Gold Mountain golf course," Ted said, laughing. We all joined in. "And that little theater downtown is kind of nice."

I took the last sip of my Bloody Mary and signaled for another.

"I'll take another, too," Mark said, holding up his glass.

"This is a navy town," Ted said, after taking a slurp of his coffee. "The town booms when the country's at war," he continued. "Three or four thousand sailors walk down the ramps of those ships when they make port. Head straight for the booze, women, and cars."

"Hell, isn't that what all young men want?" Steve said, as the waitress came back with our fresh drinks and coffee refills.

"Years ago, the core of the town was lined with bars, and then the Catholics and Protestants began a building campaign—two churches for every bar that opened. They wanted to save those poor, lost sailors. In the late thirties, Bremerton made *Ripley's Believe It or Not* as the city with the most churches in one city block."

"Well, Ted, aren't you just the Thornton Wilder of this town!" Mark tossed in, a smirk on his face.

"You know what's *really* funny?" Ted asked. "Now, despite all the churches, Washington State ranks *lowest* in the nation in church attendance, and Bremerton ranks *lowest* in the state! So, when was the last time you went to church, Steve?"

"I went last Christmas," Steve replied.

"Mark?" Ted continued.

"I go every once in a while—looking for insurance clients," Mark answered.

"And you, Richard?" Ted turned to me.

"I went to a funeral—maybe five years ago," I replied.

"No wonder you miss so many three-foot putts," Ted laughed. "You're not putting enough in the collection plate!"

"Who are the players here?" Mark asked Ted.

"A guy named Bremer was a real estate tycoon," Ted replied. "He bought and sold land and made big bucks when the navy needed a port. He's long gone now, but his fingerprints are all over the city. His money helped build a college and a bunch of other stuff, too. You know, Bill Gates' great-grandfather lived here."

"Really? I didn't know that," Steve said.

"Yeah," Ted said. "He had a secondhand store down near the waterfront. But right now, the city is dying. It's got a thirty-percent poverty rate, more than its share of slum lords, and a whole lot of homeless people."

I took the last bite of my Eggs Benedict. "Why doesn't the city just chase the homeless over to Seattle?" I asked. "Get them some jobs; put them to work at McDonald's."

Ted laughed. "You know, Rich, you've been listening to Rush Limbaugh way too much. You want a simple solution to a complicated problem. The homeless need help—a place to live, a place to get cleaned up, a well-paying job, and they need respect and kindness and motivation. You've got people with broken minds, broken hearts, broken spirits, and sometimes broken bodies. Don't be so dismissive. It could happen to any of us."

That was a thought none of us wanted to entertain. We were momentarily silent, until Steve chimed in with levity again. "Except Rich," he said. "He's the man who has *everything*. He's the self-made man!" They all snickered.

"You guys are just trying to get me to pick up the tab," I said.

"Well, it's your turn anyway," Ted said. He glanced at his watch. "Hey, we've got to get going; the golf gods are calling. I want to hit a bucket of practice balls before we tee off."

"Me too," Steve said, as they both moved out of the booth and stood up.

I grabbed the check and, pulling my money clip from my pocket, peeled off four twenties and dropped them on the table. Then I rushed out to catch up with my buddies.

Wheeeeeeeeeew! The sound of a shrill noon whistle came from the shipyard.

I could smell the salt water. I could hear the seagulls cawing as they flew above the big ships. My angels were not here, only ghosts from the past. I looked up at the tall tower of the gray carrier filling my visual space. I saw the number "61" in large black letters; below that I could barely make out the name "Constellation."

I could feel one of the ghosts looking down at me from the edge of the ship's deck. He was joined by another, and another, and yet another, until I could feel a hundred eyes looking down at me. I could feel them in my being, telling me I didn't belong here by the side of this road.

I knew I didn't belong here; I didn't really belong anywhere. So I figured I would have to keep moving.

Which direction should I go now?

What signs should I follow?

I didn't know.

I reached for the ignition key and was startled by someone knocking on the passenger window. I didn't see him coming, and neither did Willow, who had been sleeping on the seat beside me. My little dog barked, just once; then she jumped up to put her front paws on the window.

A tall young man peered in, and I pushed the button to roll the window down. "Pardon me," he began. "Could you possibly give me a ride into downtown?"

I turned and looked straight ahead before answering. I saw the big green sign with white letters just ahead: TACOMA NARROWS BRIDGE—31 MILES.

"Sure," I said. "Hop in."

He opened the door and slid into the passenger seat.

I looked in the rearview mirror to check for traffic. It was clear. As I began a wide U-turn, the young man asked, "Do you know where the Salvation Army is?"

"I do," I replied.

"Well, my dad just kicked me out, and someone told me they have food there. Do you think that's right?"

I smiled. "You bet. If we hurry, we'll just make it in time for lunch."

Chapter 6

THE FOOD ANGELS

"I give it four stars," I said, lifting my fork and savoring a bite of asparagus topped with melted cheese and crumbled bacon.

"I beg to disagree. It is most definitely a five-star," C responded. "The sliced ham is moist and perfectly textured, the yams are delectable, and certainly you must agree that the spinach dish is simply elegant. I say, *bon appétit.*"

We both laughed. "All we need now is a nice bottle of Sangiovese," I observed.

"No, no, no!" C countered. "A Shiraz, definitely a Shiraz. But I don't think we'll get that here."

C had taken me to The Lord's Diner, a free community meal for the poor, in the basement of St. Paul's Episcopal Church. I had spent my second night in Bremerton in the church's parking lot.

It was the first of many church dinners C would lead me to. We would always rate the food—one to five—like a culinary Siskel and Ebert team.

The Lord's Diner served meals from three to five p.m. on Saturday and Sunday, Easter Day, Thanksgiving, Christmas Day, and New Year's

Day. The Diner was the domain of Delsie Peebles, a diminutive black lady. The regulars referred to the Diner as "Mrs. Peebles.'" She looked like I imagine Oprah will look when she is seventy. She was always dressed well, in a skirt and a floral blouse, and her short hair was fashionably combed. Around her neck she always wore a red strap that held a dozen keys to the many doors she had to open to get the food for 130 or more hungry people.

Mrs. Peebles put out a sandwich-board sign at the corner of the church ever Saturday at nine a.m. A cooking and cleaning crew of mostly older volunteer women assembled to slice and dice. There was also an assortment of men who needed to work off court-ordered community service time. The wet and the cold could come in at about noon and get a cup of hot coffee, as long as they kept quiet and stayed out of the way. And behaved!

It was also clean-up day for many who had no other access to a bathtub or shower. From noon to one p.m., the ladies were able to use the shower in the men's bathroom, and from one to two, the men got their turn. Mrs. Peebles provided the soap, but you had to have your own towel.

There was a sign by the kitchen door that read: DO NOT STEAL FROM THE LORD'S DINER. YOU WILL BE REMOVED. I didn't know if that meant you would be removed from the Diner, or, you know, *removed!*

Mrs. Peebles possessed a booming set of vocal cords. "Don't mess with Mrs. Peebles," I was warned in an earnest whisper by one of our tablemates, as C and I were joking about our choice of wine. Delsie had a few rules: You had to behave, be upright, no swearing, no fighting, and no drugs. And you had to share and be courteous. She seemed to have Superwoman's hearing when an unacceptable swear word was uttered. "You know, there is no swearing like that allowed here," she would turn and call out to the perpetrator. Even the biggest and the baddest would tremble when she cleared her throat. She did *not* need a microphone.

Mr. Peebles was a distinguished-looking man, apparently well trained. He would sit near the window reading the newspaper until his wife approached, and with a nod or a wave of her hand, she would dispatch him to go pick up people needing a ride to the meal. He would always pull a checklist from his top shirt pocket with the list of addresses that she had obviously given him.

Mrs. Peebles orchestrated the activities in her basement diner all day, welcoming her guests as if they were the most notable dignitaries in the world. Each of the tables was covered with a cloth and a place setting for the season. Colorful paper napkins and bowls of fish crackers, bread sticks, or chips were set out. Often carrot sticks and celery slices awaited her guests. It was so nice that if the Lord himself had shown up, he would have been proud. And he would have been welcome, too, even if he were dirty and smelly—as long as he didn't swear, stayed upright, ate all his food, and behaved himself.

The guests were always served at their tables, and Mrs. Peebles was usually able to arrange for some local church youth group to carry the plates of food to the tables. This served at least two purposes: It eliminated the line of 130 hungry people, and it gave the young people a chance to get a "warm and fuzzy feeling" from helping the poor. More important, it helped them learn that the homeless were not going to bite, or spread germs, or whatever else they may have feared.

The homeless were there—like C and me, and the guys living in the woods under tarps. Earl and his family were there, and they all waved enthusiastically as C and I entered the room. There were many red eyes from too much cheap wine on Friday night. There were the elderly, many with walkers, who had to choose between spending their money on medicine or on food. Families with small children, who had no heat, gas, or electricity after their utilities had been shut off, were there. Vets from World War II, the Korean War, the Vietnam War, and the Gulf War were there. Even some of the men and women hiding from the law risked a trip to Mrs. Peebles.

Whenever it was someone's birthday, word would somehow reach Mrs. Peebles. She would demand that we all sing "Happy Birthday." If it was a child's birthday, somehow a present would appear.

When each person in the room had been served, Mrs. Peebles would lift the plastic tablecloths off three long tables piled with bread, boxes of donuts and coffee cakes, dried milk, pears, and apples, and she would announce, "The cakes and clothes are now open. SHARE, PLEASE!" Many of the crowd would rush to get a box of donuts or some fruit and to pick through the secondhand clothes neatly hung on racks or folded on the long tables. Those who grabbed too many donuts received a Mrs. Peebles tongue-lashing. "Now, I told you to share so everybody can have some!"

Everyone was to be treated with dignity and respect. There would be no making fun of the middle-aged, quite portly woman in an ill-fitting flowered dress and jean jacket holding a frying pan over her head, saying, "The Iraqis are coming. The Iraqis are coming! Get a pan. Get a pan!" Or the skinny fellow who said he had found a tunnel to outer space in the woods off Wycoff Road. "You can walk into the tunnel and go to Mars, or Venus, or Jupiter," he was heard saying. "I'm charging twenty dollars a ticket to get in."

Mrs. Peebles had her eye on C. She knew that at any minute he could create havoc by jumping on the table and announcing he had seen the devil the night before and Satan was, indeed, coming to take us all, or by inciting the crowd into a rousing rendition of the hokey-pokey.

There were "normal" people, too, who entered into discussions about who had the best french fries—McDonald's or Burger King.

But everyone knew C. They knew he probably had a few bags of premium smoke in his pocket. But he never sold it or gave it away in The Lord's Diner. "You don't need that stuff," C would say. Or "I don't have any right now."

If one listened, one could learn a lot. There were men who had been to Tangiers or Istanbul, women who had been instructed to ride in the back of the bus in Mississippi, and children confident that pop star Pink was the best female vocalist in recorded history.

My favorite dinner companion was Ray, a Polish man who was born in Brooklyn. He hesitantly gave me his last name, suspicious I might track him down and rob him. "What's the difference?" he shrugged when I asked. "It's Polish. You can't spell it or pronounce it." He was right. Ray was a Dodgers fan, until the team packed up their bags and moved to Los Angeles. "Them bums!" he said. "They broke my heart." He had seen many of the greats play: Williams, Cobb, Podres, Koufax, and Rose. "Hey, can you tell me why these pitchers nowadays can't pitch more than six or seven innings?" he asked. "Don Larsen, Johnny Podres, and Sandy Koufax always finished their games, or else they were mad!"

I joined the scramble to the tables of treats and picked up a box of coffee cake and a box of croissants. As I was weighing in my mind just which one I wanted, I saw Ray guiding his walker as deftly as possible among the tables and the throng of humanity. "No croissants left?" he asked with great disappointment when he reached the table. "They're my favorite."

"Here," I said, handing him the box I had just picked up. "I was trying to decide, and you just made my decision easy."

"You sure?" he asked.

"Well, the coffee cake looks pretty good too," I said as we moved down the line. As Ray bent over, I could see the edge of a plastic diaper sticking up from the back of his trousers.

The Diner was not a stimulating place to discuss politics, but that seemed to be the topic of the day. It was always quite boring, because there were so few Republicans. The homeless and the poor didn't like Republicans. They were still waiting for Ronald Reagan's "trickle-down economics" of the eighties to finally trickle down to them. Diners could be heard saying things like "The Republicans made sure it trickled over to Enron and places like that!" Any Republicans who didn't like the comments usually kept quiet, or moved to another table—all two of them, and their ranks no longer included me. With forty million of the two hundred and eighty million people in the country living below the poverty line or homeless, including one in five children—some in this very room—they knew they had no defense. Tough talk about individual responsibility and making your dreams come true by working two or three jobs, twenty hours a day, were meaningless here. Many had already done that and now were here, cold, tired and hungry.

About fifteen minutes into my four- (or five-, according to C) star meal at The Lord's Diner, a young man came rushing by, cupping his mouth with his hand, whispering, "The cops are here." He spread the word to about four tables and three men got up and headed briskly for the back door just as two policemen were coming in the front. They quickly scanned the room and headed for a table at the back.

Their target was a tall, lean, clean-shaven young man wearing cowboy boots and a T-shirt. He froze, mid-bite. He knew they had him, and he put down his fork. They asked his name. One cop pulled a notepad out of his top pocket and read him his rights while the other turned him around, leaned him forward on the table, frisked him, and put him in handcuffs.

The others at the table carried on as though nothing had happened. They continued eating and talking about the Bingo and dance coming up at the Elks on Friday night. "I'd like to go," said one lady, "but I don't have any money. Plus the bus doesn't run out there that late at night." Her tablemate responded, "That's okay. I can pick you up in my car, and I'll lend you five bucks to play."

"Okay. Let's go," announced the cop, and they led their suspect from the room.

"Whew," said C, leaning toward me. "I'm glad they're out of here. My yams are getting cold. That's pretty unusual for the cops to show up here.

This is usually a sanctuary. He must have been a *really* bad guy."

The episode had apparently unnerved Mrs. Peebles, who was fidgeting with the keys around her neck and watching from a distance. Careful not to be observed while observing her, I cocked my head just right and saw her let out a big sigh and head back toward the kitchen to check the oven.

"There's all kinds of drama going on here you're not even aware of," said C. "Take Sally, the short-haired woman over there," he said, nodding in her direction. "She has a restraining order against Brian, who's sitting way in the back. Maybe a hundred feet, I guess. They used to be married and she says he hit her. And the man outside the window smoking a cigarette—well, he's waiting for his ex, Peg, to leave. The judge said they can't be in the same room together. He says she hit him. Drama, drama, drama . . ."

I excused myself to go to the restroom.

As I reached the hallway to the men's room, I saw a man with wild gray hair lying on the floor, partially hidden by the people eating at a big table. His head was peeking out of a coat someone had placed over him. I recognized him; it was the fellow I saw on my first day at Sally's. He had staggered in, quite intoxicated. I struggled to remember his name. Artie? No, no. Andy! That was it. A lady at the table saw me staring and caught my eye, putting her finger to her lips. I understood and moved on to my own business.

Andy wasn't upright. They were hoping that no one, particularly Mrs. Peebles, would discover him. But moments after I returned to my table, and just as a forkful of lemon meringue pie was melting on my tongue, the paramedics arrived, carrying a stretcher and a heart defibrillator. An EMT ambulance and a fire truck were parked outside with their engines running. Someone had already called Andy in.

The lady that had shushed me grabbed her coat from Andy's body. He didn't notice. He was in a peaceful, passed-out stupor. The paramedics did their job, awakening Andy. A few people cleared a nearby table to make room for the stretcher and then watched as the paramedics cautiously lifted him up. They flashed a light in his eyes, startling him back to reality, and took his blood pressure. They all knew Andy.

"Come on now, Andy. Don't fight us," one of the medics said, as Andy crossed his arms in a small sign of rebellion. "How are you, Andy?" another asked.

"I'mmm okaaaay," replied Andy, softly. "I'm a liiittlllle coooold." His words were slow and slurred.

Andy was one of the medics' best customers. They had picked him up many times before, and it was always the same routine, prescribed by law. The medics knew it, and Andy knew it. "We're going to have to take you back to the hospital, Andy," they informed him.

"Oh, nooooo," was his reply. Andy looked sadly into the eyes of one. "Do you haaave to?"

"We do, Andy," was the medic's response. He reached for Andy's wrist and tried to guide it through the strap on the stretcher. Andy pulled his arm away. "Come on, Andy. Don't fight us. You know the routine." He reached for the wrist again.

"I cannnn waaalk, youuu know," said Andy.

"But, this is better, Andy. Safer," the medic replied.

Andy lowered his eyes, swallowed, and surrendered, dropping his arms to his sides and then lying back on the stretcher.

They finished strapping him down. As they wheeled him between the tables and back to the ambulance, the man sitting next to me said, "They'll take him up to the hospital. A doctor will look at him, and he'll be out by nine o'clock."

I went back to finishing my pie and attempted to make eye contact with one of the serving girls. I needed a coffee warm-up. Actually, after that whole scene, what I really wanted was a cognac. Preferably a Courvoisier!

The Lord's Diner had a routine. After people had finished eating and had gathered some clothes, Mrs. Peebles would bring out boxes of cereal, cans of food, sometimes candy bars, soap, razors, and toothpaste—all to give to those in need of them. Then, if you hung around long enough, she would pass out Styrofoam to-go containers, and everyone would get leftovers.

I got up the nerve to ask Mrs. Peebles why she did what she did each weekend. "Because," she said, matter-of-factly, "it needed to be done, dear." And she dashed off to the kitchen.

There was an unspoken love in the room. I couldn't know it then, but during the next year, her food kept me alive. Her table setting and the atmosphere she provided kept my mind off my troubles, her dinner guests made me laugh, her clothes kept me warm, and it all gave me hope. I never got a chance to say how much I loved her. I was afraid.

This was my first dinner at Mrs. Peebles', and I left with a full belly, a loaf of Jewish rye bread, a cream-cheese coffee cake, a can of pork, four high-energy bars, a large can of creamed corn, a like-new Cleveland Indians baseball cap with "Chief Wahoo" embroidered on the front, and a to-go box with three pieces of melt-in-your-mouth sliced ham which I shared with Willow.

But The Lord's Diner was just the start of C's tour of free food for me over the next week . . . and we always took our "hobo review" along.

"Impeccable!" C exclaimed, as he tasted a small morsel of lasagna at Family of God Lutheran Church on Fairgrounds Road. He used his fork to gently lift the pasta like a brain surgeon doing intricate work. "What do you think, Richard?" he asked.

"Can we do a six-star?" I asked.

"No," he said. "We must stay within the ratings."

"Then it's a solid five!" I announced.

Marianne caught our act and laughed.

"*Mamma mia*, this is *magnifico!*" C said, saluting the cook and then blowing her a kiss, which sent her giggling into the kitchen.

The Lutherans also had clothes, even more than Mrs. Peebles' array of garments. And bread and sweets, and little bottles of shampoo, conditioner, and hand cream they had collected from Best Westerns, Westins, Red Lions, Sheratons, and even Disneyland.

I walked out of the Lutheran Church on my first visit feeling quite Italian, wanting to fashionably burp, and wearing a quite serviceable pair of $225 tan Montefiore loafers with very little wear and a Tommy Hilfiger polo shirt, carrying four cherry turnovers and a platter of German chocolate brownies marked to expire at midnight on Monday. "Where do they get nice shoes and shirts like this?" I asked C, holding out my arm and lifting one foot off the ground.

"Death, divorce—who knows?" C responded. "It could be you are walking in a dead man's shoes. How do you feel about that?"

"It doesn't bother me in the least!" I replied.

On Wednesday night at six, there was dinner at Our Savior's Lutheran on 11th, which specialized in barbecued chicken and all the milk you could drink.

And the really hungry could double up, because the Church of God, a tiny church up on 8th, served dinner the same night—the likes of homemade beef stew with fresh-cut carrots, potatoes, celery, and onions. That was topped off with a homemade dessert—bread pudding of exquisite consistency, not too dry and not too milky. Grace and Gladys, the proprietors, spent the day making the entrée and the dessert. And you'd swear you were being welcomed aboard a cruise ship as Grace greeted you by name with a warm smile. On Friday night, the Christian Community Center, another small church, served dinner at six thirty. Their basement was easily filled when word got out they were serving their delicate chicken strata, layered to perfection.

The United Methodist Church served dinner the final Friday of each month, the time when money was the leanest for state and federal check recipients, and their tuna casserole and baked salmon rivaled any such dish in town.

Then it was back to Mrs. Peebles on Saturday and Sunday.

It was the older women in these churches—for the most part, feisty ladies—who cut potatoes, tomatoes, and meat into chunks and cooked all day for the privilege of breaking bread with the poor for maybe half an hour to an hour.

They didn't seem to need a thank-you.

They didn't seem afraid of being hot, tired, or dirty.

They seemed to be called by a voice few ever hear.

In a few weeks I saw C's waistline beginning to expand. I wanted to laugh, but mine was expanding too, from 32 to 34, then 34 to 36, and—oh no! I was pushing 38! It was a good thing they were giving away pants, too.

Chapter 7

SANCTUARY AT THE HOSPITAL

I needed to find some sanctuary from the cold February rain, which had fallen nonstop for seven straight days.

All my socks were wet, and my tennis shoes squeaked when I walked.

The street people told me they sometimes found protection from the elements at the local hospital up on the hill. There was a waiting area just inside the main door with a television, a coffee shop, and newspapers that people had left behind. The family members and friends of patients would often hang out in that lobby as they awaited word on the surgeries being performed on their loved ones on the floors above.

"Just watch out for the security guards," I'd been warned by Ron, the guy who had told me about the refuge. "The guards do a sweep from time to time. They can spot vagrants and homeless people, and they aren't too polite about kicking them out. Visiting hours end at eight, and you'll have to be on your way by then."

I found parking in the covered garage and went into the hospital. There was a bathroom just off the lobby. I used the hand dryer to dry off my tennis shoes, and then, quite awkwardly, I held one foot at a time up to the machine in an attempt to warm and dry my feet. It was about twenty minutes before I was able to get my shoes and socks at least partially dry, and then I walked out into the waiting area.

It was about six p.m., and the local news was on the old Magnavox TV. A couple of sofas filled the center of the room, and several comfy chairs were lined up along the wall. There were no security guards in sight, so I sat down on the sofa in front of the TV. There was only one other person in the room when I entered, a man sitting in an armchair near the back. He had his legs crossed and was reading a magazine by the light of a lamp.

I looked around casually to see if anyone was watching, and then I slid my right hand down behind me, searching for lost coins beneath the cushions. I found a dime. I moved over on the sofa a little and used my left hand to fish for more, this time retrieving a quarter and a penny. I tried yet again, this time along the side of the sofa, and my hand hit a bigger coin. It felt like a silver dollar. I was hoping to get enough change for a cup of coffee. When I pulled the coin up from its hiding place, it turned out to be a ten-year Alcoholics Anonymous chip. I placed it on the coffee table in front of the sofa, knowing that somebody worked very, very hard for ten years to earn it. I made a mental note to drop it off at the reception desk later.

"DOCTOR HUNTER TO E.R., STAT. DOCTOR HUNTER—E.R." A voice called over the hospital intercom as I dug into my pockets for any change I had left. My quarter and nickel, combined with the coins I had found in the sofa cushions, still left me thirty-two cents shy of the ninety-eight cents I needed for the coffee. I turned my eyes to the TV.

"If you are tired of the rain *now*, we have some bad news for you," the newscaster was saying. "We will be back with the weather report and the havoc it is causing, right after this."

As a commercial came on, I noticed a candy striper pushing a lady in a wheelchair. They were coming my way. The lady in the chair had an IV in her arm. A tube led to a bag attached above to a metal arm and hanger bolted to the chair. The lady had a round, pretty face, and her head was covered with an off-white scarf. A gold chain hung around her neck, from which dangled a gold cross highlighted by a small ruby in the center. Her neck was weathered and wrinkled. I guessed her age to be fifty-five or so. A pink-and-green print dress peeked out from under a white hospital gown, and a small red-and-silver sequined purse lay in her lap.

"How's this spot?" asked the young volunteer, as she positioned the wheelchair beside the couch in front of the television. "You can see your husband coming, through the big windows, and you can watch TV until he gets here," she said.

"This will be fine," said the lady. "Thank you so much. My husband should be here soon, and I'll have him push me back to the room."

"Okay," replied the girl. "But if you need help, just ask." Then the girl looked at me. "Are you going to be here awhile, sir?" she asked.

"I am," I assured her.

"Would you look out for her until her husband comes?" she requested.

"Sure!" I replied, thrilled to be given legitimacy for my presence in the lobby. A commercial for the local Indian casino was just winding down as the girl made her departure: "Come and play the night away!" A picture flashed of a player hitting 7-7-7 on a big slot machine.

"Oh, I wish I could get there," my new companion said, looking at me. "I feel real lucky," she added, smiling. She had a distinct accent. "My Filipino lady friends are probably there tonight, losing all their money!" She laughed. I smiled in return.

Pictures of a news reporter standing on the bank of a raging river came on the screen next. "We have three rivers that are swollen and rising fast," the reporter said. He was wearing a bright yellow rain slicker and was under the cover of a large umbrella. "And there is no end of the rain in sight. We expect the Tolt River and the Skagit River to both reach flood stage by midnight tonight."

"Too much rain," the lady said, shaking her head.

"I know," was my simple reply.

"But this is nothing, really," the lady continued. "It *really* rains in my homeland, Guam. *Monsoons!* Oh, my God—the monsoons. That's when it really rains. But it is beautiful there, too. It's warm. The *rain* is warm. We used to go back every year on vacation to visit, before I got sick. But now, medical bills are so big—so, sooo big—that we can't go. There is not enough money."

I was scanning the room and the entrance area for security guards as she spoke.

"I'm waiting for my husband," she told me. "He works at the navy base and is supposed to get off at six. But sometimes they keep him over. My name is Marcia."

"I'm Richard," I said, nodding. "Is there anything I can get you?" I asked.

"Well, maybe a cup of coffee," she said, reaching down and opening her purse. I wanted to say "I'll get it," but for obvious reasons, I didn't. She pulled five dollars from her small black purse and held it out to me. "Buy yourself one, too," she offered as I got up from the sofa, accepting the bill from her.

"Do you want cream and sugar?" I asked.

"Lots of both."

I set off, grateful for the errand, and returned with the two cups of coffee.

"I'm not supposed to be drinking this," she said, as I handed her the steaming paper cup. "My doctor would kill me if he knew."

I laughed, as a good conspirator should. "Why are you here?" I asked.

"This is my second home," she began. "I have been in and out of here so often in the past three years. They are sending me to another hospital tomorrow morning to see some other doctors. I am going to Fred Hutchison in Seattle." I knew it was serious when she told me where she was going. Fred Hutchison was the regional cancer center, and local doctors sent patients there whom they could not cure. "I have cancer," Marcia said. "They thought it was gone, but it's back, and, oh—worse than before."

"I am sorry to hear that," I said, quietly.

"I have to tell my husband the bad news when he comes," she said.

I sat on the sofa in silence for a moment, searching for some words of consolation. But no words came. "Thank you for the coffee," I finally said, reverting to small talk.

"And what about you, Richard? Why are you here?" asked Marcia. "Do you have someone here?"

I hesitated before deciding to tell her the truth. I leaned toward her and said, "I really came in here to get out of the rain. I've been living in my van for a few months and just needed to sit down someplace warm and dry."

Marcia was quiet for a moment. She said, "I'm sorry to hear that."

"I'll have to leave when the security guard comes around," I added.

"How did this happen to you?" she asked.

"Oh, it's a long story, Marcia," I said with a sigh.

Marcia sensed my reluctance to talk, and we lapsed into silence again. Then, with disarming brightness, she announced, "Well, if I die . . . well, I die! I have had fifty-two good years. I have seven children and twelve grandchildren, and I have had a lot of fun."

"Seven children! Wow!" I said. I had three, though I might as well have had none.

"Would you like to see their pictures?" Marcia asked, opening her purse again.

I got up from the sofa and moved closer to her. She took out her wallet and opened it up to the plastic inserts filled with pictures. I positioned myself beside her.

"This is my first son, Corazon. He was in the navy and now has a good job working on computers in San Diego." Marcia flipped to the next photo. "And this is my second boy, Rafael. Isn't he handsome?"

"Yes, he sure is," I concurred.

"He takes after his mother," Marcia laughed. "Then we had a girl. This is Cristina," she said, flipping to the next picture. "She is a nurse in Dallas. She calls me a couple of times a week. She loves her Mama."

"She's very pretty," I said, leaning over a bit more to view the picture.

"Then we had another boy, Jaypee." Marcia extended the wallet to show me. "His name is spelled J-a-y-p-e-e, but he calls himself just 'JP,' like the initials. He was the toughest one. He wanted to be in a rock band, then a race-car driver. He got in a little trouble now and then. But you know what he is doing now?" she asked.

"Nope," I replied.

"He teaches history in high school back in Agana, Guam. It is a big city!" she said, proudly. "He writes me a letter every week or so. And this is our next baby, Marcella." Marcia moved on to the next snapshot. "She weighed . . ."

The picture of the baby was black-and-white, and it sent my mind back in time. I was about six years old. My mother was making dinner in the kitchen, humming a song and dipping and rolling chicken in egg and flour. We were going to have fried chicken and mashed potatoes and gravy for dinner because it was my dad's birthday. I wandered down the hallway and into my parents' bedroom. The sparkling earrings and white pearl necklace lying on my mother's dresser caught my attention. I picked up the earrings and held them up to get a closer look at the shiny stones, and put them back down gently. I looked at the big white wooden box sitting in the middle of the dresser; then I glanced toward the door to see if my mother was coming.

I was just big enough to pull the box to the edge of the dresser and push up the lid. It was full of black-and-white photographs, so full that several came tumbling out of the box and fell to my feet, startling me.

"Now, this is Joey," she continued, holding up her wallet for me to get a closer look. "He was born in . . ."

Again, my mind wandered back to my parents' room, with the pictures scattered on the floor.

I sat down on the rug and picked up one of the fallen photos. It was of a young boy all dressed up in a wool suit, his pants just coming down to his knees. He wore a white shirt with a black bow tie and black knee socks and shoes. His jacket was buttoned and his dark hair was slicked back. He was handsome and wore a broad smile, as though someone had just told him to say "cheese" before snapping the picture. There were several pictures of the boy, one with him standing between my mother and dad. A few others showed a dog I had never seen. And one was of the boy in a bathing suit at a beach.

As I shuffled through the pictures, I saw a picture of a baby. It appeared to be in a crib and wore a tiny ruffled bonnet on its head. There was another picture of my mom holding the baby in her lap. And there was a photo of another girl with a round face and curly hair, with a barrette holding her hair on the right side of her head. She had a big smile and lots of freckles on her dimpled cheeks.

I knew I was likely getting myself in trouble, but I just had to know who these children were; they were strangers to me. So I picked up a few of the pictures and headed back to the kitchen. Mom was still humming and had started mashing potatoes when I came in with the pictures, but she quickly recognized what I had in my hands and the humming stopped abruptly. "Richard, have you been in our room?" she asked sternly, putting down the potato masher and wiping her hands on the apron tied around her waist.

"These accidentally fell out of the box," I said, holding them out to her as she walked toward me.

"They fell out because you opened the box!" she said, reaching down and taking them. "I've asked you not to snoop around in our room," she said, as she got on her tiptoes and slid the photos to the back of a shelf. "It's your dad's birthday, and he'll be home soon, so we are going to forget you did what you did this time. We don't want to spoil his birthday. But you can't get into my jewelry or other things again. Okay?"

"Okay," I said. Then she picked up a carton of milk, poured some into the bowl of potatoes, and reached for a spoon to stir with.

I stood there watching for a minute and then I asked, "Mom, who are the people in the pictures?"

She was quiet for a moment as she stirred the potatoes. Then she stopped, wiped her hands on the apron again, walked over to the shelf, and took down the pictures she had just placed there. "Sit down at the table," she said. I did as she asked and she laid the picture of the young boy down before me. "This is your brother, Larry," she said. "And this is your first sister, Alice," she added, placing the picture of the baby in the crib beside the first one. "And this is your second sister, Shirley," she continued, putting down a photo of a girl with freckles.

I lifted my head and looked at my mom. "Where are they?" I asked.

"They went to heaven," she replied.

We heard the sound of the front door opening. "Hello. Hello," my dad's voice called out. He was home from work.

"Now," said my mother, quickly gathering the pictures together. "Go give your dad a hug and a kiss and then go wash your face and hands before dinner. Wish him a happy birthday. We'll talk later."

". . . and this is our first grandchild!" Marcia said. "They named her after me: Marcia-Anne. Look at all the hair she had when she was born!"

I leaned forward and looked closely at the baby picture. I had five grandchildren of my own, but had not a single picture to show. "She almost needs a hairdresser!" I offered.

"She takes after her grandmommy," Marcia said, proudly. "I used to have long, flowing hair." She continued flipping through the photos. "And this is our second grandchild . . ."

I remembered my mother's long, flowing black hair as Marcia continued.

I remembered the day she finally told me about my sisters and brother. It was eight years later—eight years after I had found the pictures in the big white box. I was fourteen.

I had been playing with my friends—Jimmy Shy, Billy Caldwell, Freddie Seeberg, Jimmy Eaton, and Carolyn Parker—in Mr. English's apple orchard. We would park our bikes by the road and climb the fence. There were three big oak trees that bordered the orchard, and we would swing from the limbs to the ground below, bellowing out a "Tarzan" call. Billy liked to climb, and we would dare him to go higher and higher, until we all got quiet as we began to fear he had climbed too high. Carolyn was always the voice of reason; we had learned that the hard way, through many exploits that needn't have ended in scrapes, cuts, and bruises had we only listened to Carolyn's warnings. "That's high enough, Billy," she would yell, looking up through the branches and leaves of the big oak. "You're going to fall." And Billy would come down.

It was a hot day in Ohio, and it wasn't even noon yet. My mother had told me to come home for lunch when I heard the whistle sound from the paper company on the edge of town, as it always did at high noon, signaling lunch break for the workers. The whistle blew, and I said goodbye to my friends and raced to my bike. Mom didn't like me to be late.

When I got home, Mom was sitting on the swing on the big front porch of our house. She had just washed her hair, and it was drying in the sun and the breeze. I put the kickstand down on my Western Flyer and climbed the steps to the porch. The white box was sitting beside my mother on the swing.

"Hi, Mom," I said.

"Hi, honey. Here, give me a kiss and sit down," she replied. I leaned forward and kissed her on the cheek, noticing how fresh and clean her hair smelled. Then I sat down on the swing beside her. She told me it was time I learned about my sisters and brother.

I sat.

She reached over and opened the lid on the box. She took out a picture of the baby in the crib and handed it to me.

"This is Alice," she began. "She was such a pretty baby. She was our first child. Your father was so proud. She was born just one month before the Depression started. We lived in Chicago, in an apartment building in the German neighborhood. Times were very tough. People struggled every day just to eat and stay warm. Your dad lost his job and we struggled to put food on the table. We were behind on our rent and feared being evicted every day."

We swung quietly for a moment.

Then she told me the story. My father was out looking for work, as he did every day. My mother asked the teenage girl next door to babysit Alice while she went to stand in the bread line. There were hundreds waiting that day. She knew it would be hours before she would be at the front of the line, and she didn't want to leave her baby with the sitter that long, so she begged from people on the street. A dozen or more said they were sorry they didn't have anything to give, but eventually a nicely dressed man walked by and overheard her plea and handed her ten dollars. He said, "God bless you," and walked away. Ten dollars was a fortune in the Depression, and she went to the store and got milk, cheese, potatoes, chicken, and even coffee for my father. She rushed home, but when she got there, the apartment door was standing wide open. Alice and the babysitter were gone.

Mom's voice was quavering, and I could tell that she was trying not to cry.

"I ran to the apartment next door, but the girl's parents didn't know where she was. We searched frantically for hours, but couldn't find them. The police came and the search went on for days . . . and months. But we never found out what happened to Alice, or to the babysitter." The tears were trickling down her cheeks. "Every day, I think about Alice. I wonder if she is alive somewhere, somewhere out there—maybe in California, or Oregon, or Washington. Today is her birthday."

Mom took a deep breath and wiped the tears from her cheeks. Then she reached over and picked up a picture of the boy. She held it close for a moment and then passed it to me. "Larry was such a joy," she began again. "Your dad would hold him and rock him at night in an old rocking chair we had. He was a strong baby, with big hands and feet, and we knew that he was going to be big and tall like his father when he grew up. Larry was so full of life; he liked to get dirty and would take on any dare. He was a lot like your father in so many ways. He was a strong swimmer—just like your dad.

"I was home making dinner one day when a policeman came to the door.

He asked, 'Ma'am, do you have a son named Larry?' I froze, but managed to nod my head yes. Then he said, 'You had better come with me, ma'am. There has been an accident.' He took me to the Chicago River. Larry had drowned while swimming, and they had just recovered his body."

Again, she fought back the tears. She covered her eyes with her hands for a moment, then reached into the box yet again, this time pulling out the picture of the other girl. She handed it to me. "And this is your sister, Shirley. Shirley died of diabetes." She could no longer hold back her anguish and grief. She buried her head in her hands and began to sob.

I realized in that moment that my mother and father had given me the great gift of innocence all those years. They had chosen not to put the black-and-white photographs of the children who had died on the walls. They had chosen to shield me from their sorrow. They had let me grow up chasing and collecting lightning bugs in a jar, pedaling off to the factory pond on my bike with my friends to catch blue gill and sunfish, living without the knowledge of their pain and anxiety. But all of this time they had been holding their breath every time I was ten minutes late getting home.

My mother finally sat up. She picked up the towel, which she had used to dry her hair, and wiped her face. Then she took the photographs from my hand and put them back in the box, closed the lid, and moved closer to me. She put her arm around me and squeezed my shoulders. "You were born here in Urbana on April 25, 1943. We moved here from Chicago, because we had to leave some of those memories behind. You were a miracle for us, and you still are." She hugged me.

I felt sorry for my crying mother that day. But I didn't cry. I don't know why.

My mother hugged me once again, and then sighed. "What do you say you and I have some lunch?" she asked.

"Yeah," I replied, like the child that I was.

My world changed that day on that swing. I didn't know how much at the time. It was only now, here with Marcia, that I was just beginning to take it all in.

I focused all my attention back to Marcia, just as she reached the final branch of her family tree. "And this is our little Angelee," she said. "She was just born five months ago, Our twelfth grandbaby. Isn't she pretty?"

"That is one fine family!"

"Big, huh?" she asked, as she closed her wallet.

"Yes. Big!" I replied.

"For a while we did it, you know, like rabbits," she laughed, tossing her head back in the chair.

I returned to the sofa and sat down. We were both quiet for a moment.

"They can't do anything more for me here," she said. "I feel sorry for the doctors who have tried so hard. I am going to be a guinea pig, now, at Fred Hutch. They have new experimental drugs they want to try on me. More powerful, they say." She paused. "I am ready to die, I think. I am ready to go soon. God has been good to me. And when I die, I guess I'm going to be homeless, too—at least until Jesus comes and gets me and takes me to his home."

She was quiet then. I was quiet too. I didn't know what to say. Her right hand went to her neck, and her fingers clasped the cross that lay there. "The hardest part is telling my Vonne," she said. "He loves me so and will miss me so. It is going to be hard for him."

I finally found my voice. "I admire you, Marcia," I said. "I admire that—with all your pain, and facing death—you have the combination of strength and grace to think of somebody else."

I thought I saw her wince in pain, but then she seemed to collect herself again to fight off whatever agony she was in. She shifted in her chair and looked at me. She was smiling.

"Are you okay?" I asked.

"Oh, yes," she replied. "It's just that mean cancer reminding me that it's still inside me."

I paused a moment.

"That's a beautiful cross you're wearing," I commented.

"And?" She twinkled. "How about the wearer of the necklace? Is she not beautiful?"

I laughed. "Radiant; glorious; beauty nearly indescribable!"

"Oh, you must be a poet or a writer with such words!" She beamed. "It's good my Vonne is not here to hear you. He might be jealous!" And she giggled.

We both breathed in the now relaxed silence between us. Then Marcia pointed at the television and laughed. "Look at that!"

America's Funniest Home Videos was on. A young couple—she in her wedding dress and he in his tux—had just placed a knife on the tall wedding cake when it proceeded to collapse and cascade to the floor. "And here is a best man that may have partied a little too much the night before the wedding," the show's emcee said as they showed a film clip of a man standing behind the groom at the altar, fainting and falling to the floor.

We both laughed.

"And I guess these two damsels *really* want to get hitched," the emcee continued, as the screen showed two women crashing into each other as they raced to catch the bride's bouquet, both of them ending up on the floor.

It was in that moment, when my guard was down, that I heard a voice behind the sofa. "Are you visiting someone here, sir?"

I turned to see a big man dressed all in black, with a huge protruding stomach and a gleaming silver badge that said SECURITY pinned to his chest.

"He's visiting me," Marcia jumped right in. "He's my best friend."

"Okay. Sorry to bother you," the guard said. He turned and walked away.

"Thank you, Marcia," I said. She just smiled.

"You know, I am getting a little hungry. Are you hungry?" she asked.

"A little," I replied. I was famished.

"Richard, would you be kind enough to walk down to the café and get me a cheeseburger and fries? I would be happy to treat you as well."

"Well sure," I responded. "I can hardly turn down an offer like that."

She held out a twenty-dollar bill and said, "Get whatever you like. Oh, and get me a big Pepsi, too, please."

"Yes, ma'am," I replied cheerily, heading off on the café run. As I set out to procure our dinner, I thought how lucky I was to meet a lady who was so kind and gracious. Here was a woman facing death, and she wanted to help a stranger in a waiting room. Once our order had been filled and I had paid for our dinner, I gathered everything together and slowly walked back to the waiting area, trying not to spill the drinks.

As I got closer, Marcia was laughing at me. "You look like a high-wire walker juggling that tray," she said.

I grinned and set the tray on the coffee table. I opened her box and placed it on her lap. "When you need a sip of Pepsi, just ask and I'll hand it to you," I said, sitting down and plowing into my own box.

"I'm not supposed to eat this, either," Marcia commented. "But I'm going to! Please don't tell on me."

It didn't take me long to eat most of the burger. I saved a piece of the meat for Willow, setting it aside on the napkin. "What's that for?" she asked.

"It's for my dog," I said. "She's in the van in the garage, and she *loves* hamburger."

"What's her name?" Marcia asked.

"Willow!" I replied. "Willow, like the tree. She is a little white dog. My best friend."

Then Marcia took the top bun from her burger and pulled off a big piece of the meat. "Here, give this to her, too." She held it out toward me.

I gratefully received her offering and added it to Willow's dinner stash.

"Oh my goodness, I forgot to give you back your change." I reached into my pocket and pulled out the six dollars and change that I had left.

"Please keep it," Marcia said. "You earned it getting the sandwich for me."

"Are you sure?" I asked, holding out the money.

"Would you pass me that Pepsi?" Marcia said, ignoring my question. I put the money back in my pocket and handed her the drink. She sipped her soda and looked toward the window. "Oh, here comes my darling Vonne now," she said, nodding toward the entrance. Marcia's husband was walking up to the automatic glass doors. "Richard, would you take this food and my drink away?" She quickly reached for her purse and pulled out lipstick and a small mirror. She applied the lipstick with a well-practiced hand and adjusted her headscarf.

Vonne broke into a beatific smile as he rounded the corner of the room and saw his treasured partner. He came straight to her side and bent to receive a kiss. "Hello, sweetie."

"Hello, my darling," Marcia said.

"Sorry I am so late, but they kept me over again," he apologized.

"That's okay, honey," she assured him. "My friend, Richard, has been keeping me company." She nodded and smiled in my direction.

Vonne took a step in my direction and extended his hand. I stood up and extended mine in return. "Nice to meet you, Richard," he said. "And thank you for keeping my Marcia company."

"It was my pleasure," I replied.

Then Vonne turned to Marcia and softly asked in his native Tagalog, "*Anong sinabi ng* doctor?"

Marcia clasped her hands in her lap as she replied, "*Kailangan kong pumunta sa ibang* hospital, Fred Hutchison in Seattle."

Vonne's shoulders slumped. He bit his lip, and his eyes watered as he looked to the floor. I didn't understand the language, but I could tell he had asked his wife what the doctor had said and she told him she was going to Seattle.

Marcia then unclasped her hands and reached out to Vonne. Her husband gladly held them. "*Pero* okay *lang ako*," she said smiling. Vonne squeezed her hands tightly and smiled back. I knew she had reassured him that she was going to be okay. Then she glanced toward me. "Richard was telling me Fred Hutchison is a great place. Right, Richard?"

"I've heard it's among the best in the world," I replied.

Marcia continued, "The doctor said they have experimental drugs there that could kill the cancer. Then we can take that vacation to Guam this fall."

"Good," Vonne said, putting his hands on his wife's shoulders. "Whatever we have to do, we will do it."

"*IT IS NOW EIGHT O'CLOCK AND VISITING HOURS ARE OVER,*" bellowed the intercom.

Marcia turned to me again and said, "Richard, I will be praying for you."

"And I will pray for you," I said.

I watched as Vonne pushed his darling Marcia down the hall toward the elevator. I knew I would never see her again.

I had the waiting room to myself with Marcia and Vonne gone. *The Swan* was on TV. A woman named Becky was getting her nose broken and reshaped, and she planned to have her tummy tucked and her breasts re-sculpted. I thought to myself that she would *never* be as beautiful as Marcia, and I got up to change the channel.

I crouched down to press the tuner button on the Magnavox. The next scene I saw was Donald Trump calling a group into his boardroom so he could fire someone. I pushed the button again. People were eating dead bugs of some kind from a bowl, trying not to throw up. I pushed the button again. PBS had a program on gorillas in captivity. Finally, something civilized. I returned to the sofa.

The narrator was explaining how Snowflake, the only white gorilla ever discovered, was captured and sold to a zoo in Barcelona, Spain, where he was placed in a barren enclosure with no trees for shade and no other gorillas for company. The big hospital security guard passed through the room. "How's your friend?" he asked, looking at me.

"Having a tough time," I replied. "They're sending her to Fred Hutch tomorrow."

"Well, if you need to stay, I can get you a blanket," he offered.

"No, that's okay. But thanks," I responded. The guard walked off, and I was relieved to know I had more time of sanctuary on the sofa.

As soon as he left, two women and a man came down the hall that led to the elevators. One woman was crying and the other woman had her arms around her shoulders. They walked slowly together to the back of the room. "He's going to be okay," I heard one woman saying. "He's a strong man, and he has a lot to live for."

I could hear them talking in hushed voices in the background as I watched the gorillas on TV.

The man walked to the side of the sofa where I was sitting and looked briefly at the TV. He had his cell phone in his right hand. We exchanged brief hellos, and he dialed a number on his phone. "Hello, Marion? Marion, can you hear me?" he asked, then paced off. "Yeah, we are still at the hospital; we're going to be here awhile. So please put the kids to bed at ten. Don't let them talk you into any later. We'll be home as soon as we can. Okay. Thanks. Bye."

He closed his phone and walked back toward the women. I heard one ask, "Ron, do you think it would be possible for you to go over to my dad's house later and feed Shorty?" Ron assured her he would do that. "Dad always takes him for a walk around the block when it's not raining. But if it's raining, he just takes Shorty out to the front yard so he can go potty."

"Don't worry," Ron responded. "I'll do that in a little while."

I was near tears as Snowflake, now a massive, full-grown, powerful gorilla was playing with one of the babies he had fathered. He leaned over the baby, gently pulling on one arm, and then playfully pushed it from side to side. The baby wrapped its arm around Snowflake's neck and swung into his arms. Snowflake gracefully put the baby down on the ground and rolled it over on its stomach.

A car pulling into the circular drive caught my attention. A man got out. I could tell by the exhaust fumes coming from the back of the car that he had left the motor running. He was well dressed, in pressed khaki pants, tasseled black-and-brown loafers, a white dress shirt, and a red power tie. He talked on his cell phone as he walked briskly into the waiting room, but finished his call as he approached the small group in the waiting area. "Well, what's up?" he asked.

"He's in the ICU, Martin," one of the women said in a trembling voice. "He's stable now. He had a major attack. He fell down the stairs and cut his head. But he was able to crawl to the phone and call 911." Then she broke into tears. It was quiet again for a few seconds, except for her crying.

"Well, I had a house closing at five, a city council meeting at seven, and I'm already late for an eight o'clock staff meeting back at the office." His cell phone rang again. He checked the number before answering. "Martin here," he said. "Yeah, I'm running late. My dad had a heart attack and I'm at the hospital now. I'll be there in ten minutes." He put the phone back in his pocket.

"Can't you stay a little bit longer, Martin?" the tearful woman asked.

"No, I can't," he said. "I don't have the time. If he hadn't smoked all those cigarettes, he wouldn't be in here now. And I'll bet he doesn't have enough insurance to cover all this, and *I'm* going to get stuck with the bill!"

"For God's sake, Martin! He's your father!" the woman flashed back.

"He's seventy-two years old!" Martin snapped, and his phone rang again. "Hey, I've got to go," he said, checking the number of the new caller. "Call me if anything happens," he called over his shoulder, rushing back to his car.

"I hate my brother," the woman said, coldly.

"Why don't you sit down, Nancy," the man suggested.

I needed to go to the bathroom. I picked up the AA pin to drop off at the reception desk and then headed down the hall. I passed the elevator Marcia and Vonne had taken to go back to their room. I saw a small sign marked CHAPEL just across from the men's room. I peeked in. It was a small, dimly lit room with an altar and a cross stationed in the middle. A large Bible was placed on a stand next to it. The book was closed, but a piece of paper was sticking out of the pages. I moved forward and opened the Bible, taking the note out and reading it. "Dear Lord, I ask you to take this pain away from me, or please take me in my sleep this night. The burden has become too great, and I pray for your peace. Please send your angels to carry me away."

As I put the note back, I noticed it had been placed right beside Psalm 23, a Psalm of David. I began reading: "The Lord is my shepherd; I shall not want. He maketh me to lie down in green pastures; he leadeth me beside the still waters. He restoreth my soul; he leadeth me in the paths of righteousness for his name's sake. Yea, though I walk through the valley of the shadow of death, I will fear no evil; for thou art with me; thy rod and thy staff they comfort me . . ."

I put the note back in between the pages and closed the book. I backed away from the book and the altar and sat down in a chair in the front row of the chapel. Since my night on the Tacoma Narrows Bridge, I simply didn't believe in God anymore. I felt sad for these believers who expected some help and relief from some invisible holy one for whom they could only leave notes. Maybe their God was "online" by now, with an e-mail address, a modem, a ThinkPad, and a server.

I laughed. I laughed at God as I sat there looking at the cross and His big book. The irony was that I had nothing to live for, except Willow. I had no family to care for me, nothing to hope for. I wanted to die and could not, but Marcia wanted to live—had so much to live for—but the cancer was slowly, painfully ravaging her body. And then there was my mother; she was a believer, too, and she died of cancer. Her God let her suffer and die in agony when she was not yet sixty years old.

As I sat there, the anger at their God began to well up in me, until I began to shake. I wondered if I might strike a deal with their God. I would be an agent, a broker, a dealmaker. It would be a simple trade: my worthless stock for Marcia.

So I got slowly down on my knees and began to pray. "Dear God, this is Richard. Do you remember me? You are the God my mother and father believed in so deeply. Remember them? They are the ones who had their baby daughter kidnapped when she was just seven months old in Chicago. They never saw their child again. They were the ones whom the police came to tell that their son had drowned in the Chicago River when he was twelve. And their next child, another daughter, died from diabetes when she was thirteen.

"I am offering you a simple deal tonight. Upstairs in this hospital is a woman named Marcia who is dying of cancer. She's a wonderful person who wants to live for her husband, children, and grandchildren. How's this for a deal? You take me instead of Marcia, and you cure her cancer?"

I waited for a moment and then slowly got to my feet. I sat down in the front row of the tiny chapel. My mind drank in the silence of the room. Then it began constructing ways to consider the moment. Was this to be my new life—meeting others briefly, looking at their pictures, sharing their secrets, peering in the windows of their lives, overhearing tearful conversations of those overcome with fear and worry? Had some devils, spirits, or ghosts been given my soul after my failed suicide attempt? Were they toying with me like Scrooge—parading me around for their enjoyment in some fourth dimension?

Then I recalled a character my father used to draw over and over again on scrap paper. It was a cat, facing away from the viewer on a picket fence, with its tail hanging down. Sometimes he would make the ears round, other times pointed. Sometimes the tail would be curled at the tip. I learned as a child that he drew that cat often, whenever he was tired; he called it "the Observer."

When I would ask what it was, he would always say the same thing. "It's a cat, son . . . a cat sitting on a picket fence, just watching the world pass by."

My father's Observer was always facing away from him, looking out at the world. Was it just watching the world go by? Or was it waiting for something?

It was time to take Willow for a walk. I could feel her calling me. I stood up and walked out of the chapel, down the hall, and through the big automatic doors at the entrance to the hospital. The rain had slowed to a cold drizzle.

I got Willow out of the van and took her for a brief walk near the bushes beside the garage. I gave her the hamburger Marcia had given me for her. She gobbled it down. When we climbed back into the van, I moved the clothes around to make room for our sleeping bag and we nestled in, pulling the top of the bag over our heads so the security guards couldn't see us. We were a little damp, but it could have been much worse.

As we snuggled down, I told Willow about Marcia and her seven children and twelve grandchildren and about Marcia's cancer.

Then I thought of all the family pictures I had once had of my mother, my father, and my own children. I had left them behind over eight months ago, in a storage unit in a nearby town. When I couldn't pay the bill, those pictures were undoubtedly thrown in a dumpster and my last valuable possessions auctioned off to the highest bidder.

And I remembered the last time I saw my mother. It was in a hospital. She had colon cancer; she'd had an operation months before, but, like Marcia's, her cancer had come back. My father called and asked that I stop in at the hospital on the way to work, because my mom wanted to talk to me. "She's in room 202," he'd said. I remembered pulling into the parking lot of the single-story Mercy Hospital in my hometown of Urbana. I pulled one of the front doors open and walked into the lobby. There was no television or sofa, and no coffee shop. I walked down the hall to room 202 and peeked in. It was a small room. No TV—just a picture of Jesus on the wall above my mother's small bed. Dad was there, too, sitting on the side of the bed, talking softly. My mother smiled as I entered the room. "Hi, honey," she said, reaching out her hand to me.

"Hi, Mom," I said, bending over to kiss her. My father stood up. I could see the worry and fear in his eyes. Then he sat down again.

I could tell she was in pain. "How are you feeling, Mom?" I asked.

"Oh, not so good today," she said. I pulled a small metal chair closer to the bed and sat down where I could hold her hand. "What are you doing tonight?"

"Oh, I'm supposed to cover a high-school basketball game in the city," I said. "Two pretty good teams. But I don't have to be there until seven, and I can stay longer if you need me."

Then my mother did what she always had done for me: She protected me, even from the sadness of her own passing. "Oh, I'm going to be okay," she smiled, with as much brightness as she could muster. "I'll be going home in a day or two. How is my grandson, Richie?"

"He's fine, Mom," I replied, returning her smile. "You know what he did this morning? While I was in the bedroom making the bed, he got into the kitchen pantry and found the empty Pepsi bottles. Well, each one probably had a little sip left in it, and he was sitting on the floor with six pop bottles trying to get that last little bit out of them." My mother laughed. We talked for about an hour or so before a silence came.

"Well, you had better get to work, huh?" she finally asked.

"Yeah, I guess," I replied, looking at my watch. I stood up and leaned over the bed again and gave her another kiss. She reached out and clasped my hand, squeezing it tenderly. "I'll see you tomorrow," I said, and I walked out the door.

It was just about eleven p.m. when I was sitting at my Underwood, putting the finishing touches on the story of the basketball game I had covered. One of the other reporters called out, "Richard, line three for you." I picked up the receiver and pushed the blinking button. "LeMieux," I said.

"Richard," my father's voice said. "Your mother passed away just a little while ago."

Silence filled the air. I didn't know what to say. Finally the simplest of words came. "I'm sorry, Dad," I said. "I wish I could have been there."

"You know your mom," he replied. "She wanted it this way."

I knew he was right. She would rather have had me off playing sportswriter than sitting beside her, watching her die, sharing her pain. Her name was Grace, and she lived up to it.

"Well, I'm going home in a little bit to feed the dog and go to bed," my father said. "Why don't you stop by the house in the morning, okay?"

"Okay, I'll see you in the morning." I hung up the phone.

I didn't cry that night. Or later, at the funeral. And I didn't cry when my father died ten years later.

Now, here, sleeping in the back of my van in the parking garage of a hospital in Bremerton, tears welled up in my eyes for Marcia, for my mother, for the brothers and sisters I never got to know.

I felt the presence of my sweet mother saying, "Don't cry, Richard. There is nothing to cry about."

Chapter 8

DR. Z

With C as my tour guide to the many free meals in the city, my ache for sustenance over the next few weeks was largely appeased.

But there were many other aches and pains that a large helping of tuna-noodle casserole could not soothe.

A doctor at the Department of Health Services had diagnosed me as suffering clinical depression. He passed me on to other physicians to see if I was salvageable.

The journey back, or forward, or sideways—I was not sure which direction it was going to be—was about to become more complicated and intriguing with each day. I felt I was adrift in the raging river of life. Occasionally I could grasp the branch of a fallen tree for a rest from the torrent, but the respite was always brief, and the churning waters would then carry me away again. I could never quite reach the shore.

I had gone to the library to keep warm and dry and to read every book available on depression, only to find the process even more depressing.

The state sent me to "Dr. Z" for a look-see. They called him Dr. Z because most of his patients could neither spell nor say his last name correctly.

Dr. Z was my doc because he was the only physician in town at the time who would accept Medicaid, which paid considerably below the going rate other doctors wanted for each visit.

Dr. Z's office was just about filled with poor people when I arrived one morning in March for a ten a.m. appointment. Children who were sneezing, coughing, and obviously running fevers sat in their mothers' laps. Four little old ladies were mostly staring off into space, though occasionally taking a peek at a middle-aged man rocking back and forth in his chair while mumbling some indistinguishable words.

I checked in at the desk. "Do you have an insurance card?" the receptionist asked.

"Yes," I replied, pulling the Medicaid card from my pocket and handing it to her.

"Please fill this out," she said, handing me a clipboard that contained a patient information form. "Here's a pen, too." She held it out to me. "I need to make a copy of your card," she added as I walked away.

I settled in a chair along the wall, crossed my legs, and began filling out the form.

    Name: ___Richard LeMieux___
    Address: _____none_____
    Phone: _____none_____
    Father and mother: _____deceased_____ .
    Children: _____none_____
    Relative or friend to contact in case of emergency: ___none___
    Allergies, current, or past infections or illnesses that require
        treatment: _____none_____
    Current medications: _____none_____

I got up and returned to the desk and handed the receptionist the clipboard. She handed my medical card back to me. "Someone will be with you shortly," she said with a smile.

I then went looking for some reading material on the racks. There was no *Bon Appétit*, *Redbook*, *People*, *Golf,* or *Travel & Leisure.* There were a few AARP magazines, but I didn't want those. The book collection consisted mostly of Dr. Seuss classics. I grabbed *The Cat in the Hat,* took it back to my seat, opened the book, and started reading.

I had just gotten past the "sit, sit, sit, sit" part and was moving on to the real excitement when the nurse interrupted my reading. "Richard? Richard LeMieux?" She was standing by the entrance to the chamber that would lead me to Dr. Z's examining room. I got up and took Dr. Seuss with me, which drew a smile from two of the old ladies still sitting patiently in their chairs. "Hello. I'm Jane," the nurse said, pushing the door open and revealing the long hallway of Dr. Z's clinic. "Let's go to room number two." She briskly led the way.

"Hop up on that examining table and please take off your shirt," Nurse Jane said, reaching for a dressing gown and holding it up for me. "You may put this on." She began going through her nursing routine of strapping a blood pressure apparatus around my arm and squeezing the ball. "So, why are you here today?" she asked.

"I am here for depression," I replied, as I felt the pressure on my arm increase with each pump of the ball in Nurse Jane's hand.

"Depression, huh?" she said. "Why do you feel you are depressed?"

"Oh, well, I, uh . . . well, I tried to commit suicide a little while ago, and uh . . . well, it didn't . . . well—"

"That's okay, dear," Jane interrupted, and she put her hand on my shoulder. Then she turned and picked up a clipboard and wrote something down. "How do you feel today?" she asked.

"Well, I have been sleeping in my car for a few months and I'm a little tired, but I—"

"Here. Open up," she interrupted again, pointing a thermometer toward my mouth. "Your blood pressure is just fine," she said, grabbing the clipboard and writing again. "The doctor will be able to help you," she assured me, taking the thermometer with her other hand and checking its reading. "Temperature is fine, too."

Then Nurse Jane wheeled around and opened the door. "The doctor will be with you soon," she said. I went back to reading Dr. Seuss.

Juggling fish bowls, bottles of milk, and birthday cakes—I wondered if Seuss was "on the pipe" when he wrote this stuff. Was there a subliminal message being passed on, like "Let your soul out to play"? Or was he just messing with the minds of the parents who would be reading this book to their children, parents who might secretly want some chaos in an otherwise too-orderly universe?

"C is just like the Cat in the Hat," I thought. Entering a room, he could turn the boring and mundane into something bizarre, or at least exciting. He'd turn things upside down and make a mess with his words and deeds. He would even try to walk on water from time to time and move mountains with his faith—either of which could have earned him a room in the mental hospital if reported. He could turn even an uneventful shopping trip into an adventure.

C had asked me one day to take him to the store to get some supplies for the Armadillo. We went to Wal-Mart, where we were greeted cordially at the door. C bowed at the waist and then went down on one knee before the greeter, saying "Greetings to you, too!"

I should have run, right then.

As we cruised down aisle 2B, C spotted a young, blond sales associate with a red vest approaching us, her ill-fitting half heels slapping the tiled floor. Her nametag read "Victoria." "Pardon me, darlin'," C said, stopping her in her tracks. "Can you tell me where to find the camp-stove gas canisters?"

"Sporting Goods. Follow me!" Victoria commanded and turned to lead the parade, her heels rhythmically clicking on the tiles. She led us past Bed and Bath, through Pet Supplies, and then breezed by Automotive to Sporting Goods. "Here they are!" She pointed to the canisters. "And you're lucky. They're on sale for $1.09," she added, pointing to the happy-face sign.

"Wow," C responded. "$1.09? I pay $2.60 apiece for these at the hardware store."

"Our everyday low price at Wal-Mart is only $1.99," Victoria boasted.

"Well, it's no wonder, darlin', that you people can't afford to have health insurance and can barely afford to live," replied C. Well, that comment took the perk right out of the sales associate. Victoria's green eyes opened wide and she stiffened. Without comment, she turned and stomped away, her shoes clapping even more loudly on the floor. "Gosh, I hope she wasn't offended," he said to me as he picked up the gas canisters. "Next, some Palmolive dish soap."

We set off on the next part of the journey unguided.

As we were leaving that department, I noticed out of the corner of my eye that we were under surveillance by a middle-aged man in a white shirt and tie. I instinctively recognized him as a management type and suspected that's C's comment had been duly reported. My only hope was to get C out the door as quickly as possible.

"Do they have caramel corn here?" C asked. "I like caramel corn late at night."

"Probably," I said, looking over my shoulder for the man in the white shirt and tie.

Just as we were closing in on the caramel corn, I saw another man in a white shirt and tie at the end of the aisle. This one was wearing a bright red vest and was watching us. He stepped out of sight after I made eye contact. Now I knew we were in trouble. After all, C had a case of gas canisters in his arms. We could be terrorists, or worse yet, communists. I suspected cameras were recording our every move, and I feared our profiles were being scanned and sent by satellite to Homeland Security.

Having finally reached our objective, C grabbed a bag of caramel corn off the shelf. "I also need some of those long kitchen matches," he muttered. I took a deep breath, and he stopped. "On second thought," he said, "I think I have enough matches to get by. Let's get out of here. I actually feel bad shopping here; I feel like I'm doing something wrong."

I breathed a sigh of relief. I hoped we would escape this institution without further incident. Unfortunately, as we rounded the corner of aisle 27A, I saw the long line at checkout stand 5—the only line open in the middle of a shift change.

We got in line. The lady in front of us had a cart full of grape- and lime-juice boxes, three cases of Pampers, six packages of Lunchables bologna-and-cheese snacks, and eight cans of dog food. Another woman slipped into line behind us with a twenty-four-pack of chocolate chip cookies. And behind her, an elderly lady pulled in with a cart filled with Spam, boxes of Velveeta, cat food, a bag of cat litter, and a cat scratching post.

It was in that line, just as I placed the plastic divider bar on the conveyor belt so he could put his goods down, that C's conscience got to him. "No. No. I can't do this," he began, berating himself. "I've got to put this stuff back! Buying here is destroying the very fabric of man, enslaving people in low-wage jobs." His voice began to grow louder. "These people can't afford to live on what they are making here," he continued, pointing to the sales associates. He glanced down, took a deep breath, and let forth a yell:

"ATTENTION! ATTENTION, WAL-MART SHOPPERS! We have a special on conscience today, and it's FREE! It will make you feel good! It will make you smile! Please join me in putting our stuff back and agreeing NOT to shop here until they get their employees HEALTH INSURANCE and a LIVING WAGE!"

I looked around. Beneath all the smiley-face price-rollback signs was a sea of snarls on Wal-Mart shoppers' faces. They were not about to put back their $5.99 slippers, or any of their other newly found treasures.

The greeters had all gathered at the end of checkout stand 5 with a chorus of frowns, and the white-shirt-and-tie brigade converged on C.

"We must ask you to leave, sir!" said one, followed quickly by the other adding, "Or we will have to call the police!"

"I will be more than happy to accommodate you, sirs," said C, producing a Cheshire-cat grin. He turned and strode toward the door, leaving his gas canisters, Palmolive soap, and caramel corn lying on the conveyor belt. I could tell by his stride that he was pleased with himself. He had made his point.

I heard the sound of the door handle in the small examining room turn, and the door opened slowly. Dr. Z peeked in to make sure someone was in the room. He looked at me over his glasses. "Hello." He stepped in, closed the door behind him, and started reading the chart Nurse Jane had given him.

"Depression . . . suicide attempt . . ." Dr. Z looked up at me. "Not good," he observed. I nodded in agreement. "Well, we can fix that," he said, matter-of-factly, and he took a small flashlight out of his coat pocket and pointed it in my eyes, placing his left hand on the side of my face. "Eyes left." I noticed the frayed collar of his white shirt and the missing button. "Eyes right." I complied. "Look down." Then I noticed the tassel was missing from his well-worn right brown oxford shoe.

I thought to myself, "Poor Dr. Z chose the wrong specialty for making money in the new millennium. He should have gone for breasts. 300,000 women, including 18,000 girls under the age of eighteen, had bought—mostly charged—breast implants in 2002. At $4,000 to $6,000 per job, it added up to $2.4 billion. If Dr. Z had gone that route, he would have been able to buy a new pair of loafers *and* a new smock."

My mind was wandering. I wondered what Madame Curie would say about all of those breast implants.

Dr. Z scribbled something on my chart again and then laid it down. He searched through his smock pockets—first the top, then the lower right. I thought *he* looked depressed. The sole of his left shoe was beginning to separate from the uppers. His maroon tie was spotted. He found what he was searching for—a prescription pad—in the same pocket where his pen had been. He then quickly wrote out the scrip and handed it to me. I lowered my head, looking at the small piece of paper.

"I'm going to give you Zoloft," he said. "Take it twice a day and get lots of sleep." He reached out and put a hand on my shoulder as he spoke reassuringly. "We are going to make you feel better." He turned around, pulled a paper cup from the dispenser on the wall and filled it at the sink. He set the cup down saying, "I'll be right back."

He dashed out the door and was back in seconds. "I've got some samples to get you started today," said Dr. Z, tearing open a box and then pressing a small, pastel-green pill out of its plastic holder into the palm of his hand. He handed me the pill and the water. I put the pill in my mouth and washed it down.

"Well, just about everybody is on some drug nowadays," I thought to myself. "Rush Limbaugh is on pain pills, Barry Bonds is hitting record-breaking home runs on steroids, half the NFL is on something, and who knows what the NBA players are using, or what Michael Jackson is taking at his Neverland Ranch."

I knew the next step from my readings at the library. Dr. Z and I both knew that many suicide suitors who have failed try again as soon as they get a little boost from the pills.

I wondered if maybe Dr. Z could concoct a capsule so powerful that I could be changed into "The Millennium Man," a modern-day Wyatt Earp, with a cell phone strapped to one hip and a beeper attached to the other, armed for battle. I would wear a radio headset tuned in to Rush Limbaugh and have my laptop in one hand and my compass set in the other, so I could find my way home at night; with all batteries fully charged, I would be plugged in to the world. I would be pumped up with 1,000 milligrams of vitamin C, 500 of B, 200 of E, and two aspirin for my heart, and I would carry Viagra in my pocket, just in case. My wife would be a real-estate baroness, off closing a house deal. She would have all the toothbrushes charging, the house alarm on, and the OnStar System set in the car. Her pillbox would be full of pain pills and other supplements, marked for every day of the week. She would have the TiVo set to record Dr. Phil at two and the microwave set to start dinner at five. The windows would all be duct-taped and our guns loaded. The kids would be safe at school or on the way to their bowling class. Everything would be perfect.

And maybe if I took two or three of Dr. Z's miracle pills, I could quickly move up in the world and become a Tony Robbins, with my own late-night TV infomercial, sharing the secrets of my success, explaining how I, Ricardo (of course I have changed my name), became a multibillionaire in just six months by buying up foreclosed bungalows *with no money down* and selling them for four times their worth, and how you can do it, too, with my step-by-step motivational books and CDs, only $19.99! They teach you how to foreclose, how to toss people in the street, and even how to sleep at night after doing it! If you get good enough, you might even be able to buy a brunette!

Or maybe Dr. Z's drugs could get me the whole enchilada! I could design and build my own city and name it after myself. I could give my subjects a pill each morning and they would race from one end of town to the other all day, gathering resources for me, which I would send from my own port to China, where men, women, and children would work twenty-one hours a day for ten cents an hour in my very own sweatshops, assembling plastic widgets to be sold at Wal-Mart.

I felt like Huck Finn must have felt at the end of his story, when Aunt Sally was going to adopt him and "sivilize" him. Dr. Z's pill was now melting in my body. Would it "sivilize" me?

Like Huck, I had been there before.

But as I said, I had read the books at the library and I knew my future: Realizing that I was broken, irreparable, the state would find some garret to store me away in once and for all, crossing their fingers that I would not hurt myself or anyone else. Sometimes I would visit the swamp of despair and be sarcastic, angry, and morose. Sometimes my pills would stir the chemicals in my brain so that I could still dream of becoming the next great comedian, quarterback, or author. But in the end, I would know that I had fallen too far behind in the race of life. The cheering crowds would have long gone home before I reached the finish line. My tombstone would appropriately read *DNF* (Did Not Finish).

I looked down at the sample package Dr. Z had handed me. There was a picture of what looked like an egg on its side, with a smile (or maybe a smirk) on its face, eyeing a ladybug flying through the air. It read "ZOLOFT" in big letters, with "Sertraline HCL" in parentheses.

When I looked up, Dr. Z stood before me, peering over his spectacles again. "Come back in one week to see me," he said. "You will feel better."

"As you wish," I said, and he smiled. Maybe he had seen *The Princess Bride* too.

I quickly slipped off the dressing gown and put on my shirt, thinking Dr. Z sure seemed confident that I would get better. I knew I would come back in a week. I didn't want to disappoint him. Hell, maybe I had found another angel!

Nurse Jane had not yet returned to set up my next appointment, so I went back to reading *The Cat in the Hat*. Soon the door swung open again, and in she came, asking, "How do you feel?"

"I guess I'm okay," I responded.

"What are you doing tomorrow?" she asked.

"Nothing," I said.

"Well, I made an appointment for you at Kitsap Mental Health at ten a.m. for counseling," she informed me. "Can you make that okay?"

"I think so," I said.

"It's up behind the Fred Meyer store on the East Side," she continued. "Do you know where that is?"

"I do," I responded. "I'll just have to try to find some gas money to get there."

Jane took my hand and placed several rolled-up bills in it, gently closing my hand around the money. "That should help you get a motel room for a night, and some gas." She kept holding my hand. "Get a hot bath, some food that *you* pick out and *like*, and get a good night's sleep."

"I don't know . . ." My words choked off.

"You don't have to say anything," she interrupted me. "My husband is a doctor, and about seven years ago he became so depressed that one day he just left home. It took me three months to find him. He was in Colorado, living on the streets. If someone had not helped him, he would have died." She paused. "Now, let's get you out of here. Hop down off that table, and we'll see you in one week, at eleven a.m." She escorted me from the room with a reassuring smile on her face.

I didn't open my hand to look at the money until I closed the door of Dr. Z's clinic. It held four twenties, a ten, and three ones. Nurse Jane must have emptied her purse to help me.

I walked to the van, opened the door, and told Willow the good news. "Willow, we are going to a motel for the night!" I attempted to calculate in my mind just how far Nurse Jane's gift would carry us: fifty dollars for a motel, ten for dinner, ten for gas, fifty cents for a Zagnut bar, one for a hamburger for Willow, eighty-nine cents for a Classic Coke for later—and that left us twenty dollars for the next day.

So, we headed out—first to Denny's for a chicken-fried steak dinner with extra gravy, fries, a coke, and a piece of coconut cream pie, then on to McDonald's for a Willowburger, and finally to the store before searching for a motel room.

Chapter 9

OH, GOD!

I pulled into the Driftwood Motel parking lot about four p.m. It appeared to be in my price range—just off the highway, a little shabby, with an outdoor pool that obviously had not been used for years.

I parked the van and walked in. There was no one at the front desk, but I heard a woman's voice, apparently talking on the phone in the back. "You know I don't like calling the police," I heard her say. Then there was silence for a moment. "Well, then *you* come down here and call the cops, and *you* get them out of the room!" Silence again. "Okay, okay. I'll tell them that they have to be out by ten in the morning or we will call the cops. See you in the morning." Then I heard her hang up the phone and walk around the corner of the office.

She looked a little surprised when she saw me. "Oh, hello. I didn't hear you come in. Do you want a room?"

"Yes," I answered. "What is your rate?"

"Forty-eight dollars a night, fifty-four with tax," she answered.

"Okay," I said, reaching for the money in my pocket.

"Just one night?"

"Just tonight," I replied, beginning to fill out the check-in card she handed me.

"We have a continental breakfast in the morning," she said, pointing to a small table along the wall. It held a coffee pot on a hot plate and what appeared to be two stale glazed donuts lying on a serving tray. "Check-out time is ten a.m." She glanced at the card I handed her. "Cash or credit card?"

"Cash," I said, counting out the bills from the money Nurse Jane had given me.

"Oh, I forgot to ask," continued the desk clerk. "Do you have any pets? There's a twenty-five dollar charge for pets."

"Ah, no, I don't," I lied, hoping Willow wasn't barking in the van.

She stuffed the cash in a drawer and then handed me a key. "Room 203," she said. "It's at the end of the parking lot."

I quickly moved to the van and jumped in, hoping to get out of sight before she got a glimpse of Willow. We succeeded. There were only three other cars in the parking lot, and we drove toward our room.

I parked the van and put Willow inside my coat to hide her from view, stepped spryly up to the second-floor room, turned the key in the lock, stepped inside, and closed the door quickly. "No barking tonight!" I told Willow, as I placed her on the bed. "Or we will get kicked out."

It was a nice little room. Two double beds with bedspreads that were not too badly stained, and only a small rip in one of them. Willow cocked her head as she sat in the middle of the bed and looked at me. "We are going to have a bed tonight," I said, "and *you* are going to get a bath!" Willow's white coat had turned gray. It'd been months since she'd had a real bath.

I turned on the TV and was greeted by the *Jerry Springer Show*. "Let's bring June's husband Randy out now," Jerry said, as a man walked onstage to the whistles and applause of the audience. The man sat down in a chair next to his wife. Jerry sauntered toward the couple with a microphone in one hand and a piece of white paper in the other. "June, do you have something to tell Randy?" he asked, leaning forward.

"Randy," she began in a trembling voice. "I need to tell you that— well, I slept with your brother Buddy, and your—your father Sam."

Randy jumped up. "You bi—!" I turned the TV off.

"Willow, it's time for a bath," I said, heading for the bathroom. "Come on." She followed right behind.

I found small bottles of shampoo and conditioner in the bathroom and ran water in the tub. Then I lifted Willow into her bath and lathered her up.

As the grime began to wash away from the little dog's coat, I could see the sores from the fleabites she had endured during our travels. Her fur was so stained that I was sure she would never be the pure white snowball she had been. But Willow never complained. I thought once again that it would be best for her if I tried to find her a good home. Maybe someplace where she could stay warm, get a bath every couple of weeks, go to the vet, get better food, and be brushed every day. But somehow I couldn't bring myself to do that.

It was about eight p.m. or so when it began.

Willow and I had both had our baths, and we were fortunate to find a movie on TV—*The Natural*. It was one of my favorites. Robert Redford had just been shot in a hotel room by some lady, and the scene where he begins his comeback as a baseball great was just beginning.

I thought I had heard a champagne cork pop a little earlier and some giggling from the room next door. Now I could hear a woman's husky voice. "Oh God, oh God, oh God . . . Oh God, GOD, GOD," came the cries. Then there was silence, but not for long. "GOD, GOD, GOD,

OH GOD, GOD, OH GOD!"

"Is she in trouble?" I wondered. I got out of bed and hesitantly put my ear to the wall. Nothing. So I got back in bed.

A minute or so later, it began again. "GOD, please God, PLEASE GOD, PLEEEAASE. Oh God, oh God, oh God."

I got out of bed again and put my ear to the wall. "God, God, goddamn God," she moaned, and this time I could hear the squeak of the bedsprings. The voice was getting louder and louder, and more and more insistent.

Willow the Wonder Dog jumped out of bed and went to the door and barked, as if to come to the woman's rescue. "Shush, Willow!" I plucked her up and brought her back to bed in a single motion.

Damn. Here I am, having not had sex for, hell, I couldn't remember how long, and I get a motel for the first time in six months, and I have to be right next door to what sounded like God having sex with a human. This can't last long, I told myself, turning up the television and climbing back into bed.

But it did.

It went on for hours. Every time Robert Redford hit one of his booming homeruns on the screen, the yelling seemed to resume next door. When Redford was in one of his blue-eyed, reflective moments, all I could hear was, "Oh God. Oh God. Oh God."

Was this possibly God, the Creator himself, in the very act of creation in the room next door? Or was it evangelistic sex? Or was it, more likely, a Viagra copulation, guaranteed to last five hours before deflation?

At the very least, I thought, she needed to expand her vocabulary! Perhaps she could add some adjectives, adverbs, and superlatives: "You drive me crazy!" "Honey, you're so powerful!" "You're so big!" "Don't stop!" or even "Yes, yes, yes, darling! Drown me in your passionate seed!"

I considered slipping a note under the door with my suggestions, but thought better of it.

It was about eleven thirty when the action subsided. I guessed they had stopped to watch *Nightline*.

I was tired and drifted off to sleep.

It was a good, deep sleep, in a real bed. No dreams. But I remember my subconscious checking in sometime during the night, asking why I wasn't dreaming, or if I wanted to dream.

The "Oh GOD" nightmare returned around seven forty-five the next morning. I wanted so badly to just pull the covers back over my head and enjoy the warmth and softness of the bed, and maybe sleep till noon. But I knew I didn't have enough money to stay another night, and soon the maid would come and discover Willow's presence, and then the innkeeper would want another twenty-five dollars for our deception.

I looked around the little motel room and then out the slit in the curtains and saw the rain falling from the gray sky.

Dr. Z's pills and Jane's gift of a night in a bed had given me a ray of hope. I had an appointment at the local mental health clinic, and I wondered what the shrinks would have to say. Some magic words? Something from Freud or Jung?

I pushed myself out of bed, took a shower, and dressed. I hid Willow under my coat again and we snuck out of the room, heading for whatever this day had in store.

Chapter 10

OFF TO THE MENTAL INSTITUTION

To the rhythmic beat of the wipers on the windshield of the van, my mind began to explore its expectations of the mental institution to which I was heading.

Would the doctors wear white coats? Would they have beards like Freud and want to talk about my childhood? Would they attach wires to my skull and chest? Was there a nurse like Nurse Ratched in *One Flew Over the Cuckoo's Nest*? Would Jack Nicholson be there to entertain the crazies?

As I pulled into the parking lot, it was easy to see this was a resort for the id. Patients were roaming peacefully around the grounds, drinking coffee, smoking, and chatting. There was a small pond just off the parking lot, giving Willow a chance to get out of the van, take a pee, and chase after a couple of ducks. The patients warmed to Willow quickly, calling her over for a quick pet and asking me the usual questions: "What's her name?" "Is it a boy or a girl?" "How old is she?"

"I used to have a dog that looked exactly like her," one lady said, bending over to scratch Willow's back. "Her name was Muffin. I had to give her up," she said wistfully. "I couldn't take care of her. I didn't have the money for vets, food, or medicine." Then she turned her attention to me. "Do you have an appointment?" she asked.

"Yes," I said, wondering if it was that obvious that I was crazy.

"You know, you can take dogs in there," she said, pointing at the building. "They like them."

That made me feel a little better—a little more relaxed and at home, with the possibility of entering into a happy family. I picked Willow up and carried her into the building to find psychologists and psychiatrists bustling about with notepads and folders, attempting to be as calm and normal as possible with a lineup of neurotics waiting to be cured.

This was a portal, I thought to myself. Maybe it was a black hole. I could enter it and find a new life, a new existence, a new focus. Or I could career through time until I earned a room at Western State Hospital, where they had bars and locked everyone up at night.

This was not the country-club scene, where the doctors arrive in their BMWs and Henry Grethel suits and, to the tune of two hundred dollars an hour, talk to their clients about how to get along with their bosses or how to get over finding their husbands in bed with other women.

Some of the patients here had scars where they had slashed their wrists, or had gunshot wounds, broken arms, or black eyes. Some had jumped from the bridge but somehow didn't drown. Hell, I wasn't sure I qualified for help here—I hadn't even gotten wet yet. Dr. Z and Jane must have some pull here, I thought, to get me in so quickly.

The best-dressed people entering the building were the two pharmaceutical reps, who checked in with their gleaming, starched white shirts and blazing ties. One was from Pfizer and the other from Glaxo, and they were whisked through the locked room that led to the inner sanctum of the clinic, carrying their sample cases. I knew the doctors inside used pills in their practice, of course. And it was these guys who brought them—some pills to bring you up, some to level you off, and some to bring you down.

But I knew, and I was sure the doctors also knew, that they didn't have enough pills to cover every need. Was there a pill for loneliness? Or one for regret? A pill to help you forget? Or one to bring you love? Kindness? Grace? Understanding? How about a money pill? A family pill? A pill to restore the nectar of life that had soured or had never been tasted? Was there some magic elixir that could be drunk or splashed on for happiness?

I wished I could capture that "joy smell" that Willow discovers as she rolls in the grass, all four legs flailing in the air, wiggling and rubbing the essence into every possible inch of her body. If I could put that joy in an aerosol can, I would just start spraying

As I sat there with Willow in my lap, waiting for my appointment, I looked out the window at the patients roaming outside the clinic. They appeared to have found a spirit of camaraderie in this place where they came to receive guidance—along with doses of kindness and dignity (and pills). It was a sanctuary of acceptance. In the outside world, they were often treated with disdain, by people who—three blocks away—were paying $4.75 for mocha lattes and rushing home to watch men dunking basketballs for $12 million a year and contestants eating live lizards and animal excrement for chance to win $100,000.

I had been waiting for about an hour now and was getting thirsty. I spotted a water cooler in the hall and went for a drink. Just as I was bending over to slurp some H_2O, I heard a voice behind me. "Don't drink the water." I turned to see a tall, slender man, with an enormous beard reaching halfway down his chest, peering at me. "They put chemicals in the water to keep us calm," he whispered before walking off. I went back to my seat.

A few minutes later, a young man in his early thirties came bursting through the door. He wasn't wearing a shirt, and he was dripping wet. He walked straight up to the counter and unbuckled his pants and dropped them to the floor. "Help me!" he yelled to the receptionist. "I'm all wet and they are crawling all over me. Get them off! Get them off me!" Two men came rushing from behind the locked door to usher this flailing soul into another room, dragging pants and all.

This was more like the mental institution I expected. I spied a magazine rack in the corner and ambled over in search of something to read. There, between a three-month-old copy of *National Geographic* and the large-print version of *Reader's Digest*, was a copy of *Scientology*. It occurred to me that someone was playing a cruel joke on this institution. I picked up a very dated copy of *Arizona Highways* from the rack and settled in for what felt like an interminable wait. (At least now I knew how to get instant service if I felt so inclined.) I had finished the article about the town square in Prescott, taken a flight to Phoenix, and was heading for the rocks of Sedona when I felt a presence standing over me, casting a shadow over the red-rock cliffs I was admiring. "Richard?" a voice asked.

"Yes," I answered, looking up.

"My name is Rodney," the man said. "Would you come with me?" He turned and walked toward a door that led to the inner realm of the mental institution. At his nod, the receptionist pushed a button that opened the door, and Rodney held it open for Willow and me.

Rodney was my psychologist. He was not what I expected. Instead of a white coat, he was wearing earth tones—a green-and-black plaid cotton shirt and tan khaki pants, frayed around the cuffs. His brown shoes were well worn, even cracked on top from the weather. He wore two necklaces—one appeared to be a plastic whale on a leather cord, and the other was a small chain with some type of medallion, but I could not tell what was inscribed on it.

I expected a couch. "Pull up a chair," Rodney said, pointing to a brown metal chair along the wall. "I'll be with you in a minute. I just need to fill out this paperwork before I forget what I'm supposed to do." He picked up a folder and a pen and began writing.

I looked around Rodney's office while he was doing his work. There were two large buttons on the wall: one marked CODE RED and the other CODE BLUE. I surmised that they were to be pushed when a client threatened one of the doctors—or the president—or began taking off his or her clothes. Rodney reached over and grabbed a Tupperware bowl containing a concoction of fruit salad, romaine lettuce, chunks of cheddar cheese, and pine nuts and shoveled in a few bites as he wrote. I noticed several framed pictures behind his desk. One was of a whitewater raft bouncing in the waves; another was of Rodney standing onshore beside the boat, holding an oar. "This is just my luck!" I thought to myself. While other patients were getting doctors in white coats with miracle cures, I was getting a tour guide.

Rodney finished his paperwork, took one more bite of salad, and picked up a file folder with my name on the front. "Sorry that took so long," he said.

"That's okay," I said. "I have no place to go."

"Let's do a quick test," he said, looking me in the eyes. "Will you count backwards from one hundred, by threes?"

"97," I said. "Uh, 94, uh, 91, I think. Uh, 88." I began counting on my fingers. "Uh, 85 . . . 82 . . ." Rodney was urging me on as I struggled. "79 . . . 76 . . . 73, uh, 70, uh, uh . . ."

"That's good enough," he said. "Would you do the alphabet backwards?"

"Uh, Z," I began. "Y, X . . . W—or is it U?" I asked.

"That's okay. I can't do that either!" Rodney then scooted his desk chair back and wheeled over to a pile of papers on his desk and began shuffling them around. "Darn. I had them here just yesterday," he muttered to himself and shuffled some more. "Here! Here they are." He grabbed a file, picked through the papers, and pulled one out. "Would you please connect the dots?" He handed me the paper. "One through twenty," he added.

"Sure," I said.

"You need a pen," he said, reaching into his empty shirt pocket. He pushed his chair back again and began the process of moving the papers around to unearth his pen. "Here it is," he said, picking it up and handing it to me.

I quickly connected the dots as he asked, remembering I had done the same thing on the menu at Denny's the night before. When I was done, I handed it to Rodney.

"That's good," he said, putting it in the file. "That's enough tests." He leaned back in his chair. "I understand you are depressed."

Then I began to tell my story. I told him how my business had failed, how deeply I was leveraged, and how I couldn't pay back loans. I told him about the bankruptcy. I told him how when my loans were called, the bank took all I owned. I lost my rented home and all my possessions. I told him about the shame and despair, about how Sandra had left, about how my friends had rejected me, about my eventual eviction. I told him about the debilitating depression, about the burden I became to my children, and about how they, too, had had enough of me.

With every word, every sentence, every paragraph I became more depressed, until I was weeping uncontrollably.

It was then that Rodney stood up, pulled me close, and hugged me.

He held me until I felt a sense of peace, a sense of quiet come over me. It seemed like an hour.

A hug—the elixir for the human soul.

When I quit trembling, I knew I was lucky to have found this tour guide. If I was ever going to get out of the raging rapids that were tossing me about in this part of my life, he might be able to lead me back to shore.

I felt Rodney's arms beginning to release me. "Hey, Richard," he said.

"Sit down for a moment while I make a couple of notes to myself. And I'd like you to meet someone."

I sat down again, and Rodney grabbed his yellow notepad and began writing. After a minute or two, he reached over and picked up his bowl of food and took another bite. When he finished his paperwork, he reached for the phone and pushed a button. "Bob? You got a minute? Good. I've got somebody I want you to meet. We'll be right down." He stood up and looked at me. "Let's take a walk down the hall. I want you to meet Bob."

I followed Rodney out of the office, around the corner, and down the hall to another small office. The door was open, and a man was sitting at a desk, writing.

"Bob," Rodney interjected, "I want you to meet Richard."

The man stood up, extended his hand, and smiled. "Good to meet you," he said.

"Bob is our psychiatrist," Rodney said. "He might have some ideas that will help you. I'll leave you two alone."

"Have a seat." Bob motioned to a couple of chairs against the wall. He then picked up a box of cookies from his desk. "Would you like one?" he asked, holding the package out to me.

"Sure," I said, taking the box from his hand.

"Take all you want," he said as I dug in. "Would you like some coffee to go with them?"

"Sure."

"I'll get it for you and be right back," he said, getting up from his chair and backing out the door to the hall.

I took a bite of cookie and surveyed Bob's office. He had three Monet reproductions hanging on the walls. I stood up and examined each one as I took bites of the cookies. "Fuzzy flowers; fuzzy boats; fuzzy people," I thought as I looked at the paintings.

"Here's your coffee," Bob said, reappearing at the office door.

He handed me the cup and I sat down in the chair.

Bob slowly backed into his chair, an old high-back leather chair with wheels—a comfortable chair. "I spoke with Rodney at the coffee machine and he told me a little bit about you while I filled your cup," he said, rolling his chair forward and leaning toward me. I knew I was going to have to tell my story again—the depressing story—the story I was so trying to escape. "Can you tell me what happened?"

And so I began again, trying to be objective. I focused my eyes on the Monet painting on the wall behind Bob's mahogany desk, wishing I could somehow slip into that serene pastel world. I could hear my voice telling the story of loss again, but it was as if a kind narrator had stepped in to help out this time, and I just listened. I listened to the sad story, wanting so much to help the man, but I could not.

The narrator explained that some of my advertising clients had gone bankrupt and others had left my company to invest in the Internet, taking with them what was left of my business. He told him that my three children had once worked for me and that they had once admired me, depended on me, and believed in me. But when I could not pay back loans from banks and from friends, I hid in shame. I refused to answer telephones and prayed for a miracle. I went from being someone admirable to being someone terrified that I would be accused of fraud. Now my children saw a different father, one shrouded in misery. I was the dependent one now. I could no longer help myself.

My companion, Sandra, had loved me, loved my confidence and my wry smile. Now she saw a fearful, angry stranger with slumped shoulders. She would not stick around and watch my demise, and so she packed her possessions into a moving van and left to start a new life. Depression became my constant companion.

I closed my eyes to shut out the light, wishing I could just go to sleep, but the voice went on with the story. When I opened them again, I saw another man in the room who looked much like me. He was dressed in the same burgundy cashmere sportcoat I used to wear with blue dress pants. He wore a white starched shirt and a Frank Lloyd Wright tie. He interrupted the voice of the narrator.

"He is a good man," Mr. Sportcoat said to Bob. "He is just lost. First," he said, holding up one finger, "he lost his job. Then," he held up a second finger, "his companion—the woman he loved, the one who wrote 'I love you' notes and put them in his sock drawer. And then," fingers three through seven went up sequentially, "he lost his home, his friends, his children and grandchildren, his identity, his belief in God, and then his belief in himself. It has just been too much! Right now he needs a place to get out of the cold, to take a shower, to sleep."

Bob lifted his pen from the notepad and looked off into space. The room was quiet. "We don't have a place for him," he said to Mr. Sportcoat. "He's supposed to be in his prime right now; he's not supposed to be here! He's supposed to be investing in his retirement portfolio and planning his next vacation. He's supposed to be playing with the grandchildren on weekends. If he had robbed a bank or killed someone, then the state would spend the money necessary to lock him up. We just don't have a place—but we will find some way to help him, somehow."

"Well, do what you can do," Mr. Sportcoat said as he adjusted his handsome tie. He got up and left the room.

I remembered having three or four of those ties. I sold them one day for a dollar each at a secondhand store. I needed gas money; I always needed gas money.

The sonorous narrator was coming to the end of my story when I felt two hands placed tenderly on my cheeks, gently tugging my attention back to the man I sat with in this small office. "Richard, you've lost virtually everything that seemed to give your life meaning," Bob said, looking deeply into my eyes. "Most people could not live through that. You must feel like Job himself."

My narrator was gone.

"You have every right to be angry, and sad, and depressed," Bob said. "I am just happy you are here."

Tears filled my eyes again.

"There is hope," he continued. "We know that." Then he, too, lifted me from my chair and gave me a hug. "I know it is difficult to believe right now," I heard his muffled voice say through the hug. "But you are better now than you have ever been. You just need a warm place to live and some time to heal. Don't expect miracles. It will take time."

Then Bob pulled away. I immediately knew he had other people to see and other places to go. He had patched me up as best he could.

"We need to schedule another appointment," he said, looking at his calendar. "How about next Wednesday at two in the afternoon?"

"Okay," I said. Bob wrote it down.

I left the mental institution that day with a small glad bag of hope.

I knew it would not last long.

I needed a miracle. I needed lots of miracles.

Chapter 11

ANDY, THE BEAUTIFUL WEED

It must have been sometime after midnight when I was awakened by a loud tapping on the van window.

I was parked in the Methodist church parking lot that overlooks the city, tucked snugly into my sleeping bag. I ducked even deeper into the bag, covering my head, and put one hand on Willow, who had begun to growl. I figured it must be the police checking me out. I had been told by the guys at Sally's not to open the door. "They have to give you notice," Lenny had told me. "Don't open the door or get out. Just say 'I'm sleeping here,' and they have to give you twenty-four hours to get out."

"Richard! Richard! Wake up!" a familiar voice called out.

It wasn't the cops. It was C. "It's me, C," he called out. "Wake up! Wake up!"

I rolled over and opened the latch on the back hatch and pushed the door up. I was greeted by drops of rain and C's face. "Hey! I need your help," he said. "Andy's in trouble. Jake told me he saw him lying in the alley behind the 7-Eleven. If I can, I want to get to him before the police do."

"Sure," I said, sleepily. "It will just take me a minute to rearrange my stuff."

I quickly slipped on my shoes and tossed the stuff from the front seat into the back, and we took off to find Andy.

We were racing down the hill across the Warren Avenue Bridge toward the downtown 7-Eleven. "Jake stopped in at The Maple Leaf and told me about Andy," C said. "He couldn't do anything for him, so he walked up to The Leaf to get help. Then I walked up here. It's been maybe a couple of hours now."

The windshield wipers beat their steady rhythm as we pulled into the alley behind the 7-Eleven. Andy was still lying there, with the side of his face in a mud puddle. The walker he had been using was flipped over on its side.

"Damn!" C exclaimed. "Poor Andy!" We jumped out of the van before it had fully stopped, and C knelt down, lifting Andy's upper torso off the ground. "You alive, Andy?" he asked.

"Who'rrre you?" Andy slurred.

"It's C, Andy," C said, wiping the mud from Andy's face. "Damn, Andy! What are you doing here?"

"I, uh—I don know," Andy responded. "I'm jus—I'm jus here."

"Jesus, Andy! You're all wet," C continued. "And you smell! Did you pee your pants, Andy?"

"I guessss. I don—I don know." Andy was floating in and out of focus.

C looked up at me. "Richard, have you got any clean pants in your van?" he asked.

"I think so. I'll get a pair," I said, turning and heading toward the van.

"Maybe a shirt, too," C added. "It seems Andy threw up on himself as well."

I found a reasonably clean pair of pants and a wool shirt in the pile of clothes in the back of the van. C had already pulled Andy's pants off by the time I got back. He lifted Andy off the ground. "Can you hold him up while I get the pants on him?" he asked.

I grabbed Andy under the arms and attempted to stabilize him while C wrestled the clean pair of trousers first onto one leg and then the other. Andy was trembling from the cold. Once C got the pants up to Andy's waist, he unbuttoned and removed the shirt, tossing the old clothes aside and slipping the clean shirt on. Then C undid the knotted handkerchief from his own head and wiped the vomit from the edges of Andy's mouth. "Man! You got bad breath tonight, Andy!" he said, chuckling. Then C took off his coat and put it around Andy.

"Let's go, Andy," C said, and we each grabbed him under an armpit and led him to the van. We were moving as quickly as possible, all of us now pretty well soaked from the rain.

"Would you grab his walker?" C asked, as he settled Andy into the van. "Let's take him back to my RV. He can stay with me for a couple of days." We both took a deep breath as we started up the van. I turned up the radio as we headed back to the Armadillo, thinking that this last hour had been so "C-ish."

Andy was the classic alcoholic. He had been picked up by the police and taken to the emergency room forty-four times in a year. They would check him out, let him dry out for four or five hours, then send him back out on the street. Everyone had given up on Andy . . . except C.

Andy was what my psychologist called a "weed." "We see them every month or so, because they are sent here when they get in trouble with the rules. How they live and how they survive in this society is amazing. Every time they leave, we wonder if we will ever see them again. We don't really expect them to live. But somehow they just keep coming back, like weeds in between the rocks on a mountain trail—beautiful and persistent weeds."

My shrink's analogy was a compliment of the highest degree. Others would have ended their lives long ago, with a plethora of pills washed down with a pint of whisky. But Andy never gave up on life. He was truly a weed. Every time something chopped him off at the roots, he would come back.

Andy wasn't pretty. He looked like a skinny Andy Rooney. He shook when he drank but shook even more when he didn't. He was a querulous sort, complaining about everything when he was forced off the "sauce," for lack of money or some other reason. "Things fell through," he would often tell the few people who cared enough to listen to his story. For Andy, it was a whole lifetime of things falling through.

The weather had gotten nastier by the time we arrived at C's RV. It was raining harder and harder, and the wind had picked up. It slammed the aluminum door of the Armadillo against the side of the camper when C opened it. We scrambled to get Andy out of the back seat of the van and get all of us into the RV as quickly as we could.

"Whew!" I said, slamming the door shut when we were finally all inside.

C's two cats, MyLynx and Calico, jumped down from the loft above the front cab and welcomed their master back by rubbing against his legs, meowing loudly. The head of a black man appeared over the front seat. "What's up, fellas?" he asked.

"Hey, Brian," C replied. "I see you're in for the night."

"Yeah. It's nasty out there!" Brian said.

C propped Andy up on the seat of the fold-down bed. "I'm going to make some tea," he said, removing dirty pots and pans from the propane stovetop. "That will warm it up in here. Richard, that's Brian up front. Brian, this is Richard."

"Nice to meet you," Brian waved. I nodded my head in return.

"Brian is renting the front seat for ten bucks a month," said C, as he looked for a match. "He just got out of jail and needed a place to stay." He found the match and struck it, turning the knob and lighting the stove. "Hey, Brian. What would you think if we had Andy stay with us for a while?"

"Maybe he could do the dishes," Brian chuckled.

"How about ten dollars a month for rent, Andy?" C asked.

"Let's see," C mused, filling a teapot with water. "Ten dollars for first, ten for last, and ten for deposit. I'll waive the last and the deposit, but we'll have to check your credit report and your references."

"I think the guys down at the liquor store will vouch for him," Brian chimed in.

Andy was defenseless at this point. He just laid his head down on the bed.

"Let's get these shoes off of him," C said, pulling Andy's legs up on the bed and starting the process of unlacing his boots.

"Andy's had a rough life," reflected C. "He told me some of it one day when we were both panhandling in front of the 7-Eleven. He's from Texas—Houston, I think he said. His dad, who was a drunk and used to beat on him, kicked him out of the house when he was fifteen. Andy lived on the streets for a while. Houston was a tough town back in the seventies." The boots finally gave way, and C tossed a blanket over Andy. MyLynx jumped up to investigate the newcomer. The knowing feline sniffed and kneaded, then curled up by Andy's neck.

The battered teapot began to rattle on the burner. "You want a cup of tea, Brian?" asked C.

"No thanks," came the reply. "I'm going to try to get some shuteye." He disappeared back down the front seat—now a veritable condo!

C got up and picked the teapot off the burner, filled his cup with hot water, and sat back down. He methodically dipped his teabag in the cup. "Earl Grey. I love this tea," he said. "Hey, I found some premium snipes in the ashtrays just outside the emergency room entrance at the hospital." He reached for a tin can of cigarette butts on the counter. "Twenty or more—half smoked!" He was picking through the can, looking for the best one. Then he struck a match and lit up.

Andy began snoring. "I think that Andy's at his best asleep," observed C. "He told me once that when he dies, that's just how he wants to go. Just lie down, fall asleep, and die."

C sipped his steaming cup of tea, with an "Ah, that's good" thrown in amidst his memories and reflections. Then he sighed. "Andy's got a death wish. He's going to drink himself to death. He's getting worse. He shakes so badly when he can't afford booze. He panhandles for booze money up in front of the Albertsons—until he gets enough to buy a quart. We have to get him off the street for a little bit."

As Andy's snoring got louder, C rolled his eyes, and we shared a good chuckle. "He seems to be going downhill fast," I said. "He didn't used to need a walker."

"He's a strong man, though," C replied. "And fiercely independent. I couldn't do what he has done. He slept on the benches down at the ferry terminal all last winter. No blanket. No pillow. They finally kicked him out of there. He's slept in dumpsters. He's tough."

"How old is Andy?" I asked.

"Fifty-seven or so," C replied. "He told me once he hasn't had a birthday party in sixteen years. Yet more people in Bremerton recognize Andy than recognize the mayor! Bus drivers know Andy—and cab drivers, grocery store clerks, doctors, medics, and liquor store clerks. Everyone sort of loves Andy. He is harmless. He never hurt anybody—anytime, anywhere.

"He told me once that he started out working on an oil rig off the Texas gulf coast, near Corpus Christi, I think," C continued. "They called him 'Little Andy'—you know, part of that macho-man repertoire—that passive-aggressive mumbo-jumbo reserved for the smallest and the most gentle. They used to tease and taunt Andy because he liked to read books and write poetry."

I tried to picture Andy wearing one of those round metal caps, a sleeveless white undershirt, jeans and steel-toed high-top work shoes, covered in grease, his muscles rippling as he plied a large wrench to an oil-rig bolt in the hot Texas sun. That was Andy then—the same Andy who now panhandles up and down 6th Street on his broken-wheeled walker.

At age twenty, Andy left Texas and made his way up to the Northwest in stages. First he hitchhiked to San Diego, and then to Mexico, where he sampled the charms of the señoritas in Tijuana—until he was out of money and needed medical care. ("For excessive itching and burning between his legs," C said, "if you know what I mean.") Andy worked his way north doing odd jobs—as a short-order cook, as a farm hand picking grapes—until he landed a logging job near the Washington coast.

"Andy was one of those guys who climbed up those big trees and cut off the tops of those giants near the Olympic National Forest," C explained. He'd done that for several years and was making pretty good money for a while. But then one year he worked for a logging company that promised to pay him at the end of the job. He was living in a company cabin and eating company food with the other loggers. But after six months, the company went bankrupt and nobody got paid. He lost the few possessions he had and landed on the street.

"That's probably when Andy started seriously drinking, and he just never stopped," C surmised. "Just looking for a little comfort, you know? A little diversion from the pain. The liquor bottle became his best friend, his lover—and finally the only thing he could count on to slow the shaking."

"Well, do you think he just gave up?" I asked.

"No," C said. "Look at him. He's still here, thorns and all. A man like that doesn't just give up. He survives. He told me once that the cops kept rousting him out of the woods and finally got tired of it. As they were walking out of the woods, one cop gave him a baton to the back of the legs and a baton to the stomach. As Andy was lying there, the cop said, 'We want you to get out of town and never come back, Andy. Do you get the message?'"

"Did he leave town?" I asked.

"No. Not Andy. He has been beaten up several times." C described how some teenagers caught Andy one night in the alley behind the 7-Eleven, where we had found him tonight. They'd beaten him up just for the Friday-night fun of it.

Andy needed an "extreme makeover"—on the inside. Many of his internal parts appeared to be failing. As he inched his way down the sidewalks of Bremerton, eventually nature would call. If he ventured too far from the Salvation Army or the Ferry Terminal, he was in no-toilet land. Nine banks, six mortgage companies, eight insurance companies, ten attorney's offices, three jewelers, four art galleries, six antique stores, two tattoo parlors, eight bars, and two restaurants make up the business core of the town, and none of them wanted the likes of Andy using their bathrooms. He had tried them all before, in his quest to relieve himself, and they all said no and gave him that look that homeless people know so well. It's the look that says: "Get out of here and don't come back." So if Andy couldn't find a back alley really fast, he'd pee his pants.

C was shaking his head. "He told me he tried some things—tried to stop drinking, tried different jobs, even tried having a girlfriend. But each time things fell through. He would always lose the job, or the girlfriend would kick him out, and he would hit the bottle harder each time. His life sounds like one of those country songs—'my girlfriend left, my dog died, my trailer caught fire, and my truck got repossessed,'" C sang in his best twang.

I laughed. "Let me tell you unequivocally that you have absolutely *no* future in country music!"

C smiled and brought us back to the subject. "Do you believe in karma, Richard?"

"Well, I don't know," I replied. "No, not really, I guess. I have seen too many bad things happen to good people and too many good things happen to bad people to believe in that."

"Well," said C, "whether it was karma or just plain old bad luck, things have just never worked out for Andy. People tried to help now and again, and he'd stay with someone for a day or a week. But he always got kicked out. Now maybe nobody can really help Andy.

"There was probably a time in those years when just the right person or place would have worked for Andy. Just one break—a person who loved him enough to overlook his flaws—a place where he could blossom and turn into a beautiful rose. We are not *born* drunks, you know. But none of those good things ever happened for Andy."

The rain was now pounding on the roof of the Armadillo and we sat in silence, listening to the music nature was giving us.

I could see C's mind still working.

"I think I'm going to try to help him," he finally said. "Everybody can be helped and can help others. Yes, I'm going to do it." His voice was taking on more and more resolve.

I was a little mystified. "You're some kind of a saint," I said. He just gazed into space, the way he often did.

I finished up my tea and glanced down at my Timex. "Wow! It's four thirty in the morning; I've got to get some sleep." I stood up, stretched, and yawned.

"Well, thanks, Richard, for helping get Andy," said C.

"You bet." Willow had fallen asleep on the camper floor. I carefully picked her up, put her inside my coat, and headed out the door into the driving rain.

I tried to sort out my jumbled feelings as I drove back up to the church parking lot. What was all this about? I didn't feel sorry for Andy—Andy was just Andy. And Andy didn't need judgment or pity—mine or anyone else's. Andy was somehow able to take the good and let the bad pass by. Most of us live a lifetime without learning how crucial that can be, or how to perform that simple magic. Doubtless there was a lesson for me here. If so, it was a hard one for me to embrace.

But more than Andy, it was C whom I couldn't quite understand—his way of pulling strays in out of the rain. What made a man do that? Hell, even my *family* wouldn't do that for *me*, even clean and sober! It was "inconvenient" for them.

But that was the place I didn't want to go. Dwelling on that piece of grief would only get me in trouble.

Chapter 12

ANOTHER DAY IN PARADISE

She was new at Sally's.

When I arrived at eight a.m., she sat motionless at the round table farthest from the door, her face buried in her hands, her strawberry-blonde hair a mess. Four plastic bags packed to the brim were at her feet, and two small notebooks were lying on the table.

This was no professional bag lady. Her purse was Gucci, her clothes were fashionable, albeit wrinkled, and her Reeboks were a gleaming white.

I got a bowl of Cream of Wheat, two jelly donuts, and a cup of coffee and found a seat. It was Friday. I saw a newspaper in a trashcan in the corner. It was Wednesday's *New York Times*. "Good enough," I thought.

For some reason I couldn't help looking her way. I could see (well, almost see) the anguish of this lady. In the months of starting each day at Sally's between eight and eight thirty, I had seen many things—the drug-crazed, the schizos, the bipolars, and the drunks. But this was dark—really dark.

I could see, and feel, the big black cloud of depression hovering in her sky, blocking out every ray of sunlight. I knew that feeling. At times like that, it felt as if I was drowning. Just below the surface. I knew something was up there; it was life, but I didn't care.

And I knew she didn't care. She knew her future. She would live out the lyrics of the Phil Collins song "Another Day in Paradise," calling for help but never being heard.

One of the black guys, Alan, came strolling in and walked her way. He touched her gently on the shoulder and she slowly raised her head.

"You've got to eat, Karen," he coaxed. "You'll feel better." The woman shook her head. She closed her eyes and laid her head back down on the table.

Alan, a slim man with a small goatee, placed his hand on his chin and rubbed his whiskers in a moment of contemplation. He tried again, politely tapping her on the shoulder. When she raised her head this time, he bent at the waist, cocked his head, and smiled.

"Please eat with me; I don't like to eat alone. I'll get something for you," he said.

"Okay," she murmured.

Alan lied. AP—that's what his friends called him—seldom ate. He usually drank his meals. He liked vodka best, but he'd settle for Night Train Express (fortified wine) for lunch and dinner. He was a happy drunk. He was also a super-salesman. It was hard to say no to AP.

AP called the four-block radius around the Salvation Army building home. He roamed the area each day, panhanding in his special way. He'd stop a person along the street and tell him a joke or compliment him on his coat, hat, or tie. And then he would always ask him for eighty-seven cents.

"I need eighty-seven cents, just eighty-seven cents," he would say.

Hell, his jokes were worth eighty-seven cents!

"I learned it in Los Angeles," he said of his trick. "They always give you a dollar. No one is going to count out eighty-seven cents," he added, laughing.

AP talked with his hands, waving and pointing to emphasize each word, and after years of refining his routine, he had it down. It usually ended with a palm extended and a smile on his etched face. When he got enough money for a fifth of vodka, he would stop for some "lunch."

AP was fifty-four years old and lived with two other gentlemen behind Sally's. They would roll out their sleeping bags at night and pass out under a stairwell that led to the basement of the building. They caused no harm, committed no fouls, and were on a first-name basis with the police who cruised the alleys at night. After years of experience, the cops were happy the men were there. They would report it if the really bad guys showed up.

AP never ventured more than four blocks in any direction from Sally's, especially north toward the Manette Bridge. Four years ago, just past 11th Street, he told four young men a joke and then asked them for eighty-seven cents. They beat him nearly to death. He was helicoptered to University Medical Center in Seattle and spent a month in bed. While he was there, the doctors ran some tests and discovered he had colon cancer. They gave him two years to live. AP walked out of the hospital and hasn't seen a doctor since that day.

Late one Friday night, the boys were up drinking and smoking in the alley and listening to some tunes on an old radio they had found in a dumpster, when Karen showed up. It was one in the morning. She was hungry and tired from her several-mile walk. She had been evicted from her home in Poulsbo. AP gave her the half of the bologna-and-cheese sandwich he had left from Wednesday's sack lunch at Sally's. He tried to cheer her up with a few of his jokes and even shared his Night Train Express. Like the gentleman he was, he even gave her his sleeping bag to get her through the night.

This man who was supposed to be dead by now, this man who had given up dreaming, hoping, planning for the future—AP was worried about this woman. He instinctively knew that she had two roads to choose between: One was long and could take her to a new life in the sun, the other was very short and very dark. He got her a bowl of hot cereal, some orange juice, and a cup of coffee and returned to the table. "Here, this is for you. I'll be right back. You want some cream? I'll tell you a joke after I get mine," he said. Then he quickly grabbed two jelly donuts and some cereal for himself and hurried back to the table.

"Ronald Reagan, George Bush, and Bill Clinton went to see the Wizard of Oz," AP began. "'What do you want of the great and powerful Wizard?' the Wizard bellowed. 'Well, Mr. Wizard, I've been forgetting a lot of things lately, and, well, I thought, if possible, well, could I get a new brain?' Reagan asked.

"'And what do you want?' the Wizard roared, looking at George Bush. 'I've got to tell you, Wizard, when that lying Bill Clinton beat me in the election, it broke my heart. I need a new heart!'

"'And you, Bill Clinton, what do you want?' the Wizard thundered. Bill replied, 'Where's Dorothy?'"

AP belly-laughed and slapped his hand to his leg. Karen smiled wanly.

James, one of AP's "roommates," came in, poured himself a cup of java, grabbed a donut, took a bite, and headed for my table. "The Mariners lost again, man; four-one," he said of Oakland's win over Seattle. "They're a game and a half back now. They're going to do just like last year. Lead all year long, and then fizzle out at the end."

"It doesn't look promising," I said. "Their pitching looks tired, and nobody seems to be able to get a hit with runners on base." My eyes glanced over to AP and Karen.

James noticed. He leaned toward me. "That lady is having a bad time. A real bad time, man," he whispered. "Got put out on the street by the sheriff yesterday. An eviction. They put her stuff on the curb, man.

On the curb! In Poulsbo! No one helped her, man. No one! What's all that about?"

She was now in her first day, her first hours of being homeless.

"What's that like, man, to, you know, lose everything?" James asked. "Somebody told me you were rich—boats and stuff—and lost it all. I never had anything to lose."

"She's in shock right now," I said. "I don't know her story, but she's wondering why the angels didn't come and save her; why God deserted her; why nobody cared. Her nerve endings tingle. Everything seems fuzzy. It's like a bad dream that will go away as soon as she wakes up. She wonders where her friends are and why they aren't helping. She wonders why all the people who said they loved her are not here trying to help. She feels hopeless. Totally hopeless." I took a drink of my coffee. "She has no bed. No pillows. No pots and pans. No television. No refrigerator. No closet to hang her pretty clothes in. No clean socks. No cherished mementos or pictures of loved ones sitting on the tables or hung on the walls, no table or chairs, no candles or incense, no flowers. No place of her own, no true privacy. All the things that made her Karen are gone. I don't know her story, but I have been right where she is, and it's going to be tough, very tough for her to make it."

My mind flashed back to my own eviction. But I fought to stop that memory. *Please, let's not go back there*, I whispered urgently to myself, and buried my head in my hands. But I could not win this battle with my mind, not at this moment in this place.

I remembered being in the courtroom before Judge McCluskey. Sitting on his throne in his black robe, he had evicted three other families before me that day. I thought, "This poor man has a miserable job—putting people on the street. I wouldn't be able to sleep at night if I were him."

The notice was on my door by four p.m. that day.

I remembered curling up in the corner of my living room the night before my eviction, covered by a blanket and holding Willow in my arms, hoping the world would change overnight and people would be kinder to each other.

I remembered my son-in-law's father, who came to see me be evicted that day. He said, "I don't feel sorry for you!" I wondered, "How could anyone not feel sorry for a person being evicted, tossed out in the street? I would feel sorry for anyone experiencing that."

And then I remembered pulling out of the driveway of my home with my dog in the van—and no place to go.

If the lady across the room had any of the feelings I had had, she wasn't going to make it past this day. No one where she came from cared. Only AP cared at this point, and he was a total stranger to her and her world.

Karen now had her hands spread out before her on the table, and I could see the chipped red nail polish and the gold band on her finger. "She probably paints her toes, too," I thought to myself. "I bet she looks pretty nice when she's all gussied up."

"Look, man," James said. "She's still wearing a wedding ring." I continued to look at her, at her hands and her ring and her face.

Karen's eyes met mine as she looked across the room. I feared she knew we were talking about her. I wanted to rush to her, to try to save her. But I could not. I had no magic wand.

She looked away from me for a moment and then looked back again. Her gaze lingered. She was talking to me with her eyes. *You know, don't you?* they asked. *You've been here, here like me, haven't you? But you can't help me, can you?* Then she looked away.

I saw something in her eyes I didn't have: courage, resolve. I knew what she was going to do. She had already decided.

She was accustomed to having things—nice clean clothes, perfume, cream for her face, and feather pillows. She had grown to enjoy, no, to expect, instant gratification. Now all she owned were the clothes on her back and the few things she could carry in plastic bags. The bankers, the masters of credit had taken everything else from her, just for a few more dollars in their accounts. The rich had to be protected, you know, so they could buy another house, or another boat, or another cruise. It's the American way, to throw people out on the street.

"I wish the Major were here," I said anxiously. "He might be able to help her. But someone said he is out collecting food today."

"What we need, man, is a SWAT team," said James. "Yeah, a 'SWAT team for goodness'—good guys jumping off the roof with ropes and busting in the door to help her. That's what we need right now, mister."

I kept scanning the room for C. Maybe he could help her, with a poem or something. But he wasn't in sight either.

"I'm going out for a smoke," James said, pushing away from the table.

"I'll go with you," I said.

We cleared our trays like schoolboys and headed outside into the drizzle that had just begun to fall.

"Let's see, who do the M's play now?" I asked. "They have Oakland again tonight and then come home for two against Anaheim, I think. They need to start winning, man, or it's over."

While we were talking baseball, Karen came out the door. AP was right behind her. "Where you goin', Karen?" AP asked. "Why don't you just hang out here awhile? Heck, it's raining, and you don't have a coat."

Karen kept walking, empty-handed, in the rain, through the pay parking lot that adjoined Sally's.

"I'll be back," AP said to James, as he rushed to catch up with her. She was now a half a block away.

By the time they had reached 8th Street, AP was pleading.

"C'mon girl! Please don't cry. Let's go back before we get soaked in this rain. I'm going back!" he said, stomping his foot on the pavement.

Karen kept walking.

AP rushed again to her side. "Look, baby, we can get some money—James and me can! You can get a room at the motel. We can make things better for you! Let's go back."

But there was no going back for Karen.

At 10th Street, AP stopped. He had gone his four blocks, the end of his safety zone. "Where you goin'?" he yelled as she crossed the street the turned right toward the Manette Bridge. "What you gonna do?"

AP raced back to Sally's to get help.

There were just three blocks remaining before Karen would reach the bridge.

By the time AP got back to Sally's and we drove to the bridge, we knew she was gone. Cars were already stopped on the bridge with people peering over the worn rail. We could hear the sirens from police cars in the distance.

They retrieved her body two hours later.

At dusk I found AP sitting on the crumbling cement steps by the walled-off back entrance to Sally's, with a fresh bottle of Night Train Express. He was wiping tears away with his shirtsleeve. James and Lionel were there, too, but no one was talking. AP wasn't telling any jokes.

"I'm sorry," I said, knowing no words could soothe the pain. And then I turned and walked away.

"Hey, Richard!" AP called out. I turned and walked back, and he handed me a small paper sack. "I don't know what to do with these. I just can't throw them in the dumpster. Maybe you know what to do with them?"

I opened the bag and took out a small plastic makeup case with a cracked lid, a lipstick holder, and two small notebooks.

"She left them on the table," AP said.

One notebook had a Monet flower design on the cover. I opened it. The first page had been torn out.

On the second page she had written:

WATCH, PENLIGHT, CAT, BRACELET TO LITTLE JOE

On the third page began a poem:

> *The winter here is cold and bitter,*
> *it's chill ass to the bone and I*
> *haven't seen the sun for weeks too long*
> *too far from home.*
> *I feel like I'm sinking and I*
> *claw for solid ground.*
> *I'm pulled down by the undertow*
> *I never thought I could feel this low.*
>
> *Oh ~~Death~~ Darkness, I feel like letting go.*
> *All of the strength and all the courage comes*
> *to lift me from this place.*

Three pages later she wrote:

> *Today I choose to love, not hate.*
> *Forgive, not accuse.*
> *Lay down my life for them who don't believe anyone*

cares.

Not return evil with evil.

Put Satan to rest by not allowing them to be the opposite

Of what they really are.

Not let their walls block my view of their Soul.

Be a friend to all.

The other notebook was handmade from a notepad from the Navy Federal Credit Union with the words WORTH NOTING in gray letters at the top of each page. The pages were stained by something spilled on them.

On the second page she began:

She took her life within her hands
She took within her two hands
No one can tell her now
I believed in you
Underneath this canopy of snow
Where 57 winters took their toll
I believed in you
Where did you go?
I believed in you
Where did you go?
Gone to meet her
Back from where she came
Maker gone to save her soul
Come to me
She took her life in her own two hands
Angel, fly over me my Angel

Come
It's late and past your bedtime
I will keep you safe forever
I will keep you safe
Angel my Angel.

After a minute or so, I looked at AP, James, and Lionel and asked if they wanted to say a prayer for the lady. They all nodded.

We joined hands in the gravel parking lot and I said, "Dear God, please help Karen find peace in your gracious and loving home. Amen."

Then I asked AP, "Could you spare a glass of that Night Train Express?"

"I don't have no glass, but you can have a swig or two," he replied and handed me the bottle.

I found a seat on one of the old blue plastic milk crates and shared the bottle with AP, and he started telling me a joke. "Colin Powell, Norman Schwartzkopf, and George Bush were captured by the Iraqis," he began. "They took Powell before the firing squad . . ."

As AP was telling his joke, my mind returned to the night I had attempted to end my life like Karen had.

I wondered how it must have felt—falling through the air, knowing death was just seconds away. I wondered how she felt in that final moment when all she ever knew—thinking, breathing, talking, walking, living—was leaving her body.

I wondered if she was now in Hell in the hands of the Devil, like all the preachers warn. Was the Evil One chuckling, "I've got you now. You are going to get what you deserve, you homeless, worthless scum"?

Or perhaps she was in heaven, where Jesus himself would be toweling her off and consoling her as she cried, "I couldn't stand it anymore. It's terrible down there."

And He would reply, "I know, Karen. I know."

Chapter 13

I GET SAVED

A week had gone by since I had seen Dr. Z and he had started me on drugs. They had not kicked in yet. I was expecting them to, though, any day now . . . with a great rush of jubilation!

I had a nine o'clock appointment today, which I knew would be brief. I had read most of the textbooks on depression at the library while I was trying to escape the rain and the cold, and this was a textbook follow-up. "The patient, who has failed in a suicide episode, may feel 'up' and stronger and could again attempt to take his or her life in the first month of taking the antidepressant drug," read one of my sources.

I was pretty sure Dr. Z just wanted to see if I could make it back alive.

The waiting room was full again when I walked in the door. I think I recognized three of the elderly ladies from my last visit. I was hoping Nurse Jane would be there with her kind words of understanding, but a different voice called out to me as I was sitting and looking out the window. "Richard?"

"Yes. That's me," I said, looking up at the nurse standing by the door that led to the examining rooms. She was a short woman with a round face, dark skin, and a plump body. Her plumpness pushed the limits of the buttons on the smock she wore. She had a pleasant enough smile, but it seemed misplaced. But hell, what did I know? I was on drugs!

"I'm Tina," she said. "Please follow me." She led me back to a room. "Hop up there on the examining table. We have to do the routine." I complied, and she pointed a thermometer toward my mouth. "Open up."

While the thermometer was doing its job, Nurse Tina wrapped the blood-pressure cuff around my arm and pumped the ball quickly. She was a strong woman, and it only took seconds for her to complete the task. She ripped the tester off and whipped the thermometer from my mouth. She looked at it and pronounced, "You're good!" She took just a moment to make the appropriate notations in my chart.

"The doctor will be here in a minute," she said. Opening the door, she put my chart in the slot just outside the examining room. Then she turned back into the room, paused, and looked at me intently. "You know, Nurse Jane told me about you and that you need a place to stay."

"Yeah. I'm still living in my van," I replied.

"Well, I have a place you can stay free for a few months," she said, reaching out and putting her hand on my shoulder. "You can stay there until you get back on your feet. How does that sound?"

I was stunned. At first, I was speechless, so I just stared at her. Finally the words began to form. "I hardly know what to say." I paused, and then said, "Sure. I can't turn down an offer like that."

She smiled and reached for a notepad on the shelf. Taking a pencil from her pocket, she said, "I'm writing down the directions to my place in Gig Harbor, and my cell phone number. I won't get off here until six tonight, and then I am going to church before going home. Until then, I have a friend—the pastor from church—who can help you, and you can meet me at the church tonight. Would that be okay?"

I was still pretty numb. "Sure," I mumbled.

Nurse Tina took another piece of paper from the pad and began writing. "I'm giving you the pastor's address and directions to get there. His name is Bob; he owns a car dealership. I'll call him and tell him you will be on the way."

"Thank you," I said, as she handed me the instructions.

"The only thing I ask is that you don't tell the doctor. Okay?"

"Okay," I replied. "This is very nice of you. I can't thank you enough. I—"

Just then the door opened and Dr. Z interrupted me in mid-sentence. He had my folder in his hand as he walked into the room. Nurse Tina said, "No temp, and blood pressure is okay." She made her exit.

"How are you feeling?" Dr. Z asked, looking at me over the top of the chart. "Any better?"

"About the same," I said.

"Next week you will feel better," he assured me. "I'm going to make an appointment for the same time, same day. Okay?"

"Okay."

"I'll see you then. Take your pills," he added as he walked out the door.

I left in a bit of a daze.

Once I was back in the van with Willow, I followed the directions Tina had written out. It took about fifteen minutes to get to Pastor Bob's dealership. He was talking with a couple about a minivan when I arrived. He acknowledged my presence by pointing at me and saying, "You must be Richard. Tina called me. I'll be with you in just a minute."

Bob excused himself from the couple and disappeared, but returned instantly with the keys to the van and a handful of paperwork, which he handed to the happy car buyers. He shook their hands, smiled, and wished them well, and they were off.

He was walking toward me when the ringing of the cell phone on his hip claimed his attention. He reached for it with one hand while extending the other to me. "Hi," he said. "I'm Pastor Bob. Hold on a second." Then he put the cell phone to his ear. "This is Bob . . . Hey, Ernie! Where have you been?" He turned and paced a few feet away as he listened. "Well, let's pick it up tomorrow, then—about noon. I'll meet you here." He continued to pace back and forth as he listened. "Yeah, the guy is another deadbeat. I warned him we would come and get it if he didn't pay." He listened again and then said his goodbyes and clicked the phone cover shut just as the beeper on the other side of his belt vibrated. Bob slipped it off his belt to check the number and then looked at me. "Hey, let's go for a ride." He grabbed his leather coat off the wooden stand near the door, and I followed along.

Pastor Bob sold used cars Monday through Saturday during the day. He was a repo man at night, on Mondays, Tuesdays, Thursdays, and Saturdays. Then on Wednesday nights and Sunday mornings he held services at a small, ascetic Jewish church, where he would cajole, shame, and whip a small flock into a frenzy—a frenzy for Jesus.

As we walked toward his car, I asked, "Okay if I bring my dog, Willow?" Bob hesitated. "She goes everywhere I go."

"Okay, sure, bring her along," Bob replied, opening the door of his huge Chevy SUV. We all climbed in, and Bob whipped out of the parking lot and onto the main thoroughfare. "Tina said you're homeless, and she is going to put you up in her camper for awhile."

"Yeah. It's really nice of her," I said.

"She is a very nice person." Pastor Bob pressed the volume button on the radio, increasing the intensity of the *Rush Limbaugh Show*. Limbaugh was explaining to his "dittoheads" that he had to change his opening theme song because the artist didn't agree with his views and didn't want him using her song.

"Can you imagine that?" Pastor Bob exclaimed. "Some nut doesn't want Rush to play her music on his show!"

A copy of the local newspaper was lying on the front seat, so I picked it up and pulled out the sports section. "The SuperSonics lost again," I said, trying to make conversation.

"I don't like basketball," Bob said. "Or baseball, or football. It's a waste of man's time. I'm too busy for that stuff."

I flipped the newspaper over to the horoscopes and read mine in silence. I'm a Taurus with a Capricorn rising sign. The forecast looked good, so I decided to share it with Pastor Bob. "It looks like a good day for me," I offered.

"Why's that?" Bob asked.

"My horoscope says, 'Words of Wisdom come out of the blue to guide you in important decisions; an unexpected stroke of luck will—'"

"Reading those things is a sin!" Pastor Bob interrupted, and he pulled off to the side of the road. "They're the work of the Devil," he continued, his voice rising. "Whenever you read those, you are giving the Devil power. You are mocking God's will. As soon as you can, you need to get down on your knees and ask God to forgive you for reading those things!"

"I—I'm sorry," I said, folding up the paper and laying it on the back seat, wondering just what I'd gotten myself into.

Pastor Bob put his rig back in gear and pulled out onto the pavement just as Limbaugh delivered his final comments: "Despite what the liberals want you to believe, our brave sons and daughters are bringing democracy to Iraq. Gotta go. I'll see you tomorrow!"

I tried once again to make conversation. "So do you think the United States can bring democracy to Iraq?"

I should have known better.

"Oh, *yes!*" Pastor Bob was off and running. "They had better learn over there. They need to be saved! The rapture is coming! God, His Holy Son, and *all* the Angels are coming out of the sky, and they're going to cut off the heads and burn the bodies of those who are not saved. It will be one great inferno!"

He was gaining momentum. "The Almighty is going to destroy the baby killers, the homosexuals, and anyone who doesn't live by His word. He will bury them in mud and send waves to destroy their homes in every place in the world. I know! I have been to Israel six times! I have walked where Jesus walked. I have felt His pain!" His eyes began to get teary and his voice was trembling.

I thought it best to just keep my mouth shut. I turned and looked out the window, wishing I could escape Pastor Bob's big blue SUV.

Bob composed himself and cleared his throat. "President Bush can't come right out and say it, but he believes homosexuality is a sin against God Almighty. If I could cure them of their disease, I would plunge my hand into them and pull out the cancer that dwells inside them. Then I would take those people and put them into a homosexual treatment center to cure that abomination forever more."

I remained quiet, but my imagination could not be silenced. I tried to picture what a "homosexual treatment center" would look like to him. Would it have photos of porn stars like Chesty Morgan holding up her 44Ds, Nina Hartley with her legs spread, and Janie displaying her pierced vulva? If so, it would be just like the bathroom at The Maple Leaf, which is about as far as you can get from a gay-friendly establishment.

"You're not one of *them*, are you?" Pastor Bob peered at me for my answer.

"Oh, no, no," I said, laughing.

"Because, if you are," he continued, this time leaning toward me, "not even the most powerful preachers in Dallas or Houston can save you. You are damned!"

"Not me. I like women," I assured him.

Bob pulled back from me. He appeared greatly relieved by my answer, and he focused his eyes back on the road ahead.

Shortly, he raised his right hand and began to quote scripture to me: "And God said . . ."

Pastor Bob had driven us to the edge of town. We were in a neighborhood of rundown houses and pulled up in front of one. There was a plastic children's pool in the front yard, which had collapsed on one side. The water remaining in the pool was a very special shade of stagnant green. The yard was littered with broken plastic toys—a Tyco wheelbarrow with no wheel, a lawn mower with one wheel, and a plastic bike with no handlebars. It was a true Toys"R"Us junkyard.

"I'll be right back," Bob said, as he opened the SUV door, activating the electronic *ding-ding-ding*. I watched Bob walk to the front door and knock. A few seconds later, a man in a T-shirt opened the door and they conversed. I could tell by the way Pastor Bob was shaking his head that the man in the T-shirt didn't have the answers Pastor Bob was looking for. He was frowning as he walked back to the vehicle. The *ding-ding-ding* sounded again as he opened the door and slid behind the wheel.

"Another freeloader," he said with disgust, turning the ignition key. "The SOB is a week behind in his rent. I own several houses I rent out. I told him to pay in two days or I'm going to toss him out."

"I'm sorry to hear that," I replied. "Speaking of money, Tina said you might be able to help me out with some gas money. Would you? Maybe ten dollars? I'm on empty."

"I never carry any cash," he responded, seeming to brush off my request. "I use my credit cards all the time; I get frequent-flyer miles. I like to go to Las Vegas to see all the shows, and we went to Disneyland the last three years with the kids. Remind me tonight at church, and I'll get you ten then."

Pastor Bob made an abrupt turn off the main road into a cul-de-sac and rolled to a stop. He grabbed his cell phone and pushed one number. "Ernie? It's Bob. Hey, I just made a pit stop and that Toyota is sitting in the driveway. We are on for the repo tomorrow!" He slapped the phone closed and put it on the seat beside him. "The deadbeat who bought that car from me," he said, pointing to the tan Corona, "is two months

behind in his payments. We're going to repossess it at noon tomorrow."
He paused and looked at me. "Hey! I've got an idea: How would you like
to go to work for me?"

"I—I don't know," I stammered. "I do need the money . . ."

"Well, I need somebody to help Ernie repo cars," he said.

"Gosh, I don't know. I've never done that before. It sounds dangerous."
I was stalling.

"It's easy! I can train you. I'll pay you ten bucks an hour."

"I'll have to think about it," I finally said, trying not to say no and
certainly not wanting to say yes.

"Well, think about it." Pastor Bob said, as he started his SUV again.
He made a U-turn and headed back to his dealership.

"You need a job," he said as the car picked up speed. "After you have
repossessed four or five cars and have some money in your pocket, you
will feel better. You will have that feeling of accomplishment and pride."
He paused briefly. "You said you like women, didn't you?" He lowered
his voice just a bit. "I bet you don't have a woman right now, do you?"

I fumbled for an appropriate answer, but Pastor Bob just kept talking.
"I know you don't," he said, "because it's 'no money, no honey'! That's
the way it is. Women like money. They have to have it!" He laughed
heartily.

"I—I—" I began again, thinking of mentioning women like Mother
Theresa, but Bob was on a roll.

"After you get a few repos under your belt, maybe we can find you a
good Christian woman who will . . ."

Pastor Bob kept on talking, but I tuned him out. In a fifteen-minute
car ride, he was stripping away any small piece of dignity I had left. He
reached for the radio and rock music filled the SUV. He reached out
again and pushed the volume up; then he began to sing along.

It was a tune I didn't know, but it had a nice beat. The lyrics were
strung together with liberal doses of "my Lord" and "my Savior."

"That's Michael W. Smith," Pastor Bob stopped singing long enough to inform me. "He's going to sell more records than Elvis or the Beatles before he's done. We flew down to Branson, Missouri, to see him *live*, a couple of weeks ago."

While Bob was tapping his finger on the steering wheel to the beat of the music, I began to hum an old Beatles song, listening to the words in my head.

"What's that song you're humming?" Pastor Bob asked.

"Oh, just one of those old Beatles songs," I said. "It's called 'Imagine.'"

"I don't think I've heard that one," he said.

I sat quietly until we turned into the dealership and pulled to a stop. "Well, Richard, I'll see you tonight at church," Bob said, opening his door.

I climbed out of the SUV, picked Willow up, and carried her to my van. We needed to find a park where Willow and I could take a walk and think.

We found one not too far away and pulled into the parking lot. Willow jumped out of the van, and a chipmunk caught her eye. She was off in a second for the chase, but stopped at the base of a tall fir, which the chipmunk had scampered up to escape my wild Willow. "You treed that one, Willow!" I laughed as she circled the towering tree.

The beautiful branches of the fir draped across the sky. I stood there, admiring the natural wonder, and tried to envision Pastor Bob's angry angels flying in at light speed to kill all the gays with laserlike, pinpoint fireballs, burning all the sinners and nonbelievers and horoscope readers, and then airlifting Pastor Bob and his flock to a Disneyland/Las Vegas heaven. Was I expected to believe that God was going to destroy this wonderful creation we call Earth—the tree I was admiring, the waist-high ferns that surrounded me, the mountains and all the other creatures—in a gigantic hissy fit? I found that hard to believe.

Early that evening I pulled into the small parking lot of the church. It was just before seven. There were about ten cars in the lot, all with ELECT BUSH-CHENEY and JESUS SAVES stickers on their bumpers. I was hoping the owners would take up a collection to save *me* that night.

As I opened the door of the small church, I was greeted by the sight of a dozen or more people. Pastor Bob was busy setting up a projector and a movie screen, but he waved and smiled at me. I waved and smiled back. It didn't take him long to get the show under way. "I've got a great movie for us to watch tonight," he announced. "Would you all take your seats, please?" We all found seats in the pews as the lights were flipped off and the projector rolled.

The perfect preacher and the perfect choir in the perfect church in Dallas filled the screen. The preacher paced back and forth on the massive stage, asking his flock over and over again if they wouldn't be willing to give up everything to be born again—the job at the plant, the wife, the house, the truck. "What price would you pay for everlasting life?" he asked. Then he told the perfect story of his perfect daughter leading the perfect life, and everyone—on the screen and in the little church hall—was yelling "Hallelujah!" and "Praise the Lord!" Then the perfect daughter went off to the perfect college and was the perfect student— until she forgot to be perfect all the time, and she smoked, and she drank, and she even tried that *evil* marijuana. But God told the perfect pastor and his perfect wife what to do, and they went to California to get their once-perfect daughter and bring her back to the Lord, and everybody yelled "Amen!" After a dramatic pause, the pastor stated in an intimate tone that quickly rose to a shout, "Sandi Jean didn't ask to be born. But she did ask to be *born again*. She asked Christ Jesus to forgive her her sins, and *He did!*"

The crowd in Dallas was now standing, crying out, "Praise God! Praise God! Hallelujah!" And everyone in the small church in Gig Harbor was doing the same, except me. This was new to me. But I'll try anything, so I stood up, raised my arms halfway with my fists clenched, and mumbled a "Hallelujah" or two. I felt I wasn't doing it right, so I watched the man in front of me, raised my arms a little higher, and opened my palms. "Praise God," I ventured. "Praise God."

The preacher on the film held out both arms as the chorus of praises continued. Then, like a maestro before a grand symphony orchestra, he raised his right hand and the throng quieted. "If you, too, want to be born again, all you have to do is ask!" and the audience erupted again in applause. Then three white projector screens came floating down from the top of the cathedral like billowing clouds, and a woman in a sequined white dress walked to the center of the stage with a microphone in hand. "Please sing along," she sang to the audience, as music and lyrics appeared on each screen.

"Je-sus, Je-sus, Je-sus," the song began, and a little cross appeared above each word to help the crowd sing along. "We want to know you. We want to know you." The cross bounced from syllable to syllable.

"I know this one," I thought to myself. "That's a George Harrison song. 'I really want to know you . . .'" I hummed to myself.

"Je-sus, Je-sus," the woman in white sang, raising her hand slowly to the screen.

"Well, I guess it isn't the George Harrison song after all," I concluded. "But they stole his line!"

The people in the little white church joined in the song, closing their eyes and raising their hands and their heads to the ceiling. I did the same, except I kept one eye open to follow the dancing cross.

Pastor Bob turned on the lights and raced to the projector as the film came to its end. People scrambled about the church, lining up for the bathroom. Meanwhile, I studied the tapestries hanging on the walls, trying to figure out what they meant. What I saw looked like ghosts and animal sacrifices, probably scenes from the Old Testament.

With everyone now back in their seats, Pastor Bob stepped to center stage and did a local replay for his little flock. "Did you like the film?" *Hallelujah!* "Have you all been born again?" *Yes!* "How about you, Mary Lou?" *Yes!* "And you, Jim? Have you been born again?" *Yes, hallelujah!* "And you, Richard?" He was pointing at me. "Have you been born again?"

"I . . . I . . ." I stammered and hesitated. Everyone was staring at me in the silence. "I think so," I finally managed to say.

"No, that can't be!" Pastor Bob said. "You know when you are born again. It's not like anything you have ever known before!"

Everyone yelled "Hallelujah!" and I felt a hand on my right shoulder, then another on my left. "Save this sinner, Father God!" I heard the voice on the left say. "Hallelujah! Hallelujah!" came the response from the right. They gently pushed me forward until I was standing below Pastor Bob. I could hear the movement of the congregation and soon they had encircled me. They all knelt and clasped their hands in prayer.

I wanted to run. But how? My gas tank was nearly empty and I had no place to go. I wanted to say, "Hey, guys, this isn't for me." But that would spoil their party. I felt trapped.

Pastor Bob reached out, put his hand on my shoulder, and began praying, "Dear Father God, forgive this man his sins and help him accept you and be born again." Then I felt other hands touching my shoulders and pushing me back. Still other hands caught me from behind and lowered me to the floor, until I was prone. As I was making that long journey from standing upright and independent to being helpless on the floor, I thought of the pictures of the animals on the wall hangings I had studied earlier. Was I to be some form of ritual sacrifice? There were hands all over me now. I closed my eyes, giving in to whatever was to follow. I could see no way out.

"Drive the sin from this man, oh Father God," Pastor Bob prayed fervently. Others eagerly joined in with shouts of "Hallelujah! Hallelujah!" and another woman's voice layered in the "Oh God, Oh God. God, God, God!"

"Wow—that voice sounds very similar to the voice from room 204 back at the Driftwood Motel a week ago!" I thought. I opened one eye ever so slightly to see who was crying out the "Oh God, Oh God," and it was the preacher's wife, Doreen, kneeling over me with her arms stretched skyward, her head bowed and her eyes closed.

A man's voice shouted, "Be gone, Satan! Be gone!"

"Save this child, Jesus," Pastor Bob said. "In God's name, save him!"

I didn't know what to do. I was afraid to open my eyes. I expected to see a vision of George Bush on the ceiling. And I didn't know what to say. I remembered Burt Lancaster in *Elmer Gantry*, vowing, "I'm going to fight the Devil. I'm going to kick him; I'm going to bite him!" I thought of Robert Duvall repeating "Holy Ghost power! Holy Ghost power!" in *The Apostle* and Steve Martin working his miracles in *Leap of Faith*. But my thespian skills were rusty. My biggest acting role ever was playing the little tailor in *Seven in One Blow* in the sixth grade. I had also played the ensign in *Mister Roberts* when I was a junior in high school. I think I had two lines: One was "Mister Roberts! Mister Roberts, the palm tree is missing!" and I couldn't remember the other—but even if I could, it undoubtedly wouldn't serve me well in my current situation.

They were now all chanting over me. The passionate tones of a woman with a speech impediment resounded above me. "God, hep him, hep him!" I knew they weren't going to give up, and they certainly weren't going to give me any gas money until I was saved. There had to be some climax to this night.

So I started trembling in my hands, then in my arms, then in my legs. I moved my head from side to side and whispered, "Thank you, Jesus." I waited a moment and added, "Thank you, Father God!"

"Hallelujah," said Pastor Bob. "Hallelujah," another man's voice echoed.

I opened my eyes, and the arms of the people quickly lifted me to my feet. Each member of the small congregation hugged me. Pastor Bob quickly turned and flipped on the stereo he had placed on the altar steps and an Amy Grant song filled the room.

A fellow named Jim began a sequence of clapping and wringing his hands and raising his arms in the air as he stomped the floor with his cowboy boots, shouting "Thank you, Jesus. Thank you!"

As I shook each of the hands thrust toward me and looked into each of the beaming faces, I felt waves of mixed gladness, sadness, pride, and deep emptiness. I was glad for them as they celebrated the joy of saving my soul, proud of my theatrical performance, and very sad, because deep down inside, I knew I could not share in their born-again party.

The faithful began to file out of the small church, and Pastor Bob packed up his projector and shut down his boom box.

I hung around, hoping for the gas money he had promised me earlier in the day. The repo drive-by already seemed a distant memory. "I was wondering if I could get that gas money we talked about," I finally ventured.

"Oh, yes. I had forgotten about that." Pastor Bob fished in his back pocket for his wallet. He took out a ten and handed it to me.

"Thank you," I said, ready to head for the door.

"Oh! I've got a couple of other things for you, too," he added, heading for the pew where he had left his briefcase. He reached in and lifted out a brown envelope.

"Here's a couple of bumper stickers for your van!"

I reached in and pulled them partway out for a peek. There were two bumper stickers all right: ELECT BUSH-CHENEY and JESUS SAVES. I now had my ecumenical starter kit! "Thanks," I said, putting the stickers away.

"You are welcome," Pastor Bob replied. He returned to gathering his things, and I headed for the door, free at last.

Tina had not made it to the service—I didn't have any idea why, and I certainly wasn't going to quiz Pastor Bob at this point. I decided I'd head out there myself and just hope that she was there. I made sure the directions she had written out for me earlier were still in my pocket, and I set off to the gas station and then to Tina's to see my new home.

Chapter 14

ANGEL OF PREY

I headed back toward the lights of town and found a gas station. I put nine bucks' worth of gas in the tank and saved a buck to buy Willow dinner. She was hungry, so we went to the McDonald's drive-thru and got her a hamburger. That was one of her favorite treats, when we could afford it. We lucked out because it was two-for-one burger night, so we both had dinner on that one dollar.

I pulled out Tina's instructions again and headed out in that direction. It began to rain as we navigated the turns on Ohio, Indiana, California, and finally John Road, past the dead-end sign around the curve. The road turned to gravel with huge potholes as I searched for the first trailer on the right.

About a mile down the rutted road, I was greeted by headlights coming directly at me in the middle of the road. I slowed and pulled over, flicking my lights. A pickup truck pulled up alongside me; it had a big blue top covering the back. The window rolled down and a man stuck out his head. I put my window down and heard the loud roar of an engine in desperate need of a new muffler. Exhaust fumes filled the air and assaulted my nostrils.

"Lost?" the man yelled over the roar.

"Yeah," I said, reluctantly sticking my head out. "I'm looking for Tina . . . I don't know her last name."

"That's okay," he said. "I know who you mean. I just left there. Just keep on going. And good luck!" He smiled.

I rolled the window back up and took a deep breath. I was tired. "We're almost there, girl," I told Willow.

We drove on, around a curve and down a small hill. Then I spotted Tina's trailer. I pulled into the driveway, and the headlights of the van revealed a small camper just behind the big trailer. I knew that had to be our new home.

I dashed through the rain up to the door and knocked. "Just a minute," yelled a voice from inside. About thirty seconds later, the door opened. "Here you are," said Tina, abruptly handing me a broom and a dustpan. "I haven't had a chance to clean it up for you. You might need these. The door is open. I'm off tomorrow, so I'll see you then," she added, closing the door.

I picked up the equipment and headed back to get Willow out of the van. I grabbed her in my arms and juggled her and the broom and dustpan until I got to the camper door and used my little finger to pull the latch. Thankfully, the door swung open easily, and we quickly climbed inside to get out of the now pouring rain. I closed the door and set Willow down, while digging in my pockets for a book of matches.

The lit match provided just enough light for me to locate the switch. I flipped it and saw Willow was sitting at my feet. I bent down to scratch her head. "Willow, girl, we have a home! And the lady said we can stay awhile." She responded to the excitement in my voice with a squeal and a good shake. It was thrilling to know that we weren't going to have to pack up and leave in the morning. Whenever I awoke after a one-night stay in a motel or on somebody's couch, I always had a sinking feeling, knowing that we would be sleeping in the van again by nightfall.

I looked around the small camper. There were some dirty dishes in the sink and an unmade bed in the back, but it was quite comfortable considering how the rain was pounding on the metal roof.

The wind picked up as I opened the door to go get my sleeping bag from the van. A gust caught the door and slammed it into the side of the camper. I took a deep breath and stepped out into the storm, holding my cap in place with one hand and pulling the door closed with the other. Then I raced to the van to get what I needed.

It didn't take long, but I was dripping wet by the time I climbed back into the trailer. I took off my soaked shirt and laid it by the sink. Then I stripped the sheets off the bed, discovering a Tootsie Roll candy wrapper, some popcorn kernels, and some mouse leavings. I rolled up the sheets, sweeping the debris onto the floor, and rolled out my sleeping bag.

It had been a long day—being saved and all—and I was cold and tired. I finished taking off my wet clothes, called Willow, and we eased into the sleeping bag.

This blur of a day began to sort itself out as my muscles began to relax. This was too good to be true. Somebody had given me a place to stay, with no strings attached. "What a nice thing to do," I thought. "I need the rest. I'm going to sleep till noon!" Willow had already found her way to the bottom of the sleeping bag and was warming my feet.

It was quiet, except for the pounding rain. It reminded me of my first childhood home, back in Ohio. My parents' home had a green metal roof, and I loved to fall asleep to the sound of the rain. I rolled on my side, and within seconds I was asleep.

Dawn had just broken when I heard pounding on the aluminum door. "Richard, it's me!" Tina's voice called out. I heard the door open and then footsteps as she stomped into the camper. I opened one bleary eye to see Tina's face hovering over me.

"I've been called in to work today," she said. "I was talking to my husband last night, and we were thinking it might be best if you paid us something for letting you stay here," she added.

"I—I thought . . ." I began to answer as I regained my senses.

"Maybe two hundred or three hundred a month?" she suggested.

"Well, right now, I . . ." I was having trouble responding.

"You don't have to pay today," she said. "In a day or two would be fine. I've got to get going to work." She turned and headed for the door.

The commotion awakened Willow from her slumber, and she made her way out from under the covers, placing her head beside mine. Neither of us was quite awake yet. But that didn't stop the worrying. Where was I going to get a couple of hundred dollars in two days?

I heard Tina's car start, back up, and then churn up a little gravel as she sped away. I knew I wasn't going to be able to fall back into slumber, so I began preparing myself to get up and face the day. So much for sleeping till noon! I slowly pushed myself out of bed and slipped on my jeans, my shirt, and my still-wet socks and shoes, and I opened the door of the camper.

I was facing the back door of Tina's trailer. Two women were standing on a small wooden porch by the door, both puffing away on cigarettes. They smiled at me as I rubbed the sleep from my eyes and stepped out of the camper. "You must be the new boy," said one.

They were skinny women—almost frail—I thought, as I approached. Both wore jeans and old sweatshirts, and neither was wearing shoes. "Homeless guy, right?" the frailer of the two asked in a voice affected by some type of speech impediment. I nodded.

"It didn't take her long to replace Roy," the other lady said, and they both chuckled. "You must have passed Roy on your way in," she said. "He lived in the camper for a couple of months."

"Did he have an old truck that needed a new muffler?" I asked.

"Yes," she answered.

"He stopped to give me directions last night," I said. "My name is Richard." I extended by hand.

"I'm Madonna," the woman said, extending her hand in return. "This is Roberta." I shook hands with the other woman as well.

"You want a cup of coffee?" Roberta asked. She took a big drag of her cigarette, tilted her head up, and slowly blew the smoke into the air.

"Sure," I answered. "I'd love one."

Roberta snuffed out her cigarette on the wet railing of the porch and then opened the trailer door and went inside.

"You been living in your car?" Madonna asked.

"Yeah—for a while," I answered. "I've sorta lost track of the time."

"Tina said you can stay here?" she asked. "For free?"

"Yes," I replied, and then hesitated. "Yesterday she said I could stay for free. But this morning, she said she and her husband had talked it over and that they thought I should pay something." Madonna smiled, and then she turned her head away.

Roberta came through the trailer door with a cup of coffee in her hand. "Here's your coffee," she said, holding it out to me.

"Thank you," I said, taking it in both hands.

"Tina said he could stay here for free yesterday, and then told him today he needed to pay something," Madonna informed her, laughing.

"That's the last thing you're going to get for free here," said Roberta, pointing to my coffee.

"Oh, look, Roberta!" Madonna said, looking toward the camper door. "A puppy!" Willow had decided to face the world herself and was standing at the door of the camper looking out.

"That's my friend Willow. Come, girl," I called, and she jumped out into the wet grass and scurried to the porch.

"She's darling," Roberta said, bending to pet her. Willow stretched as Roberta rubbed her back. Madonna also bent down to pet Willow on the head.

While the women were cooing over Willow, my eyes panned out to survey the neighborhood. It appeared that I was at the end of a dead-end road. There was another blue trailer about fifty yards away, covered by a moldy plastic carport held up with two-by-fours. A 1970s Chevy Monte Carlo was sitting on blocks in the front yard, its hood missing and its back right side undergoing an extensive Bondo treatment. Two rusted burn barrels sat beside the driveway.

These women both appeared to be nearing forty, or had just breached that magical age for women. Roberta was the shorter of the two. She had long stringy black hair that needed brushing. Her chin jutted out from her lean face, and her eyes were deep set. Madonna had her strawberry-blond hair cut short, and it was obvious to me that it was not professionally done, even by the gals down at Supercuts. She either cut it herself, or Roberta did it. The sleeves of her pale-green sweatshirt had been cut off, revealing the bottom half of a red-and-blue heart-shaped tattoo with the words "Dale & Madonna" forever etched into her skin.

I took Willow to a park in town for a romp and spent much of the day looking for some type of work. At each job-search stop, someone would hand me an application, I would fill it out, and then they would tell me, "Somebody will call you." Since I had no telephone number, I knew that was going to be hard to do.

I found the St. Vincent de Paul assistance center in town and asked if they could help me out. They gave me a ten-dollar cash voucher for the nearby 76 station, five dollars in cash, and a list of the churches that provided free meals to the poor. I already knew that list by heart. Fortunately, the Lutheran church was serving an outstanding tuna noodle casserole that evening at six.

I reluctantly made my way back to Tina's about seven, not knowing what to expect. Would Tina be Jekyll or Hyde?

But luck was on my side, at least for the moment. Willow and I made it uneventfully back to our new residence and into bed without any contact with my new benefactress/landlady.

The sound of Tina yelling at the top of her lungs woke me from my slumber.

"You can't do anything right, you stupid bitch! You don't do anything I tell you! I ought to kick your ass out into the street where you came from!"

I could hear a woman sobbing. And I thought I could hear her saying "I try; I try," through the sobs. "Don't throw me out. I have no place to go."

The voices stilled for a moment. I rolled over on my other side and closed my eyes. But it wasn't over.

"What did you say?" Tina demanded in a loud voice.

"I, I, I . . ." stammered Roberta in response. "You shouldn't get so mad at me."

"*Mad?!*" Tina shrieked. "I'll show you mad! Get in your room!"

I could hear the stomping of feet and a door slamming. Slowly I sat up in bed and moved the curtain aside to look out.

In the porch light, Madonna was lighting a cigarette. She took a big drag, tilted her head up, and exhaled. Then she leaned against the side of the trailer and sighed a deep sigh. Eventually, she stood up and stepped off the porch, cocking her head slightly to the left as she began to walk. She looked up, took about fifteen paces, and then stopped. Then she cocked her head a few degrees more, and as she walked back into the light I could see the pain and concern in her expression.

I let the curtain fall back into place and lay back down. I sighed to myself. There was nothing I could do. The yelling continued, but now, at least, it was muffled by the closed door of Roberta's room.

I had been awake for about half an hour, lying in bed with my hands held behind my head, listening to the birds chirping in the early-morning light. I had my escape plan in place and was just waiting for Tina to leave for work. I had locked the camper door.

The peaceful sounds of the birds stopped abruptly as the trailer door opened and then slammed shut. Then I heard the sound of the latch on the camper door being pulled. "Shit," Tina muttered. There was a rustling of keys, and a second or two later she opened the door and stepped in.

"Richard, don't forget to get that money today," she said as she stepped toward the bed and stood over me.

"Okay," I said.

Then she turned and stormed out the door, slamming it closed. She got into her car. The engine turned over, the transmission screeched into reverse, and gravel flew as she accelerated. I took a few deep breaths and listened for the birds to begin singing again.

A few seconds later—right on schedule—I heard Roberta and Madonna open the door for their morning smoke. I could hear their voices—Roberta was crying and Madonna was trying to console her.

I got out of bed, put on my clothes, and wrote a quick note to Tina: "Sorry I have to leave, but I have no money and no prospects for any. Thank you. Richard." I put it on the fold-out table in the kitchen.

I pulled open the curtain and peeked outside. The two women were still standing by the back door in their bare feet, puffing away. Madonna looked my way, and I knew she had seen the motion of the curtain and sensed my prying eyes. I closed the curtain and stepped back.

I decided I'd better find out what was going on, so I opened the door and stepped out. "Good morning."

"Good morning," Madonna replied. Roberta was quiet as she looked toward the ground. Then she looked up at my face and took another drag off her cigarette. Her face was strained, and it was easy to see she had been crying.

"What kind of cigarettes do you smoke?" I asked, trying to engage in some small talk.

"Salem Lights," she said, pulling the pack from the pocket of her jeans and showing me the nearly empty green-and-white package.

"Tina seemed to be in a rush this morning," I observed. The ladies just nodded and puffed.

"You want a cigarette?" Madonna asked.

"Yeah. I don't smoke very often, but every once in a while I do. Thanks."

She reached in her pocket, pulled out her pack, and pulled one out for me. "Here you go," she said. I took it. She reached for her lighter; I leaned forward and got a light.

A few seconds of silence passed and then Madonna filled the void. "I suppose you heard the screaming?"

"Yeah, I did," I said. "Is everything okay?"

"Oh, it's something you're going to have to get used to, if you plan to stay," she said.

"But she doesn't have the right to hit me," Roberta blurted out. "She should be put in jail. She treats me bad. I hate her!"

"Jesus, Roberta. Slow down," Madonna interrupted. "You know nobody can understand you when you talk so fast. Slow down!"

I could see the tears welling up in Roberta's eyes as she looked at her friend.

"It wasn't that big a deal," Roberta said. "So what if I forgot to put a coaster under my glass on the coffee table? It didn't hurt it." She stared at the ground, dejectedly. "Now I'm not allowed to have any pop for two weeks!"

"You know that isn't why she got on you, Roberta," Madonna said. "She must have had a bad day at work, or maybe she lost a lot of money at the casino on her way home. She was pissed off at something else and she took it out on you." She paused and looked toward me. "Tina takes everything out on Roberta. When something goes wrong, she starts in on her."

"What a shame," I said. "But you don't have to take it," I suggested.

"Oh, you really don't want to mess with Tina," Madonna said. "She will rip you a new one, little man. Her husband is scared to death of her. He drives a truck, and I can tell you he is only happy when he is on the road."

I laughed, but then quickly began wondering what I had gotten myself into.

Roberta was angry. "She's so mean to me. She yells at me and hits me and takes my shoes and locks them up so I can't leave. It ain't right," she added, brushing a tear from her cheek.

I looked at them in disbelief. "Yeah, she does," Madonna began. "She locks up our shoes when she's gone so we can't just walk off."

"She takes all our money, too!" Roberta interrupted, nodding her head. "That ain't right, neither."

I stared at them again, bewildered.

"Yeah," Madonna said. "We both get money from the state. Roberta isn't quite right—can't you see that? And, well, I've got my problems, too. We both get $336 a month, plus $150 in food money on our food cards. When our money comes in, Tina takes it for rent. She buys all the food on our cards. We make dinner, clean the house, and take care of the place.

"We have to keep track of everything we use. She even charges us to do our own laundry—a dollar fifty to wash and a dollar to dry and a dollar for a scoop of soap. She buys our cigarettes out of our money and gives us thirty dollars in cash each month."

"We can't go nowhere," Roberta said. "We can't afford our own place. No one will give us a job. We've been here for two years now."

"Roy was paying two hundred dollars a month to live in the camper," Madonna said. "He was cutting firewood and selling it by the cord, but then his truck broke down a couple of times and he had to buy parts. He couldn't pay, so she kicked him out."

"Why don't you ladies get an apartment together somewhere else?" In my astonishment, I was grasping for helpful suggestions. I had sensed the unhealthiness of this place, but I had no idea it was *this* bad.

Madonna chuckled. "The cheapest place we'd be able to find would be four-fifty to five hundred a month—plus another fifty a month for electric. They're going to want first and last and a damage deposit. Plus Roberta got herself caught shoplifting, *twice*," she continued, raising her voice and lifting her eyebrows. "And my ex beat me up so bad that I spent several days in the hospital and he went to jail. He's been out for a while now, but I know if he ever finds me, he's going to kill me. I'm counting on him not being able to find me here. This is the best we've got right now," she said emphatically, nodding at the trailer.

I considered Madonna's plight. She was poor, hiding out in her own prison, wearing the brand of a person who would kill her when he got out of jail. As for Roberta, she wasn't making any move to get her things packed, so I assumed Tina had not actually thrown her out, in spite of the threats.

It was time for me to share my plans with them.

I stepped closer. "I'm taking off this morning," I said. "I want you to know it was a pleasure for me to meet you."

"Oh, Tina's not going to like this," Madonna said. She took a long drag off her cigarette and shook her head for emphasis.

"I'm heading for Bremerton," I said. "I was thinking . . . well, I could give you girls a ride into town, and maybe you could get some shoes, and some help finding a place, and . . . well, I was thinking maybe you girls could get a fresh start." A glimmer of hope appeared in Roberta's eyes.

Madonna had begun to stiffen as soon as I suggested the ride. There was no hope in her eyes. "It's a risk," I continued, "but sometimes you have to—"

"Maybe we could, Madonna!" Roberta was actually getting excited. "Maybe we could . . ." But this time her voice trailed off as she saw Madonna's expression.

As the two became quiet, I realized the answer was no.

Madonna snuffed out her cigarette. "Come on, Roberta. I'll brush your hair." She opened the door, Roberta put her cigarette out, and they both disappeared inside.

The closing of that trailer door could not have been any more final if it had been a cell door slamming shut. These two women were serving a life sentence. Parole denied. And worse yet, hope gone. And that was the ultimate devastation of homelessness—whether or not the victims had a roof over their heads.

With a heavy heart, I turned back to the camper. It didn't take more than a few minutes to gather my clothes, get Willow, and head for the van. I turned the key, shifted into reverse, and slowly backed up. I then put the van in drive and quietly pulled away, trying not to disturb the gravel as we made our escape.

Chapter 15

DAVID'S SONG

I was heading back to Bremerton, knowing I would be sleeping in the back of the van again.

I'd had a home for a couple of days. But now I was free! *In many ways*, I thought, *the homeless are the freest of all. We have no dignity, no honor, no pride, no ego to protect. We are like Hare Krishnas, living in the assurance that Mother Earth, the Universe, or the grace of God will somehow provide.*

I was anxious to get back to Sally's for some breakfast and to see C. I couldn't wait to show him my freshly blessed Bush bumper sticker, to share with him how I had been saved, and to tell him about my escape from Tina's compound.

It was about seven thirty in the morning when I drove down 6th Street toward Sally's.

Workers were using a mobile crane to place patriotic decorations on the light poles for the city's Memorial Day parade. Three motorcycle cops had parked their rigs in front of the old downtown theater and were rousting two of the Vietnam vets I had seen at Sally's many times, Ogre and Hillbilly, from their sleeping quarters under the marquee.

Ogre was struggling to roll up his sleeping bag with his one good arm and the stub that remained of his left one, and Hillbilly, his matted hair sticking out from under his soiled baseball cap, was picking up a couple of empty beer bottles and some trash and putting them in his backpack under the watchful eyes of the police officers, who stood waiting with their hands on their hips.

I kept rolling on by.

The line to get into Sally's had gotten longer while I was away at Tina's. The door didn't swing open until eight, but by seven forty-five the line went around the corner of the building.

I saw a Chinese couple for the first time. That was unusual. The man, maybe sixty years old, was slumped at the shoulders and avoided eye contact. The woman stood quietly, with those worried eyes I knew so well. They didn't want to be seen in this line. They still had some pride left.

I wished C was here. He would have known what to say to make them more comfortable. As I waited in line, I kept looking out for him.

Who, or what, was C? I had wondered about that from time to time when I could not find him. Was he some imaginary friend I had created, the way a child would? No, I knew that wasn't true, because I could *smell* him when he came around. I was repulsed by his dumpster diving. He would fish a half-eaten Big Mac and fries from a trash can and eat them like a hungry stray dog. He could not pass up a trash can. He often looked like Pigpen from "Peanuts," dust flying from his stained clothes. He wasn't afraid to get down and dirty with the beggars and the drunks, cleaning up their puke, duct-taping the soles to the tops of their shoes.

C had energy. He was like a five-year-old just before bedtime, never wanting to go to sleep, always afraid he might miss something.

And he was a man of God—though maybe not in what many would

consider the traditional sense. If anyone in the history of man was going to move a mountain with faith, it would be C. He talked to the crows, and they would often gather in his presence. He was like a box of Whitman's chocolates—one minute a cherry cordial, then a tart orange, then a nut. I wanted to toss away the pieces of him I didn't like but found it impossible.

I came to admire him. He would quote Yeats while sitting on a park bench eating peanut butter from a jar with his fingers. Of all the people I had ever met—lawyers, judges, priests, bankers, star athletes—C was the most alive, the most attuned. Women were attracted to his blue eyes and the dulcet tones of his voice, but he would challenge their intellects and their spirituality in a mental sparring contest I didn't quite understand. They wanted to talk about Oprah, or Dr. Phil, or the next American Idol. He wanted to talk about Carlos Castaneda, or Jean-Paul Sartre. He seemed to want to get into their brains, not their pants.

C was a "long-hair" in an age when short hair was in, and he didn't like to have his picture taken. He would always turn his face away or get up and move out of range whenever a camera was pointed anywhere in his direction.

My attention returned to the activity around Sally's. The local citizens were beginning to gather for the parade, carrying their lawn chairs, dragging their coolers-on-wheels past the breakfast line. A pickup truck towing a green-and-white float decorated with shamrocks made a wide turn from Warren Ave to 6th; 4-H BUILDS CHARACTER was written on its side.

Hillbilly and Ogre came strolling up the alley and got in line behind me just as the door of Sally's swung open. C was right behind them, tossing bread to the crows and pigeons on his way. C had his sea bag tied around his shoulder. The crows were crying out in a marvelous chorus as C reached into the bag and broke each slice into generous pieces, tossing some left and some right. Then he shook the crumbs from the Wonder Bread bag onto the ground, put the bag in his pocket, and walked toward us, smiling.

I stepped behind Hillbilly and Ogre and put my hand out to C. "Richard!" C's smile warmed me. "It's good to see you!" He reached out to shake my hand. "Where have you been?"

"Boy, have I got a story for you," I replied as the line began to move. "I got saved in Gig Harbor!" While the line crawled along, I told C the tale of Pastor Bob and our car trip, informed him that horoscopes are the work of the Devil, and let him know I'd been saved in a little white church. C laughed as I relayed the details of that incident—the hands on me, Pastor Bob's wife crying out "Oh, God!" Jim dancing over me, the woman chanting "God, hep him, hep him!"

Hillbilly and Ogre were chortling and shaking their heads; they couldn't help overhearing the story. "He was lucky to get out of there with all his body parts, right, Ogre?" C said.

"Damn right, C!"

"Ogre didn't lose half his left arm in Nam like some people think," C said. "Right, Ogre?" Ogre nodded. "Do you mind telling Richard how you lost it?"

As his name implied, Ogre was not a good-looking man. It appeared his nose had been broken more than once, and part of his right ear was missing.

"I got saved, too, Richard," he said. "Four or five years ago—after I got arrested for breaking and entering. But I went crazy with that Jesus stuff. The Pastor said, 'It's in the Bible: If your eye offends thee, pluck it out!' Well, my offender was my arm; I stole with it. So one night I got drunk and cut off that arm with a bandsaw."

I didn't know what to say; fortunately, the line picked up speed as Hillbilly and Ogre rounded the corner, and into the confines of Sally's they went. "I guess some people carry that 'being saved' a little too far," I whispered to C.

"Ogre sure did," C said. "He's a good guy. His real name is Paul. But he likes to be called Ogre now. He's gotten used to it." The line moved forward again and we stepped inside.

The Major was making an announcement on a microphone. "There is a parade for Memorial Day today at ten a.m., and you are welcome to stay here and watch it with us from the side of the building. I know there are a lot of Vietnam vets here today, and we are going to have a special church service here on Sunday to honor those who served in all the wars." Then the Major put the microphone down on the table and got into the food line behind us.

"Hello, C," he said. "And you, too, Richard."

"Something smells good," C said.

"Chef Pat's made biscuits and gravy," the Major replied. "They're always pretty good."

The line moved forward again, and we were at the serving window. I picked up my tray and held it out. The server took a piece of Wonder Bread and placed it on my tray and then piled on a hearty portion of sausage gravy. "We ran out of biscuits," he said, "but you could put Pat's gravy on just about anything and it would be great." I nodded my thanks and got a cup of coffee before heading for a table at the back of the room. C and the Major did the same, and just as we were sitting down, we heard a clunk and then a screech emanating from the loudspeaker system. Lilly, a diminutive Native American, had the microphone in her hand.

"Oops," said the Major. "I should have put that away."

"I have a shong—a shong I want to shing," Lilly slurred as she rocked back and forth. Lilly was about four feet tall and about fifty years old. She wore black jeans and a stained black sweatshirt this morning, and she was obviously intoxicated.

"It's called 'David's Dance,'" she said. She paused a moment and then began to sing. "When the shpirit of the Lord moves in my heart, I will danshe like David danshed." Lilly sang off key and attempted to dance—or at least sway—from one foot to the other, but she nearly fell to the floor. She repeated the line, slurring some of the words and looking at the floor. When she tried "I will shing like David shang," seven or eight people shoveled the last spoonfuls of their grub, deposited their trays in the washtub, and escaped quickly out the door. Others just laughed as Lilly continued. "I will shing . . . I will shing . . . I will shing like David shang." Lilly stumbled and almost fell down again. She tried to continue, but when she saw how many people were laughing at her, she put the microphone down.

The Major jumped from his chair and quickly retrieved the microphone from the table. "Thank you, Lilly, for your song," he said, heading for the office with the valuable equipment.

Lilly then saw C and leaned forward, squinting to bring him into focus. "C! C! C!" she said, and with unsteady steps she made her way between the tables to the spot where we were sitting. She sort of fell into the seat the Major had vacated. "C," she said, leaning towards him, "I am in need. You gotta help a girl out!" She gave him a pleading, if not quite focused, look.

"This must be the terrible Tiger Lilly," C said, leaning back and holding up his hands to form a cross with two fingers. "Oh, no!" he said. "It is the terrible one, not the sweet little Lilly everyone loves. It's the evil twin!"

"Come on, C." She lowered her voice. "You know what I need. I need some weed . . . shumthin to get me through. Gimme some."

"I don't have any right now," C replied.

"Oh, c'mon, C! You ahways do," she slurred.

"I don't. I really don't," was his reply.

Lilly became quiet. She slowly got up, steadied herself on the edge of the round table, and walked away without a word. "Poor Lilly," C said. "Too much firewater." He picked up his sea bag and his tray. He was obviously ready to move on. I picked up my tray and followed.

"I've got to tell you the rest of the story about the trailer I stayed in and the two women I met. You won't believe it!" We walked toward the door, and C nodded his encouragement.

"Well, I thought I had this place to stay," I began. "The woman told me I could stay there free, but it didn't take long before—" I stopped in mid-sentence when we pushed the big door open and found Lilly lying in the grass.

"Oh, Lilly," C said. "Are you okay?" He got down on one knee and touched her face.

Lilly opened her eyes. "Jus resting," she said, looking up at C.

"Come on, Richard," C said. "Help me get her up. Maybe we could take her home. She only lives a couple of blocks from here."

I bent down to help Lilly to her feet. She weighed in at maybe ninety pounds. We guided her to the van and got her into the front seat. Willow went right to work licking her face and bringing Lilly's spirit back to life. C got in the back seat. Willow licked Lilly's mouth, nose, and eyes, and she chuckled at the attention.

It was only three blocks to Lilly's apartment, which was located directly across from the navy shipyard. Hers was a rundown, one-story stucco building—currently painted white, but you could tell from the flaking on the side that it had once been blue, once yellow, and once green. We rolled to a stop.

"Okay, Lilly, we got you home safe," C said from the back seat. He stepped out and opened the door for Lilly.

Lilly had recovered somewhat. "I'm not gettin' out till you gimme shome weed," she slurred, and she crossed her arms defiantly across her chest.

C laughed. "Oh, come on, Lilly, we did you a big favor bringing you home. The cops would have scraped you up and taken you to detox."

"I ain't movin'," Lilly spat back.

"I told you I don't have any," C said.

"Well, then gimme a dollar," Lilly said.

"We don't have any money, either," C replied.

"You got fifty cents?" Lilly asked, turning her head to me. "I'll get out for fifty cents."

I looked out on the crowd that was lining the parade route; they had become intrigued by our theatrical performance. "How am I going to get this drunken woman out of my car?" I wondered. I dug into my pocket and pulled out my last quarter and held it up to Lilly. "I've got a quarter," I said. "That's all I've got."

Lilly thought for a moment and then reached out and took the quarter from my hand without a word. She slid off the seat, stumbling again, but C caught her arm and held her up. Still silent, Lilly headed for her apartment door.

C began to scoot into the seat, but stopped. He looked at me, then back at Lilly. "This isn't right," he said. "You doing anything for the next couple of hours?"

"Not really," I had to admit.

"Then let's not leave the lady alone right now." He stuck his head up above the van and called out to Lilly. "Lilly! You want some company for a bit?"

Lilly didn't even turn her head, but raised her hand high to wave us in. She opened the door and walked in, leaving the door ajar for us. C got out of the van and headed for Lilly's apartment. I pulled the van into a parking spot, picked Willow up in my arms, and went inside.

"I hope it's okay that I brought my dog in," I said to Lilly, who had thrown herself down on a sofa.

"Okay," Lilly mumbled. I found a seat in a comfortable easy chair beside the sofa.

C began making himself at home, just as he always did. He walked into the small kitchen off the living room and opened the refrigerator door, bent forward to peer in, and then closed the door.

"We need some music," he said, looking around the apartment. "Aha!" he said, spying a radio sitting on a side table. He walked over and turned it on.

"Hurry on down to Cal's," the announcer was saying. "We're open till nine tonight and we have the car for you with NO MONEY DOWN!" Then the deejay took over. "We're back with the top one hundred of all time. Here is 'Oh, Oh, Oh, It's Magic,'" and the song began to play.

C walked over to a table by the window, covered with plants. He stuck his finger in the dirt. "Lilly, your plants need water."

This seemed to concern Lilly, and she began to get up, but appeared to feel dizzy and plopped back down. "C, would you give 'em water?" she asked. "Not tap water!—water from that plastic bottle in the kitchen. I collect rain water for them."

While C was watering the plants, I scoped out Lilly's apartment. A small wooden dining table was covered in a pretty print cloth and it was set for four, with brightly colored plates, cups, and saucers, and silverware placed appropriately on cloth napkins. Two small windows were covered in handmade beaded curtains of silver and turquoise. The sofa Lilly was lying on was covered with a beautiful red-white-and-blue Native American blanket. The wall behind the sofa contained framed family photos. There was a picture of a man in a brown army uniform and cap. He was an older man. I got up and went closer. There was a photo of a younger man, also in an army uniform. Next to that picture was a black-and-white photo of a Native American man with a long feathered headdress.

The song had ended on the radio, and another commercial came on. "This Memorial Day is the perfect time to buy your loved one a place in the heavens with National Star Registry," the announcer proclaimed. "For only $19.99, you can have a star named after your wife or husband, and we will send you a certificate of authenticity." It seemed bizarre that there were now stars in the sky named Becky, Barbie, and Randy. "We're back," the deejay's perky voice resumed. "Here's Etta James and 'Standing on Shaky Ground.'"

Lilly had roused and was on the move. She stumbled toward C and nearly fell to the floor. C reached out and caught her. Lilly then nuzzled up against C, wrapped her arm around his neck, and pulled his head down so she could whisper in his ear. It seemed Lilly was offering C a little feminine touch for a pinch of his bud.

C smiled as he gently pulled away from Lilly. "Oh, madam, I would be one lucky man to taste the nectar of your kiss and to know your charms, but I am not worthy of even a small embrace from a lady of your stature. Alas, my lass, I also have noticed the fragrance of vomit on your breath." Lilly abruptly pulled away from C, in a huff. "But I do have with me the elixir to cure what ails thee," C added, as Lilly reached the wooden chair in the dining room and threw herself down in disgust. She took the back of her hand and rubbed it roughly across her mouth.

C dove into his sea bag and pulled out a plastic Fanta bottle filled with a caramel-colored substance. "It's called Adam's Tree Bark Tea," C exclaimed, as he held up the bottle. "It cures everything! Drives out evil spirits, grows hair on bald spots. wipes out fungus, improves concentration, and relieves constipation!

"My gran'father used to make that back in South Dakota," Lilly said. "Tree bark tea. I haven't had it in forty years. Where'd you get it?"

"Oh, I can't reveal that," C said. "A secret location. We have passwords and everything just to get in."

"You're full of shit, C," Lilly retorted. "I'm gonna take a shower. I need it bad." She stood up slowly and used a hand to brace herself.

"That's an understatement," C noted wryly.

"There's a pot in the kitchen, so make us some tea," Lilly said as she headed to the bathroom, finally resigned to the fact that C was not going to provide the stimulants she longed for.

C took his bottle to the kitchen, and I heard him rattling through pots and pans, looking for an appropriate one in which to heat the tree bark tea. Lilly had closed the door to her tiny bathroom, but even with the door closed and the strains of "My Girl" coming from the radio, it was easy to hear her throwing up.

"Lilly is worshipping the porcelain god," C said, laughing. "Hey, Richard. Come look at this."

I went into the kitchen. C was running some hot water into the sink and pouring detergent onto a pile of dishes. He stopped, put down the soap container, and quickly dried his hands on a small towel on the counter. "Would you take these out to the recycling bin?" he asked, pointing to three empty Smirnoff bottles. "It's right out front."

"Okay," I said, as he handed me the empties. I headed for the door.

"Wait. Let's get rid of this one, too." He opened the refrigerator and removed another bottle. "There's one last swig in it," he said, twisting off the cap and downing the contents. "Looks like she's been drinking for quite a few days."

C handed me the bottle, and I headed for the door again. Outside, the parking lot was now full of people sitting on their ice chests and looking relaxed in their lawn chairs. I received a few smiles as I headed for the bin, loaded down with empty vodka bottles. I dropped them in the bin and quickly headed back.

I could hear the shower running through the thin walls. "So, you know Lilly?" I asked C as he was washing the dishes.

"Oh, not very well," C replied. "I have bumped into her around town. She thinks I sell weed, which I don't," he continued. "I only use it for my bad back, which hurts a lot from all the crosses I bear in life. It's purely medicinal," and he laughed.

"I've seen her intoxicated a lot, usually alone, walking the streets," he continued. "And I've run into her at Sally's and a few other places when she's been charming, polite, and quite the conversationalist."

I walked back into the living room to check on Willow. She had curled up for a nap, with one eye open to survey the human activities.

But Willow's nap was short-lived. "Aaaaaaaiiieeeeiiiii." The sound of a fire-truck siren filled the room. Then "Rrrrrmmmm, rrrrrmmmmm." Motorcycles revved their engines and a band played Sousa's "Stars and

Stripes Forever"—first the piccolos, then the trombones, the drums, and finally the full band.

The parade had begun. I pulled back one of Lilly's delicate curtains to view the tuba players puffing on their instruments and strutting by. The band was followed by a red Mustang convertible with a Marine sitting atop the back seat, wearing his dress uniform—white pants, blue coat with brass buttons, and dress cap. He was waving at the crowd. Next, a white convertible came into view, a new Cadillac with a sign on the side: CONGRESSMAN NORM DICKS SUPPORTS OUR TROOPS. The congressman, dressed in a blue suit, white shirt, and red tie was smiling and waving at the crowd as well.

Then, like a small earthquake, the walls began to shake and a roar from above filled the room. The crowd outside cheered and looked to the sky as a jet plane came in low and fast over the city. Two of Lilly's pictures fell off the wall, and Willow got spooked and ran to sit at my feet. "Flying low, wasn't he?!" C yelled from the kitchen.

"Wow!" I said. "It's okay, girl," I assured Willow, who hopped back onto the sofa.

Lilly opened the bathroom door, a large towel wrapped around her small body and another around her head. "That feels a lot better," she said, as she walked barefoot to her bedroom and shut the door.

Drums could be heard again outside. I peeked out to see six drummers pounding in unison. A drum major in his navy whites blew his whistle sharply three times and then spun around to face the rest of the band. Lifting his shiny baton high, he blew his whistle again and turned smartly forward as the band began to play. C broke into song in the kitchen in his off-key, crackly voice, "Anchors aweigh, my boys, anchors aweigh!" He came singing and prancing into the living room with a long toilet brush he must have found under the sink.

I couldn't resist joining in his parade around the living room, holding my hands to my mouth and making a squeaky sound like I was playing a flute. C lifted his brush high, then low, stopped for a second, and then paraded again.

"Hey!" Lilly called out, and we froze in our tracks, not only at her voice, but also at her appearance. She had put on a beautiful white dress trimmed with multicolored beads and a pair of white moccasins. Her jet-black hair was still wet. She held a brush in her hand and brought it to her hair. She looked beautiful.

"That's my toilet brush, C—in the *living room!*" Lilly sounded quite indignant. The sound of the band began to fade away, but the radio was still blaring. Buffalo Springfield was singing "There's something happening here . . ."

"I can't stand all this noise!" Lilly said, turning off the radio.

"The tea is ready," C said, heading for the kitchen.

Lilly noticed the two pictures that had fallen off the wall and went over to them. "Good. The glass didn't break," she said, picking them up off the floor and carrying them to the table. She sat down, gracefully.

I joined her at the table, and C came in carrying two cups of steaming tree bark tea. He gave one to Lilly and one to me and returned to get a cup for himself. "You look nice in that dress," he said as he returned.

"Thank you, C," Lilly responded demurely. She carefully picked up one of the pictures she had retrieved from the floor.

"Who is that, Lilly?" I asked.

"That's my father," she said. "Isn't he a handsome man?"

"He is!" I replied.

"He's Cherokee," said Lilly. "That's another picture of him on the wall—the old one, with the headdress. I hardly knew my dad. My mother gave me this picture before she died, four years ago. His name was Charles. They liked to call him Charlie. He died in the Korean War when I was a child."

"And that one?" I asked, nodding at the other picture.

"My brother. Isn't he beautiful?" she asked, turning the frame to us.

We nodded.

"He took care of me when I was little, always watching over me." She smiled, gazing at the picture.

"Where is he now?" C asked.

"He died, too," Lilly said. "He joined the army like my dad and was killed in Vietnam. They wanted to be warriors. David wanted to be a warrior like his dad." She clutched the picture to her bosom. Tears began to form in her eyes. "David was killed on Memorial Day."

The parade was still passing by outside, but it seemed quite still in the apartment.

"War has got all it's going to get from my family," Lilly said, reaching for her tea and taking a sip.

"So that's why you were singing 'David's Song' this morning," C said.

"Yes. In his honor," Lilly replied. "But I was kinda drunk."

"Well, could you sing it now?" C asked.

"Now?" Lilly was incredulous at the suggestion.

"Why not?" C asked.

"I—I guess," she said. She began to sing very softly:

> When the Spirit of the Lord moves in my heart,
> I will sing like David sang.
> When the Spirit of the Lord moves in my heart,
> I will sing like David sang.

She raised her voice as she continued.

> I will sing, I will sing; I will sing like David sang.
> I will sing, I will sing; I will sing like David sang.

Comfortable with us now, Lilly stood up, stepped back from the table, and said, "Sing with me."

When the Spirit of the Lord moves in my heart,
I will dance like David danced.

As she sang, she began to sway from one foot to the other. We began to sing along.

When the Spirit of the Lord moves in my heart,
I will dance like David danced.
I will dance, I will; I will dance like David danced.
I will dance, I will dance; I will dance like David danced.

C and I applauded. Lilly bowed and smiled and then sat down at the table. She reached for her cup and took a drink of her tea. "You know, this is pretty good tea," she said.

"And you're a good dancer," C said.

"And you're a good singer," I said to C.

"That's a lie, Richard," Lilly said, and we all laughed.

Lilly took another sip of tea and then set her cup down. "The Indian Commissioner banned dancing by Cherokees in 1883." She was reflective for several minutes.

And so the afternoon continued. We stayed at Lilly's the rest of the day. We all stuck our heads out the windows to watch the rest of the parade: Boy Scouts, then Cub Scouts, then Girl Scouts, the 4-H float, twenty or more glittering baton twirlers, a line of antique cars, and a troop of sultry belly dancers, followed by a half dozen silver-saddled palomino horses.

Later, C found enough money in the bottom of his sea bag to send me to the store for the makings of chicken and dumplings, which he prepared. After dinner, Lilly told us all she knew about her family as we played a few hands of her favorite game, Rummy 500.

Lilly said we could sleep over if we wished, but we would have to be quiet; no parades and stuff. I curled up on the sofa with Willow and closed my eyes. C was chuckling from the easy chair as he watched *The Simpsons*.

As I readied myself for sleep, and what I hoped would be good dreams, I replayed my mental tape of the day. My friend C had shown me a new window to look through, pushed me through a door I would have never entered, and sang with me a song I would never have sung. "David's Song" would have been just another set of lyrics to me.

But when C bent down to help Lilly get off the ground in front of Sally's, I had to bend down with him. If I had been by myself, I would most likely have just stepped over her. And I would have been the loser.

Chapter 16

VINNY

C always seemed to show up when I needed him most.

It was Tuesday and it was raining. It had poured most of the weekend and on into the week. A clear sky and my sense of hope were on a par—there was none of either in sight. When I still had a home, rainy days like this would find me watching a video, having dinner, maybe playing cards with Sandra. Then we would light some candles, burn incense, and make love.

I had been depressed most of the weekend, losing the struggle to bury those memories of the past. It surprised me how inventive my mind could be in finding ways to protect itself when I was feeling particularly challenged by homelessness. I felt like an "urban cowboy" in some ways, totally out of my element, yet knowing I must adapt. I couldn't just stand there in one spot waiting for Mr. Sulu to beam me back to the bridge of the Enterprise, where the old crew would hug me and welcome me home.

With no home and no money, I had found occasional cheap

entertainment for Willow and me at PetSmart, and we headed there again today. We would look at the hamsters, and Willow would scratch on the glass cages. (It occurred to me that the hamsters were more valuable than I was. They were housed, they were fed and watered regularly, and they were worth $19.99 apiece; someone would buy one, take it home, name it, and even buy it some toys.) We would also check out the birds and the fish. Other dogs would come in and check each other out as well, and we were always given a free dog biscuit for the road. It was warm and dry, and it took my mind off my troubles. It was a brief diversion—a short-term shelter for Willow and me. We could easily kill an hour at PetSmart.

Today I thought about C as we toured this animal warehouse, and I wondered what he might say. A young child was crying by the fish tanks. "I want a new fish," the girl pleaded with her resolute mother. "I want it! I want it!"

"You flushed the last three down the toilet," the mother responded. "I am *not* wasting any more money on those little fish!"

"How would *you* like to be flushed down the toilet, ma'am?" That's what C would have said.

I wondered how many millions of goldfish in New York City alone had been flushed down toilets by little girls and boys and if any of them survived and flourished, gorging on the sludge under the Big Apple until they reached monstrous proportions. Could goldfish two hundred feet long be swimming deep in the harbor and someday (in Stephen King fashion) attack cruise ships and ferry boats?

We continued sauntering down the aisles. There were turtles from Africa, snakes from the Amazon, birds from Guatemala, fish from Costa Rica—all snatched from the rocks, deserts, rivers, and jungles of the world, put in cages and transported to other cages here, to be sold and displayed in still other cages in living rooms and dens and dentists' offices. All for profit.

On that wonderful note, we prepared to leave PetSmart and go back out into the rainy day. To my surprise, C was standing just outside the door. "Hey there," he said. "I've been next door at the thrift shop." He lifted two plastic bags in the air. "Got some towels, dishcloths, and a few other things for the Armadillo."

"I just took Willow to the zoo," I said.

"Would you mind giving me a lift?" C asked.

We dashed through the heavy rain to the van and jumped in.

"You interested in watching some TV?" C asked as we started rolling.

"Sure."

"Let's go over to my friend Vinny's." C nodded his head to indicate the appropriate direction, and off we went.

When we arrived and knocked on the door, a disembodied voice yelled, "Come in." It was Jake from Sally's, spread out on the sofa in his boxers, drinking a beer and watching TV. "Hey—C and Richard! Good to see ya. Grab a seat and make yourselves at home." Jake dragged himself off the couch and reached for a pair of pants. "If I've got guests, I guess I'd better get some clothes on."

C and I planted ourselves in a couple of recliners. "What are you watching?" C asked Jake.

"Oh, nothing really. I've been flipping around—six hundred channels, and nothing good to watch."

"Can I try?" C asked. Jake tossed him the remote. "I'll find something to watch. There's got to be a war on somewhere. Let's try CNN. What's the channel?"

"Who knows?" mumbled Jake. "You've got the remote."

C continued to flip through the channels until he found CNN. One of the embedded reporters was standing in front of a U.S. Army tank on the road to Baghdad. "These tanks are really troop carriers with as many as six soldiers squeezed into tight quarters in the back of the vehicle," the reporter said. "It is very hot, especially in these desert conditions and with the troops wearing chemical warfare–protective clothing."

C punched buttons again and found the *Iron Chef* sushi program. A chef was slicing and dicing broccoli at amazing speed and preparing an award-winning Asian dish. The chef bowed at the waist as he received accolades from the show host.

"I never liked sushi," Jake offered.

C flipped back to the war. "These tanks have a special plating that protects them from just about any weapon in the Iraqi arsenal, except a Scud missile," the reporter said. The picture being picked up from the satellite feed was blurred and skipping around like an old home movie, and the corresponding words came through a second after he moved his mouth, creating an eerie effect. It was like they were broadcasting from the moon in 1969.

C held the remote out and hit it again.

"Very good, very good!" The sushi show host was talking with his mouth full, complimenting yet another guest chef on his presentation of broccoli and sushi.

"Give me that thing," Jake said, motioning for the remote.

I heard moaning and movement in the next room. Someone went into the bathroom and closed the door. "Fuck. Oh, fuck," I heard the voice say. "I can't stand this anymore."

"You okay, Vinny?" Jake yelled.

"I'm just tired of it, Jake," came the muffled reply. A few minutes later the bathroom door opened, and I heard Vinny toss himself down on the bed.

"It's getting worse," Jake whispered. "It's been bad the past couple of days."

Jake flipped on a *M*A*S*H* rerun.

"I always liked this show," Jake said.

"Ooooohhh, God! Please make it *stop*," Vinny moaned. "*Please* make it *stop*."

"Vinny, you'd better eat something," Jake said. "You got to eat, man. You want me to make you a bologna-and-cheese sandwich?"

Vinny just moaned.

"Nothing you can really do," Jake said, looking at me. I could see the concern in his eyes.

This was a death watch. Vinny had colon cancer. He had constant diarrhea and spent half his time in the bathroom.

"You had better eat," Jake repeated, rolling over on the sofa and directing his voice toward the bedroom. "You want me to make you some tea?"

"Fuck, Jake. I can't keep it in me. What's the use?" Vinny yelled.

"You'd better get your lazy ass out of bed and move around," Jake yelled back, "or you're just going to die right there in that bed!"

"Fuck you, Jake!" Vinny spat back. Then he lapsed into silence.

The harshness of Jake's words barely concealed his anguish over his friend's misery. Jake was staying with Vinny during his ordeal. Both had been homeless; Jake still was. The government had helped Vinny get a small apartment after it became obvious that his cancer was so advanced that he was going to die on the streets.

"You got anything that might help Vinny?" Jake asked C.

"We can try," C said. "Richard, can I borrow your keys? I need to get something out of the van."

I tossed the keys over to C, and he went out briefly. He returned a couple of minutes later with his duffel bag and took out a small baggie of weed. He found his pipe, then he headed for Vinny's bedside.

Jake and I focused back in on *M*A*S*H*.

The smell of marijuana wafted into the living room. I could hear C talking about *The Lord of the Rings*. "I liked that a lot," Vinny said. "Jake brought the video back one night."

"Did you like the wizard Gandalf?" C asked. "Did you see the end when he fell into the fiery abyss?"

"Yeah. What great graphics," Vinny said. "Is the second one out on video yet? I'd really like to see it, but I can't go out."

C's weed seemed to be easing Vinny's pain. And every second of comfort was precious.

Jake was humming along with the *M*A*S*H* theme when Vinny called out, "You make that sandwich yet, Jake?"

Jake laughed. "Oh, *now* you're hungry? No, but I'll do it now." He headed for the fridge. "You want a sandwich, Richard?"

"Sure," I said, "if you've got enough."

"We've got plenty." Jake took the bologna, cheese, and mayonnaise out of the fridge and grabbed the bread. He dipped the knife in the mayo and started spreading. Vinny and C came out of the bedroom. "You want a bologna sandwich, C? Or some sushi?" Jake joked.

Vinny looked like a ghost, standing there in his white shorts and socks. He was pale and fragile-looking. His hair was mostly gone. His legs were swollen to about twice their normal size. "Let's watch a movie," he said. "What have we got? How about *Something About Mary*? I know we got that. That's funny."

I reached out and offered my hand. "My name is Richard," I said. "Glad to meet you. *Something About Mary*—I think I've seen that. Isn't that the one where he accidentally kills her dog?" I asked.

"That's it," Vinny said.

The mention of dogs reminded me that Willow had been in the car for quite a while and probably needed to do her business by now. "I'll be right back," I said. "I've got to take my dog for a walk."

As I was walking out the door, a thought struck me. I turned and asked Vinny, "Hey, do you mind if I bring my little dog in after our walk?"

"Does she bite?" he asked.

"No, but she might lick you to death."

"That would be good," Vinny said. "Bring her in."

Willow and I took our walk in the alley behind the apartment complex. She peed at the base of all eight dumpsters.

I thought about what I had just witnessed. Here was C, bringing his medicine bag of weed to give a man some brief comfort from a living hell. He was doing what no doctor could legally do in this state.

Willow and I climbed the stairs to the apartment. She was excited because she knew she was going inside. She burst into the room and headed straight for Vinny, who was sitting on the couch. She licked his face until he pushed her down. She settled into his lap like they were old friends. Could this little dog sniff out the sickness? I wondered.

"Nice dog," Vinny said. "What's her name?"

"Willow," I said. Vinny seemed content to sit and pet her.

Jake grabbed the video and pushed it into the VCR.

C reached into his bag and got some rolling papers and weed and rolled a few joints, which he then passed around the room. "You want one of these, Richard?" he asked.

"No. I never got the hang of it," I said. "Thanks anyway."

"That's what I like about him," C said. "He hangs out with me, but he doesn't smoke all my weed."

"I tried it in college," I said. "Back at Ohio State nearly forty years ago. I always thought it smelled like somebody was burning dog poop."

"Remember Cheech and Chong?" Jake said, nearly choking with laughter. "Remember when the big black dog ate their stash? Then the dog took a dump with the cannabis in it."

"Yeah, I remember that movie," C laughed.

"Then they rolled it into a big 'doogie,'" Jake said. "Cheech called it a Labrador—and they *smoked* it!"

"I tried weed, though," I said, beginning my story again when the laughing subsided. "I never got high, but I did it because I was trying to bed this long-haired blonde from Chagrin Falls who wore crepe dresses and tie-dyed shirts. A group would meet at her pad, take off most of their clothes, and get into a circle on the floor. They would light up their joints and say things like 'Make love, not war!' I would take a drag, hold it in and then—nothing! So, I faked it. I'd say 'Good shit, man!' and start making up stories about whales coming to me in a vision and sharing knowledge about people who lived under the seas. It seemed to impress them."

They all laughed and then took a hit on their joints. They were getting pretty stoned.

"Hey, there are more sandwiches on the counter," Jake said. "And there's milk in the fridge if you want some."

"I'm feeling a little better. Maybe I can sleep through the night," Vinny said, hopefully.

At about midnight there was a rap on the door, and Lenny stuck his head in. "Anybody here?" he called.

"Lenny! Welcome!" Jake said. "What's up?"

"Fuckin' nothin', man," Lenny replied. "I was down at the tavern playing some fuckin' pool. I'm looking for some fuckin' stuff, man. You got any?"

"I've got a little left," C said, passing the plastic bag to Lenny.

Lenny was from Jersey. He was a fast talker. He communicated in short, rapid-fire sentences, liberally laced with the f-word. He hadn't been back to his native Jersey in thirty years, but you would swear that he just left yesterday. His accent was quintessentially Jersey, circa 1960. He demanded your attention when he was talking to you. If he didn't get what he thought was the proper level of focus, he would move closer until he did—so close you could feel his breath. Then he would tilt his head as he leaned into your face.

Lenny rolled his joint quickly and lit up. "Fuckin' good stuff!" he pronounced, exhaling.

We all sat staring at the screen for a while, feeling very mellow from the weed, randomly commenting on the film while discussing topics ranging from managing testosterone to how to score a good lay. Finally, Vinny struggled up from the couch. "I think I'll lie down," he said. "I'm getting tired. Thanks, C."

"Sure," said C. "No problem."

"Good night, Vinny," Jake said. "If you need anything, just call."

"Good night. Nice to meet you," I said as Vinny headed for the bedroom.

The angels of death were already gathering in that room, just waiting for the last sigh, the final breath, the end of life.

There was no wife, no woman, no nurse to wipe the sweat from his brow. Just a few buddies hanging around for company. There was comfort in company.

"I've seen this a bunch of times," Jake said, flipping off the VCR.

"Put on some fuckin' porn," Lenny said.

Coverage of the war in Iraq came on when Jake turned off the movie. "Coalition troops are experiencing heavy resistance from forces loyal to Saddam Hussein near the town of Kabul, in southern Iraq," announced the embedded correspondent. "There are casualties . . ."

"I say *nuke* the fuckers!" Lenny exclaimed. "Motherfuckin' A-rabs! Send them all to Allah, man!"

"Reports from the front say Iraqi forces surprised a coalition convoy. Six American soldiers have been reported killed in action. Fifteen more have been wounded."

"Hell, those guys have it easy, man," Lenny said. "It's not like Nam."

"For real," Jake said, reaching around and taking out the rubber band that held his ponytail in place. His hair fell; it must have been ten inches long. "I was in Vietnam too. Crawling through the rice paddies."

"Yeah, half my platoon got it in the fucking jungle in one day,"

Lenny said. "I was in the marines. We were the first into the villages after they bombed the hell out of them. A lot of it was cleanup after the bombings. We would come in and shoot the ones who didn't have a fucking chance—men, women, *and* children. We just shot them in the head to put them out of their misery. I was in the Special Forces with Lieutenant Callie. When they picked us out for duty, they asked, 'Who here is willing to shoot his own motherfucking mother?' About half the guys stood up."

"You shot the children?" C asked.

"Fuck yes, man," Lenny replied. "Hell, some of them had their arms or legs blown off. Some had their guts hanging out. They were just going to lie there and die. I was seventeen. People were dying around me every day. My best friend, Scooter, he never came back. I didn't think I would come back alive either. If my captain said, 'Shoot 'em in the fucking head,' I shot 'em in the fucking head. I'm a Sicilian from New Jersey. My captain was a Sicilian. He told us if we *didn't* shoot 'em, he would shoot *us!* You didn't mess with that fucker!"

"I have nothing good to say about that hellhole," Jake said. "I learned to smoke dope there, to shoot up there. No, I should say I have *one* good thing to say about Nam—I saw Bob Hope there in Da Nang. You know, he came over to entertain the troops. He was good. He had this joke: 'Technically, this is not a war. So when you get shot, technically, you're not shot.'" Jake laughed. "If they hadn't sent me home, I'd be six feet under."

"Sent you home?" Lenny asked.

"Yeah. They court-martialed me. I thought you knew that, Lenny," Jake replied. "I'm a deserter. I left my post. It was near some little village. A colonel with a burr up his butt decided to go bust some heads on a Sunday and took two of us in a jeep. We parked at the edge of the village. They left me to guard the jeep. 'Shoot anything that moves, Private,' the colonel ordered as they left. 'We'll be back in fifteen minutes,' he barked. Hell!

They were gone for three hours! I was sick, man. I had the flu or something. It was hot, man. Sweat was just pouring off of me. I heard a noise in the jungle. I saw the trees move. 'Halt!' I yelled. 'Come out with your hands up, or I'll shoot!' The bushes moved again. I swore I heard a gun cock. I panicked and fired a round into the jungle. I heard crying. It was a woman crying. I leveled my rifle toward the sound as a woman carrying a baby walked out of the jungle. She walked toward me with her knees buckling; she was bawling. Blood was streaming from her shoulder. Her hands were covered with blood and she walked toward me, kneeled down, and laid the baby at my feet and then covered her face with her blood-soaked hands.

"The baby was dead. I had killed her baby, man. Shit, I *broke*. I tossed my machine gun into the ditch, left the jeep behind, and started walking back down the road. I swore I would never kill another living thing again, not even a fly.

"The colonel and the guys caught up with me several miles down the road. He pistol-whipped me. Nearly killed me. He had cut off the head of a gook he was interrogating and stuffed it in a duffel bag. He pulled it out and held it over me. 'I oughta do this to you, you fucking asshole!' he screamed. Blood from the head was dripping on my face.

"They took me back to camp. I was put in the brig for a while. Some doctor took pity on me and sent me home to Bremerton. Fuck, I got a dishonorable discharge. The colonel eventually got a Purple Heart. That son of a bitch lost both of his legs."

Lenny's eyes were filled with tears. "Killing women and children is not something I'm fucking proud of," he said. "Hell, at seventeen, with your lieutenant screaming 'Kill the fuckers!' and everybody shooting and yelling, that's what you do. You're seventeen. There's a lot of difference between seventeen and fifty-seven. We were killing the 'enemy.'" Lenny leaned forward in his chair as he looked at Jake. "Don't you think I have fuckin' nightmares?" His voice trailed off.

Jake got off the couch. "Want a cigarette?" he asked, holding out a neatly rolled cigarette in his hand.

"Sure," Lenny said.

"When I got back, my family didn't want anything to do with me," Jake said, lighting Lenny's cigarette. "My girlfriend left me. I bounced around town drinkin' and smokin' pot. When the little money I had was gone, I lived in the woods, or lived on the streets and ate out of dumpsters—for years. I still do. In fact, what time is it? I'm thinking about going dumpster diving! You coming with me, C?"

"Sure," C replied.

"How about you, Richard?" Jake asked.

I had never been dumpster-diving before. "Oh, I don't know," I said.

"It can be profitable," Jake coaxed. "I found $3.75 in pennies two nights ago. People throw away good stuff. You'd be surprised."

The idea of climbing in a dumpster at three in the morning didn't appeal to me. But I was broke. "Okay. I'll go along," I said.

"Good! You can drive. I know of a good place to start. It's on the east side of town, behind Safeway," Jake said.

"How about you, Lenny?" C asked.

"Fuck, no! I ain't crawling around in no stinking dumpster!" Lenny exclaimed. "I'll stay here, watch some porn, and keep an eye on Vinny in case he needs anything. Okay?"

Jake tossed the remote to Lenny.

"What channel has the porn?" Lenny asked. "I've got cable; I'm not used to this DirecTV shit."

"Just hit 177," Jake said. "That's the Hustler channel. Lots of fucking and sucking."

Lenny hit the remote buttons and smiled as two women doing a portly guy appeared. "That's what I like!" Lenny cheered.

"Let's go," Jake said, grabbing his coat.

I had missed the Nam experience. The closest I ever got was riding the bus to the processing center in Columbus when I was in college; there were six black guys and me. They all went; they were too poor to have the protection of college. Unlike Lenny and Jake, it was only one day out of my life; I went right back to Ohio State.

As we left the death watch, it occurred to me that we were all homeless in some way. It seemed that we were all psychically frozen somewhere— the half-dead, the on-the-way-to-dead, the blessedly dead—and at that moment, I wasn't sure which one defined me best.

What better time to be initiated into the art of dumpster diving?

Chapter 17

DUMPSTER DIVING

"**I** got shotgun," C announced as we stepped out into the drizzle and piled into the van. Jake and C seemed to be getting an adrenalin rush at the thought of climbing into dumpsters to look for treasures. I was just worried about how to avoid the inevitable teriyaki or ketchup stains that both C and Jake seemed to wear as badges of courage, earned by participation in this local sport.

"Have you run into those new space-age dumpsters?" Jake asked C. "The ones that compact all the trash as soon as you throw it in? Hell, they take all the fun out of my nights. It makes trash worthless. The jelly donuts, the lemon-roasted chickens, and the coffee grounds all get compressed into one big block."

C and Jake continued their discussion of the latest in sanitation technology. My mind drifted back to when I was a young man in Ohio.

I was twenty-seven or so. My neighbor Henry, who was about ninety, hobbled over one day when I was taking out the garbage. I had two big bags' worth, and Henry met me at my three trash cans.

"Got a lot of trash," Henry said in a tone of voice that left me wondering if it was a question or a compliment. He stood still, peering over his glasses at me as if he wanted to discuss my garbage.

I was *not* going to talk trash with Henry! I knew what he really wanted to do: go through my trash and salvage the good stuff. So I tried to change the subject. "Hi, Henry! How are you?" I asked.

"Still kickin'," he said with a muffled laugh. Then his eyes returned to my trash cans.

Henry seldom threw anything away. He saved old newspapers, used pencils the size of cigarette butts, and washed out milk containers in which he saved some of the other things he saved. He even peeled the labels off tin cans and used the cans to store nuts, bolts, buttons, and pins. Henry had seen the advent of the automobile and the television. He had fought in what they called The War to End All Wars—World War I—and he had lived through one of the epic events in the history of the United States: the Depression.

The Depression was the great equalizer for the national ego of the United States. People did not eat. They slept in the cold and shivered. They lost everything. They were homeless. Hundreds of thousands needed help.

And the poor helped each other.

John Steinbeck wrote in *The Grapes of Wrath*: "I'm learnin' one thing good. Learnin' it all the time and ever' day. If you're in trouble or hurt or need—go to poor people. They're the only ones that'll help—the only ones."

The souls who lived through those years suffered and therefore looked at the world in a cautious way.

I grew up at the beginning of the "throw-away" age. My trash included such things as milk cartons, newspapers, magazines, diapers, plastic bottles, cardboard boxes, paper towels, tin foil, and aerosol cans—just to name a few.

"It's a throw-away world these days—people, too," Henry said, shaking his head as he watched me stuff my trash cans to the brim and then struggle to lock the lids in place. I knew what Henry meant. If he lived much longer, his kids (now fifty) would put him in a "home" where he could get the "proper care."

"It is," I agreed. I knew even then what he meant, but I didn't take it to heart. I didn't embrace it. I was busy at twenty-seven. I had not lived through the Depression. I had always eaten, and I had always been warm. I did not understand it then, but all I had and all I was going to have—and eventually lose—was given to me by the grace of people like Henry, who *had* lived through the Depression. When I was a young boy, it was those people who paid me fifty cents to shovel the snow off their walks. It was they who hired me as a sportswriter. It was they who taught me to think and to do. They lived in small houses on tree-lined streets with sidewalks, and when a neighbor was in trouble, they were there to help.

But Henry knew he would be thrown away. He would be placed in some human storage unit where he could be managed. His social security checks would cover the costs, and he would get a small allowance to cover his basic needs. It would be so antiseptic, clean, and tidy—breakfast at seven, lunch at noon, dinner at five. The family would *finally* clean up the firetrap he called a house and throw away the old newspapers, the old tin cans, and the milk cartons. They would sell his vintage baseball trading cards of Berra, Podres, and Schoendist and his prized, dusty editions of *The Saturday Evening Post* with Norman Rockwell paintings on the cover. They would then have a big garage sale and dispose of the rest of his "junk."

"Turn right here," Jake said. "Pull around back and we'll case it out."

We had barely rolled to a stop when C and Jake threw the van doors open and headed for the dumpsters. They were like kids at Toys"R"Us, excited about getting something—*anything.*

"I'll take the one on the right," Jake said. C acquiesced to the elder statesman of dumpster diving and walked toward the one on the left. Jake lifted the lid on the big green metal dumpster and looked in. "You've got to be careful," he said turning back to me. "You've got to avoid sharp objects and diapers. Looks good! It's about half full," he added as he grabbed onto the rim and then climbed into the dumpster.

Jake stood for a moment atop the pile of trash and then pulled out his rolling papers and cigarette tobacco. "I've been doing this for thirty years now," Jake said as he prepared his smoke. "I've eaten out of these things to survive," he said as he licked his rolling paper, formed his smoke, and lit it.

I was in the presence of the Master of Survival.

"Here're some donuts, right off!" Jake announced. He opened a large box, picked a donut out, and took a bite. "A cream-filled Bismarck. Still good. Here, you want one?" he asked, handing the box to me. "Take a couple. We'll take the rest home." He started digging deeper. "Let's see if we can find something to wash them down with," he said.

C was throwing trash bags full of stuff out of the other dumpster.

"Aha! Found the roasted chickens," Jake said, holding up greasy, cellophane-wrapped chickens in each hand. "Man, they throw six or seven of these away every night. Here, put these in the van," he said, pushing them toward me.

"I found some potato salad and bean salad over here," C yelled. "We can have a picnic!" C climbed out of dumpster number two. "I need a bag to put this stuff in," he said as he picked up one of the plastic bags he had tossed out earlier. He turned it upside down and the contents tumbled to the pavement.

"What's this?" he asked as he bent over to look at the stuff on the ground. He picked up several photos. Some were torn in half. He studied them for a minute. "Looks like another broken heart and another dream that came to an end," he said. "A bunch of family photos. A husband, two kids, a dog—no, two dogs," he added as he sifted through the pictures.

"Any rings in there?" Jake asked. "Check for rings!"

"Not in this bunch," C replied. "We'll have to look in the other bags."

Jake jumped out of his dumpster. "Let's take a look," he said, grabbing one of the bags. "This one is kinda heavy." He ripped it open. "Picture frames, photo albums, a couple of ties, an old smoking pipe . . ." He was taking inventory. "Hey! Here are the rings!" He picked two rings off the ground and held them up to the light. "In this light it's hard to tell if they're worth anything," Jake said, squinting. "You never know. Could be worth ten bucks or ten thousand." He added the rings to C's collection of photos. "You found them, C."

"I'll share the money if they're valuable," C said. "It was your idea to come here."

Jake reached down and picked up an eight-by-ten photo. "Nice-looking man and a pretty woman. Great looking kids—all smiles then! I wonder what happened. Did she leave him? Did he leave her? It's a shame."

"It's a throw-away world—people, too," I said, echoing old Henry.

Jake picked up a photo album and slowly flipped the pages under the flickering security light. "Here's the vacation pictures," he said. "Looks like they went to the Grand Canyon. Yep, here they are at the canyon rim." He picked up another album and opened it. "Here's Christmas," he said. "They had a big tree that year. Here they are in front of the tree—he in his Santa hat, she in her Santa sweater. Looks like they had a great Christmas! Better than I ever had," he added, tossing the albums back into the dumpster. "Let's see what else we can find."

C and Jake kept at it for another half an hour or so. I never did jump in. When they had had their fill of perusing other people's discarded possessions, we left.

Chapter 18

VINNY DIES

Chef Pat, adorned in her hairnet and plastic gloves, was looking pretty perky for eight o'clock in the morning as she greeted her hungry flock for breakfast at Sally's.

Her boys were happy with Tater Tots smothered in sausage gravy, with a cinnamon roll on the side. Pat took pride in her cooking, and as chief cook, server, and bottle washer, she was on the front line each day to see the response.

"She's a fuckin' good cook when she's got somethin' to fuckin' work with," Lenny said as he liberally shook salt over his food. "This is fuckin' good, man!"

I wondered if Lenny used the f-word in every sentence to accentuate the passion of his feelings, or if the habit had just become so ingrained that it was an integral part of all his communication. "Maybe I was just being a snob," I thought. A "fuckin'" snob, at that.

The breakfast crowd at Sally's was usually made up of homeless men. Many had shivered through the night in their cars, if they were lucky enough to still have them, or under some makeshift cardboard shelter in a doorway or alley. They needed something hot in their stomachs. Some had gone job hunting at seven a.m., only to be turned away. There were no jobs—at least, no jobs for them.

The tweeters and the alcoholics were still sleeping.

C and Jake came in, looking a little beleaguered, and hit the serving line. I figured they just got into some bad dope the night before. The two men received their portions from Chef Pat and headed for our table. Jake sat down without delivering his usual morning greeting. C wasn't himself either.

"Everything okay, Jake?" I asked, breaking the silence.

Jake cleared his throat and brought his eyes up from his food.

"Vinny died last night," he said, his voice cracking. "I was there when he left us."

"I'm sorry," I said.

Jake was silent for a moment. "Oh, I know it's best that it's over. The pain has finally ended for him."

We sat there without speaking for a few minutes, some of us halfheartedly eating.

"Vinny was a fuckin' good guy," Lenny said, shattering the silence and then belching. Jake and C rolled their eyes.

"We're going to have a short service on Wednesday," Jake said. "Just C and me and a couple of other guys who were in Nam with Vinny. Would you like to come?" Jake was looking directly at me.

"I'd be honored," I said.

"It's going to be at the cemetery on Naval, about one o'clock. It's that cemetery up on the hill. Nobody's going to be there but us. Do you know where it is?"

"I'll find it," I said.

"Hell, I'm not very hungry this morning," Jake said, picking up his tray and dumping the remains in the big garbage can by the kitchen door. He returned to the table and slipped on his worn jean jacket. "I'm going to find a place to get stoned."

"I'll go with you," C said, and they left, heads down.

Many Wednesdays had come and gone in my sixty years. I don't believe I particularly remembered any of them.

But I will always remember the Wednesday of Vinny's funeral service with Jake, C, Charles, and Rodney.

As I pulled into the Naval Avenue cemetery on that Wednesday, I saw the four men on a small hill. Three of them were standing and the other was in a wheelchair, with two large white dogs sitting by his side. Willow jumped out of the van when I opened the door, thinking it was the park. "I guess you can come along, too," I told her.

As I approached the men, I saw that the three Nam vets were dressed in their old army uniforms, now nearly forty years old. There was a light mist beading up on their wool jackets. The grave was covered with dozens of flowers—roses, daisies, tulips, and lilies.

"Richard," Jake greeted me. "Glad you could make it. Meet Charles. That's Rodney on wheels." Charles was a big bald man who obviously had long outgrown the uniform he once wore. He could fasten just one button and his stomach stretched the jacket to its limits. Rodney was too big now to button even a single button on his jacket.

It was obvious that Jake was stoned for the occasion.

"Look at all the flowers," I said.

"Yeah. C and I found them all in the dumpster behind the flower shop last night," Jake said. "They're still pretty."

It was time to say goodbye to Vinny.

Jake reached out his hand to C, and then we all joined hands and made a circle. "Let's have a moment of prayer," Jake said.

The dogs seemed to know that this was a solemn moment. All three of them were lying quietly in the grass.

"Well, Vinny, old man . . . It's time we say goodbye to you." Jake cleared his throat. "We wish you were still here, but we understand why you had to go. We will miss you. You were our friend. So no matter where you go, you just give 'em hell." Jake's voice was cracking and fading away.

"I have something I would like to read, if it's okay with you guys," C said. The men all nodded, so C took a book from his well-worn duffel bag. He flipped the pages and cleared his throat. The book was by Carlos Castaneda, *Journey to Ixtlan.*

C read to us—to Vinny, really—about death being our eternal companion and how a man must learn to deal with that through his life as a warrior-hunter: "A warrior-hunter deals intimately with his world, and yet he is inaccessible to that same world. He taps it lightly, stays for as long as he needs to, and then swiftly moves away, leaving hardly a mark."

"Peace. Be safe," I heard C whisper, and we all joined in "Peace. Be safe."

Tears filled all five pairs of eyes.

"Let's have a smoke," Jake said. "One last smoke with Vinny."

So C got his stash out of the duffel bag, and we all sat down in the grass.

"Well, we sent him off the best we could," Charles said. "He didn't have anybody—any family, I mean—did he?"

"No," Jake replied. "His doctors tried to find some aunt he talked about in California, but they couldn't find anyone."

"After Nam, he became a roll-in-the-gutter drunk. Even *I* didn't want to have anything to do with him then. Mad at the world. He weighed ninety-eight pounds when he died. The cancer had eaten him up. He was over one eighty in Nam," Charles said.

C was passing the first of his joints around the circle.

"Yeah, he was a mean drunk," Rodney added. "He spent some time in those bully missions in Los Angeles and San Francisco. He got the shit beat out of him a couple times."

"Hell, we're all lucky to have lived this long," Jake said. "I thought we'd all get it in sixty-five. We should have died then, in the rice paddies. You remember those goddamn rice paddies, don't you boys?" Jake reminisced. "My feet were wet for three months. I could never keep my socks dry. I got that fungus. Hell, Rodney, you lost your legs there. They sent you home before you got to see much of the jungle."

"You remember those fucking ants, Jake?" Charles asked.

"Those jungle ants?" Jake shuddered. "Those fuckers seemed to be the only things that survived Agent Orange. They'd wrap themselves in the leaves of the short trees somehow. I don't know how they did it. Then they would reach out and bite you when you brushed up against them. They had the sting of a fucking wasp. Talk about chemical warfare! A year in Nam and I never saw a spider, a snake, or a monkey alive. But I saw plenty of those fucking ants. Sometimes when they would sting you, you thought it was a bullet from some sniper and you were going to die right there. Hell, it's been thirty-seven, thirty-eight years, I guess, and I still don't sleep well at night.

"We would have all been better off if we had died over there," he finished solemnly. And then there was silence as each man seemed to drink in and reflect on Jake's statement.

That is when it came to me—the concept, the knowledge I needed to help me understand these men.

All of our wars were carried on the backs of the poor and the sons of the poor. The poor were the first to fight and the first to die. Boys from Bremerton, Terre Haute, and San Diego all found a home in the military. They found dignity and camaraderie. It was the poor, rough, toothless, and uneducated who won at Saratoga, as it was the thieving and obdurate who fought at Antietam. The poor died first and last in World War I, World War II, and Korea, and fifty-eight thousand Americans died in Vietnam, many of them paupers.

The big military and industrial conglomerates pocketed billions during the war in Vietnam. But when these men—gathered on this knoll—came back from the killing fields, after surviving hell in the jungles, they came back poor—poor monetarily and poor in spirit. America had lost. It had run. It hadn't just retreated to fight another day. It had left people behind to be tortured and killed. There were no parades or parties or dancing in the streets like after World War II. No breast-beating pride or songs of victory. It was a moment of shame in United States history. The returning soldiers were ignored. There was the GI Bill, but many fell through the cracks. They fell into a void; Jake and Charles and Rodney and Vinny all fell into it. It was a void where a couple of joints and a bottle of whisky made the journey of any given day a little more bearable.

According to the National Survey of Homeless Assistance Providers and Clients, veterans make up twenty-three percent of America's homeless population. The National Coalition for Homeless Veterans conservatively estimates that one out of every three homeless men is a veteran. Nearly fifty percent of these men served in the Vietnam War. It was, in part, because of the sacrifice of these men that the real estate salesman, the attorney, the developer, the banker, the car dealer, and the professional athlete could build fortunes. If the world were fair, Donald Trump would be handing these guys hundred-dollar bills, Alex Rodriguez thousand-dollar bills, and Bill Gates million-dollar bills.

"You know," Charles said from the silence, summing up exactly what I was thinking, "none of us have shit after all these years. I'll bet we don't have ten bucks between us."

"You got that right," Jake said.

"Vinny handled it better than any of us . . . the war, I mean," Charles said. "He didn't seem so—you know—scarred. Vinny was a warrior."

"I swear I could feel it the moment he was gone," Jake said. "I was watching TV and I could hear him moaning. Then I heard him sigh. Then he was quiet. I got so used to hearing him moaning and talking to the pain, the quiet let me know the time had come. I walked into the room. He was still. I called out to him, but I'd seen them die in Nam and I knew. I closed his eyelids, covered him with the blanket. I called 911 and told them someone died, gave them the address, and then I left. I didn't want him to just lay there alone for days. I hated leaving him that way, but I couldn't be involved, not with my record. I walked by yesterday, and they still had the yellow police tape and coroner's notice on the front door. I left some stuff there: shirts, pants, needles, and syringes. I figure I won't get them back."

C had passed around the joints, and Jake handed one to me. "No thanks, Jake," I said. "I can't get high. It's just a waste on me."

"I know," Jake replied. "But, for Vinny's sake, smoke with us."

I could not refuse that request.

"Here's to Vinny," C said as the five of us lit up.

As I inhaled the smoke deep into my lungs, I tried to put myself in the shoes of these men when they were nineteen-to-twenty-year-olds walking through the jungle and the rice paddies, knowing that six of their friends were killed just the day before.

When I was twenty, I was at home or at college, reading and writing, having sex with girls in the back of the Buick, watching *The Mary Tyler Moore Show* on TV. McDonald's had opened its first restaurant in my hometown a couple of years before, and I was eating three Big Macs a day, with fries.

As I took another hit from the joint, I started to get angry at God. Not for me, but for them. If there was a God, how dare He allow these men to suffer so long for a fight they didn't choose? It was time for Him to get His lazy ass down here and help them. I wanted to pray for these men and all the other homeless souls I had met and broken bread with each day.

But would it do any good?

Were the trillions of prayers offered up over the centuries just a total waste of time, time that could have been spent just as productively producing widgets? Was God, like me, depressed by what He saw? His most blessed creation—mankind—was killing, enslaving, and torturing fellow men over gold, oil, land, and water. Did God need a few milligrams of Zoloft? Or how about a joint?

I was sick and tired of hearing excuses offered by preachers about how God works in mysterious ways and loves the poor, the hungry, and the sick. I wanted God to break into the six-o'clock news and make an announcement: "Good evening. This is God. When I am done with this message, I want you to turn off your television, walk out your door, love your neighbor, take the homeless into your homes, stop killing each other, quit stealing from one another, and halt the raping and pillaging of the world I have given you. Good night, David. Good night, Chet. Good night, everyone, and have a nice tomorrow."

The warmth of the sun on my face brought me back to the present. I was one of five men sitting in a circle in a graveyard. I saw part of a rainbow dipping into the water in the distance. It was still drizzling, but the clouds were moving on and the sun was breaking through.

It was then that I realized I might have finally gotten high! "You guys see that rainbow?" I asked.

"I do believe Richard is high," Jake laughed.

"What rainbow?" C asked.

"That one," I said, pointing. "It's growing bigger. It's going to fill the sky."

"You see it, Charlie?" Jake asked.

Charles shook his head.

"I guess you're right, Jake. I must be high. Do you guys see rainbows when you get high?"

"Sure do," C said. "And we all get mad at God and cuss Him out!"

The rainbow grew stronger, arching across the sky in hues of pink, green, and yellow.

"Oh, I see that rainbow now," Jake said, taking another hit of his joint.

"Me, too," Charles said.

"It's a beauty!" C added.

"Well, I'll be damned," Rodney exclaimed.

We all took another drag and admired our own personal version of the colors.

"Did I ever tell you I can talk to whales?" I asked.

"Oh, shit," Jake said. "We'd better get out of here before he gets going on that!"

Chapter 19

THE OPERA

The next week, C invited me to a night at the opera in Seattle.

We left right after lunching on macaroni and cheese at Sally's. We drove up to Bainbridge Island and caught the ferry from there to Seattle.

C wanted to cruise "The Ave" in the U District, just north of downtown Seattle. The Ave is an eight-block stretch of ethnic restaurants, bookstores, funky bars, and shops full of T-shirts, incense (with provocative names like White Dove, Virgin, Captain Black, and Hot Breath), exotic knives with curved black handles and shiny steel blades, and pipes bearing an uncanny resemblance to those used to smoke illegal drugs.

A mixture of university students and professors, homeless and street people, and amused observers frequented The Ave. There were teens with spiked hair, dyed orange, chartreuse, red-white-and-blue, and all the other shades of the rainbow. Street musicians were strumming their guitars and singing folk songs, with their instrument cases lying open on the sidewalk, ready to receive the coin of the realm.

C was in his element. Flowers Bar was our first stop of the day. It had been a flower shop for many years. Poor students would often buy a single rose there on the way to a date, when gallantry was in vogue. When the new owners bought the site and turned it into a restaurant, they couldn't think of a better name. So they simply called it Flowers. It was an airy place, with old, cracked leather chairs placed by the front windows. That made it the perfect perch for people watching.

"I think I'll have a White Russian," C told the waitress tending to our perch.

"Do you have a nice Pinot?" I asked.

"Very nice," she said, with a smile.

"I'll take a glass," I replied, and she headed off to fill our order.

Flowers was busy.

"Listen," C said, leaning toward me. "People are talking about *issues*— about books, art, music, and faraway places. They are sharing ideas instead of talking about other people, their husbands, their problems, their cars, and their possessions. Ahhhh . . . this is heaven!"

We spent the next four hours watching the parade of people on The Ave, and C would have made the Russkies proud, consuming seven White Russians to my four Pinots.

We arrived at the opera just as they were flicking the lights to announce the start.

C looked more like a cast member, dressed in his "pirate-wear," topped with a bandana. All he needed was a gold earring and he could have been Captain Cook. He handed the tickets to the usher, who directed us to third row, center. I, dressed in my jeans and scuffed Reeboks, found myself seated next to a gentleman in a black tuxedo.

"How did you get these great seats?" I whispered.

"I did somebody a favor," C said. "Somebody needed a glad bag for a sick friend, and I just happened to have one. Actually, I think these seats belong to Mr. and Mrs. Bill Gates, but they're touring Europe right now."

The house lights dimmed. I crossed my arms and leaned back in my seat. C leaned forward as if to inhale every moment of the production. It was *Carmen*. The gypsy girl lifted the hem of her skirt and danced toward her male admirers in a sun-drenched Seville square outside the cigarette factory where she worked.

The production carried the audience through a whole range of emotions. C laughed when Carmen sang the "Habanera" aria, about love as a lawless gypsy child. He cried when the outcast Don José lamented the prison love had made for him.

At intermission, while others were savoring six-dollar glasses of Chardonnay in the lobby, C took a can of Budweiser and a bag of Fritos from his wool pea coat and noisily enjoyed his refreshments, much to the chagrin of some and the amusement of other operagoers.

The third act was just as engrossing as the first two. C nodded as Carmen mourned the fate that cannot be escaped. He tapped his feet and hummed along to the "Toreador Song." And he cried again when the tormented Don José drove his knife into the heart of his beloved, Carmen, and threw himself on her dead body.

It was about eleven when the opera ended and we headed back to the van. C was exhilarated, humming the score. "Can we stop at 7-Eleven?" he asked.

Willow was doing her I-have-to-take-a-pee dance as we headed out. She had been very patiently waiting in the car, drinking her water in the cup-holder and napping the entire time we were in the theater. I found a spot as quickly as possible and took Willow for her nightly duty. C stayed in the car listening to NPR, catching up on the war.

Willow seemed to enjoy our late night walks the best. Maybe it was the wolf in her little body, smelling the grass as it began cooling down after being warmed by the earth during the day. She rolled more at night, throwing herself on the ground and tossing her tiny frame back and forth, wiggling and rubbing her nose in the green stuff. When she stood up, it looked for a moment like she was intoxicated. And then, she would run!

The music was blaring from the van speakers when Willow and I returned. C was inside stomping his feet and playing an imaginary drum. I opened the door and Willow hopped in. "No wonder he killed himself," C said, "playing music like that all the time."

"Who's that?" I asked.

"Kurt Cobain," C replied. "That's one of his hits—"The Man Who Sold the World." He was from Seattle."

"No, I'm not familiar with him at all," I said, settling into my seat, and headed for 7-Eleven. C turned Cobain up another few decibels, pounded his feet harder, and moved his head to the beat of the music.

As I expected, our pit stop at 7-Eleven was for an intoxicant. C bought two bottles of cheap high-proof wine.

"Wait a minute." C stepped out of the van again and dug into the top pocket of his shirt and then patted his pants pockets. "Damn. I've done it again." Then he went over and took the lid off the trash can in front of the store, rustled up an aluminum can, and got back in the van. "I lost my pipe," he said. "I must have lost a hundred of them by now." He took his knife from his pocket, punched a hole in the empty can, and bent it into a chic marijuana appliance. "Just as good, if not better," he said of his new pipe.

"Pick your poison—cherry or strawberry?" C asked, holding up the bottles of wine.

"You choose," I said.

He closed his eyes. "Eenie, meenie, mynee, mo. It's strawberry!" he said, twisting the cap off the bottle and pouring generously into a paper cup. He took a swig and handed me the cup. "When we get back on the other side, let's stop in Hansville and see my friend Adrian, okay?"

We headed north toward Edmonds and barely caught the twelve-thirty-five ferry. After six White Russians, four glasses of Pinot, and a night of *Carmen*, washed down with two glasses of forty-proof strawberry wine, we both fell asleep in the van to the hum of the ferry turbines. The blaring of the horns signaling our arrival in Kingston startled us both back to life. "Arriving Kingston," the first mate announced over the speaker system. "Passengers need to return to their cars at this time. We are tying up for the night. The next ferry will be at five thirty a.m."

"I must've dozed off," C said, stretching.

"I did too," I said. "It felt good. Are you sure your friend—what's his name?"

"Adrian."

"Are you sure he'll still be up?" I asked.

"He stays up all night most of the time," C replied. "He's truly a night owl." C reached for his cup and poured some more wine. "Adrian is the quiet type," he said. "He likes to be alone. He's got a little two-bedroom cabin in the woods. He works in the garden, smokes some pot, has something to eat, takes a nap, reads a book, smokes some more pot, eats dinner, smokes some more pot, plays his guitar, reads, and then smokes some more pot. Now, take a right at the old country store coming up," directed C. "It's not far after that."

I made the turn at the store and headed north. C delicately shaped his marijuana bud and placed it over the hole in his beer-can pipe, struck his lighter, and sucked in hard. I noticed a car coming up fast from behind and immediately checked my speed.

"I hope this isn't a cop on our tail," I said.

"Cop? Where?" C choked on his smoke.

The car drew up behind us and then changed lanes, whizzing past, doing a good eighty.

"Whew! He was moving!" I said.

C took another hit from his can. "Glad it *wasn't* a cop," he coughed out. In a moment, he pointed ahead. "Turn right on the next road. It's gravel and kinda bumpy."

I slowed and made the turn. It was bumpy all right— full of potholes a good eight inches deep. After about ten minutes of torture I asked, "Hey C, how much farther do we have to go? The van and I can't take much more of this."

"Just a little bit farther. We're almost there," he promised.

As we approached Adrian's cabin, we could see car lights in the distance. "He must be home," I said.

"Wait a minute; something's not right," C said, leaning forward and peering out the window. "It's too bright. Adrian's wouldn't be all lit up at this time of night; he'd be too stoned. Slow down. Pull over here, and turn off your lights."

I pulled over as instructed, flipped off the lights, and turned off the engine.

"Let's walk up there and check this out," he said, opening the van door quietly.

I climbed out and told Willow we'd be right back. "No bark! No bark!"

Now that we were out of the car, we could hear yelling. We slowly approached Adrian's place.

"I don't like this," C whispered. We crept along in the shadows of the tree line until the house came into view. "Stay down."

"That's the same Chevy that roared past us on the highway," I whispered back. Its brights were on and the motor was running.

"Fuck you, asshole!" someone screamed, and a man was pushed out the front door. He was wearing jeans but no shirt or shoes. "We're going to teach you a fucking lesson!" the voice bellowed again.

The shoeless man fell to the ground, and two men raced out and kicked him. "There, motherfucker! Maybe you'll listen to us when we ask you something next time," the man kept yelling. "That's if you *live*, asshole!"

"We've got to *do* something," I said to C, starting to get up.

"Stay down!" he ordered, pulling me back to the ground. "Those guys'll kill you and think nothing of it. That's Michael and Roy. Michael calls himself the 'avenging angel.' He's the one with the black vest and the big chain hanging around his waist. The fat guy with the ponytail is Roy. Adrian should know better than to deal with those dudes; he must have been pretty desperate, like a cabin payment due and the bank on his ass.

"Michael's a hired gun—a bounty hunter. For forty bucks, he'll collect the hundred dollars somebody owes you. He's like a bill collector, a lawyer, a banker, a judge, and a jury all rolled into one."

"Where's the fucking stuff we paid you for, asshole?" Michael yelled as he kicked Adrian in the back with the pointed toe of his boot.

Adrian seemed to say something, but we couldn't hear it.

"Next week, my ass!" Michael bellowed. "That's what you said last week, you son of a bitch!"

"Drug deal gone sour," C whispered. "This is bad."

"You like to drag on your shit all day," Michael snarled. "Well, we're going to give you a little drag. Right, Roy? Give me that fucking rope!" Roy tossed the rope to Michael, who tied Adrian's feet together and then pulled him toward the car. He tossed the end of the rope to Roy, who tied it to the bumper of the car. Michael jumped into the driver's seat and raced the engine of the Chevy.

"Let's get the fuck out of here and call the police," C said. "Hurry!"

I took a quick look as Michael put the car in gear and started dragging Adrian around the graveled cul-de-sac, and then I scrambled to the van.

"Go! Go! Go!" chanted C as I started the engine and turned around as fast as I could. "Hit your horn, now! We can't stop them. They have guns—they'd kill us! But we sure as hell can pray they'll hear us leave and stop!"

I blasted the horn as we raced down the bumpy road, shaking all the way.

"Michael and Roy skinned a man alive two years ago," C said. "It was so bad it wasn't even in the papers. The policemen who found the victim had to go to therapy for months afterwards, and one eventually quit the force. They sawed off another man's legs after killing him and then stuffed him in a dresser drawer."

The things C was telling me made me drive even faster as we pounded our way back to the main highway. The adrenalin was gushing.

We found a pay phone at the country store and C jumped out and called 911. "I hope he lives," C said as he jumped back in the van. "Now, let's get out of here!"

We passed two sheriff's cars about two miles up the road. They were heading back the way we had come, with their sirens blaring and lights flashing.

"Pass me that bottle of cherry wine!" I said. I unscrewed the cap and took a big drink and passed it to C, who took a chug.

It was three thirty in the morning. We drove the next few miles in a daze. I was waiting for my heartbeat to return to normal.

"You hungry?" asked C, finally. "Let's go to Denny's."

I hardly knew how to respond. Maybe he was used to events like this happening around him, but I wasn't. I didn't know if or how I ever could be. Maybe being homeless and living from moment to moment eventually hardens you—makes you so numb you no longer have normal reactions to the horror you may have just seen or the terror you may have felt. But it seemed to me that this was way over the top. It had to do with the drug scene—and it scared the shit out of me. I could see how some people had become homeless because of their drug use; it seemed that the drugs started out as an "aspirin," taken to ease some of the immediate pain of their plights. Unfortunately, it was an aspirin that became an incurable addiction. I vowed once again never to mess with that shit.

We did end up at Denny's. It was funny how fast a dream could turn into a nightmare and then be forgotten altogether. The one constant on this journey seemed to be the need for sustenance, and the rule was never to turn down an opportunity for a meal, since you had no idea when or where the next one would come along.

We went into the almost-deserted restaurant and found ourselves a booth. With very little thought, we ordered ourselves coffee and an early breakfast.

C breathed in deeply, then out again. "You know who the most famous homeless man in history was, don't you?" I didn't.

"'Foxes have holes and birds of the air have nests, but the Son of Man has no place to lay his head,' Jesus said."

I lowered my head and shook it back and forth. "I should have known that."

"You, Richard, are in good company," C said.

"People were afraid of Jesus," I replied.

"Yes, and people are afraid of the homeless today. And they are disgusted when they see a person digging through a garbage can or a dumpster. They're frightened when someone unclean talks to them— afraid they might ask for money, afraid they will steal their car or rob their house or stab them. But it isn't the homeless they should fear. It's the people who have jobs and money—like that truck painter, Gary Ridgeway, aka the Green River Killer. Did you know he admitted to killing forty-eight women in Washington State? He's the deadliest killer in the United States to date," C said.

"Yes. I did read that," I responded

"Can you imagine that one Christmas Eve, Ridgeway got off work early, cashed his Christmas bonus check, went to the mall, bought some presents on his MasterCard, had dinner at home with the wife, and then went out and killed a young woman and dumped her body along the road? She was one of those disgusting, homeless prostitutes people fear," C said. His raised voice attracted the attention of the three other customers several tables away. "Hell, maybe the son of a bitch did her a favor! She would probably have had to sell her body over and over again for ten, maybe fifteen years just to pay for a three-hundred-dollar-a-month apartment, electric and water, and a run-down car!"

The waitress arrived with our Grand Slam breakfasts and refilled our coffee cups.

"They arrested Ridgeway at his job on November 20, 2001," C said, resuming his tirade as soon as she left our table. "He painted a picture of death—mostly of teenaged runaways. If I remember right, the first girl he killed was sixteen years old. I don't know what it is about Washington State, but, you know, three of the most notorious serial killers come from here. Ridgeway killed forty-eight women, Ted Bundy, who used to work for the Republican Party, killed thirty, and Robert Yates killed thirteen."

We ate in silence for a few moments.

"The people should *really* be afraid of guys like that Tacoma police chief who shot his wife to death in the parking lot at the mall," C continued. "Or the son of the director of the Department of Corrections for Washington State who raped a two-year-old. He pleaded guilty and got a whole six months! If a homeless guy had done that, he'd get life in prison!"

C told me a story about how he'd once picked up a hitchhiker outside of St. Louis. Her name was Keisha. She told C she was twenty-two, but he figured she was really about seventeen. She was homeless and heading west. She had worked at Kentucky Fried Chicken for three years at five-fifty an hour. Her boss kept putting the moves on her every day until he got her in the car one night and demanded she put out. So she did. But it was nothing new to her. Her father molested her as a child and had sex with her until she was thirteen. She ran away when her father gave her to their next-door neighbor one night for letting him borrow his chainsaw. A couple of guys took her in and got her a couple of tattoos on her ankle, and she learned to make money selling her body."

In the two weeks she rode with him, she offered him her body every day as payment for the ride. She couldn't figure out why he wouldn't accept. She thought he must be gay. C admitted he'd been tempted—she was a pretty little lady. But he taught her how to play chess instead, and they played a game every night. He also taught her the differences between Zinfandel, Chardonnay, Merlot, and Cabernet Sauvignon. He dropped her off in San Diego, and she gave him a hug.

"You know, the big thing that sets the homeless apart is that they usually only commit crimes out of desperation," C continued. "Those with homes and jobs commit crimes out of boredom or hatred or greed."

I just sat there in a sort of trance.

"Elliot Liebow wrote a book about the lives of homeless women called *Tell Them Who I Am*. I think it came out in ninety-three or ninety-four. He said something like this: 'You are not needed anywhere, not wanted anywhere. Nobody cares what you do.' And you know, unless people have been there—lost, alone, rejected, feeling worthless and unwanted— they just can't know that numb feeling that drags you down. All the dreams are gone, gone forever. You're just hoping for some force to end the nightmare peacefully."

I nodded, remembering my night on the bridge all too well.

"Whatever happened to Emma Lazarus's sonnet on the Statue of Liberty that welcomed millions of people to America? 'Give me your tired, your poor, Your huddled masses yearning to breathe free, The wretched refuse of your teeming shore. Send these, the homeless, tempest-tost to me, I lift my lamp beside the golden door!'"

C raised his fork like he was Lady Liberty herself.

"Homelessness in this great country of the United States is an abomination!" C exclaimed. The other customers got up and made their way to the cash register.

"But the great masses—who are only one paycheck or one stroke of luck better off themselves—even *they* repeat the same great lies about the homeless: 'They are lazy. They don't want to work. They are drunks, bums, drug-using, worthless scum.' If you tell the same lie over and over again about the homeless, it eventually becomes the truth. You tell your wife the lie, then you tell your children the lie. Rush Limbaugh and Mike Savage then broadcast the lie, and politicians who want your vote politicize the lie. The lie just grows and grows."

The waitress finally delivered change to the other customers, who quickly escaped out the door.

C looked sadly into my eyes. "The homeless are human beings," he said. "Okay, so they are people with problems—some greater than others. But there is no problem that can't be overcome with love, patience, and kindness. Given help and a sense of direction, most will help themselves and even help others."

We finally left Denny's, and I dropped C back at the Armadillo. We were quiet with each other; there seemed little left to be said.

As I drove away I realized I would probably never know what happened to Adrian, and I had to accept that reality. His fate would be like that of so many others—disappearing off the face of the earth without a trace—no funeral, no seven-gun salute, no flowers, no friends wearing all black, their faces streaming with tears.

If I disappeared, no one from my past life would know or care. Only C and the regulars at Sally's would note my absence and say a prayer for me.

Chapter 20

THE LUCKY ROCKS

I'm in more trouble than I thought, I said to myself as I walked out of the mental institution, heading for the van. I had spent the morning at my now regular appointments in mental-health land. These mornings were always psychically challenging and often emotionally draining, but today's discussions left me in an even greater state of confusion than usual.

After an hour with my psychiatrist, Bob, he admitted to me that even *he* had a problem. He is a very good swimmer; however, his son is afraid of water, and he has to give him a bath each day. So I wondered, if Bob couldn't get his son over a water phobia, what are the chances he'll be able to fix me?

Then, after a two-hour session, Rodney, my psychologist, speculated that I just needed some good luck (for a change), and he showed me two rocks he carries in his pocket. He said he rubs them together in times of stress or misfortune. Were lucky rocks now a standard part of the treatment for clinical depression? I wondered. And will sacrificing two chickens under the light of the full moon be next?

I had been hoping these mental health gurus would have all the answers—some magic wand they could wave over me, some roadmap to Camelot. Instead they had given me the happy pills: Zoloft, the miracle mind-candy for depression in the twenty-first century. I was one of the nearly thirty million Americans taking sertraline hydrochloride, the most prescribed antidepressant in the United States. Clinical depression as well as obsessive compulsive, panic, and social anxiety disorders in both adults and children—all taken care of with Zoloft! Well, the pills did seem to help, at least a little. And now I was off looking for two lucky rocks.

But the thought of suicide was still bouncing around in my mind.

I got in the van and turned the key. Willow hopped into my lap and pressed her nose against the glass. It was her way of requesting that I open her window. I complied. She stuck her head out as far as it would go, and with her ears flying in the wind, we headed for lunch at the Salvation Army.

More than once I had thought of driving over the center line into a big truck to end my journey on this planet. It would be quick and easy and effective. But how do you do that when you are traveling with a wonderful furry white dog who loves you and whom you love back? (Not to mention the trauma to the other driver.)

Then the heaviness that I had come to know so well began its journey through my body again as I headed downtown. A tingling in my arms began and slowly spread to my legs. The recurring thought was back. I had first experienced it the day after I failed to jump from the bridge, and it had haunted me every day since:

Maybe I did succeed in my fatal jump—maybe this existence was just an illusion experienced by the dead. Or maybe I was sent back! Maybe neither God nor the Devil wanted my soul in its present state. Maybe I wasn't driving down this road at all, but—

As usual, my thoughts halted abruptly when I saw C. He was pushing a bright pink baby carriage across the Manette Bridge, wearing cut-off jean shorts and a pair of hiking boots, and his unruly hair was sticking out from under his baseball cap.

I pulled off on the other side of the bridge, laughing, and waited for him to catch up. I hadn't seen him for a while, but every time I did I got an adrenalin rush, knowing that something was about to happen. I felt like Jim going down the river with Huck Finn whenever C was around.

Coming off the bridge, he was smiling and headed my way. "Richard! It's good to see you," he said, pushing his carriage up beside the van. I got out and looked inside his latest acquisition. It was full of shirts, pants, and socks, topped off with three novels and a twelve-pack of Coors. Four were already empty. "I've been to the laundromat," he said.

I couldn't help but chuckle. "Where did you get the carriage?" I asked.

"Where else?" he replied. "I found it in a dumpster!"

"I was heading for Sally's," I said. "Do you want a ride?"

"Sure," he said, and began tossing his laundry into the back of the van, spilling a half-empty beer on his clean socks and shirts. We wrestled with the baby carriage, the bright pink fringe getting caught in the metal bars as we opened the hatch and put it in on its side, spilling more beer.

With everything finally stowed, we pulled back out on the street and headed for Sally's, hoping there were no beer-sniffing patrol dogs on duty at eleven in the morning.

"Man, have I got some great news!" C exclaimed. "Andy finally got his social security money after all these years!"

"Great!" I replied. I had rarely seen C this animated.

"Sixty-seven thousand dollars!"

"Sixty-seven *thousand? How?*"

"Well, he filed sixteen years ago, but he would get drunk and disappear for months and not get his paperwork. Then he would come around and file the papers again—and, sure as shootin', he would get lost again. It's hard to get mail when you're living on the street all the time. But now he's got it!"

C told me about Andy's new apartment, with a kitchen, a bedroom, a bathroom, and a living room with a TV. Andy spent most of his time in the living room. He put a mattress in front of the TV so he can drink all he wants and watch TV or read.

"That's wonderful," I said.

"If you're not doing anything, can we run over there later?"

"Okay!"

The plan was set as we pulled into the alley behind Sally's. James and Lionel were there, having an animated discussion by the brick wall at the back of the building. James was pointing to the ground. We started to get out of the van, and when James saw C he started toward us, waving his right hand toward his belly, beckoning us to come over. "C! C! Come over here," he said. "We need your opinion. You too, Richard!"

James and Lionel had been pitching pennies against the wall, and two pennies appeared to be leaning against the red brick. "That's mine," James said, pointing to a bright copper penny. "And that's his," he said, pointing to the other coin. "As you can see, both coins are leaning against the wall, but my coin is obviously leaning at a steeper angle, which means the total circumference of my penny is closer to the brick!"

C just laughed.

"You got books, C," said James. "You got a book on that?" he asked.

"There's *Hoyle's*," C said. "But I don't have it with me. And I'm not sure it covers this particular circumstance."

Lionel needed to state his case, too. "I say it's the edge of the penny that counts. And his penny is at such a steep angle that some of his edge isn't even touching the wall. See? See? Take a close look!" he added, bending over and pointing closely at James' penny.

There was a moment of contemplation as we all bent in to get a closer perspective on the positioning of James' coin.

"What's the matter with you, man?" James snarled, cocking his head and staring at Lionel.

"Nothin' is the matter with me," Lionel countered. "It's easy to see that this nigger—*you,*" he continued, pointing at James, "is trying to cheat this nigger—*me!*" he said, pointing at himself.

It was obvious to C and me that there was no immediate solution to this conundrum. "How about a tie?" C offered.

"Nope," said James, resolutely.

"A playoff?" C persisted, looking at Lionel, who shook his head emphatically.

"This is for big money, C," said James. "Big, *big* money!"

C cupped his chin and rubbed his beard. "Then you have a stalemate, boys," he said.

"What's that?" James asked.

"It means that I will try to look it up in *Hoyle's* and get back to you tomorrow. Anyway, it's time for lunch."

"You look it up in the book, C," James said. "Look it up."

We turned and retraced our steps toward the building. C was chuckling to himself. Then he turned and took a few steps back to James and Lionel. "Hey, by the way, you two gentlemen know that the n-word has been banned, don't you?" he asked.

"Oh, no, no, no, no, baby," Lionel came back, vehemently. "That's against free speech! Against the Constitution! That's just for you white boys!"

"Why's that?" asked C, his face totally deadpan.

"Because, you know, C, you might be disrespecting us," Lionel answered. "I can call him that 'cause he's my bro, man. He *knows* I love him."

"Well, I love you, too," C pressed on.

James' face lit up, and he looked to the sky. "C loves us!" he yelled, rocking back and forth on his feet. Then he looked at his companion. "Did you hear that, Lionel? C loves us!"

"He's right," Lionel said. "He can call me 'nigger' anytime he wants.

C is every color. He's like the rainbow. He's the Rainbow Man!"

"I consider it a compliment," C said, nodding to the men. He was smiling broadly as he headed for lunch.

The usual crowd, plus a few new faces, had gathered in the dining room. Earl and his family were sitting at the first table by the door. Katie looked at me and asked, "Where's Willow?"

"She's in the car, guarding it," I answered.

Chef Pat had prepared one of my favorites, tuna-noodle casserole with lots of peas and cheese. I was hungry.

As we were waiting in line, I felt a tug on my shirtsleeve. It was Katie. She extended her hand and showed me two small stones. "These are for Willow and you," she said. "They are lucky . . . ah . . . lucky rocks."

I was stunned and didn't know quite what to say. Katie quickly retreated to her seat beside her mother, just a few feet away.

"Thank you, Katie," I said, and then winked at her.

She tried to wink back, but closed both eyes instead.

Now I had my lucky rocks. I rubbed them together and put them gently in my pocket, my mind having tuned out the chatter in the room.

Wow! What about this moment? What did it mean? Happenstance? Coincidence? I really didn't care. I didn't want to analyze—just enjoy the bliss. My body went through the motions of getting food and finding a table and eating, but my mind was transfixed by the gift I'd been given from this little girl.

"I've got an announcement!" The Major's voice brought me back to attention. He was standing before the group with a cup of coffee in his hand, dressed in his dark blue trousers and his crisp white Salvation Army shirt and black tie. "We are going to show the movie *Mr. Holland's Opus* in the chapel at one thirty, if anyone would like to see it. It's free, and it's a very good movie!"

I took a sip of my coffee. "Do you want to stay for the movie?" I asked C.

"No," he replied. "The Major will show it again, I'm sure. I'll catch it next time. I'm going to visit the kids."

"The kids?"

"Yeah. The young people living in the woods off Riddell Road—out by Kitsap Mental Health. You know, Adam and the young guys you've seen in here."

After scanning the room, I said, "They're not here today."

"You up for a spring walk in the woods?" C asked, standing up.

"Why not?" I said, picking up my tray and heading to the trash can. We said our adieus, and I thanked Katie again for my rocks.

"Not staying for the movie?" the Major asked as we passed him.

"You got popcorn?" C asked.

"Not this time," Major Baker laughed. "But that's a good idea. We are going to show it a couple more times next week."

"I'll see it then. And thank you for showing it," C said as the Major walked briskly off toward the chapel.

And we were off on our next adventure.

Chapter 21

THE HILTON

C and I parked the van in the parking lot of the mental institution because the trail through the woods to the kids' camp was just up the road. We walked a couple hundred yards along Almira Drive, until C located the entrance to the path.

Willow bounded along in front of us. Finally I asked, "Are you sure this is the way?"

"This is the trail, all right," replied C. "They just don't want to be found. It's just around the corner." Moments later I could see big blue tarps through the trees. "Hello! Anybody home? It's C," he called out.

Four boys and a girl were sitting on wooden crates around a small campfire. They waved and smiled as we emerged from the woods into the clearing. "Hey, Jason. I see you guys are still here," said C as we got closer.

"They haven't chased us out yet," Jason said. He was maybe sixteen or seventeen, wearing a weather-stained Seattle Mariners baseball cap.

"Where's Adam?" asked C.

"I'm in here, C." A muffled voice called out from inside a tentlike structure made from two or three large tarps tied to the trees with frayed rope.

"So you're home," C responded, stepping toward the makeshift door cut into one of the tarps. Willow and I followed along.

Adam was heating water in a pan on a rusty, dented Coleman stove as we entered. He turned and bowed at the waist. "Welcome to my humble abode," he said.

C introduced us. "This is Richard, and his dog, Willow."

"Yes. I've seen you around. Nice to meet you. I'm just making some tree bark tea. Would you like some?" He turned back to the near-boiling pan of water.

"Yes, thank you," C responded.

"Richard, how about you?"

"Sure," I said.

Willow had wandered off to the side of the tent and was sniffing at several trash bags. I called her back.

"It's okay," said Adam. "She smells the food in those bags. I've got cereal, eggs, bananas, and stuff in them."

C sat down on one of the large upside-down buckets. He pulled his pipe from his pocket, placed it in his mouth, and blew the sediment from it. Reaching into his pocket for the plastic pouch of smoke, he began filling his bowl. "What's the latest?" he asked Adam.

"Well, we're still about ten," was the reply. "I haven't seen Justin or Heather for a couple of days, but their stuff is still here." He paused as he prepared our tea. "I hope they haven't fallen into harm's way. The police haven't rousted us for about a month and a half, so that's about due. We just take it one day at a time." He handed a steaming cup to C, brought me a cup, and returned to the stove to pour his own. When he finally settled down on a seat, C handed him the bag of smoke. "Thanks, C," said Adam, taking his pipe from his shirt pocket and reaching out to accept the gift.

As the two began their smoking ritual, I used the moment to take a look around. The sun shining through the tarps gave the room a light-blue hue. Adam had stored his clothing in some clear plastic trash bags in one corner of the tent. A loud female voice broke the silence: *"BOB, REPORT TO LAWN AND GARDEN. BOB, LAWN AND GARDEN"*— it was the loudspeaker system at the large Fred Meyer complex at the edge of the woods.

"We hear it every fifteen to twenty minutes," Adam said. "Probably somebody wanting to buy a gallon or two of Weed-B-Gon. Jesus! No wonder all the fish are dying in Hood Canal and Puget Sound with all the weed killer people are using." He took a hit off his pipe. "They are probably going to spend a million dollars on a study to find out what is killing the fish, when all they really have to do is go down the street to Home Depot and ask them how much weed killer they sold last year."

The kids were laughing about something outside. "I did not!" I heard Jason say.

"Yes, you did!" a girl's voice countered. "You said, 'Run, bunny rabbit. Run before they get you. Run, bunny. Run, run, run' in your sleep. Everybody heard you, didn't they, Mike?" Mike confirmed that Maria was right.

Adam, C, and I laughed.

"This is excellent, Adam, as usual," C said, holding up his cup of tea. "I've really enjoyed sharing the stuff you gave me last time I was out here."

"Well, thanks. It's just something I experimented with," Adam replied, cupping both hands around his mug. "I heard somebody bought this land," he continued. "Someone read in the paper they're going to level it and put in a go-cart track, a baseball batting cage, and a miniature-golf course."

"I haven't heard that," C said, "but I wouldn't be surprised."

"It's supposed to be all lighted for night use," Adam added.

Our conversation was interrupted by a youthful voice calling out, "Hey, Adam!"

A young man stuck his head in the tent. "C, Richard—this is Gentry." Adam made the introductions.

"It's my turn to go get water," Gentry said, holding up a couple of empty plastic milk cartons. "Maria's coming. We're going to the 76 station because they let us fill these up last time. We'll be back."

"Okay," Adam replied.

These young people were living like the Suquamish Indian tribe had lived here in these woods two hundred years before, I thought to myself as Gentry closed the makeshift door and left. The tribe now had the biggest gambling casino in the Seattle area, providing their patrons with free ferry rides and limousine service eighteen hours a day, three hundred and sixty days a year. Adam's "tribe" had dug a latrine and went plowing through dumpsters at night for tarps, chairs, and anything that could be used in camp. There was water to carry, food to share, and chores to be done, and each took a turn guarding the village. But the biggest shift over the past two hundred years was that this refuge in the woods was now surrounded by Burger King, Napa Auto Parts, the Dollar Store, PetSmart, Outback Steakhouse, and Bob and his weed killer. Adam appeared to be the oldest and the leader of this tribe.

"How many other camps are there now?" C asked Adam.

"Oh, I'm not sure—five or six, I think," he replied. "Mars—you know Mars?" C nodded. "He used to be here, and he moved into the woods behind the dealerships on Auto Center Way. I think they have about eighteen people living there. Howie has a camp of about ten that I know of out behind the fairgrounds. But, man, he's paranoid. He gets high on coke and wants to move the camp in the middle of the night. I try to stay away from him. This is the Hilton; Howie's camp is a Motel 6."

"*BOB—ATTENTION BOB—BOB TO AUTOMOTIVE. BOB TO AUTOMOTIVE.*" The perky voice on the Fred Meyer loudspeakers intruded upon the village again.

"They've chased Howie out more than once. The police did a sweep back in there a couple months ago and took their tarps, chairs, blankets, food, and everything during the day. They were getting ready for a monster truck show and a pro wrestling event at the fairgrounds and wanted to make sure the homeless weren't around."

Adam's smoke was now gone, and C passed his young friend the bag, saying, "This is pretty mild stuff."

The irritating sound of a car alarm going off in the distance filled the silence as the two focused on their pipes again, blowing away the residue, packing the weed just right, then lighting and inhaling.

"It's good," Adam said of C's stash. "You don't smoke?" he asked me.

"Naw," I said.

Adam stood up from his white plastic bucket and stretched. He was tall, with long, thin brown hair and a bristly beard. He walked over by the Coleman stove again and pushed the button on a small plastic radio. Strains of classical music filled the tent. "Oh, great! Classical," said C.

"You like classical, too?" Adam asked.

"Love it!" was C's reply.

I had seen and heard a lot of strange things while riding around with C, but a homeless boy whose taste in music runs to baroque? I had to admit that this was a bit surprising. Hard rock or country would have seemed much more likely. But then I had never seen a young man functioning as the mayor of a tent city for misfit teens, so how could I guess what his musical tastes would be? Far be it for me to judge any of this experience. The world obviously had many surprises in store for me yet.

"I usually save the batteries so I can play the radio at night," Adam was saying, "but today is special because you and Richard are here." He explained how he'd found the radio in the dumpster behind Fred Meyer and hated leaving it when he went into town—the police might do a sweep and take everything. He'd lost everything last time, all his books and his clothes. He'd heard them coming and hidden in the bushes. There were two cops and four guys they hired for six dollars an hour from AmeriCorps. He recognized three of them from Sally's. It only took them about an hour to toss everything into big black plastic bags and cart it off.

BEEP . . . BEEP . . . BEEP . . . BEEP—the sound of a car alarm once again invaded the woods. *"BOB, GO TO LAWN AND GARDEN. BOB TO LAWN AND GARDEN"* followed soon after.

Adam walked over to the radio and turned the volume up a notch. "Beethoven's fifth symphony; I like this," he said, attempting to ignore the sounds of what some call civilization. He poured himself another cup of tea and looked at C. "Would you like another cup?"

"Sure," said C, handing his cup to Adam.

"Richard?" Adam was holding out the scorched and battered pan.

"No. I'm okay for now," I answered.

"You seen anything of Mojo?" C asked Adam.

"Not for a couple of months, I guess . . ."

As Adam and C resumed their conversation, my mind wandered off, as it often does. I thought about my life when I was Adam's age.

I had a job making $1.25 an hour as a printer's devil at the *Urbana Citizen* newspaper in Ohio. On a day like today, my main concern—something that had consumed my very being for the entire week—was whether my girlfriend, Bonnie, was going to put out when we went to the New Moon drive-in movie that night.

Bonnie was sixteen, and she was my dream. She had long blond hair and was a member of the Flag Corps of the high school marching band. She looked stunning in her short black skirt and long red boots as she flipped the flag to the music, then held the pole straight out and marched forward while the band played the high-school fight song.

I had the entire night planned out in my mind: I would pick up Bonnie at six. She would hop into my 1952 dark-blue Ford Fairlane, which I had spit-polished twice in the previous four days. She would sit close like she always did, and we would go for burgers and fries. We would talk about the silliest things. She thought "Cookie" Burns was a dream, and The Beatles were her favorite band. I never disagreed.

I had given her my class ring from high school.

We would listen to the radio on the way to the New Moon—Chubby Checker singing "The Twist," Chuck Berry's "Maybelline," The Coasters' "Yakety Yak," Jimmie Rodgers' "Kisses Sweeter than Wine"—and we would turn the volume up all the way for The Big Bopper and "Chantilly Lace." I would always sing along with The Bopper, lowering my voice: "Chantilly Lace, with a pretty face, and a pony tail hanging down, that wiggle in the walk . . ." and Bonnie would giggle and put her hand on my leg.

It was hero night at the New Moon—a double-header of Zorro and Tarzan. But we didn't come to the New Moon for the cinematic experience. After we struggled to attach the big aluminum speaker to the Fairlane window, Bonnie moved closer to me, and I wrapped my arm around her shoulder.

She was a siren. Some gene had been passed from Jezebel herself directly down to Bonnie. She let me know just what she wanted as I looked into her eyes, pressed forward to kiss her precious lips, and reached inside her white cotton bra for the buried treasure. Her breathing would quicken and a sultry, sensuous moan came from deep within as she reached out to touch me . . .

"Hey, Richard. Richard! What are you smiling about?" C's raspy voice interrupted my trip back to the New Moon. I wanted to reach out and wipe the fog off the car windows.

"Oh, I was just thinking of a pleasant place I was once," I said, somewhat sheepishly. "I think it was 1963 or '64 . . ."

"Geez! I wasn't born yet," C kidded.

"It was my age of innocence," I said. "There were no McDonald's, no Wal-Marts. The television stations put test patterns on at midnight . . . no radio talk shows, no CNN, no *Fox News*—"

"Helene is coming!" Gentry interrupted me by pushing the plastic tent flap open.

"Great," said Adam, hurrying out. C was right behind him.

I lingered in Adam's tent for a few moments, looking at the books lying beside his sleeping bag and his few other possessions. I didn't know how he got here, or if he would ever escape this life, but I admired him for being able to smile. I knew I couldn't have survived in the woods like this when I was seventeen. I didn't remember children living like this at all back then. Had I just been oblivious, or had the world changed?

And now, while Adam, Maria, and the others were hoping just to be left alone in this small patch of tranquility, other children their age had been taught to race past this type of haven to their first job at McDonald's, and then on to another job at Target, and another at one of the mall stores . . . Soon, of course, they'd have to race to the bank to cash their checks to make their car and insurance payments . . . To what end was all this leading?

I headed out to join the others. As I ducked through the door and let the flap fall behind me, I saw three women enter the camp carrying cardboard boxes.

"Are you guys hungry?" asked Helene, a short woman who appeared happy to be setting down her large box. "Whew! That was heavy!" The other two, also struggling, set their heavy burdens on the ground.

"C and Richard, I would like you to meet Helene," Adam said, stretching his long arm around the lady, who then reached out and gave him a hug.

"And this is Charlotte, and Jean." Helene went over to the other women and held each hand as she introduced her compatriots. "We have brought you some lunch. We'd better eat it while it's hot," she said, ripping open the top of the box and lifting out plastic tubs of food. The ladies had thought of everything. Paper bowls, plastic forks and spoons, salt and pepper all appeared as they set up lunch. "Please join us," Helene said, looking at C and me. "We have plenty."

"I can't say 'no' to a lady who says 'please,'" C said, and he and I both accepted a bowl of homemade stew.

"We have rolls and butter in this box," Helene continued, "some Coke and apple juice in the other."

"And I've got Hershey bars, graham crackers, and marshmallows for s'mores in my backpack," Jean chimed in.

C sampled the stew and looked at me. I tasted a spoonful and took a bite out of the homemade buttered roll. "A five-star picnic," I concluded.

"Most definitely!" C concurred.

Helene watched Maria wipe her mouth on her shirtsleeve and got up and pulled a bunch of napkins out of a box. "Here, Maria," she said, handing the girl a napkin. "I forgot to pass these out."

"Okay, *Mom*, we'll use our napkins," Adam said, laughing. "Helene has been like a mom to us," he continued, looking at C. "She brings us lunch and dinner a couple times a week and even does our laundry sometimes."

"Goodness!" C's eyes widened in amazement. "Laundry? That's kind of you! All this is so . . . well, *very* kind of you. Why?"

"This is just a small payback for what someone I never met did for my son," Helene answered. "He ran away when he was fifteen and went to California." She described how he'd lived in the woods around Mount Shasta. A woman of about sixty came upon his camp one day while hiking. She befriended him, and for three years, four times a week, she hiked the four miles in to his campsite with food, clean socks, and books. She even went there on Thanksgiving, Christmas, and New Year's Day. "She saved his life," said Helene. Then one day, she convinced him it was time to see his mother. She drove him all the way home, dropped him off at the curb, and drove away. Helene had never gotten to say thank you. Her voice began to tremble.

Jean, sensing the need to lighten the moment, said, "Let's have some s'mores!" She broke out the crackers, chocolate bars, and marshmallows, and C whipped out his always-sharp knife to fashion some marshmallow sticks.

For a couple of hours we all sat by the smoldering campfire and talked. Helene seemed a little uncomfortable when Adam and C dug their marijuana pipes out of their pockets for another smoke. But Jean asked, "Do you mind if I have a hit? It's been, well, maybe thirty years."

Adam, somewhat shocked, smiled and said "Whoa!" and then passed his pipe politely over to her. She took a drag and held it in for a moment before exhaling. "The last time I did that, I was a junior at Kent State," she said. "I was there when Governor James Rhoades sent the National Guard in."

"Kent State—where is that?" Jason asked.

"It's in Ohio," Jean responded. "I was there when they shot the students."

"Shot the students?" Maria asked.

"Yes, the National Guard shot some students during a demonstration."

"You know, Maria, 'Four dead in O-hi-o'?" Adam interjected.

"Oh yeah. I know that song," Jason said. "But I didn't know anybody really got shot. I thought it was just a song."

"They were protesting the war, right?" asked Adam.

"Well, that was part of it," Jean answered. "They were protesting the war, the government, the American invasion of Cambodia. Two of the students who were killed were just walking to class."

Charlotte, who had been so quiet, was intrigued. "Did you wear tie-dye?" she asked Jean.

"I sure did," Jean laughed. "Instead of this Old Navy sweatshirt, Wrangler jeans, and New Balance tennis shoes, I used to wear tie-dyed T-shirts, multicolored pleated dresses, and sandals. I wore my hair long—not short like this," she said, brushing her hand across the side of her hair.

"Were you an antiwar demonstrator?" Charlotte asked.

"Yes, I was," she responded.

"I never knew that about you," Charlotte said to Jean. "And I've known you for fifteen or sixteen years."

"I grew up in Pittsburgh, but when it came time to go to college, I couldn't get into the eastern schools," Jean said. "But I got into Kent State, and I loved it. Kids from New York, Boston, Philadelphia all went there because it was cheaper than the schools in the east—only a hundred and twenty-five per quarter. We were alive with ideas, art, and music. We were going to save the world."

Willow's nose had led her to the s'mores Jean was preparing, and the little dog placed her front paws on the lady's knee as if to say "How about me?" She gave Jean that irresistible look. "Well, aren't you just a cutesy little creature?" said Jean.

"That's Willow. I should have introduced her earlier."

Jean broke off a piece of cracker and held it out to Willow, who took it gently from her hand and began to crunch on it. It didn't take her long to finish off that morsel, and she hopped up again on Jean's leg and cocked her head. "You want more?" Jean asked, as she was already breaking off another piece of cracker.

"Richard calls her the Wonder Dog," said C, and we all laughed.

"Because she does tricks?" Helene asked.

"Sometimes she will sit or roll over when I ask," I replied. "And sometimes she just looks at me as if to say 'Why don't *you* sit or roll over this time?' *That's* why she's the Wonder Dog."

Helene took the last bite of her s'more and slowly stood up. "Well, I'm sorry to say, we had better be getting back," she said. "Do you have any laundry for us?" The kids all went to their tents to gather up their dirty clothes and quickly returned with about six bags' worth. "Wow!" Helene exclaimed, surveying the assortment of bags. "I guess we'll be busy tonight!"

"We'll help you carry them out," C offered to the ladies. "It's about time for us to go, too."

Helene went to Adam and gave him a big hug. "If any of you need us, don't hesitate," she said. Jean put her arm around Maria, and Charlotte put her hand on Jason's back. "You have my number. Just get to a phone and call."

After heartfelt goodbyes, the ladies, C, and I picked up the laundry bags and empty boxes and headed down the trail toward the road. The women were silent as we trudged along with the heavy sacks. When we got to their car, they thanked C and me for our assistance. Helene gave C an embrace. With tears beginning to fill her eyes, she asked, "Are they going to be okay?"

"Yes, thanks to you, I think they are," C responded.

The ladies all got into their car, and we waved as they pulled away. "Those women have spunk," said C, watching them drive off.

After a moment, we headed for the van. "Hey, you want to go over and see Andy's new digs?" C asked.

Chapter 22

ANDY GETS LUCKY

We pulled up in front of Andy's new abode just before seven o'clock. It certainly was not the opulent spread that Bill Gates built in Bellevue with a bowling alley, a home theater, and a basketball court, but to Andy it was like Graceland.

C knocked on the door and then opened it slightly. The TV was on. "Andy? You here?" C called out.

"Come on in," Andy called back.

We walked in, and Willow headed straight for Andy, who was sitting on a mattress in front of the TV, picking at the sores on his feet.

"Willow!" Andy exclaimed, as she hopped on his lap and pawed at his hand for him to pet her. "I've missed you!" he said. After just a few strokes down her back from Andy, Willow turned and headed for his feet and started licking in earnest. "She's a healer, isn't she?" Andy was smiling.

"Yes, she is," I replied.

"I don't think she can fix these feet, though," said Andy, looking at them. "I should have changed my socks more often."

"Speaking of socks," C interrupted, "I've got your socks in Richard's van. I'll go get them." He headed for the door.

"It's good to see you, too, Richard," said Andy. "Where you been?"

I started rambling on about how I had been here and there as I took stock of the room. There was a large picture window with a view over the water, and I could see the Manette Bridge in the distance. It was a big room with hardwood floors. It must have been a stately place in its day. It had been remodeled with textured white walls, but I could picture pretty flowered wallpaper, a large chandelier hanging from the high ceilings, an ornate sofa and loveseat, oriental rugs, maybe a Victrola, oak chairs with hand-carved legs, and paintings fashionably displayed.

The fireplace was covered over now and the red bricks painted white. And the white walls were bare.

Andy had all he needed. Beside his mattress he had a carton of Marlboros, two Bic lighters, a big ashtray, a pair of broken eyeglasses held together with duct tape, and several books, including *The Penal Colony, Sons and Lovers, The Bonfire of the Vanities, Humboldt's Gift,* and the Bible. And a big bottle of Smirnoff, half empty.

"This is a nice place you have here, Andy," I said.

"I like it," he replied. "I can relax here. It's the old Gates mansion, you know. The granddaddy of the richest man in the world lived here." There was a vague smile on his face, the irony not lost on him.

C returned, carrying Andy's socks. "I got those Hershey bars you wanted," he said, dropping the socks on the floor and handing Andy a small paper bag.

Andy reached in and pulled out two plain Hershey bars. "Good. No nuts. I hate nuts!" Turning to me, he added, "Last time he brought me back Hersheys with nuts."

Willow's tongue was hanging from her mouth—worn out from licking Andy's feet. "You need some water," C said to her, and headed for the kitchen. He took a dirty bowl out of the pile of dishes in the sink, quickly cleaned it, filled it with water, and brought it back to Willow, who lapped up it up as fast as she could.

I noticed Andy's not-quite-Supercuts hairdo. It was much shorter on one side than the other, and uneven in the back as well. "I see you got a haircut," I commented.

"Yeah. C cut it a couple of days ago," Andy said. "Boy, I really needed it. My hair was getting all stringy, but it feels better now. How does it look?" he asked.

"Great!" I lied.

Andy spotted C eyeing the television remote, and he slowly reached out and gripped it tightly. "I got cable, Richard," he said. "I never had cable before. I get eighty channels. But, you have to keep this"—holding up the remote—"away from C! Every time he comes over here, he flips around too much. He watches five minutes of *SpongeBob*, five minutes of the *Iron Chef*, five minutes of the History Channel . . ."

"C'mon Andy, give me the remote," pleaded C.

"No way, C! It's almost time for *Wheel of Fortune*," said Andy, switching to channel four.

"Well, it's good to see you so feisty today," C said. "Yesterday you were so weak you couldn't even push those remote buttons." He laughed.

Andy picked up his patched-up glasses, slipping them on just as the show began. Pat Sajak was just walking on stage, arm and arm with the queen of all game shows, Vanna White. "There she is—Vanna!" said Andy. He lit up a Marlboro and coughed as he took a deep drag. As the crowd cheered, Vanna walked across the stage to her position before the huge blue-and-white puzzle board. "That's my girlfriend! When I go to heaven, that's what I want. I want a Vanna White!"

Pat was introducing and making small talk with the three contestants—Wendy, a dental hygienist from Riverton, Utah; Michael, a banker from Bakersfield, California; and Judy, a cashier at Wal-Mart in Toledo, Ohio—when Andy looked at me and asked, "Richard, do you think I will go to heaven?"

"Have you been good, Andy?" I teased.

He laughed. "Noooooo!" Then he reached for his glass beside the mattress. With shaking hands, he picked up the bottle of vodka and poured until his glass was nearly full, spilling a little on his trousers. "Would you like some?" he asked, holding the bottle out toward me.

"Well, I'm sure you're going to heaven anyway," I said, taking the bottle from his hand. "Yes, I will take a short one."

"I'll take a glass, too," C added, as I headed for the kitchen to get glasses.

I found two in the sink and washed them and returned just as one of the contestants won the first toss-up round by quickly identifying the phrase YOUR CHARIOT AWAITS, chalking up sixteen hundred dollars. The audience supplied polite applause. "That's a good start, Wendy," said Pat. "Now for our second toss-up round. The subject is 'animal.' It's two words and nine letters." Quirky music played loudly as letters appeared on a small puzzle board near the players. "Okay, Wendy!" "KING COBRA," Wendy said. Pat saluted her. "You have won one thousand nine hundred dollars!" The crowd applauded.

As I poured two vodkas, straight up, Pat pushed the game along, and the three of us were pulled into the glittering world of the Hollywood sound stage, intrigued for the moment by the lives of total strangers playing a game of chance. Andy moaned "Shit" when one player inevitably lost her accumulated winnings by landing on bankrupt, but he was really more enthralled by the hostess than anything. "She has the legs of a goddess," he murmured.

Actually, millions of minds across the nation were captivated as they worked to solve the puzzle of the moment from their own couches or mattresses. In that way, television is the new great equalizer. Subject: Fun and Games. Eight Words. Slowly, consonants and vowels began to appear in odd places on the puzzle board. We were all rooting for one contestant or another, while trying to win ourselves. Would the Wheel of Fortune be kind to this Wal-Mart cashier?

Andy leaned forward and squinted. "I got it!" he said. "ENJOYING WINE AND CHEESE AT A SIDEWALK CAFÉ. C'mon, Judy!"

On the screen, Judy swallowed hard and looked at Pat. "I'd like to solve it," she said. She was holding her hands together as if she was praying as she ventured her best guess: "ENJOYING WINE AND CHEESE AT A SIDEWALK CAFÉ?"

"You've got it!" Pat cheered as the final letters spun into place, lights flashed, the camera quickly panned to Vanna's smile, the crowd rose to its feet, and Judy cheered. Not surprisingly, the big prize that day included the "big-meal deal" trip to Paris, worth almost six thousand dollars.

"See!? See!?" exclaimed Andy. "I could be going to Paris right now if I was on that show!"

"You were right!" C said. "And you got it first!"

The Wheel went to commercial break, and I could tell C was getting bored. He wasn't one to participate in this kind of mindless escapism for long. For someone like Andy, though—whose isolated life on the streets stretched from endless days into endless weeks, months, and years—having a home at last, and a TV with a remote, was a powerful experience and the ultimate in entertainment. C reached over to pick up one of Andy's books, and Andy recoiled with the remote. "I thought you were going for this," he laughed. "Don't even think about it!"

"No. I don't want your stupid remote," C chided. "Can I read this?" He held up *The Fortress of Solitude* by Jonathan Lethem.

"Sure," said Andy. "It's good."

C picked his pipe out of his pocket, and said, "I'm going in the bedroom to read for awhile." C was like that. He liked to be alone, smoking his pipe and reading with the noise of people nearby, or in the background. I decided to hang out with Andy.

A commercial for Viagra was just ending as my attention returned to the tube. A glowing woman was embracing her smiling man and the announcer was reading the medicine's warning: "blah-blah, blah-blah, blah-blah . . . and if your erection continues for longer than four hours, consult your doctor."

"Yeah, right!" chortled Andy. "Can you imagine calling a doctor at midnight and saying, 'Doctor, my hard-on won't go down!'?" I laughed. "You ever had a hard-on for four hours, Richard?" I was just taking a sip of vodka, and almost choked. I laughed so hard tears were rolling down my cheeks. Andy continued, "I guess I could call 911."

I slowly recovered as *The Wheel* moved into the Jackpot Round; Wendy was on a roll and had piled up forty-three hundred dollars in winnings on lucky spins. "There are no Vs," said Pat, his voice trailing off. Andy appeared to be getting tired. He took a big slug of his vodka and then lay back on his side.

"I'm going to check on C," I said, lifting myself off the floor. Willow had fallen asleep on the mattress at Andy's feet. I found C sitting cross-legged on the floor, puffing on his pot pipe and reading the book he had borrowed from Andy. "Good book?" I asked.

"I don't know yet," he responded. "I'm just getting into it." He took his finger and tapped down the smoke in his pipe and then hit the bud with his lighter. He took a big hit, held it, and finally exhaled. "It's about a young boy who's the only white kid in his Brooklyn neighborhood," C said, holding up the book. "He has to hide his lunch money in his socks, but he still gets 'yoked' every day. It's got possibilities."

The smell of marijuana filled the room, and C was getting mellow. We could hear Andy yelling, "DIAMONDS ARE A GIRL'S BEST FRIEND! It's DIAMONDS ARE A GIRL'S BEST FRIEND, you dummy!"

"He's relaxed here," C said of Andy. "It's about time he had a place to call home. I try to stop in every day at least for a bit to check on him. He wasn't very good the last couple of days. He could barely make it to the bathroom and couldn't even sit up. He just lay on his side. I made him soup and a sandwich." He paused, thinking back on the past few days.

"He's all worn out. The doctors at the clinic know Andy. They are afraid to give him any strong pain medicine because he drinks so much. But he seems better tonight."

"It was nice to meet Adam and those kids today," I said, changing the subject. "Thanks for asking me along."

"You're welcome," C said. "It's sad to see them living in the woods, but they are better off there. Maria, one of the girls, came home one night after working a double shift at the mall and got in the shower. Her dad climbed in with her and raped her. She ran away that night after her father fell asleep. She's sixteen, I think she said.

"Then there's Gentry. He got into trouble at school. I don't know the whole story, but he appears to be the rebellious type—whatever *that* is. Anyway, he said school was boring and he quit. He got a job doing construction for some guy. After he spent two weeks putting up drywall eight hours a day, the guy didn't pay him, and they got into an argument. The boss said he was fired, and Gentry pushed him. So the guy whipped out his cell phone and called the cops. Gentry ran off. He said he found out later that the boss does that to kids all the time."

"That's terrible," I said.

"It happens," C shrugged. "What's a kid to do? And Adam—well, Adam was at the wrong place at the wrong time. He got picked up for smoking a joint in a park down by the water in Port Angeles. He's a longhair, has a medallion with a leather strap around his neck, and wears sandals all the time. He looks like he just arrived from the sixties in a time machine. Adam has a quick wit, and he admits he said something the cop may have construed as insulting or they might have let him go. But they busted him and took him to jail."

TV sounds drifted in from the living room. "We are going into the Mystery Round. Are you ready?" Andy must have turned up the volume a notch.

Adam had told C that he had been waiting in his cell when three policemen came in carrying a young guy who was screaming, "I'm from Texas. You can't do this to me. I'll whip your ass!" Things got out of control as they tried to put the guy in a cell. They sprayed him in the face with pepper spray, took off all his clothes, hog-tied him with a homemade rope, put a hood over his head, and left the guy naked, bleeding, and unconscious on the cell floor. Then one of the cops looked at Adam and said, "You better be quiet, or we'll give you some of that!" and they all left. Adam sat in his cell while the man bled to death.

Eventually, Adam's dad bailed him out. Adam was afraid to tell his parents what he had seen, and the next day he just took off. He stopped here and has been here ever since that day two years ago—living in fear in the woods. "There was an article in the paper a month or two ago that said the county paid the family of the Texas man one-point-six million dollars in a settlement of the excessive force case," C said. "It was a federal lawsuit. But Adam can't go home. Not one of the officers was fired. He is still afraid."

Adam's story frightened me. What would I have done if I had been in his shoes? I wondered what would happen to the kids when summer ended and the weather turned. There are hundreds of young people like Maria, Gentry, and Adam living in forests and old abandoned houses, praying their parents and the police don't find them.

From the living room I heard the *do-do-do, d'd'do-do-do, dout, d'do-do-do-do-do* jingle and the TV announcer saying, "This is *Jeopardy!*"

Willow came into the room and sat down in front of me. Then she whined and looked at the door. "Do you have to go outside, Willow?" I said to her, getting up.

Willow was the first one out the bedroom door, and I followed, glancing at the TV as *Jeopardy* host Alex Trebek was introducing one of the contestants.

As I headed for the front door to let Willow out, she headed back to Andy instead and lay down on the floor. "Come on, girl," I said. But she just lay there.

It was then that I noticed Andy's overturned glass and a small pool of vodka on the floor. His eyeglasses were also on the floor, and Andy was lying motionless. I walked closer as C came out of the bedroom. "It looks like Andy spilled his drink," I said.

C picked up the glass, knelt down, and looked at Andy. "Oh, no," was all he said. He picked up Andy's hand and held it, searching for a pulse. Then he put his ear to Andy's chest, but Andy's body was limp. C reached up and gently closed Andy's eyelids and looked up at me. "Andy has passed on," he said softly.

"What?!" I was stunned.

"Andy died, Richard," he said.

I was in shock and began to tremble, but C was like a physician at the bedside of an old friend who had just taken his last breath. "It's okay, Richard," he said, seeing my distress. "It's been coming. It was time." He moved Andy's arms across his chest and then took a blanket and gently pulled it over him.

I had never been this close to death before. Even when my mother and father died, I had not been at their bedsides.

My mind began to process what had just happened. Andy the Weed had died. He had finally gotten a place to live, a bed, and a TV. He died on his own time, just like he wanted. After sixteen years of sleeping on hard benches, in dumpsters, under cars, and in doorways, Andy went to sleep for the final time on the same living room floor that William Gates III might have played on as a child.

Andy left over sixty-three thousand dollars behind in the bank—the remainder of the money he had waited for and needed all those years on the street.

C, still kneeling, clasped his hands, said a brief personal prayer, and then looked at me, grinning slightly. "Well, I'll bet Andy's already in heaven, under the sheets with a woman who looks like Vanna White," he said.

There was no phone in the apartment. "Would you give me a ride up to the pay phone by the ferry terminal?" C asked.

"Sure," I said.

"I'll call the landlord," he said. "His number is on the fridge." He walked toward the kitchen. "He'll need to know about Andy, and then I'll come back and see what needs to be done."

"I'll be glad to help," I said.

"Good. Thanks."

We called the landlord. The paramedics came to pick up Andy for the last time. And I took C back to the Armadillo. I gave C a hug before he climbed into his home, and, as always, he held up two fingers and said, "Peace. Be Safe."

I drove the van to the Methodist church parking lot, where we had been sleeping for the past week, and quickly began preparing our bed for the night. It had been a long day in my homeless world. The pastor of the church was working late in his office, and the light illuminated the van. He walked to the window and waved to Willow and me. We waved back.

The wind was picking up as Willow and I climbed into the back of the van once again. I struggled into my sleeping bag, and Willow pawed impatiently to join me. Then she ducked under the covers and jockeyed for a warm and comfortable spot.

Lying on my back, I put my hands behind my head. The gusting winds were causing the tall fir trees beside the church to sway. The light from the pastor's office shone through them and created shadows that looked like mammoth wings slowly moving up and down.

I thought of the kindness of C and the things he had done for Andy. C had "paid it forward" for Andy. With very little, C had done something very big.

Something I would not have done.

When everybody else had given up and considered Andy just a

charming nuisance who was drunk all the time, urinating on himself, C picked him up and cleaned him off and restored his grace and dignity. The two established a graceful *esprit de corps*, doing little things like washing socks and getting candy bars—without nuts. Andy did his best to do what he could in return. The last few months of Andy's life were better than the preceding sixteen years, because of C.

And I considered that dreadful thing I feared the most now: the future.

Would I end up living like Andy? I asked myself. When my van finally broke down, would I then have to sleep in a doorway? Would I drink all day just to subdue any hope or dream I might have? Would Willow be able to survive? Or would she get killed just trying to stay with me?

I was tired of thinking. It was time to rest. I closed my eyes and rolled over on my side. "Ouch," I said, feeling a sharp pain on my hip. I reached down to rub the pain and felt the two hard objects in my pocket. They were the lucky rocks Katie had given me at Sally's that morning. I fished the rocks out of the pocket of my jeans and held them up to the window. I noticed that they sparkled in the light that was streaming in, and I slowly rubbed them together.

"This first rub is for Andy," I whispered. I held the rocks tightly in my hand until I fell asleep.

Chapter 23

THE REAL FIELD OF DREAMS

Winter can be monotonous in the Northwest. The climate is never particularly harsh, which is one of its great attractions. You're no more likely to freeze in the winter than you are to broil in the summer, but that doesn't mean it isn't cold and miserable sometimes—just not the deep-freeze kind of cold you get in the Midwest or the Northeast.

But the dreariness can penetrate your psyche. People with financial means become snowbirds (wintering in warmer climes like Arizona), frequent travelers (to places like Mexico or Hawaii), or winter-sports fanatics (racing to the ski slopes at the first hint of snow). The rest of us just have to find a way to survive.

Northwesterners have an amazingly high incidence of Seasonal Affective Disorder—SAD. (Now, that is a perfectly descriptive acronym!) They spend the season of shortened days and seemingly endless nights popping pills and seeking out "natural light therapy."

For those of us who battle the demons of depression *all* the time, the low, flat, gray skies and frequent drizzle are even more challenging. I had struggled every hour, every day, and every week during the cold and dreary months of January, February, and March.

Spring has always been intoxicating to me, for all the reasons that great poets and writers have recorded over the centuries: the fresh smells and the vibrant colors; the trees budding and the bulbs blooming; the sap rising and the life-blood surging in nature and in man. I had no definite dreams for the future, nor even any plans to change my current reality. It just felt good to realize one balmy day that I might not shiver that night when I crawled into the back of the van to go to sleep. And Willow was delighted to romp and frolic in the fragrant blades of fresh, new grass.

Then there was the sportswriter in me, and my deep love of the spring sport of baseball. It had been one of my favorite pastimes since my childhood in Ohio. Spring and baseball, now *that* was a winning combination! It seemed to hold out promise that anything was possible. It reminded me of one of my favorite movies of all time, *Field of Dreams*, where the blue-eyed Kevin Costner hears voices from an Iowa cornfield telling him, "If you build it, he will come."

It was a movie about things that aren't real . . . but people believe in things that aren't real all the time if they *want* to believe. That's why the movie touched the hearts and triggered the tears of so many thousands of viewers. The only ones who could see what was happening on that cornfield in Iowa were those who believed.

My friend C was good at that.

And Bremerton had its own *Field of Dreams* story.

It was a beautiful day in May when C showed up at Sally's for lunch with a smallish leather baseball glove and a scuffed softball he had purchased for a dollar at the thrift shop. The magnolia trees were blooming, and the pink, red, and white rhododendrons delighted the eye. The months of rain were over.

But inside Sally's stone walls, gloom still had its firm grip on many. There were no jobs to rush to. No reason to hurry outside. It was still a dark time, with nothing to look forward to. C couldn't fix all the problems of the world that spring day, but he had a brilliant idea that just might brighten this small corner: a softball game!

As I was savoring my mac-and-cheese lunch, I watched C work his game plan; he had to convince the Major to sponsor a softball game for the crew. I couldn't quite hear the conversation, but I saw C pounding the softball into the glove and the Major's head bobbing up and down as he began to catch the vision. It was as if C was hypnotizing the Major with the smell of the leather glove and the sound of the ball popping into the mitt.

The Major was a baseball man. He couldn't say no.

So, the Major took some of the money that people put in those little red bell-ringers' pots at Christmastime and went shopping for some used gloves, bats, balls, and bases at secondhand shops and garage sales. Four blocks from the Salvation Army building was Carpenter Field, sitting empty every day, just waiting for this flock to come and play. And C and the Major made it happen.

Every Wednesday for the next twelve weeks, from one to three thirty in the afternoon, the people at Sally's walked up the street to play softball. It was definitely something to look forward to.

The roster would change each week as one or two would go to jail, or get out of jail, or OD, or get so drunk they couldn't get out of bed. But somehow the teams would get put together. Word spread, and soon it grew to the point where there were regularly two full teams and even fans in the stands.

Little miracles happened. One man got out of jail at noon and convinced a sheriff's deputy to give him a ride to the ballpark so he could be there in time for the game. Another man gave up drinking on Wednesday mornings so he could play.

The best game of the season was the last one. The participants were people who had had their dreams crushed all their lives and those who had never had a chance to dream at all. This was the lineup:

US:

First base: Donna. At 340 pounds a big target, in the vein of Boog Powell. Afraid to catch any ball thrown faster than twenty miles an hour. Closes her eyes and puts up her glove as the ball arrives. Sometimes catches it. Ill-suited for the position, but she wants to play first base, and at 340 pounds, nobody is going to argue with her. Bats: right. Throws: left.

Second base: Justin. Young, strong, and looks like he has been sniffing paint thinner for years. Good glove, but throws hard and wild, which scares the hell out of Donna. Everyone is on alert when the ball is hit to Justin, because he throws the ball randomly to any base. Bats: left. Throws: wildly.

Shortstop: C. A great brain and a spirited player, but with poor eyesight, he plays the game by ear. Seems to play better after two nickel bags of marijuana. Bats: right. Throws: right.

Third base: Richard. Looking for a sweet diversion—a chance to be in the *Sun* newspaper. Takes Zoloft for depression and likes the zany feeling. Truly delusional—says he is going to be a famous writer some day. Bats: right. Throws: wherever.

Left field: Mary. A spunky gal. 97 pounds, but plays with the determination of Pete Rose in his heyday. A victim of abuse by her ex-husband, who broke her arm once and another time put her in the hospital for three weeks with a broken jaw. She lived in a safe house for six months. Mary shows up for every game and is always picked last. Has struck out thirty straight times before this game. Bats: right. Throws: as far as she can.

Center field: David. A Goliath, at 6-foot-4 and 220 pounds. In the navy and a volunteer at Sally's kitchen, he is always picked first because he can hit the ball very, very far—the only player to hit the ball out of Carpenter Field. Bats: you betcha! Throws: hard enough to sting your hand.

Right field: Bob. A gifted musician who plays saxophone and piano and would make Sinatra and Gershwin proud, but in a town captivated by rap-crap and tits-and-ass country music, he is now relegated to pressure-washing buildings and pounding nails. Like all great artists, he is moody and has drunk too much on occasion, and the police frequently dislike his tune. He's done the "jailhouse rock" more than once. Bats: he's *going* to have a big hit someday. Throws: right.

Pitcher: Tony. A chronic alcoholic, he shakes most of the time, which serves as a diversion for the opposing batters. Tony can be one hell of a pitcher. But, like all pitchers, he has to be "on"—that is, just enough alcohol so he is not drunk. Too much and he can't pitch; too little and he shakes so much he has to go get a bottle of wine.

Catcher: Bill. Definitely bipolar and psychotic. Likes to chat with the batter and the pitcher and often carries on conversations with himself about ghosts, CIA agents, and lightning striking out of a clear blue sky. This seems to disturb the opposing batters (a nice complement to Tony's shaking).

THEM:

First base: Joseph. Tall and lean and just out of jail for assault. He can hit all right. Bats: right. Throws: right.

Second base: Steven. Served two terms for robbery. He can definitely steal. Bats: right. Throws: right.

Shortstop: Gentleman Jake. The Shoeless Joe Jackson of the lineup. Wears no shoes because his feet were so damaged while slogging through the rice paddies of Vietnam that it hurts to walk. Good glove; slow on the base path. A lefty all the way.

Third base: Grady. 6-foot-2, 195 pounds, and strong, but his right foot was injured when he stepped on a mine during a tour in Vietnam. At fifty-four, he still has to walk with a cane, and to his credit he even plays third base with a cane. Slow on the base path.

Left field: Jason. Now sixteen, he spent three years living with his mother and sister in an abandoned car in a ravine just outside Bremerton. Did not go to school for three years and has never played softball until this summer. Runs like a rabbit being chased by a dog, but doesn't understand the concept of stopping at first on a single, second on a double. He just keeps running. Our team often doesn't tag him out, because it's just too much fun to see him run and score, and everybody gets a warm, fuzzy feeling.

Center field: Mike. Also calls himself Ike, Spike, and Tyke—four different names and four different personalities. He is a master of the quadruple soliloquy, often talking to all four of "himself" at the same time. Mike is the nice guy; Ike is tough; Spike is just plain mean; and Tyke is the child of the foursome. With four of him, it was difficult to make out a lineup card, but his teammates didn't care as long as one of him caught the ball.

<u>Right field</u>: James. 6-foot-2, 185 pounds, black, all-city football and basketball player who came from a poor family and made some bad choices. Stole a car and did his time. His felony record keeps him from holding a good job. Graceful and gifted, now twenty, he deserves a break. Gets a hit every time and never drops a fly ball. Bats: switch hitter. Throws: right.

<u>Pitcher</u>: Major Baker. The Pedro Martinez of Salvation Army softball, but he throws pitches that the less athletically endowed can hit. Good bat and good field, but slowed by a groin injury. Bats: right. Throws: left.

<u>Catcher</u>: Lyle. A whimsical fellow, who seems to find amusement in the specter of the game events unfolding. At 6-foot-1 and 138 pounds, he appears to need a couple good meals. Has a distinctive batting technique that features no backswing. He sort of swats at the ball like he is killing a fly. It works. Batting 600. Bats: right. Throws: right.

So read the "Bad News Bears" lineup for softball at Carpenter Field on this perfect sunny spring day.

The fans got there early (noon) because Wednesday was always sack-lunch day, when, instead of a hot lunch inside, Sally's handed out small brown paper bags for lunch with a bologna-and-cheese sandwich, chips, an apple, butterscotch pudding, and a small milk to go. It was the perfect pregame meal for players and fans to enjoy before the action began. The bleacher bums, about twelve in attendance for this key matchup, would then use the brown paper bags to disguise the beverages of choice (or budget) that they'd snuck in. The Major, tolerant though he was, disapproved, of course, but made a compromise. He knew they were going to drink someplace. Better that it was here, where they were safe.

This epic began with THEM at bat. Our pitcher, Tony, got off to a shaky start, allowing six runs on ten hits. US could not retaliate in the first inning, as Donna grounded out, Justin singled, C hit a wild fly to center, and Mary struck out for the 31st time in the season.

US rallied back for two runs in the second, with a 360-foot blast into a blackberry bush by David to lead off the inning and an inside-the-park homer by Bob when Mike, Ike, Spike, or Tyke misplayed a long fly ball and then threw it to Jason, who fired wildly over the first-baseman's head as Bob was rounding second. "You should have caught the damn ball," Ike yelled at Mike. "I should beat your ass," Spike growled. "Everyone makes mistakes," Mike replied. "It wasn't my fault," Tyke whined.

It appeared a big inning was possible when US loaded the bases with two outs, but the excitement ended when Mary struck out for the 32nd straight time.

Tony seemed to settle down after a trip to the men's room, where it was quite probable he had stashed a bottle of vodka. He shut out THEM for two straight innings. His pitching was complemented by Jason's perfect grab of a sharply hit ground ball. He then fired it straight to Donna, who stuck out her mitt and caught the ball, much to her own amazement. Her catch inspired every player on the field.

Then something happened that makes baseball such a great game: confidence crept in. "If *Donna* can do it, *I* can do it," was the silent but world-changing thought spreading around the field. There were no more dropped balls, no more wild throws by Jason. I could almost hear the voices of Harry Caray and Mel Ott calling this game at Carpenter Field.

US closed the gap to 6–4 in the fourth, when David hit his second homer of the game, driving in Justin, who had beat out a grounder.

THEM scored three more runs that same inning when Joseph, Jake, and Jason (who actually stopped at first this time) all singled and James tripled, increasing the advantage to 9–4.

The Major kept US at bay, turning a variety of superb lofted pitches into harmless popups or grounders, for easy outs—except for Mary, who struck out for her 33rd, 34th, and 35th straight times.

It appeared THEM had this game in the bag when Lyle singled, Joseph doubled to left, and Gentleman Jake sent them both scurrying home with a blooper to right in the top of the seventh. The 11–4 lead appeared insurmountable. William Saroyan once wrote:

> Baseball is caring. Player and fan alike must care, or there is no game. The caring is whole and constant, whether warranted or hopeless, tender or angry, ribald or reverent. From the first pitch to the last out the caring continues. With a score of 6–0, two outs, two strikes, nobody on, only an average batter at bat, it is still possible, and sometimes necessary, to believe that something can still happen—for the simple reason that it has happened before, and very probably will again. And when it does, won't that be the day? Isn't that alone almost enough to live for, assuming there might just be little else? To witness so pure a demonstration of the unaccountable way by which the human spirit achieves stunning, unbelievable grandeur?

But like they say, "The game isn't over until the fat lady sings." There was hope.

Justin opened the final refrain with a sharply hit ball just out of the reach of Shoeless Jake, for a single. C hit a little blooper that barely cleared Jake's glove, for another single. "You're picking on me!" Jake yelled out. But you could tell he and THEM were still confident. They were smiling.

US got a break when I hit a fly ball that Jason lost in the bright sun over Carpenter Field, and it fell in for a single, to load the bases. Mary stepped to the plate and struck out for the 36th straight time. David then smashed a grand-slam homerun over the center-field fence that stirred the drunken fans, who had been napping in the stands for the last hour or so.

That made the count 11–8 with one out and wiped the smiles off of THEM.

Bob, the musician, followed David's homerun with another blast over the fence. The back-to-back blows made it 11–9, and all of a sudden US and THEM were at the point William Saroyan wrote about—counting on the almost unbelievable, against all odds, hoping that today would be that incredible day.

Tony singled to keep the rally alive; Bill followed with a slicing single over the first-baseman's head. The fans leaned forward in their seats. THEM became tense. Everyone was riveted as Donna stepped into the batter's box. It was still going to take a miracle for US to come back to beat THEM, but the gods of softball seemed to be toying with this bunch today, using us as puppets for their amusement.

It isn't always the Mickey Mantles or the Babe Ruths of the world who get the key hits that win the biggest games. It was Mookie Wilson of the New York Mets who hit the ground ball that trickled through the legs of Boston first-baseman Bill Buckner and deprived the Red Sox of the World Series Championship in 1986. The Mets beat the Red Sox 6–5.

And if Donna gets a hit at this moment, few will remember. But *she* will.

Tony was shaking at second and Bill was talking to his own personal Babe Ruth at first when Donna hit a chopper down the first-base line. Joseph raced up the line to get the ball and Steven moved over to cover the bag. But Joseph's throw caught Donna in the back, and Tony and Mike raced home on the error to tie the game.

Justin and C both singled, to load the bases for me. It was my chance for glory. All I had to do was put the wooden bat on the rawhide ball and I would be the hero. I would receive the adulation of my teammates and cheers from the throng of twelve in the stands.

But it wasn't to be. On the first pitch, I popped one up to the pitcher. That left the fate of the game in the hands of our little Mary.

As Mary strode to the plate swinging a bat, her friend Tina cried out from the stands, "Come on, girl! Hit that ball! Pretend it's your ex's nuts! Show 'em what you can do!" Victory was within our grasp with the score tied at 11–11. Donna was on third base.

Mary had struck out seven times today, and the Major was salivating on the mound for his own personal-best strikeout record. The Major had the heart and soul of Mother Teresa, but he wasn't about to fool around with the game on the line, and he uncorked two straight "mystery pitches" that the diminutive Mary swished at harmlessly, for two strikes.

That famous mystery pitch, when lofted toward the plate, appeared to be rotating forwards. Then, about halfway to the batter, the ball would reverse directions and rotate backwards in some quirk of physics that only the great ones like Gaylord Perry, Rollie Fingers, and the Major could understand.

Mary, along with everyone in the stands and on the field, knew what was coming: another mystery pitch. The spectators all lifted their brown paper sacks to their lips and then held their breath. Mary waved the bat rhythmically and stared the Major down. Perturbed, the Major did something he never did—he *spit!* There would be no mercy. This was going to be the best mystery pitch ever.

The Major took his stance, brought the ball back, and then moved forward as he let go of the ball. Mary's muscles tensed and her eyes widened as the spinning ball arrived at the plate and she put all of her 97 pounds into one mighty swing.

It was her Moonlight Graham moment.

The bat caught a portion of the ball, sending it gyrating wildly toward the only spot on the field where a hit was possible, considering the cast of characters on the field: halfway down the third-base line.

Grady, playing third base, tossed his cane aside and hobbled toward the whirling ball. The Major, his groin pull causing him agonizing pain, winced and stepped lightly toward the line.

Donna, feeling the gravity of the moment, was off at the crack of the bat—340 pounds of determination. The ground was shaking.

The catcher, Robert, at 138 pounds after three good meals—something he never got—held his position at the plate, unafraid.

The Major doubled over in pain and went to the ground, but he kept crawling for the ball.

Grady stumbled forward, grabbed it, got to his knees, and flung it awkwardly toward home plate. His valiant effort was four feet wide, pulling Robert (fortunately for US) off the plate and out of harm's way as Donna touched home and hummed the theme song from *Dragnet*— *"Daaa, da da daa . . . da da daaaaa!"*

Maybe the fat lady didn't sing, but she sure hummed.

Mary touched first base and then jumped on Joseph, throwing her arms around his neck and her legs around his waist. Joseph made an impeccable reception of the tiny woman and spun around as all the players on the field joined in celebrating this improbable ending.

Yes, the field was full of believers that day. And just as Kevin Costner had done on the big silver screen, C asked, "Is this heaven?"

Chapter 24

HOW MUCH FOR THAT DOGGIE?

A large, gold-painted statue of a lion guards the entrance to a city oasis, which is appropriately named Lions Park. It sits squarely in the center of town.

The homeless had been using it as a shelter at night, sleeping under the metal bleachers of the softball fields. But early-morning joggers, aghast at seeing humans lying on the ground covered by dirty blankets, complained, and soon routine police patrols and locked gates kept the destitute out.

The park was heaven for my little dog, Willow. A grand spread of well-watered green grass for rolling, tall trees for shade, and a constant cool breeze off the saltwater channel on which it was located all made for a perfect place, to the canine mind. Willow knew where we were going blocks before we were in sight of the lion because she could smell the park. She would begin a dance of ecstasy, hopping back and forth between my lap and the passenger seat as I drove.

That is exactly what she was doing one late July morning as we pulled into the park after breakfasting at Sally's. I pulled the van to a stop under a shade tree about eight thirty. The park was nearly empty. Willow was first out the door; as soon as I cracked it open, she was off to smell the world.

I closed the door and hustled to catch up with her as she hurried from tree to tree, sniffing and marking the territory. But the troubles of the day were on my mind, and I couldn't seem to shake them enough to fully share her bliss. The prevailing thought as I walked along was, "What in the hell am I going to do?" My gas gauge was near empty—maybe the tank held enough to get to the nearest filling station, but that was about it—and I didn't have two nickels to rub together. I was going to have to find money on the ground, or have it fall out of the sky, just to keep going. I had not felt this low and desperate in months, and I didn't want to have to beg again. I had hoped to run in to C at Sally's and ask for a few dollars, but he must have slept in. Then I thought I would see if the Major could provide some assistance, but he was out begging for money himself—to keep Sally's doors open.

Willow could usually feel my distress, but even she was slow on the uptake this morning. We were, after all, *at the park* at this moment, and it was a beautiful morning. She threw herself to the ground and rolled in the grass, then got up and ran with the wind at her back until some other smell filled her nostrils and brought her to a halt. My task was just to follow along behind and watch out for predators—like pit bulls, or the animal control truck—that could spoil this frolic for her.

These visits to the park were the best thing I could do for her. Often I felt bad that she had gotten stuck tagging along with me on this journey—having to sleep in a cold car, having to stay in the car while I ate at Sally's or at a local church, seldom getting a bath, and never getting the pampering she had received as a puppy. I'd considered trying to find her a comfortable home, one that was warm in the winter and cool in the summer, with a soft couch to rest on.

A couple of cars were pulling in as Willow began leading me back toward the shade and the cup of water she knew awaited her in the van. As we approached our ride, a man in a big new truck pulled in right beside us. He was talking on his cell phone and left his motor running. It was a diesel Club Cab 4x4, and he had to talk loudly to be heard over the engine.

"Can you hear me now?" he asked the party on the other end of his connection. "Good. I just pulled into this city park down by the water. The reception is much better here. Anyway, I expect the Johnsons to call for me this morning. Tell them the price has gone up to three hundred eighty thousand on the house on Rocky Point. We've got three potential buyers."

He quit talking for a moment. Then he turned off the engine and began to step out. "Wait a minute. You're breaking up. I'm getting out of the truck so I can hear you better," he said. "Okay, I can hear you now." He was pressing the phone closer to his ear and walking away from the truck. "Well, I'll have to take care of that when I get back." He pulled a pack of cigarettes from his pocket, then pulled one out and lit it. "I already stopped by the Martins' this morning to let them know they are going to have to cough up another twenty thousand for that place on Pine Road." He paused, taking a drag on his cigarette. "And before I forget it, my travel agent is supposed to drop off the tickets for the Cancun cruise. I'm heading out to Gold Mountain to play golf—I've got an eleven o'clock tee time. I'll stop in the office at six to look over all those papers. Just leave them on my desk."

Willow had jumped in the van to get her drink of water, and I had spent those few moments summoning the courage to walk around the van and ask the man for help. He snapped his cell phone shut, tossed his cigarette to the ground, and snuffed it out with his foot. He was already reaching for the door handle, and his back was to me as I nervously spoke up.

"Sir, I hate to bother you, but I'm having a tough time right now." He turned to look at me. "I need to borrow five dollars for gas to put in my van." The words seemed to tumble out of my mouth, and I had a sinking feeling that I had asked the wrong person.

"What's the deal?" he asked.

"It's a long story," I said, "but I lost my home, my job, and a lot more, and I'm living in my van now."

His eyes traveled to the van, where Willow was now sticking her head out the window. "I don't like to give money to street people," he said. "I always think it goes to alcohol or drugs."

"I don't drink or do drugs," I said, hoping that I sounded convincing, even though I was feeling labeled and judged.

"I sell real estate for a living," he said. "I'm trying to rebuild the city by bringing people in here who have money. People like you hanging around just lower the property values. And if people just give you money, you just keep on hanging around." For some reason, he felt the need to explain his position to me. "This town is on the way up," he continued. "The trouble is there have been too many low-income and homeless people for too long. We need people to buy out the poor and fix up those slums and let the poor move down to Oregon or California, or to wherever will take them. You know what they call this town over in Seattle? They call it 'Bummertown.'"

I knew it all too well. I just stood there, feeling completely defeated.

The man looked at Willow and asked, "That your dog?"

"Yes," I said. "That's Willow. Willow, my van, and some clothes—that's all I have left."

"How much did you pay for that dog?"

It seemed like an odd question, but I decided to answer. "She cost six hundred when she was a puppy," I said.

He stepped closer to the passenger side of the van, where Willow was standing on the seat with her front paws on the door. "Will it bite me if

I reach out to pet it?" he asked.

"No," I said. The thought of Willow biting *anyone* almost made me laugh.

He reached out cautiously to pat her head. Willow accepted his attention, then jumped down and over onto the driver's seat.

"How much do you want for that dog now?" he asked, looking directly at me.

His question caught me off guard. I was silent.

"My daughter might just like a little dog like this," he said. "Cleaned up, it might be kinda cute."

"I really need the money—but I couldn't sell my *dog*!"

He laughed and shook his head, and then reached into his pocket and pulled out a money clip. He slowly peeled a hundred-dollar bill from the clip and held it out. "Here. I'll give you a hundred bucks for the dog, right now."

I shook my head.

He used his thumb and forefinger to get another hundred from the clip. "How about two hundred?"

"No, thanks."

"Okay," he said, looking at Willow again. "Does it have all its shots?" he asked.

"She's due. It's been maybe two years since she's seen a vet," I said.

"Well, then," he said. "I'll tell you what I'll do." He took two more hundred-dollar bills from the clip. "I'll give you four hundred for it. That should get you down the road and buy a few nights in a motel. Four hundred—that's my last offer."

I stared at the money in his outstretched hand. "Thanks for the offer," I said. Then I looked him straight in the face. "But I can't sell her. She's my friend. I couldn't sell her for *any* price."

The man laughed again. Then he tucked the money back into his money clip and put it in his pocket. "*Everything* is for sale," he said.

"Houses, boats, cars—and people, too. It's just a matter of price. That's what I've learned."

Then he turned away.

"Good luck," he said, getting into the truck and starting the engine. He looked over his shoulder and backed out, turned his truck around, and pulled away.

I stared after him for a moment. I was shaken. A part of me wanted to argue with him and convince him he was wrong—that everything was *not* for sale—that everyone did *not* have a price. But a small part of me wasn't all that sure.

And maybe that was the difference between the "haves" (at least those who flaunted what they have) and the "have-nots"—that sense of certainty that they have answers to all the questions of life. I wasn't too sure they even had all the right questions. I wondered at what point on this journey the wheeler-dealers traded in their sensitivity, caring, and compassion for the cockiness of those who are able to carry and flash a large roll of bills.

It occurred to me that in some ways, perhaps—no, I was *certain*—I had a lot more real value than the man in his truck. I didn't have money for gas, but I did have Willow. And, desperate as I might be feeling otherwise, I still had the comfort of some dignity.

I stepped over to the van, resolving to wait until someone else pulled in so I could try again. "Come on, Willow," I said to my friend, opening the door. "Let's take another walk."

She cocked her head and gave me a sideways look, then jumped from the seat onto the pavement. I closed the door and we headed for the grass. She knew what was valuable, too.

Willow stayed right by my feet as we walked across the asphalt. The thought of being without her had unnerved me. "Geez, Willow!" I said, looking down at her. "You're worth more than I am! But you know I couldn't sell you, not for a million bucks."

As soon as our feet hit the grass, Willow lowered her nose and was off again, following a new scent. I let her race ahead, and I walked slowly along the outfield fence of one of the softball fields.

As I passed center field, I saw a softball lying in the grass ahead. I walked over and picked it up. It was an almost-new ball that must have been hit over the barrier the night before and left behind. I tossed the ball up in the air a few times as I kept walking behind Willow. She raced over to the fence to smell a piece of folded-up paper lying next to the chain links.

The paper was just inside the fence, maybe blown there by the wind. I bent down to retrieve it and unfolded it carefully to find "Lineup" written at the top—then, "Bob, second base; Jim, first; Larry, shortstop; Steve, third." And tucked inside the paper were two ten-dollar bills. Some player had obviously put his lineup card and his hot-dog-and-beer money in his back pocket and then lost it.

I smiled at our good fortune as I put the money in my pocket. It was all we needed to keep us going for another day.

Chapter 25

CAMPING

When people grow so weary of their conditions that they can no longer stand them, there has always been a place to go—the wilderness.

The Venetians did it, cutting down trees and building a city upon them. The Jews did it, as Moses led them through the desert. The Pilgrims did it. Brigham Young led the Mormons to it. And Thoreau escaped to it.

The homeless men of Bremerton were doing it, too.

They were living in the woods behind the old Eagle Hardware warehouse, with shelters made of old blue tarps stolen from construction sites and black plastic garbage bags taken from dumpsters.

It was in these woods that they could drink their 40-ouncers, fashion the empty cans into giant marijuana pipes, and find peace.

But Willow and I still had wheels as our domicile. We had not reached the point where the woods were our only option for rest.

We were asleep in the Methodist church parking lot in East Bremerton when the sound of cars pulling in awakened us. Willow barked as the heads of three little children peered in the windows of the van. "Puppy! Puppy!" one of the girls exclaimed. It was Monday morning, and parents were dropping off their children for daycare on the way to work.

"Nicole! Alicia! Bobby! Come here!" a woman's voice called out. "It's time for school."

"Look at the puppy, Mommy!" a child's voice responded, as Willow scratched frantically on the window to welcome the children.

"Come *now*, I said," the mother replied sternly.

I waited for them to leave, rearranged the furnishings, started the engine, and pulled out onto Sylvan Way. I needed to find a 7-Eleven where I could take a pee, fast!

As soon as I pulled out of the parking lot I was tailgated by a boom-box cowboy in a beat-up Buick. He got so close I could see the toothpick hanging from his mouth in my rearview mirror. We pulled over to let this early morning brush with evil pass us by, and we sighed. Willow needed to go to the park to pee herself, so we headed to the nearest grassy knoll and then for some breakfast at Sally's.

It was a beautiful morning in August, the best time of year in the Northwest. When we pulled into the lot at Sally's, it was already sixty-five degrees. "It's going to be a hot one today," the radio announcer on 710 KIRO said. "It might reach ninety! So get out and enjoy it, if you can."

Sally's was crowded, as it always was on Mondays. Three black men were talking hoops at one table. "The Lakers are going to win it all, man," James told Sammy and Lionel. "They've got Gary Payton now, and Malone."

"With Shaq and Snow and Kobe, they're going to have the dream team," Lionel agreed, swallowing a spoonful of cornflakes.

"Hey, I been wondering where you been, man," James said.

"I just got out of jail yesterday," Lionel explained. "Domestic violence, man. My third time. I've got to go to anger management classes now. It's going to cost me thirty bucks a week for those classes, and I don't *have* it.

If I don't go, I'm back in jail, man!" His girlfriend had asked him to come by and fix the leak in her sink, and he'd stayed the night. He had given her his hard-earned money to help with the rent because she said she was going to get evicted. Everything had been all right for a couple of weeks; then she got her check from the state and wanted him out. He'd given her all his money. Then she said, "You *stink*, man!"

"She didn't say that when I was fucking her and giving her money," said Lionel. "She pushed me toward the door. She went *crazy*, man. *Screaming!* I pushed her back. She called the cops and they took me away." He'd told them about the sink and the money, but they wouldn't listen.

"I told you long ago, man, to stay away from that woman," James said. "She's just using you. You're her last-of-the-month friend—she only needs you when she runs out of money. When she gets that check on the first, you're shit to her, man. Don't you understand?"

"Yeah, but we got a kid together, man," Lionel replied. "And I love my kid. He's six now and he looks just like me. If I want to see him, I got to do what she wants. She says 'You gotta do this, or you ain't seeing the kid.' Ever since I got busted for stealing that car, I ain't got *no* rights. But I gotta see my kid, man; I gotta be with him."

I was just finishing my Post Toasties and my stale chocolate donuts when C walked in. It was only eight thirty, but he'd been imbibing. "Yahoo!" C called out. "It's a wonderful day in the neighborhood!"

It was as if he could read my mind this morning. "Richard! What do you think about going camping?"

"I like the idea!" I said.

C filled his bowl with cereal and poured milk over it with a flourish. "Let's go to Illahee State Park," he said. "It's just on the edge of town."

It sounded like a good idea: two homeless guys sleeping out under the stars, communing with nature, filling their lungs with fresh air, and finding peace in the wonders of God's quiet places. It would be a welcome reprieve from the rigors of the boom-box beat of the city.

I should have known that the homeless would not be welcome at the state park. In fact, no one was really welcome at Illahee. Money was welcome, but not people. My first clue was that there was no WELCOME TO ILLAHEE STATE PARK sign as we drove through the entrance.

There were signs—129 of them! The first sign was FEE AREA, marked with two red flags to get attention. The second was PAY HERE. Actually, there were twenty-nine PAY HERE signs, twenty DOGS MUST BE ON LEASH signs, twenty-four DON'T LITTER signs, and six DON'T FEED THE ANIMALS signs. I thought of the sixties tune by the Five Man Electrical Band, "Sign, sign, everywhere a sign, blockin' out the scenery, breakin' my mind." Four sturdy bulletin boards gave detailed descriptions of what you could *not* do and how you would be removed from the park if you did what you could not do. The word "please" was used once. The word "thank you" was never used.

The Washington state parks had been turned into profit centers. It cost five bucks just to get in and take a walk, sixteen bucks for a campsite, and a quarter for a one-and-a-half-minute shower. The once-friendly Ranger Rick had been turned into the park Gestapo; protected by flak jackets and carrying sidearms, the rangers cruised the park monitoring the visitors. Innocent families were tracked down by the rangers if they forgot to pay the five-buck fee and then threatened with a hundred-thirty-five-dollar ticket, or worse.

Undoubtedly the State of Washington needed the five-dollar fee for every family picnic so desperately because it had spent 360 million on a new baseball stadium, 340 million on a new football stadium, a few million on a new ice-hockey arena in Everett, on an ice-skating rink in Bremerton, and finally six billion on a new mass-transit train that could whisk passengers from downtown Seattle to Sea-Tac Airport in thirty minutes. The passengers, after all, needed to have the fast train so they could get to the airport four hours early, where they would stand in line to get through security.

The local police cruised through the park every couple of hours to make sure the campers were obeying all the signs the rangers had put up and to see if any family had become so unruly that a major show of irresistible force was needed. They surveyed each campsite as if they were looking for weapons of mass destruction.

Where were the invitations to the "Interpretive Programs," where the smiling ranger would greet the campers and share his knowledge of the forest? Where were the campfires where the people could gather to sing "Kum Ba Yah," tell campfire stories, or describe sightings of a Sasquatch in the camp bathroom? Where were the guided nature walks, where the ranger would point out the antics of the blue jay, the deer tracks, or which berries could be eaten and which ones shouldn't?

The roar of no less than five generators running from morning till night drowned out the songs of the birds and drove the deer and the squirrels from the park. The generators were sending power to RVs, inside of which children were playing computer games and the parents were e-mailing their friends and watching *Dr. Phil* on television. They would peek out from time to time, and some came out to refill the generators with gas.

There were no dogs catching Frisbees or frolicking children playing tag in the grass. The children who did venture outside were rollerblading or riding their power scooters in the parking lot.

Some RV campers were actually seeking a non-smoking campsite— unable to see the irony of that, with all the pollutants they brought in.

But we were here to camp, for real! C's survival instincts kicked in in this woody wonderland, so he did what he always did when he found himself in a foreign region: He went dumpster diving. After about half an hour, he returned with a copy of *You Can't Go Home Again* by Thomas

Wolfe, a worn-out oven mitt, a broken Realistic radio, and two bottles of unopened Washington Hills blush wine that obviously hadn't pleased the palate of more discriminating campers. It didn't take C long to unscrew the top of the blush blend and find a place in the sun to read Wolfe's prose. He read aloud as he always did, accentuating the sentences that stirred him. The crows began to gather, and C continued to read to his feathered friends.

Meanwhile, the back door of the 40-foot mobile home (appropriately named an "Auto Villa") in campsite number 5 opened, and a man remarkably resembling Osama bin Laden came out to smoke a cigarette. "Naw, it can't be," I said to myself. But the more I looked, the more he evaded my gaze, until he turned his back to me and kept puffing.

The cast of characters became more intriguing when a mustard-yellow Ford Econoline van roared into campsite number 8. It was truly a Dijon color—definitely not French's. The passenger mirror on the truck was secured by a mass of duct tape. The engine sputtered and coughed and spit out a noxious smell when the driver turned it off.

Through the cloud of smoke produced by the gasping engine appeared the driver, who made a beeline for our campsite like he was a long-lost friend. He did a quick study as he walked our way. "Homeless guys, huh?" he said, approaching. "Me, too. I live in my van," he added as he twitched and looked away, like an old prizefighter who had taken too many lefts to the head. "Livin' in your car?" he asked, twitching again.

I nodded and wondered if it was really that obvious. Did I have "homeless" written on my forehead? Or was it because we had no tent, no sleeping bags, no Coleman stove, or any of the usual camping paraphernalia? C, engrossed with Wolfe, ignored our visitor and continued reading to the crows that were now pacing about the campsite.

"What's with your friend?" the newcomer asked.

"He likes to read," I replied.

As a come-on, he said "I've got some food and stuff in the truck, if you want it. I've just been to the food bank—beef stew, canned salmon—good stuff."

I pulled myself up and started following him to the Dijon van when he turned around and extended his hand. "I'm Achilles," he said. "Most people call me Chris."

"I'm Richard," I said, shaking his hand, and we headed for his van.

Achilles had turned his 1972 Ford van into a home. From the door I could see he had bolted a dark-blue La-Z-Boy recliner in the back and welded a platform on the inside wall to hold a small battery-operated TV. On the floor of his home-on-wheels were twenty or thirty copies of *Penthouse* and *Galley* magazines, a half-dozen books, and a .38 pistol. He had several paint cans he used for storage. One can was full of Bic lighters, another contained some tattered photographs, and yet another a bunch of snipes. Achilles picked up a sizeable snipe from the can and lit it. "Wait a minute," he said, "I've got to dump this." He reached into the van for a big white bucket, picked it up, and threw the contents onto the ground outside. "I pissed in there this morning and forgot to throw it out." He set the bucket back in place, climbed into the van, and handed me two big cans of Dinty Moore Beef Stew, three cans of smoked salmon, a can of peaches, a jar of peanut butter, and a box of Triscuits.

Achilles settled himself in the La-Z-Boy and blew a smoke ring in the air. "What's your problem? Drugs? Booze? Gambling?" he asked. "How come you're homeless?"

"It's a long story," I said, juggling the cans and boxes in my arms as I stood alongside the van.

"Mine's drugs, man. Narcotics. My wife kicked me out two years ago, and she took everything." He was twitching again. "You're in luck today; you're here to see me shoot up for the last time," he said, taking off his wool shirt. "You want to watch me?"

I tried to think of an appropriate answer to his question. I didn't have one. I felt obliged, because he had just given me food for dinner, and I sensed that somehow he needed someone—namely *me*—to witness this last act of self-degradation. My mind was locked and my eyes focused on one thing: that gun. "What's the gun for?" I asked.

"Sometimes when I get down," he said, leaning over and picking it up, "I play Russian Roulette. Like this," he said, putting it in his mouth and pulling the trigger.

"SHIT! Don't *do* that!" I yelled. "It might have been *loaded!*"

"It is loaded," he laughed. "Just one bullet, though." Then he put the gun down.

I shuddered.

"Look at this, man," he said, pointing out the needle holes in his left arm, and then his right. He was skinny as a rail, and the needle marks stood out like craters.

He picked a Bible off the floor, randomly opened it, and laid it in his lap. Then he reached down in one of the paint cans and picked out a spoon, a Bic, and a small Ziploc bag with one white pill in it.

"It's my last one," he said, taking the pill from the bag and placing it on the spoon. "My ex-wife sells me these for ten bucks a pop. It's her heart medicine. It gives you a good ride." He got his needle from the paint can and flicked his Bic, sterilizing the tip. "This is how it's done," he said, as he moved the flame under the spoon and began melting the pill.

It was show-and-tell by a drug addict. I felt like I was enrolled in "How to Shoot Up 101." No wonder his ex-wife needed heart medicine, if she'd been married to him for very long.

"You've got to do this just right—skim the stuff off the top," he said, taking another spoon to add the finishing touches to his elixir. Then he filled the needle, placed it in his vein, and pressed the plunger.

When he was done, he dropped the needle in the bucket and picked up the Bible from his lap and read. "'Unto thee, O Lord, do I lift up my soul. O my God, I trust in Thee; let me not be ashamed; let not my enemies triumph over me. Yea, let none that wait on Thee be ashamed;

let them be ashamed which transgress without cause. Show me Thy ways, O Lord; teach me Thy paths. Lead me in Thy truth, and teach me; for Thou art the God of my salvation. On Thee I wait all the day.'"

"That's a Psalm of David, man. Psalm 25," he said. "Jesus is telling me to quit this stuff, man. And Jesus is too strong to mess with. This is history you're watching here. Jesus came to me in 1976. A friend asked me to go to a revival at the stadium in Anaheim. I didn't want to go, but I did. The preacher was calling out to people who wanted to be saved. They were singing 'Amazing Grace,' and people were holding their hands up to the Lord. I was sitting in the top row with nobody behind me, when I felt something pick me up by my armpits and push me toward the stage below. It was Jesus! He walked right behind me all the way down to the stage through those thousands of people, all the way to the minister, who touched me. It was like a lightning bolt went through my body, man. I was saved. Don't mess with Jesus, man. He's too strong."

I was still standing there—now needing to take a pee so bad that I was beginning to cross my legs like a little boy—and still holding cans of food and a box of crackers, listening to his life story come rushing out like a stream.

"My mom and dad came to visit me that night after the revival," he said, leaning forward in his La-Z-Boy. "They were dead, but they came to see me. My dad was named Demetrious; he came here from Greece and worked in the mills in Chicago. He had big hands. He was a rough, burly guy, and he became a prizefighter and won a lot of fights. He knew everybody, and everybody wanted to buy him drinks. Man, he could belt them down. He had a temper, too. But you know, he never hit my mom and he never hit me.

"We moved to Anaheim with some of his winnings. Our next-door neighbor was Duke Ellington, man. That's where my mom got hooked on drugs. I spent seven years taking her to doctors and cleaning up her puke before she OD'd. This shit is going to kill me too, if I don't stop.

You're witnessing a miracle here, man.

He was getting high now, and he pushed his La-Z-Boy back until the footrest popped up. Then he picked up his Bible again and asked me to close the door.

I rearranged the foodstuffs in my arms to free a hand and pushed the door closed. I could hear him inside, starting to read again. "Remember, O Lord, Thy tender mercies and Thy loving kindnesses; for they have been ever of old. Remember not the sins of my youth . . ."

Even after I returned to our campsite, I could hear Achilles reading. His voice was getting louder and louder. I could picture him rocking back and forth in his La-Z-Boy, calling out "Holy Ghost power! Holy Ghost power! Thank you, Jesus! Thank you, Jesus!"

C was still reading aloud at the table, with just as much passion as Achilles in his van.

I quickly dropped the groceries given to me by the drug-enhanced holy man next door and headed for the bushes to empty my bladder before it exploded. I checked the trees for surveillance cameras and found a fern to drown. "Why me?" I asked myself as I watered the plant. "Why did this strange fellow tell me his story and show me his habit? Hell, I could have been an ATF agent, for all he knew. Was it because he needed to unload to someone and I happened to be there? Was he just lonely?"

The park ranger was walking through the campgrounds on his rounds, making sure all the paying inmates were obeying all the signs. In spite of his menacing look, I decided to approach him as he passed by our campsite. "Hello, Ranger," I called out, walking in his direction. "My name is Richard."

"I'm Ranger Bartlett," he replied, glaring.

"Your first name?" I asked, trying to break down his wall a little and get on a first-name basis.

"Just Ranger Bartlett," he fired back.

I felt I was in the presence of a CIA agent. His first name must remain a secret, or be shared only on a need-to-know basis. "I was wondering what *Illahee* meant," I asked.

"I don't know," he snapped. "I think it's some Indian name." The beeper on his hip interrupted our "conversation." He quickly checked the number, whipped his cell phone out and dialed. "I'll be right there," he said into the phone as he dashed away.

"Whoa," I thought to myself, as I walked back to my 20-by-20-foot, sixteen-dollar-a-night campsite with a rotting picnic table. "I'm glad he didn't grab his gun instead of his cell phone; he could have blown his ear off!"

As the full moon began to rise over our prison camp, somehow I felt this journey back to nature was going to turn out to be a mistake. My instincts were right on.

It began just as our pot of Dinty Moore beef stew was reaching the point of culinary perfection on the campfire grid. The couple in site number 7, right next to ours, was having a not-so-delightful after-dinner discussion about laziness and dishes and parentage (legitimate or not) and lack of relationship. The louder and nastier their attacks and retorts, the more liberally laced they were with the f-word.

Then there was silence—a respite, albeit a short one.

I dished up the stew and buttered some slices of wheat bread for C and me, hoping for a peaceful meal. Foolish me.

"I'm leaving!" she launched. "Give me the goddamn car keys!"

"Go ahead and leave, bitch," he retorted. "But *I'm* keeping the car!"

"Fine!" she yelled. "I'll call my son to get me, you motherfucker!" She grabbed her cell phone and dialed the number, while he grabbed his paint-ball gun and took aim. He fired and spattered a purple blotch onto her sequin-studded denim shirt, just below her right breast.

"Randy," she screamed into the phone. "Come and get me at the state park, *quick!* No, pick me up along the road to the park. Come quick! Harry just shot me with his paint-ball gun!" Then she ran.

Harry stood there with his paint-ball gun, dressed in the Desert Storm fatigues he'd probably bought at Wal-Mart. He fired a round at the trees. Then he slowly reloaded, grabbed his Sharper Image night-vision goggles and marched away, I presumed in pursuit of his quarry.

It seemed such a short time—way too short. We were halfway through our beef stew and thinking delicious thoughts of making s'mores with the Hershey bars and graham crackers we had gotten from the food bank, when suddenly the miracles of modern-day cell phone communication and OnStar technology jolted our tranquility. The only thing that could have made it more bizarre would have been the sound of helicopter blades over our heads. A Washington State Patrol car was the first of the ground force to arrive, followed by a Bremerton Police cruiser, then an unmarked police car, then another State Patrol vehicle, then yet *another* Bremerton police car with two officers. The rush stirred up the dust and clogged the pathways and brought people peeking out of their aluminum camping palaces to see what all the buzz was about.

Willow hid under the rotting picnic table as the chaos intensified.

C hid in the trees, fearing he might be recognized by someone involved in one of his past exploits.

The high rollers in their Auto Villas locked their doors, closed their curtains, and loaded their guns. They were truly locked and loaded.

Achilles slammed his Dijon van door shut and hit the deck. "Oh, God!" I could hear him cry out as he hid under the blanket in the back of his rig.

I could also hear C quietly singing the theme song from *Cops* as he retreated further into the forest: "Bad boys! Bad boys! What you gonna do? What you gonna do when they come for you?"

Ranger Bartlett was the last to arrive on the scene. He appeared disheveled and was still slipping on his flak jacket as he approached. The laces of his jackboots were untied and he had a milk mustache. The knowledge that his park had been turned into a refuge for homeless drunks and drug-using, longhaired freaks seemed to infuriate Ranger Bartlett. He was hopping mad.

The chocolate from my s'more was oozing from the corners of my mouth when no fewer than ten law-enforcement officers, plus Ranger Bartlett, approached to find a deserted campsite 7.

"I think they were some of that homeless trash that gets some welfare money and comes down here," Ranger Bartlett explained to the detective in charge. A policeman was roping off campsite 7 with yellow CRIME SCENE plastic tape, tying it to the pines and the firs.

"Sir?" The detective approached me, offering his badge. "Did you hear anything going on next to you in the last thirty minutes?"

"Sir!" interrupted a patrolman. "They left a lot of things behind over here. Should we call in the canine unit?"

"Let's see what this man has to say first," the detective answered.

So I explained, as best I could, trying to reconstruct which "fuck" went where and which "son-of-a-bitch" was used at what time in the discourse between the two unhappy campers. They probably would have been making whoopie in their tent by now if they just could have sung a couple of verses of "Kum Ba Yah" around a warming fire.

It dawned on me that I was getting to tell a campfire tale after all—just as I had secretly wished. I had their full attention, and they leaned toward me like Boy Scouts around the fire pit, hanging on my every word. "In the intense heat of the torrid argument," I said, spinning my tale, "her feeble hand shook as she dialed the phone number of her son Randy and cried out, 'Come and get me at the campground—no, come and get me along the road. He just shot me with his paint-ball gun!'"

The officers raised their eyes to the sky as if they had all just seen the Northern Lights shimmer. "Did you say *paint-ball gun?*" the detective asked.

"Yeah," I replied. "He shot some trees, too." I pointed into the woods. "Those two Douglas firs and a madrone."

The detective took a radio from his belt and said, "Command—all clear." The intensity of the moment immediately began to deflate; only the adrenalin hangover remained. "Please excuse us for bothering you," he said. "Her son heard 'He shot me!' so he called 911. Thank you for your help."

I could have led the troops twenty feet to the most dangerous and deranged person I have ever met, hiding in the Dijon van, but decided not to. After all, he wasn't hurting anyone.

I also had a hunch that, if we lived to camp at Illahee another night, Achilles would provide the campfire story I would need to tell the police on their next visit.

"I'm going to make a sign, NO PAINT-BALL GUNS, and put it up tomorrow," Ranger Bartlett told the detective as they walked away.

A woman pulled into Achilles' campsite just as the ranger was leaving. I assumed it was his ex-wife stopping by to peddle him some more heart pills.

It was about ten o'clock when I decided to take Willow for a walk. The generators were turned off. Achilles and C had stopped reading. Osama and his tribe and the other Auto Villas had turned off their lights, and there was no sign of the ranger. I took Willow off her leash, and we walked into an open field in the park.

The August moon was full and Saturn sparkled in the sky. The planet was as close as it had been in some sixty thousand years. We lay in the grass, looking at the stars. "There's the Big Dipper," I told her, pointing to the sky. "And there's the Little Dipper," pointing to the sky again. The little dog looked toward the sky and then looked back at me. I told her, "When you spell DOG backwards, it spells GOD!" We sat quietly for a moment. "I think that's Aquarius, right up—" I started to say as I pointed, but a shooting star darted across the sky. "WOW! Did you see that, Willow? A shooting star!" The silence was so precious that we just lay there in the grass looking at the sky.

Chapter 26

A ROOM WITH A VIEW

"Well, well, well. We are so fortunate this morning to be joined by 'The Mayor of Bremerton,'" chimed C, leaning back in his chair.

John, the subject of C's jesting commentary, had just shuffled into Sally's for breakfast this Friday morning, which was the beginning of the Labor Day weekend. He pointed a finger at C, closed one eye, and used his thumb as the make-believe hammer of a gun as he pretended to shoot C. "Gotcha," he said, smiling, and turned to pick up his tray and receive his breakfast portion for the day.

C had given John the moniker "The Mayor of Bremerton" a long time ago, because not only had John lived in Bremerton all his life, but he had *lived* in Bremerton. John must have been sixty-something, and he looked a little like Captain Kangaroo. His white hair was cut in that same Dutch fashion, though not quite as neatly styled, and he had a near-white mustache. His right eye was always half closed from an injury he received while working at the naval yard as a young man. On fire watch, he had stood near the welders as they made repairs on the massive aircraft carriers in the shipyard, keeping his eyes open for stray sparks that could lead to disaster. It was one of those sparks that damaged John's eye.

John was a walking encyclopedia of Bremerton history and enjoyed spinning yarns about the town, with a touch of Will Rogers' wit. He had played the trombone in the high-school band, which had regaled every ship entering and leaving the yard. He knew about the secret tunnels under the shipyard and all the dirty laundry about past and present politicians and other local notables.

C and I were sitting at the table nearest the serving line, in the company of "Willie the Walker." He was an extremely quiet man, maybe seventy years old, who was nicknamed for his brisk walks from one side of town to the other every day, carrying a small plastic bag in each hand. I'd heard Willie would fill the bags with abandoned newspapers, rolls of toilet paper from restaurant washrooms, and other things he could use at home.

John, his tray now filled with a bowl of Malt-o-Meal, a cinnamon roll, a hardboiled egg, and a cup of java, turned his sprightly step toward our table. He was wearing his usual smile. "May I join you gentlemen?" he asked, placing his tray on the table.

"Of course, Mr. Mayor," said C.

"Well, I see you somehow lived through another night," John said, looking intently at C. "For the life of me, I don't know how!"

C just laughed and picked up his cinnamon roll. "John, look at this. I think I see the face of Jesus in this cinnamon roll!"

John rolled his one good eye, but then peered at C's roll. "It could be," he replied, cocking his head slightly. Sally's is a church, you know." Then he picked up his own roll and looked at it. "Mine looks a little like Donald Trump!" He bit into it. "But it tastes like it's just a week-old cinnamon roll."

"You know, a cinnamon roll with the image of Jesus on it could be worth some money," I said.

Willie looked at his roll intently. He turned it from side to side and then all the way around before slowly sliding it into one of the bags sitting on the floor beside him.

"Well, what's the latest?" C asked, as John attempted to guide a spoonful of cereal past his mustache. What John didn't know about Bremerton probably wasn't worth knowing. He had lived in the same house for all of his sixty-plus years—a big two-story house with a large front porch—less than half a block from Sally's, across 6th Street. It was smack-dab in the center of town, by the A1 Auto Repair and a drive-thru bank, directly across the street from Monica's Social Club, a well-known, brightly lit watering hole that served beer in big, frosty mugs.

John swallowed his porridge and wiped his mouth with a napkin. "You mean you haven't seen today's newspaper?" he asked.

"No," said C.

"Well, now they want to spend thirty million dollars to build a tunnel under the city to take the traffic away from downtown. That's after spending millions over the last thirty years to get people to *come* downtown!" John huffed.

"Where are they going to get all that money?" I asked.

"I'm sorry," John said, leaning toward me. "I didn't hear what you said." I happened to be sitting on his bad-ear side.

"Where's the money coming from?" I said, a little louder.

John looked at our other tablemate and asked, "Willie, did you get a paper today?"

Willie, without a peep, picked up one of his bags and laid it on the table. Then he pulled out a stack of papers—the *New York Times*, the *Seattle Post-Intelligencer*, *USA Today*, and the *Kitsap Sun*. He silently handed the *Sun* across the table to John.

"Thank you, Willie," said John. "Willie gets these to do the crossword puzzles," he said as an aside. "He's a wizard at them." Willie just smiled.

"Now, let's see," said John, snapping the paper open. "Headline: Dicks Encourages City to Accept Tunnel Money," John read. "Story: Congressman Norm Dicks has encouraged the City to accept grant money from the federal government to build a six-block-long tunnel under the City that will ease traffic congestion during the departure and arrival of Washington State Ferries. 'The City needs to accept the grant as soon as possible, or risk it being taken away in the next budget session,' Dicks said."

John folded the paper and handed it back to Willie. "For heaven's sake, why don't they take that money and build a recreation center right here, downtown, with some showers for the homeless people to get cleaned up, and maybe a pool table or two, and a place for some free movies. A room with some books would be nice, too—where somebody can sit down and read. We need someplace for the poorest of the poor to go besides begging for enough change to get a beer at Monica's and walking down the alleys at night."

"Here, here!" chimed C. "*That's* why I call you The Mayor!"

"Oh, don't get me started," John replied. He cracked his hardboiled egg on the oval table and began to pick away at the shell. "Look at that Congressman Norm 'Dickhead' Center going up down the street," he grumbled. "What a monstrosity that is!"

C broke into a laugh. "Did you just call our congressman Dickhead?" he asked. Even Willie could not contain himself and started giggling.

"It's going to cost thirty million for a government building to house a bunch of paper pushers," John continued, peeling his egg. "Why didn't they just buy the old Eagle Hardware building on the other side of town? There are thousands of square feet of empty space in town. It's just pork, pork, and more pork money from the feds. This little piggy developer gets some, this little piggy banker gets some, and this little piggy real-estate firm gets some. The rich get richer and the poor get poorer. They could have taken *some* of those millions to build a homeless shelter—maybe with a free medical clinic and a dentist or two to help fix up some of our rotten teeth."

"Jesus, John, somebody's going to call you a communist, or at least a socialist!" C leaned forward as he accentuated the titles. "Or, maybe you are the worst of the worst, John: a *liberal!*" he added.

"Well, I'm no communist or socialist," John replied. "But if helping the poor and the sick and the oppressed makes me a liberal, then I guess I am one, and damned proud of it! I'm in good company, too. Jesus believed in helping the poor; he must have been a liberal, too."

John had finally finished peeling his egg. He reached to the middle of the table for the salt and pepper shakers. He delicately salted his egg and added just a dash of pepper. Just as he was putting the egg to his mouth, C asked, "What about those waterfront condos they are building right down by the new convention center and hotel?"

John drew the egg back from his mouth and shook his head. "I don't understand it. That's a Housing and Urban Development project. I thought HUD was supposed to build affordable housing for the poor. Some of those condos are going for a million dollars each! That's not 'affordable housing' to me! That's how convoluted our government has become. Oh, the bureaucrats can rationalize and tell you that the spending is going to create jobs and make the city better, but the homeless and the poor won't get *any* of those jobs. The big construction companies will come in and build the condos and leave, and the rich will buy them. The poor and the homeless will still be poor and homeless as they walk by those condos. Something is rotten in the state of Denmark," John concluded, as he popped the egg into his mouth.

Without saying a word, Willie picked up a bag in each of his hands and shuffled off toward the door.

"Do you need a ride somewhere?" I asked C.

"No; a ship came in last night, and I'm going to hang around downtown for a bit to see what's going on." he replied. He picked up his tray and turned to go clean it off. "I'll probably see you later," he said over his shoulder.

That left just John and me at the table. "I'll see you later, Mayor," C tossed in as he passed our table again on the way to the door.

John picked up his cup and took a sip of coffee. "Some little bird told me that you are writing a book," he said to me.

"Well, yes and no," I said. "I have started a book, but I don't know if I will ever finish it. I feel like throwing it away sometimes. It's not very good."

"What's it about?" he asked.

"It's about homeless people," I responded.

John raised his bushy eyebrows. "Well, you have a wealth of good copy in this town," he said. "But, whatever you do, don't put anything I said about the city in your book. People here don't like to be criticized."

I took a sip of my now cold coffee.

"I also heard you're still living in your car. That right?" John asked next.

"Yeah, I am. It's been over a year now. I've been sleeping up in the Methodist church parking lot most of the time—sometimes at the Episcopal church. Just me and my little dog."

"Well, I've got a room at my place if you're interested," said John.

"Oh, I'm interested all right," I replied. "But I don't have any money. How much would it cost?"

"I've got five people living there now," he began. "But I've never rented this room. It used to be my room when I was a kid. It looks out over the street. I've been using it to store stuff. We would have to move some stuff around to make it habitable, but we can do that. It's better than sleeping in your car. And your dog can sleep there, too. As far as money goes—well, let's say you give me what you can, when you can. How about that? Maybe you'll get rich off your book."

"Wow. That's generous of you." I was a little stunned, and more than a little wary. After my close encounter (of a very unusual kind) with Tina and her trailer, I wondered if this was another offer that was too good to be true. Would I be evicted tomorrow if someone else came along who was able to pay more? At least it would be a bed for tonight, or maybe even for a few nights.

"Come on. Let's go take a look at it," he said, standing up.

We walked out of Sally's together. "I'll grab Willow," I said and walked quickly to the van. I opened the door and picked her up in my arms to carry her to John's house.

I didn't know much about John, I thought as we walked to the corner and waited for the traffic light. As he was pointing out things of interest in the neighborhood—the bank on the corner that was built about ten years ago, the auto-repair shop that came a year later after they tore down the Miller House—I was thinking about the many times I had seen him around town. He drove a brown-and-black late-sixties Volkswagen bus that he had obviously been patching up over the years. It would putt and sputter and occasionally backfire as he would arrive with five or six hungry people to a free church dinner. He generally gave his riders tour-guide service over the sound of the engine, often pointing out which bridge was built when, what year the local college opened, and where he had gone to school.

"Here's home," John said as we reached his house in the middle of the block. We climbed up the steps to a big porch. It was a turn-of-the-century Victorian home. "I was born in this house in 1938," he said, reaching in his pocket for a ring full of keys. He selected one and slid it in the lock. "Everybody else uses the back entrance," he said. "But since your room is right up at the top of the stairs, you can use the front. It's right above the porch here. You'll have to remember to lock the door every time, though. Sometimes people hang around on the porch at night. My room is clear in the back, and I can't hear them out here."

It was dark inside. Shades were pulled down in the living room. "This way," John said, as he grabbed the rail of the dark mahogany staircase and began climbing the stairs. I followed.

The staircase made a turn at the top, and we arrived at the second floor. John looked through his keys again, picked out another, and turned it in the lock. He opened the door and flipped the light switch. One bare bulb hung from a patched-up light fixture on the ceiling; it blinked a couple of times before it came on. "I'll have to fix that someday," John muttered, pointing to the fixture.

It was a small room, mostly full of dusty cardboard boxes. There was an old dresser on one side and a metal fold-down bed up against the wall. John walked over to the paper shade that covered the front window. He pulled it down slightly and then let it go so that it rolled to the top, letting sunlight fill the room. Dust from the shade filled the air.

"Let's get some fresh air in here," John said, reaching for the latch on the window. He turned it with one hand and pulled the window open with the other, sneezing loudly.

"Gezundheit!" I replied.

"I haven't been in here for a long time," John said. "We can stack some of these boxes on top of each other. That will give you more room." He reached down and strained to pick up a heavy box. "These are old records," he continued, "—old 78s. Let's stack them along that wall."

It didn't take long to move the thirty or so boxes out of the way. Then John swung the metal-spring bed into the middle of the room. "Now, if I remember right," he began, "this bed springs out dangerously when the latch is opened. You grab one side and I'll get the other." We positioned ourselves to avoid injury and John pushed open the latch. The mattress forced the springs down, and we guided it into place. John tested the mattress with his hands. "Still good," he declared. "Try it out."

I moved to the side of the bed and sat down. Then I slowly swiveled and stretched out. The end of the bed at my feet hovered a few inches off the floor. "Oh, I forgot about that," he said. "It's a little catawampus. You have to put some books under the legs to level it out. You can use any of the books in that pile on the floor. Otherwise, you will be sleeping either uphill or downhill all night."

I carefully swung my feet off the side of the precarious bed and stood up. John pulled a couple of books from the stack in the corner of the room. "Here: Milton's *Paradise Lost* and Dante's *Inferno* ought to level the legs out. You'll have plenty of demons under your bed," he chuckled. He bent down slowly and placed *Paradise Lost* under one leg, then moved to the other side and put *Inferno* under the other. "There."

Willow had been sitting by the door, observing our activity. She came over and jumped into the middle of the bed. "Well, it looks like your dog is at home," John declared as he reached over to pat her head. Willow sat up, wiggled her nose and let out a tiny sneeze. I soon followed with one of my own.

"I've got a broom and some dust rags," John said. "It won't be so bad when you clean it up a little. In fact," he added, fishing for his keys and moving toward the door again, "I might have what we need right in here. Follow me."

Just outside the room was another door, secured with a padlock. John inserted a key and it opened with a click. He turned another key in the door lock and opened the door.

"My treasure room," John said. He switched on a small overhead chandelier. My eyes widened at the sight of dozens of antique Victrolas, with horns in many shapes and sizes, sitting on tables and on the floor. "I must trust you," he said. "I don't show this to everyone."

There was one massive Victrola sitting on the floor. It had an off-white horn that must have been three feet long. "So *this* is what all the records are for," I said.

"Yes. I collect these. They are my babies," John said, spreading out his hands. "Most of them were broken when I bought them. I stole parts from some of them to get the others working."

"They are fantastic," I said, marveling at the collection and contemplating the irony of a man with such poor hearing in one ear being a collector of Victrolas.

"My mother got me my first one when I was a kid," he said. "It had a dog on it, like that one over there—you know, the Victrola dog?"

"Yes, I remember the dog," I said.

"She used to play Benny Goodman records on a big machine in the living room, and she would dance with me when I was about that high." John held his right hand about three feet off the floor. "She was a wonderful woman. I still have that one in my bedroom. I play it at night when I go to sleep. I have good memories here."

"So, you said you were born here?" I asked.

"That's right—right downstairs in the kitchen," he confirmed. "There was only one bridge in town then, the Manette. The hospital was on the other side of the water. The bridge was closed for repairs, and there was no way to get to the hospital, so the doctor came here. The only time I've been away was two years during the war. I lost most of my hearing in this ear and my eye was damaged by a grenade, so they shipped me home."

John stepped up to the closet door and opened it. It was stuffed with boxes piled on top of each other. He found a broom and dustpan and handed them to me. "These are a little worse for wear, but they will do the job."

"So, is this really the only house around here?" I asked.

John stood and nodded. "I've seen a lot come and go," he said. "The city got bigger, then smaller, then bigger, then smaller again. I played my trombone when six thousand sailors came, and I played it when six thousand sailors left. This street used to be lined with homes. Now, I'm the last holdout. The last of the Mohicans, you could say. I spent twenty years taking care of my mother here before she died. It took me six years to clear the things from her room. I'll probably die here, too."

I honored the quiet, distant look on his face. After a moment, it shifted. "Let's go get that room cleaned up," John said heading for the door. "Oh, here are some old, holey T-shirts we can use for dusting." He picked some rags up from the bookcase by the door. "Oh, wait. I've got to show you this."

John picked up a small box from the top of the dusty bookcase. He held it carefully in his hands and pushed something on the bottom. The top of the box slowly opened and a small red bird rose into view. The bird warbled a redbird song. "These boxes are rare," he said proudly, touching the bird with his little finger. "Those are real feathers!"

"Amazing," I said.

Then John placed the wooden box gently back on the bookcase, and we moved out of the room. He locked the door and put the padlock back in place, snapping it closed and pulling on it to make sure it was secure.

We went into the front bedroom, and John went right to work sweeping the floor while I dusted. "You might want to put some cotton in your ears if you want to sleep tonight," he said, as the broom swished across the floor. "A ship is in with lots of sailors on it. On top of that, it's Friday night and a holiday weekend."

A few minutes later, John swept the last of the dirt into the dustpan and placed the broom against the wall. "Well, I've got to get going," he said. He pulled out his key ring again. "Here's a key to the front door. Don't forget to lock it on the way in and out. And here's a key to this room." He handed them to me. "I'll see you later."

I nodded my thanks, accepted the keys, and kept on dusting. John's feet made a strange stomping sound as he went down the stairs. I heard the rattling of his key chain and, minutes later, the sound of his Volkswagen bus coughing and spitting as he fired up the engine.

I spent almost another hour cleaning, then decided to take a break and go for a walk in the park with Willow. We stopped at the library to read the daily papers and stopped by a local church for a much-needed evening dinner before heading back to John's house.

I walked into the Salvation Army parking lot about six in the evening to get my sleeping bag from the van, just in time to see James and AP straining as they lugged an old floral-print sofa down the alley.

"Put the goddamn thing down for a minute!" AP yelled. "I need to catch my breath!"

"We only got a few more yards to go," James panted back.

"I'm puttin' my end down *now*!" AP dropped the heavy sofa to the pavement.

"Shit, man," James whined, momentarily holding on, but then letting go of his end with a thud. "We were almost there, man!"

As I walked toward them I saw their friend Brian around the back corner of the 7-Eleven, carrying two wooden armchairs, and Robert, another regular at Sally's, toting a couple of wooden shipping pallets. James took off his weathered baseball cap and wiped the sweat off his brow. He spotted me as he looked up.

"Richard, Richard!" he said, waving me over to them. "Look, we scored a sofa and some chairs. They had a one-day garage sale up the street, and they said we could have these if we carried them away!"

I looked at the sofa. There was a large rip in the material on the side, and the cushions were threadbare in many places. I asked an obvious question. "What're you guys going to do with them?"

"We're gonna sit on them!" James replied, in an equally obvious answer.

"Where?" I asked.

"Right over there," James replied, pointing to the spot behind Sally's where the men hung out.

"Okay, but you know the Major won't go for that," I cautioned.

"Hell, they're gone for the weekend," AP offered. "It's a holiday, man—Labor Day. They won't be back till Tuesday. We can party till then."

Brian and Mike had caught up with AP and James and were now

supervising the operation.

"Let's go," AP said to James. He leaned down to pick up the sofa; James did the same. They put their hands under the bottom and lifted with audible grunts. I watched as the two men carried the sofa the final few yards and then, in unison, dropped it in the dirt.

"Let's face it that way," James said, pointing to the cement wall and beginning to tug on his end.

"Shit, man, it's okay like it is," AP said, sitting down on his end.

"But it would look better if we faced it that way," James insisted.

"Okay, okay!" AP grudgingly stood up. The two men then spun the couch about forty-five degrees, looked at it and then plopped themselves down, one on each end.

"I'll start a fire," Brian said, lifting one of the wooden pallets he had tossed to the ground. He got a good grip and tried to remove one of the slats, to no avail. "You guys got an axe?" he asked.

"We ain't got no tools," James replied.

Brian tossed the pallet to the ground, raised his leg, and stomped on the slats with his boot, loosening a couple of them enough to twist them off.

"Did you check for spare change behind the cushions?" I asked AP.

"Man, we did *that* half a block away from the house!" AP said. "Just a couple of candy wrappers, though. That's all."

Brian continued to stomp and break wood away from the pallets, and Robert began collecting the wood as AP and James looked on.

"Man, I'm thirsty," James said, getting up off the tattered sofa and walking toward the old wooden steps that had once served as the back entrance to Sally's, now boarded up. He got on his hands and knees, crawled partway under the steps, and pulled out a large black plastic bag, which held their stash of refreshments for the night—a case of Rolling Rock.

"Bring me one," AP called out, followed by a "Me too" and an "I'll take one" from Brian and Robert.

James pulled out four bottles and delivered one to each of his buddies.

"Well, it looks like you guys are set for the night," I said.

Brian took a swig of his beer and set it on the ground. He made a small tepee out of the pieces of wood that he had splintered off the pallet. Then he got down on his knees, leaned forward with his lighter, placed the flame near the splinters of wood, and blew gently. Slowly, the small pieces of wood began to burn. "I'm a good fire builder," he said, as the fire began to grow. He placed a few larger pieces of wood on top of the small blaze. "And there are two or three more pallets behind the 7-Eleven we can get later," he added, picking up his beer and sitting down on one of the chairs.

"I'll see you guys later," I said, excusing myself. I got my sleeping bag and made sure my vehicle was locked up tight before heading off. Willow and I walked over to John's house for the night. There were three people talking on the front steps of the house as I approached. I had seen them all before. The woman took a deep drag off her cigarette and then flicked it out into the street. "You the new guy?" she asked, as I moved closer, carrying Willow.

"Yeah. I'm Richard," I replied.

"I'm Lisa," she said. "This is Steve and this is Don. We all live here."

I nodded at the guys and said, "This is my dog, Willow." I put her down on the sidewalk but watched her carefully. It was only about ten feet from the front steps to the street, which was now humming with traffic. "Is John here?" I asked.

"No," Lisa replied. "He took one of the other guys to Seattle. He's had a toothache for a week or more; he moaned most of the night last night. So John took him to the university over there. It's about the only place he could go. He doesn't have any money. John found out they will pull it for free at the dental school. Nobody would do it over here. They didn't leave until two, so I don't expect them back till late."

"Well, glad to meet you," I said. "Come on, Willow," I called, and we moved up the steps. I unlocked the door, climbed the stairs, unlocked the door to my room, and tossed the sleeping bag on the bed. I quickly unrolled it, and Willow hopped up on the bed.

The room was stuffy, so I opened the window about halfway. I peeked out at the lights from Monica's across the street—there was a neon Budweiser sign glowing in one window, a Coors sign in another, and a Lotto sign filling a third, the latter serving as a spotlight for a pull-tab banner. To the right behind the signs, I could see the silhouettes of men playing pool; at the other end of the building, I could see the outlines of people sitting at stools at the bar.

Four sailors were walking briskly toward the front door in their dress whites. They were laughing as they walked into Monica's one by one. The neon lights illuminated their uniforms. Once inside, they headed for the bar and then blended into the crowd.

Well-dressed men and women began walking down both sides of the street. An older gentleman wearing a white Stetson hat was walking arm in arm with a woman carrying a single long-stemmed rose. I guessed they were going to see Kenny Rogers; I had seen the announcement on the marquis of the old theater on the corner of 5th Street, just a block and a half away—the one that had been remodeled into a dinner theater—a distant reminder of my former life.

People were parking in the bank parking lot, kitty-corner to Sally's, and walking to the theater. As I glanced that way, I noticed that the crowd had lured AP and James off their comfy sofa. The boys were smiling and joking and panhandling as the well-heeled theatergoers trooped by. AP was playing to the crowd. He was shuffling his feet and cocking his head from side to side as he delivered his routine, trying to pry a dollar or two from their pockets. I imagined he was telling one of his jokes and asking for eighty-seven cents. I wished him well and watched as a man shook his head, but his mate reached into her purse.

I saw the profile of a man who looked strangely like C standing on the corner wearing a rumpled raincoat and a round, golf-style cap. He wore dark glasses and held a white-and-red cane in one hand and a cup in the other. He was tapping his cane on the sidewalk and saying something I was much too far away to hear.

The strains of Willie Nelson singing "Georgia" were coming from the jukebox, and the sound of laughter and the clatter of pool balls clashing on the break were coming from the Social Club. For a few moments, it felt like I was in New Orleans as I peered from this Victorian window, watching the well-dressed passing by the poor folk on the street.

Just then, four motorcycles sped by, filling the air with noise. I pushed the window down a little, pulled down the paper shade, and moved over to the bed. I kicked off my shoes and climbed into my sleeping bag. I was tired, and a good night's sleep in a bed—albeit a precarious bed held in place by Dante and Milton—was both needed and welcome. It didn't take but a minute for me to drift off.

The sound of voices and the flashing, spinning white-and-blue lights penetrating the paper blind jolted me from my slumber.

I discerned distinct conversation from the porch below. "They're going to nail his ass!" This was followed by the sound of laughter.

I rolled over on my other side, hoping the sound and the lights would go away.

"The dumb fuck has a headlight out," another voice said, again followed by laughter.

I slowly got out of bed and walked to the window. I pulled back one side of the blind, just to take a peek. The flashing lights of two police cars were mingled with the hues of all the beer signs at Monica's. The police had pulled over an old yellow Buick right in front of the Social Club. Two men were in the car.

"You know them, Donnie?" I heard a woman's voice ask.

"No," came the reply.

Just then the shrill sound of a siren silenced the voices. Another police car sped past the window going in the opposite direction, its blue-and-white lights flashing and its engine roaring. I glanced up the street to see three figures, dressed in black, standing under the light of the big red cross mounted on the side of the Salvation Army building.

The police officer on the driver's side of the old Buick stepped back as a young man in a baseball cap, T-shirt, and jeans got out of the car. He walked to the trunk and opened it. Another young man climbed out from the passenger side. Two officers stood at alert while two others began a search, one looking in the trunk, the other in the glove box and back seat. Whatever the officers had found warranted an arrest. The driver turned, placed his hands on the car, and spread his legs. The other man leaned on the police cruiser. They were both quickly cuffed and searched.

"Boy, I don't even need TV here," I thought. "It's like *Law & Order* for real!" The police guided the two men into the back seat of their cruiser.

To add to the light show, a tow truck pulled up with its red lights flashing. In less than ten minutes, both police cars had pulled away and the truck had loaded its charge and pulled off, the Buick in tow.

With all the extraneous lights now removed, I could see the flying sparks and the glow of the fire being enjoyed behind Sally's by AP, James, and the boys.

The teenagers had just begun to walk down the street toward Monica's when I saw Brian around the corner of Monica's parking lot. He was barefoot and shirtless and wild-eyed, carrying what appeared to be an automobile flare in one hand. The young men in black took one look at

Brian and moved quickly across the street in front of John's house.

"Look at that!" a voice from below said. "He's shit-faced! He doesn't even know where he is."

Then a woman came rushing out of Monica's and headed for the parking lot. A man was not far behind. She was reaching in her purse, apparently for her car keys, when he caught up to her.

"You fucking bitch!" he roared, grabbing the woman by her shoulder and spinning her around.

"Get away from me, Jason!" she screamed back. "I'll call the cops!"

"Go ahead, bitch!" he yelled, pushing her against the car.

"Hey!" This new voice was coming from the woman on the porch right below me. "You can't do that!"

The man looked across the street and glared. "Mind your own business!" he screamed.

"We'll call the cops if you push her again," came the warning from below.

The man stepped back, and the woman—crying and shaking now—put the key in the lock of the car door and opened it. She quickly got in and started it, backed up, and pulled out into the street. She sped away. The man glared across the street in our direction again, but he walked back into the bar.

"Jesus! You dumb ass! That could have been a bad scene," a man's voice said from below.

"I don't give a shit," the woman responded. "The son of a bitch shouldn't be hittin' a woman!"

I looked back up the street toward the 7-Eleven. The white, green, and red sign illuminated the three teenagers standing on the corner. A robin's-egg-blue Caprice with shiny, spinning wheel covers was just backing up, turning around, and cruising into Monica's lot.

"There's *real* trouble," said a masculine voice from below. The Caprice had come to a stop, but the wheel covers were still spinning. A black man emerged from the front passenger door, and another from the rear. The driver stayed in the car with the motor running, as the other two men walked toward Monica's door. "Keep your mouth shut, no matter what these guys do," the man on the porch pleaded. "They're selling crack and they're—"

"Okay, okay! Just shut up and give me a cigarette," the woman interrupted.

In just a few minutes, the two black men came back out with a white man and got into the Caprice. I could see the driver light a cigarette and roll his window down slightly. It didn't take long for the men to take care of business. The back door swung open, and the white man got out and went back into Monica's. The driver tossed his cigarette out the window, pulled out onto 6th Street, and drove away.

As I turned to see the blue Caprice speed off, I saw Gentleman Jake and three other men approaching John's front steps. One of them was called "The Indian"; the other two I didn't know.

"Jake, you're drunk," I heard a woman say.

"I'm in a bad way," Jake slurred. "You s'pose I can sleep on this porch tonight? I jus wanna be safe."

"There'll probably be a few others," said the woman.

I watched as Jake half-collapsed on the steps. "I fuckin' fell off the wagon," he said. "Two years without a drink until tonight," he slurred. "But I'm haaaapppy now."

I pulled myself back from the window. I had seen enough for tonight. I left the blind up and got back into my sleeping bag. I rolled on my side and closed my eyes.

"It's been four years for me, Jake," I heard the woman say. "Four years without a drink and I am—"

"Whaoooooooooooooooo!" A man screaming across the street interrupted whatever she was saying. "Whaoooooooooooooooo!"

I opened my eyes. The sound of Bruce Springsteen pounding from Monica's jukebox ended abruptly, and the light streaming in the window began to dim. "Monica's must be closing," I thought to myself. I pictured Monica pulling the plug on the box and turning off the neon lights, one by one, as she was shooing the customers out the door. I could hear the car doors slamming and engines starting as the patrons began to take their leave.

"Hey! You fuckers across the street!" a man yelled. "You want a piece of me?!"

"Don't say *anything!*" the man's voice below warned quietly.

"I'll whip your ass!"

"Come on, Bob. Leave the poor fucks alone," another voice across the street said. "I'll take you home. Come on. Let's go."

There was near silence for a moment. Then I heard another door slam and a car starting to pull away.

I pulled the sleeping bag over my head.

I wondered if there were windows and porches like this in Paris or Berlin—or was this just a piece of Americana, with a room reserved just for me?

It must have been sometime after three when I finally dozed off. I remembered hearing the voices on the porch becoming more subdued— still talking, but running out of steam.

When I opened my eyes and peered out the window, morning had broken, and I could see that it was overcast. I got up slowly, trying to not wake Willow. As I walked over to the window, I checked my watch. It was eight thirty.

The street was empty except for a car or two passing by. A small ribbon of smoke was still rising off the campfire behind Sally's. All was quiet from the night before.

But I knew it would not be for long. It was going to be *Saturday Night Live* tonight.

As I looked out at the street below, morning brought some clarity about the previous night's events. I was homeless, and I knew it was really kind of John to let me stay here. But out this window I had seen much too much in one night. I had seen homeless men sitting by a campfire as if they were in a third-world country. I had seen a drug deal, an arrest, and a physical altercation.

While I desperately needed a roof over my head, I knew it could not be here, by this window, where I could see the homeless day and night. I could survive watching myself escape into my van in a church parking lot every evening, but seeing others walk the streets without hope every night was just too depressing.

I felt that sometime, in some way, some terrible thing was going to happen here.

I woke Willow from her sleep and rolled up my sleeping bag. I picked up the bag and Willow and left the room, locking the door behind me. I tiptoed down the stairs and unlocked the front door. There were six people, including Jake, sprawled out asleep on the porch. Some were covered only by their coats; some had no covers at all.

I quietly closed the door, took the key John had given me, and turned it carefully in the lock. I slipped the keys back into my pocket, making a mental note to return them as soon as I saw John again. I stepped gingerly over a woman lying directly in my path and then cautiously around another body draped precariously at the top of the steps. I made my descent and covered the short distance to Sally's parking lot. I got in the van and placed Willow on the seat.

Pulling out of the lot, I headed toward the water. A block and a half from Sally's, I passed the girders of the new government center rising five stories in the air. Then I turned right and passed the construction site of the million-dollar condos and the new convention center.

In that block and a half, I had traveled from one world to an entirely different one—and I didn't feel that I understood either of them.

Chapter 27

S'GHETTI

"Dear Lord, bless the hands that made this meal for all of us to share tonight," the minister began, after asking all the poor to bow their heads in prayer in the small basement of the Community Christian Church at the end of Warren Avenue in downtown Bremerton.

"Thank you, Lord God, for bringing us together to share our joys and concerns as we break bread," he continued. I raised my head a little to peek at him. He was a slim, older man, mostly bald except for a swish of graying hair that he combed over the top of his head. He had a gentle voice. "You are always with us in our time of need, and you lift us from the depths of despair," he continued. "God bless us all."

It was, thankfully, a short prayer. That was the kind the homeless liked—we were generally a hungry crew! The eighty or so of us who had crowded into the small basement that night lined up along the wall as three ladies began serving dinner from the metal trays covering the folding tables at the front of the room. It was a Friday, and the offered feast was fish sticks, macaroni and cheese, and apple pie.

C and I shuffled to the end of the line. We were not there by choice, but in an effort to prevent a potential legal problem for the fellow with us. Our friend Johnny's ex, Marion, had a restraining order against him, which involved so many feet of separation. Johnny was hoping his former lover would not be at this church dinner on this particular night.

But she was. Marion was at the front table.

Still, Johnny was hungry, so C was doing his utmost to keep the requisite distance between them and avert any contact between the two. He encouraged Johnny not to look, talk, or think about Marion—so, of course, Johnny had to look, talk, *and* think about her. "I know I was wrong to hit her, but she—"

"*Shuussh!*" said C, trying to position himself so that Marion could not see Johnny.

The line began moving forward at a steady pace as the ladies wielded their tongs and big serving spoons. "More fish sticks!" one server yelled out to the kitchen helper.

"Coming!" a voice yelled back from the kitchen.

By the time C, Johnny, and I reached the front of the line, the lady serving the fish sticks was frowning. A man from the kitchen had just dumped a fresh load of fish sticks on her serving tray, and they were burnt. "I'm sorry," she said, looking at us. "They burned the fish sticks." She began picking through the pile for the least damaged pieces. "They're only burnt on the bottom," she said. "Maybe you can scrape them off."

We all smiled and assured her they would be fine. Johnny and I then got our dinner portions, and C turned to scope out the situation in the room. Marion was sitting at a table in the middle on the right side. Her back was to C and Johnny.

"Okay, Johnny," C began, in his best conspiratorial tone. "We are going to hug the left side of the wall to the very last table back there. Do *not* look at Marion on the way. Stay right behind me. Then sit down, eat, and leave. We don't need any drama here in the basement of the church."

I fought back a chuckle as C, the peacemaker, took the lead, followed by Johnny and then me. We moved quickly to our table, carrying our burnt fish sticks, macaroni, and apple pie. I peeked over at Marion, who was peeking back. Then she smiled at me, acknowledging our effort to keep Johnny away, which I considered quite gracious under the circumstances. I breathed a huge sigh of relief, knowing all was going to be peaceful through this meal.

Yes, it was peaceful all right—if not entirely pleasant. C's strategy to keep Johnny in a safe place put us smack-dab across from one of the people we usually tried our hardest to avoid: Ted, the master of the grossest burps and belches in this ragtag traveling community. Everyone knew the burp would eventually embellish any mealtime gathering; we just didn't want to be too close when it did.

Tonight was no exception. We ate just as quickly as we could in an effort to be out of there before the inevitable occurred, but to no avail. I had just finished my last bite of apple pie when Ted lowered his head to his chest and the sound roared its way up from his depths, bringing all conversation in the room to a temporary halt. Then Ted pushed his chair back and left. Gradually the chatter around us resumed.

"I think I've lost my appetite," C muttered. "What do you say we get going, Richard?"

"I'm ready," I replied. "Need a ride, Johnny?"

"No, I'm going to hang out downtown. It's Friday night!" he answered.

"But you are going to stay away from you-know-who, right?" C more ordered than asked as he stood up.

"Oh, yeah," was Johnny's reply. He stood up and we all walked outside together. Then he said, "Thanks, guys," and began walking down the hill on 11th Street. C and I headed for the van, relieved for several reasons that this particular meal was over.

"Feel like going for a ride?" C asked after we got in the van.

I hesitated as I turned the key and looked at my gas gauge.

"Don't worry about gas," C said, reading my eyes and my mind. "I've got some gas money."

"Then sure," I said.

"Head out toward the fairgrounds on the east side," he said, as I put the van in gear. "It's not far," he added.

C leaned forward, squinting his eyes to focus on the radio. He picked a button and pushed it. It was 101.5, one of the rock channels from Seattle. "Great," he said as a song came on, and he began doing the imaginary drum routine I had come to know so well.

The taste of burnt fish sticks still filled my mouth, and I tried to clean my teeth and gums with my tongue as we drove. C's eyes were closed now, his head shaking back and forth and his feet stomping to the song. Then he lifted his head and opened his eyes. "Turn right at the next light," he instructed.

I did as he asked. "Up ahead—see that storage sign?" he asked.

"Mm-hmm . . ."

"Pull in there." I took a left into the driveway by the storage units. "Oh, good. The gate's open," said C. "Just go straight in—all the way to the back, by the fence."

I drove slowly over the speed bumps that dotted the path, past the steel-gray doors of the storage units, and stopped at the very end. We got out, and Willow, not to be left behind, jumped out after us. C walked to the end unit—number 33, put his ear to the door, and then knocked. "It's me, C," he said. "Anybody home?"

It took a few seconds, but then the door rose slowly. The bare feet, the torso, and then the face of a black woman came into view, and she broke into a smile. "C! It's good to see you," she said. Her eyes were flashing. Two young children stepped forward; they were boys who stood about waist high. "Everything okay?" she asked.

"Sure. Everything is fine!" C reassured her. "Has anyone been hassling you here?" he asked.

"No," she said. "We don't usually get back here until seven. The manager leaves at five."

"Oh," said C, "this is my friend, Richard. And this is his dog, Willow." Willow had already scooted inside, and the boys were petting her.

The woman stepped forward and wrapped me in a hug. "Glad to meet you, Richard. I'm Dorothea." Then she turned to the boys. "Boys, say hello to Mister Richard." To me she said, "This is Elijah, and this is Dustin. My two boys."

Dorothea was a large woman, with big arms sticking out from the sleeves of her print dress. Her hair was pulled back in a bun, held there by bobby pins.

Three sleeping bags were rolled out on a large piece of soiled foam rubber by one wall; clothes were folded neatly on top of cardboard boxes. A tarp covered something along the back wall.

An extension cord hung from a fixture in the ceiling that allowed for a plug and a light bulb. The cord looped down to two hot plates sitting on a small wooden table along the wall. One plate held a pan and the other a pot. Something was cooking. I walked over and sniffed. It smelled delicious.

Elijah noticed my interest. "We're having s'ghetti," he said, smiling.

"That's *spaghetti!*" his mother corrected. "Spah-get-ee." She said it one syllable at a time. "Now you say it," she instructed her son.

"S'ghetti!" he said.

Dorothea laughed. "Oh, you'll get it someday."

"We were just getting ready for dinner," she said, reaching for a spoon to stir the sauce. "I have plenty . . ." Her voice trailed off invitingly.

"Sure, I'll have a bite," C replied, politely.

"Richard?" Dorothea asked.

"It smells great," I replied. "But only if you really have plenty. We already had dinner."

"We have plenty," she assured us. "The boys eat like birds, and I made a lot." She went to work finishing dinner preparations. She poured water from a plastic jug into the pot and turned on the burner. Then she took a loaf of French bread out of its foil sleeve and began slicing it. She hummed as she went about her tasks.

Dustin and Elijah stood close to their mother. Dustin was restless, rocking back and forth with his hands clasped behind his back. Both were skinny as rails; Elijah wore blue jeans with a red T-shirt, and Dustin had on blue jeans with a yellow T-shirt. Dustin inched closer to Dorothea and put his arms around her leg.

"You boys have to give me some room, now, while I'm a-cookin'," she said, shooing them away.

C knew the boys needed something to do. "Dorothea and the boys have been gracious enough to stay here and guard my drums," he said, looking at me and then the boys.

"Your drums?" I asked. "What drums?"

"Play your drums!" Elijah said.

"Yeah, play the drums!" Dustin joined in.

C stepped to the back of the storage unit and pulled an old tarp off a full set of drums and cymbals. There was a bass drum, a pedal, two snare drums, and a drummer's stool. He tossed the tarp in the corner as Elijah and Dustin rushed over.

"You don't know how hard it is to keep those boys away from that drum set," Dorothea said.

C picked up the drumsticks lying on top of the snare drum and then sat down on the stool. "I picked these up on my way here from Portland. A drummer I met at the Salvation Army sold them to me. He was down on his luck and needed money for a bus ticket back to Michigan. I had them in the Armadillo for a while, but they were taking up all my living space. I got this storage space and thankfully bumped into Dorothea and the boys—and here we all are."

"Thank the Lord I met C," Dorothea said, snapping a handful of spaghetti in half and dropping it in the pot of now boiling water.

"Play something, C," begged Elijah. He was standing beside C with his hands clasped behind his back.

"Okay," C replied, hitting the big cymbal with his stick, making it clash. "Oh, what can I play that you boys know?" C rubbed his beard. "How about the Grateful Dead's *Casey Jones?* 'Trouble ahead, trouble behind . . .'"

The boys looked puzzled. "How about a rap song, C?" Dustin asked.

C took a deep breath, rubbing his chin again. "Okay, then." He pushed up the sleeves of his shirt and reached out his sticks to strike the drum. *Da-dump, da-dump . . . .* The sound echoed off the ceiling.

Dustin is my man. He's got the plan
to give the world all he can.
Da-dump, clash.
His brother, Elijah, is always there
and he's willin' to share.
Clash, da-dump, da-dump.
They're learn' to read and write
and never fight
and they hug their mother really tight.
Da-dump, da-dump.
Burma Shave.

Dorothea burst out laughing as C hit the cymbals and pounded the bass drum with his foot pedal.

Elijah had a question written all over his face. "What's Bur—burma Shave?" he asked.

C smiled. "I thought you might ask that," he replied. "Years ago, rappers used to put up signs along the side of the road. Usually five or six signs made up a simple poem, and the last sign always said Burma Shave—to punctuate the message *and* sell the shaving cream called Burma Shave."

"Oh," Elijah replied, still mystified. "Play some more."

"Okay," C said, now thoroughly into his musical debut. "Here's one you might know." He raised his foot and then lowered it to begin the next song. "It's called 'The Hokey-Pokey.'"

Dorothea paused in her stirring of the spaghetti sauce, dipped her finger in for a temperature test, and quickly put the spoon down.

"Wait a minute, C," she said. "Come here, boys; you, too, Richard."

We all walked toward her. "Now, join hands," she said. And we all did.

Then C began his song, striking the snare drum lightly. "You put your right foot in," he began, and Dorothea put her right foot forward and nodded for the boys to do the same. "You put your right foot out." She continued to model the movements. "You put your right foot in and you shake it all about." *Da-dump, da-dump.*

The boys and I followed Dorothea's lead as we did the dance. "You do the Hokey-Pokey and you turn yourself around," Dorothea began to sing with C, "that's what it's all about."

We did the left foot, the right hand, the left hand, and the whole self to the rhythm of C's drumming.

"Oh, my goodness!" Dorothea exclaimed, placing her left hand on her chest. "All that dancing just wore me out."

Elijah blurted, "Let's do it again!"

"No, it's time for dinner, boys. Fill the pan and wash your hands."

"Okay, mama," replied Dustin. He took a small metal pan from along the wall and filled it with water from the plastic milk jug. He washed his hands and Elijah did the same, while their mother got five paper plates from a box below the little table on which she was cooking. The boys stood beside her as she handed them each a plate. Then she dipped a big spoon into the pot and pulled out the pasta for Elijah's plate and repeated the process for Dustin.

"Hold them out straight, boys," she said, as she ladled a spoon of sauce onto each of the piles of pasta. She then stuck a white plastic fork into each pile and said, "Take those plates to our guests, boys. And then come back for yours." The boys walked quickly over to serve us our dinner. "Don't drop them," she warned.

"Oh, I forgot the bread," Dorothea added, pulling two pieces of French bread off the loaf. Elijah and Dustin delivered our bread and hurried back for their own plates.

C used the swiveling stool from his drum set as a seat, and I sat down on the edge of one of the sleeping bags. I twisted my fork in the spaghetti and carefully guided it to my mouth. "Excellent!" I said.

"Thank you," Dorothea responded. "It's Paul Newman's sauce."

"Four star, definitely," C said.

"Fine casual dining in an out-of-the-way location," I added.

"An *intimate* location," C corrected me.

"Yes. Yes, that's better," I said.

"Where the specialty of the house is 'S'ghetti,'" C said

Dorothea chuckled as she listened to the banter, serving up dinner for her sons.

C lifted an abundant forkful of food to his mouth and dropped half of it in his lap. He scraped it up and aimed for his mouth again. "How's the job going at the motel?" he asked Dorothea, as he wiped some of the sauce off his pants and licked the fingers clean.

"Oh, it's okay," she said. "I get the boys up and we get dressed, and they catch the bus for school in front of the Catholic Church, and then I get the bus across town to the Howard Johnson. That bus stops a lot, so it takes about an hour.

"Check-out time is eleven at the motel, so I'm busy cleaning the rooms and changing sheets from then till four. It's mostly navy boys who stay there, and whew, those guys are messy." She shook her head.

"Okay, boys, here's some bread," she said, putting a piece of bread on each of their plates. "Now go sit down and eat *all* your dinner." The boys found seats on their sleeping bags, and Willow sat down between them. She began making eye contact for a possible handout.

"There are three Filipino women and me," Dorothea said, continuing about the motel. "They've got us on a timer to get the rooms cleaned as fast as possible. I got twenty-five hours last week, which was good. But they don't get much business. They got two hundred rooms, but they're lucky to fill fifty most nights. The rumor is it's going to close. That's what the girls say. If I have a good week, I bring home a hundred and ten or twenty with tips, and that goes fast with food to buy, my medicine, and bus fares.

"But we got it better than some people. There was a family staying at the motel last week—a man and a woman and two kids. Some church put them up for three nights. They were always there. They didn't have any money to go any place. They had some canned stuff from the food bank—ravioli and stuff. The father was handicapped . . . kinda slow, if you know what I mean."

Dorothea took a bite of her spaghetti and looked at her boys. "Elijah, you've got spaghetti sauce all over your face." She reached for a roll of paper towels and handed a couple of sheets to him. "Wipe your mouth. Here's some for you too, Dustin," she added. C didn't escape her attention either. "C, don't wipe your mouth on your shirt!" Dorothea laughed as she tossed the roll of paper towels to him. C peeled off a piece and then handed the roll to me.

"I felt so bad for them," Dorothea said. On the day they had to leave, she said she could tell by the look in their eyes that they had no place to go. The church had run out of money for the room. "The girls took up a collection, and we gave them our tips. Twenty bucks is all we had," she said.

Dorothea, who had been standing as she ate and talked, finally sat down next to the boys on the sleeping bag. "Oh, it feels good to get off my feet," she said. Willow moved over beside the lady and looked at her plate. "What's the dog's name?" she asked.

"Willow," I said. "I call her the Wonder Dog."

"We had a little dog back in Mississippi where I grew up," Dorothea said. "His name was Shorty, and he was the meanest little son of a gun." The miles and the years showed in her eyes when she laughed. Then she pulled out a piece of spaghetti and offered it to Willow. "Here you are, Wonder Dog," she said. Willow gobbled up the treat.

"We need a dog, Mommy," Elijah interjected.

"Oh, heavens," said Dorothea. "We can barely feed ourselves right now." She looked at C and added, "Someday, maybe. Someday when we get a home again—a home with a fenced yard so the dog can be outside in the grass and be safe."

"How's it coming on that housing list?" C asked.

"You mean with the Housing Authority?" Dorothea laughed and raised her eyes to the ceiling. "We were number 5,700 two months ago, and we're number 5,700 now! They told me it was going to be a year or two for us to get to the top of the list."

"A year or two?" C sounded incredulous.

"I went into the office just last week again, after work, and they said they couldn't tell me anymore *where* I was on the list," Dorothea said. "They told me they have a new policy in place. They said I could look up my position online at home anytime. Heck, I don't have no computer to go online. I don't have no phone. I don't even have no home."

It was the first hint of despair I had heard in her voice, and I sensed that she worked very hard to keep her attitude up for the boys.

I saw Elijah looking at me, seeming to question my place in his world.

"How old are you now, Elijah?" I asked, responding to his gaze.

"Nine," he answered. "Nine years old."

"How do you like school?"

"Good."

"And what's your favorite subject?"

Elijah lifted his head and then lowered it quickly to punctuate his answer. "Geography!"

"Why geography?" I asked.

"I want to be like Harry *Potter*," he said, nodding his chin again to accentuate the word. "I want to ride a big train and go to a big castle. I would become a great wizard!"

"So, your mother has been reading *Harry Potter* to you," C commented.

"C gave us that book," Dorothea told me.

"I want to go to England, Russia, Africa, and—uh, uh—China," Elijah said.

"You have big dreams," his mother said.

C looked at me. "Richard, have you ever been to any of those places?"

"I have," I said. "I've been to England, Africa, and China, but not Russia.

"Wow," said Elijah. His eyes were wide with wonder.

"How about you, Dustin?" I asked. "What's your favorite subject?"

The younger boy clenched his lips together and hunched at the shoulders before looking at his mother.

"Dustin is a little shy," she explained. "He's not quite eight yet. What do you like about school?" she prodded.

"Lunch," he said, eliciting a laugh from all of us.

"What's so good?" C asked.

"Ummm . . . toasted cheese sandwiches and—um, pickles." He broke into a wide smile, followed by a giggle.

The conversation lulled as we all got serious about eating.

In the quiet, I mused. How and why, I wondered, did this mother with two children end up living in a storage unit? With half the hotel and motel rooms in town empty every night and twenty or thirty empty buildings within five or ten minutes of here, why was there no room for them? C and I were—well, we were street people. C seemed to like his life. And I—well, I'd had a lot, and I'd lost a lot. But I had ridden the big trains from Rome to Venice, stayed in the turret room of the Castle de Mercure outside Avignon in France, and known dreams and fantasies to come true.

I had no dreams now. There was no magical feeling. And if there were a wizard, I would wish him to appear and wave his wand over me and ease me into a peaceful sleep, forever—never to return.

But Dustin? Dustin still had dreams—dreams fostered by his mother's reading by the beam of a flashlight in a cold, dark storage unit. He wanted to travel to Hogwarts and stand beside Harry Potter and learn the excitement of using human powers for the common good, for love and community. Maybe together Dustin and Harry could wave their magic wands so children would not ever again have to live in storage units like this.

Dorothea took another strand of spaghetti and held it out for Willow. "I've got some dessert tonight," she said, pushing herself up from the floor. "Do you want the rest of this, pretty girl?" she asked, looking at Willow and holding out her plate. "Oh, is that okay?" she asked me.

"Sure," I said.

So she put the paper plate on the floor, and Willow began licking up the meat sauce. Dorothea walked over to a paper bag near the door and reached down to pull out a package. "Butterscotch pudding!" she exclaimed, holding up small containers of the pudding. She returned, handing one to each of us. "You are going to have to use your forks," she said. "I am all out of plastic spoons."

I looked at the smile on her face and the love in her eyes. I marveled at her ability to make a home for herself and her family here in unit number 33. And I wondered how much longer she was going to be able to hold it together living here, where most people stash the stuff they don't need or want or cherish any longer.

"Dustin?" Dorothea's voice got my attention. "Do you have to go?"

We all looked at the boy, who was now holding both hands in front of his pants and squeezing his legs together. He nodded. "Can you hold it just a little while longer?" she asked. He nodded again.

"We had better get down to the 76 station on the corner," Dorothea said.

"I can get you down there in the van," I said.

"Great." Dorothea smiled her appreciation. "Grab your toothbrushes, boys," she said to them. "We might as well get ready for bed."

The boys scurried to get their toothbrushes out of their school backpacks and put them in their jeans pockets.

"You can put your plates in this paper bag," Dorothea said, picking up a bag and handing it to C. We quickly tossed in our plates and forks. "We will take that along and toss the trash in the dumpster at the 76. They have been pretty good to us down there, letting us get cleaned up and use the bathroom."

Dorothea quickly unplugged the hot plates and grabbed two washcloths and stuffed them in a large purse that she tossed over her shoulder. It was with a sense of urgency that we all piled into the van and drove as quickly as possible to the 76 station.

"We've got to get cleaned up and then get back to read *Harry Potter*, say our prayers, and get to sleep so we're ready for school and work in the morning," Dorothea said, as we pulled into the filling station. I came to a stop and turned off the engine. "Thank you for coming by," she said. She and the boys stepped out of the van. "Dustin, you had better get to the bathroom!" He dashed into the building, with Elijah right behind.

"Thanks for dinner," C said.

"That was the best s'ghetti I ever had," I added, laughing.

Dorothea broke into a big smile, then turned and rushed off to catch up with the boys.

I put my hand on the ignition key, but then stopped. I sat there a moment thinking. I had changed my wish for the wizard's wand. It wasn't about me anymore. Now I wanted the magic wand to take Dorothea and her boys to a home of their own, a home with a stove, a refrigerator, a TV, beds, lights, and toys.

"There's nothing you can do, unless you've got a few thousand in your wallet," C said, adding gently, "Maybe someday you can."

I turned to look at him and saw the deepest sadness in his eyes. There was nothing I could say.

C motioned to me to turn the key, and I smiled. "Engage, Scotty," he said.

"Aye, aye, Captain."

Chapter 28

BANK OF AMERICA

A fine drizzle was falling as I pulled out of the Episcopal church parking lot, where I'd spent the night. I turned into the sweeping exit lane that merged into Wheaton Way, one of the main four-lane thoroughfares through town. It was lined with pawnshops, quick-money branches, and fast-food stops—shrines of Americana. I wouldn't be welcome at any of these establishments this cold, wet morning—not with a mere fifty cents in my pocket. I had overslept and missed the eight-o'clock breakfast call at Sally's.

With no specific destination in mind, I was just cruising along, following where the road led me. As I passed Money Tree, I saw the unmistakable figure of one of my friends from Sally's. He was walking as quickly as he could along the sidewalk.

Randy's black nylon raincoat and black hair were soaking wet as he dragged his club foot and swung his deformed left arm to help propel himself forward through the rain. He was carrying his small black gym bag in his right hand.

I hoped Randy had not seen me as I passed. I wasn't in much of a mood for his company this morning. I had given him dozens of rides down this road after many breakfasts at Sally's. With some frequency Randy would carefully observe my actions at breakfast, and when it appeared I was near my last sip of coffee, he would struggle to get nearer to me, and with a sad look on his face he would ask, "Richard, can I talk to you?" I would always say, "Sure." Then he would lean even closer and ask, "Could you give me a ride to the tire center?"

It was hard—well, impossible, really—to say no to Randy, because when I said yes, he would break into a great toothy smile. And I knew how much a ride—and that ride in particular—meant to Randy. It was a two-mile trek to his destination, mostly uphill, across the usually windy Warren Avenue Bridge. It would be a workout even for an able-bodied person, and for Randy it was doubly so.

I knew that as soon as he got in the van he would toss his gym bag on the running board, pat Willow on the head, and then lean toward me and ask, ever so politely, if it was okay if he changed the radio station. I would always nod hesitantly as he took his good hand and punched the buttons to his favorite country-and-western station. And at the first few chords of that distinctive whine and twang, he would begin tapping his deformed hand against his knee, keeping the rhythm and wearing a big grin.

I don't cotton to country. Fact is, from the days of Ferlin Husky and Patsy Cline to today, I could count on one hand the country warbles I've enjoyed, and most of those came from the lungs of Dolly Parton. I was sure the world had more than enough songs about Ford pickup trucks, coon hounds, whisky drinkin', and true love lost in Laredo. I was more of a Rolling Stones man.

I would steel myself as Randy reached over to turn up the volume on a song that was playing, like "High in a tree on the top of the hill . . ." Then Randy would say, "That's Randy Travis! He stole my name," and he would smile at me.

I knew that as soon as we pulled into the tire center parking lot, Randy would peer out the window, looking for his friends who worked there. Men in matching blue pants and short-sleeved white shirts, with their first names embroidered on an egg-shaped emblem sewn over their hearts, would welcome Randy with a wave or a nod. "He's got my name on his shirt," Randy once proudly pointed out to me, as a man with "Randy" on his shirt pushed a bald tire out of the garage and around to the "dead pile" at the side of the building.

Gene, Bob, Roy, and Randy would let Randy hang out awhile every morning while they used their pressure drills to remove lug nuts and change tires, all to the blaring sounds of country music. "I wish I could work there, but I can't," Randy told me one morning as we pulled into the tire center lot. "I can't," he repeated, pointing to his bad hand. But the men also let Randy watch a little television and drink the complimentary coffee in the waiting room, and they joked with him when they weren't busy balancing tires or aligning front ends. After an hour or so, Randy would sense that the men wanted him to leave, and he would walk up the street to K-Mart. He would hang out at the back of the store and play the free-demonstration computer games until one of the "associates" started giving him that you-just-can't-be-here look. And after Randy had worn out his welcome there, he would walk back down the hill, dragging his foot, and try to get back to Sally's in time for lunch. Randy would spend the afternoon walking around town, searching for snipes in ashtrays and coins on the ground.

I remembered C pointing out one day at breakfast that some might call Randy a little slow, while others might say he was a bit off. "Someone told me that someone told *them* that Randy ran away a couple of times and lived in the woods," C reported. "But he couldn't make it on his own, and he moved back in with his mom. But that's what someone told someone, who told someone, and, well, now I'm telling someone something I really don't know about someone else."

I found that while Randy may not know who Dick Cheney and Alan Greenspan were, he sure knew Tim McGraw and Garth Brooks, as well as the words to all their country songs.

Randy seemed to be ahead of his daily schedule this morning. It was just nine thirty, and he'd already left the tire center. I wondered if the men had kicked him out. As the stoplight at the corner was changing, I peeked in my rearview mirror to see if he had spotted me, and, well, yes, he had. He was waving his bad hand and calling out frantically, "Hey, Richard! Richard! Wait! Wait!"

Randy reached the side of the van just as the signal was changing to green, and he pressed his sad, wet face to the window. "Richard? Can I get a ride?"

"Hop in," I replied, motioning him in. Randy used his good hand to open the door, tossed his gym bag on the floor, and maneuvered his clubfoot into the van. "BEEEEEEEEEEP!" A woman behind me leaned on her horn as Randy got the rest of his body into the van and closed the door. I hit the gas.

"You're soaking wet, Randy."

"You missed breakfast this morning," Randy replied. "I looked for you."

"Yeah. I overslept," I explained.

"I was hopin' you'd be there." he said. "Would it be okay if I changed the radio?"

"Sure. It's okay," I said. He reached over and pressed the buttons, searching for his favorite station. "Where can I drop you off?" I asked as I braced for the first notes of country twang.

Instead, there was an advertisement on the airwaves. "This is Ray Vincent of American Equity Mortgage," the announcer said. "Are you tired of making interest payments of eight to ten percent?"

"I'm going to the bank," Randy said, over the radio ad. He smiled, placed his wet gym bag on his lap, and unzipped it. Then he reached in and pulled out a check. "It's my birthday today, Richard," he said.

"Well, happy birthday, Randy," I said.

"Randy at the tire center gave me a check for twenty dollars to buy me a new radio headset at K-Mart! Then I can listen to country music all day!" Randy was gushing.

"That's great, Randy," I said. "What bank are you going to?"

"Bank of America!" Randy said, showing me his check. He pointed up the street in the direction of the nearest branch.

The mortgage company ad on the radio came to an end with its little jingle, "American Equity Mortgage, the future is up to yooooooouuuu!"

As we motored down the boulevard, a country song began: "American girls and American guys, we'll always stand up and salute."

"I love this song," Randy said, leaning forward and turning up the volume. "This is Toby Keith," he added, beginning to rock back and forth to the beat of the song. The Old-Glory-and-Uncle-Sam lyrics were interspersed with Randy's own special brand of patriotic commentary. Both ceased as we pulled into the Bank of America parking lot.

As soon as we came to a stop, Randy opened the door, swung his good foot out, and dragged his bad foot behind him.

"Would you come in with me, Richard?" he asked. "In case I have trouble?"

"You won't have any trouble, Randy," I assured him. "The check is drawn on this bank, so they'll cash it for sure." I paused, reading the uncertainty all over his face. "But if you want me too, I will."

"Please," Randy said.

"Okay." I set the parking brake and got out of the van. I was hoping they might have some complimentary coffee inside.

We were in luck. I spotted a coffee thermos and cups, and even a plate of cookies, on a small table. Randy got in the teller line while I grabbed a cup of coffee and a cookie. When I walked over to join him, he was wearing a big grin of anticipation. "I used to have a headset, but somebody stole it," he said, looking at me. "I can't wait to get a new one!"

It didn't take long for Randy to get to the teller. "I'd like to cash this, please," he said, passing the check to her.

The lady accepted the check and then looked at Randy. "Do you have an account with us, sir?" she asked.

"No," said Randy.

"We just need to see a picture ID, then," she said, turning the check over and preparing to write down his information.

Randy picked up the gym bag he had dropped on the floor and held it in place with his bad hand while he unzipped it. His face began to contort into that forlorn look he often wore. He reached into the bag and pulled out some of its contents, one piece at a time, and placed them on the counter. First came a small plastic bag, half-filled with the snipes he collected. Then a muffin left over from breakfast at Sally's. Then a rumpled newspaper he had probably fished out of the trash on the way here. "Here it is," he said, breaking into a triumphant smile. He pulled out his bus pass, complete with picture, and pushed it across the counter to the teller. "It was at the bottom of my bag all the time."

The teller looked at Randy, looked at the pass, and then looked back at Randy. I watched her as she compared Randy's picture to the real-life Randy with the same scrutiny she would use on a suspected terrorist. Her name was Mary Lou, according to the American-flag nametag pinned to her blouse.

"This pass expired some time ago," the teller said. "Do you have another picture ID? We need two picture IDs to cash a check for a non-customer."

Randy turned to me with a sad look in his eyes.

"Geez, it's his birthday," I began. "And one of the guys up at the tire center gave him twenty bucks to buy himself a present. The man who gave him the check has an account here. It's a small check. Couldn't you just cash it for him?"

"I'm sorry, sir, but our bank rules require two picture IDs to cash a check," she said, matter-of-factly. "We cannot cash this check without proper identification."

Randy lowered his eyes to the floor.

"How about the manager?" I asked. "Could she approve it? It's only a twenty-dollar check."

"You can try," Mary Lou said, pointing to a lady standing at the credenza in the center of the bank.

"Come on, Randy," I said, motioning to him to follow me.

The manager was holding a brochure and pointing to its contents with her red-white-and-blue pencil as she spoke with a customer. Randy grabbed his snipes, his muffin, and his newspaper and put them back into his gym bag. He limped along behind me. We got in line to see the manager, and I tried to help him relax with some small talk. "Well, Randy, how old are you today?" I asked.

"Twenty-five," he answered, smiling.

"You were born in Bremerton?" I asked, keeping my eye on the manager.

"I've lived here all my life," he said.

"Would you like to move anyplace else?" I asked.

"I don't know," Randy said hesitantly. "I've never been anywhere else."

The manager closed the brochure and handed the customer her business card. I cleared my throat in preparation for pleading Randy's case to her. She smiled at me and nodded for us to approach.

"Hello. My friend Randy here got a twenty-dollar check for his birthday from his friend up the street at the tire center," I began. "And because Randy really doesn't have any picture ID other than his bus pass, we're having trouble cashing the check. The check is from a man who has an account at your bank," I added.

"Let me see the check," the manager said. The nametag pinned to her blue-blazer lapel read "Marilyn." Randy handed her the check; she looked at it, then asked to see the bus pass. Randy took it out of his pocket, and the manager took it from his good hand. She held up the bus pass, looked at it, looked at Randy, and looked back at the pass again before returning it to Randy. "Did our teller explain our rules about cashing a non-customer check?" she asked.

"She told us we needed two picture IDs," I said.

Manager Marilyn nodded. "I can't cash this check. The bus pass is expired, and we really need a driver's license, a MasterCard with a picture on it, or a passport." She handed the check back to Randy.

"Well, I thought because it was his birthday, and, well, since it was such a small check, you might cash it for him," I said.

"It's nice that it is his birthday, but this is a Bank of America rule," she announced.

I realized at that moment that Randy and I were financial lepers— third-class citizens, untouchables. The bankers—the keepers of the cash— had created a colony where all the lepers with no ID or a credit score of under 300 must go and live out their days. Off somewhere in banking land, rules had been made, printed, and sent out across the country to protect investors from all the Randys and their twenty-dollar checks.

I thought if I could just talk to the rule makers, I could tell them about Randy and plead his case. I could tell them it was his birthday. I could tell them how badly he wanted that radio headset. I could tell them of his open face, his innocence, his smile. If they could just see his face, surely they would not need two pieces of picture ID.

"Can you give me the phone number of the bank president?" I asked Manager Marilyn. She seemed quite stunned by my request. I forged ahead. "I'm sure if I talked to him or her, I could get approval to cash this check for Randy."

"You want to speak to the president of the bank?" she asked.

"Yes," I replied.

"I doubt he will talk to you," she replied, coldly. I began to see the you-are-wasting-my-valuable-time look sweep across her face.

I wished so hard that I had the words to change this woman's mind. I wondered what it would take to "free her doubtful mind and melt her cold, cold heart."

And then the cowboy in me came calling. I saddled my emotional horse and got ready to ride in the name of the true Red, White, and Blue. "You know, Randy here can't get a driver's license," I began again, "because he can't drive. He's got a deformed hand and a deformed foot. Randy doesn't have the money to get a picture MasterCard or Visa, and he can't afford a passport. He has never been out of this town. What he does have is a small birthday check he wants to get cashed. You know, the last time I was in New York, I visited the Statue of Liberty, and on the side of that dear lady it says, 'Give me your tired, your poor, your huddled masses yearning to breathe free, the wretched refuse of your teaming shore. Send these, the homeless, tempest-tost to me. I lift my lamp beside the golden door!' That's what America is supposed to be about."

I could see that I had struck the wrong chord with Manager Marilyn, as her face began to turn a crimson shade that matched the stylish scarf she wore around her neck. Her eyes widened, and I knew she wanted to have her boots go walkin'—all over me. She reached for a brochure on the counter beside her, circled something with her red-white-and-blue pen, and handed it to me. "If you have any complaints, you can call that 800 number," she said, turning brusquely from the credenza and heading for her glass-enclosed office.

She picked up her phone. I figured she was calling the cops to take Randy and me to Folsom Prison.

I had little hope that other bankers would be any better at breaking the stranglehold of corporate regulations, but, for Randy, I had to make the effort. "Come on, Randy," I said. "Let's try someplace else." Randy stuck the check back in his pocket and followed me out the door.

Randy was shattered and looking sad, sad, sad as we got into the van. "How about we go back to the tire center and ask Randy to give you cash?" I asked him

"He didn't have any cash this morning," replied Randy, as I started the engine. "That's why he gave me the check."

"Then how about we take the check back to Randy and ask him to bring you cash tomorrow?"

"Today's my birthday," Randy said, simply.

Randy had given me quite rational answers to my two questions. As I pulled back onto the boulevard, I decided I needed a financial advisor to help solve this problem. I headed for the Armadillo.

Randy managed a smile as another American Equity Mortgage ad came to an end with its now familiar refrain of ". . . the future belongs to yooooouuuu!" and another country song began with "Well, it's a long way to Richmond, rollin' north on 95 . . ."

"That's 'Modern-Day Bonnie and Clyde,' by Travis Tritt," Randy said.

Thankfully, it only took a few minutes to get to the Armadillo, and Tritt was in his last few bars—the redhead having now become a sheriff— ending with an insightful "Yeah—whoa—well—woo-hoo."

I pulled up to C's abode on wheels next to Allen's Mini-Mart, only to see a note written on an old paper bag tacked to the door. I left the engine running, so Randy could enjoy his music, and stepped out to read the message: "Gone on a Mexican cruise. C." I chuckled, pretty sure the note meant C had gone ten rounds with Jose Cuervo and was sleeping it off.

An idea formed in my brain. Maybe Allen would cash the check. Then I thought, "Naw; he probably doesn't even know Randy." But I was desperate. I needed to get away from the country music before I became bow-legged, got yearnin' for a pair of boots, and started calling everyone "Y'all." Heck, the worst Allen could do was say no, and we had just been through that with the biggest bank in the world.

I turned off the engine. "Randy, come along with me," I said. "Let's see if we might cash that check in the store."

Once inside, we found Allen at his usual station on the stool at the end of the counter. I walked over to the bell by the cash register and hit it once. Allen hopped off the stool and stood before us.

"Hello," I began. "This is Randy, and it's his birthday today. We have this check he got for a present, and he would like to cash it."

Allen just looked at us.

"Give him the check, Randy," I said.

Randy reached into his pocket handed the check to Allen.

Allen held it up and looked at it. "It is good?" the Chinese man asked.

"Yes," I said, nodding my head.

"You have to buy something," Allen said.

This sounded hopeful. I turned to Randy and asked, "Randy, what do you want?"

Randy looked at the displays on the counter. He reached out and picked up a package of Starbursts and put it down in front of Allen.

"Sixty-nine cents," Allen said, hitting the button to open the cash register. He quickly placed the check in the drawer and took out a handful of cash. "Ten," he said, laying a ten-dollar bill on the counter. "Fifteen," he said, laying down a five. "Sixteen, seventeen, eighteen, nineteen, and thirty-one cents," he said, counting out the rest of Randy's change. "Happy birthday." He walked back to his stool, sat down, and crossed his arms.

Randy smiled. He began to pick up his change with his good hand. Then he stopped, as something in the glass case beside the cash register caught his eye. There, in the case, next to several decorative knives with dragons engraved on the handles, was a headset radio. "That's what I want!" Now Randy was smiling all over.

I leaned forward to see if I could find a price on the headset, but I couldn't see one.

The ever-vigilant Allen hopped off his stool and walked back to the cash register. He hit a key on the cash machine and the drawer opened. He took a small key from one of the compartments and stuck it in the lock on the back of the display case, releasing the door. He reached in and picked up the radio in question. "Twelve ninety-nine," he said, holding it up to Randy.

"Does it have batteries?" Randy asked.

Allen turned it over and looked at the writing on the package, then nodded an affirmative to Randy.

"That's cheaper than K-Mart, Richard," Randy said to me. "I'll take it!" he said triumphantly to Allen, and he put his money back down on the counter.

Allen counted out the money from Randy's nineteen dollars and thirty-one cents and pushed the remaining change and the headset radio across the counter.

"I've still got some money left," Randy said, picking up his change and putting it in the pocket of his jeans.

Randy tried to open the package right away. He held the case steady with his deformed hand and attempted to pull the plastic off with his good hand, but it seemed to be a losing battle. He looked up at me at last and said, "Could you help me, Richard?"

"Sure," I said, taking the package from him. I pulled on one corner of the package, and I pushed on the other, trying to pry the headset from the plastic. I turned the package over, looking for a penetrable seam, muttering, "I don't know why they make these blasted things so hard to open." Then I heard a click from behind the counter. Allen was standing there holding a long knife similar to the ones inside the glass case. It was a switchblade, and he held it up toward the ceiling, the metal gleaming in the light. He held out his hand without a word, and I placed the package in it. In seconds, Allen cut the headset free from its plastic protection, handed it to Randy, and tossed the plastic away. He folded up the blade of the knife and stuck it in his pocket with the dexterity of a gang member.

"Thank you, mister," Randy said to Allen, and I nodded my thanks as well. Allen headed back for his stool and we headed for the door.

Outside, Randy put his gym bag down on the ground. He held the headset against his chest with his deformed hand and widened the adjustable arms to fit his head. Then he turned the channel knob to where he thought his country station might be and held the headset to his ear. He fiddled with the knob until his station came through loud and clear, and then he slipped the headset over his head.

And he beamed.

I beamed, too.

I let him enjoy the moment. After a bit, I asked in a loud voice, "You want me to drop you off someplace, Randy?"

He pushed the headset back off his ears until it fell onto his neck. "No, I think I'll take a walk," he replied.

"Okay then," I said. "Well, I'll see you later." I started walking back to the van.

"Hey, Richard?" he called. I turned. "Thank you."

"You're welcome."

As I got in the van, I watched Randy put the headset back over his ears and pick up his gym bag. He started walking toward the bowling alley up the street. "I'll bet he's going looking for snipes," I said to myself.

The drizzle had stopped, so I started the car and rolled the windows down. It was then that I heard the singing. It was Randy, walking up the street, singing at the top of his lungs to a tune on his radio.

Chapter 29

HERO LOST

Major Baker was treating the homeless to an after-lunch movie in Sally's chapel. As I entered, he was leaning over to make sure the film reel was threaded properly in the projector. I took a seat in the back pew. It was a plain little room—a sanctuary from the elements. There was a bite in the cold breeze outside. It was now late October, and winter was fast approaching. I figured that most of the audience, like me, was here to stay warm and dry for an hour or so, at least as much as for the entertainment value of the film.

Surveying the room, I spotted C sitting in the front, right next to the screen, which was placed before the small altar. He was chatting with a young man I had not seen before.

The Major stood up and adjusted his glasses, which perpetually slipped down his nose and had to be pushed back in place. He appeared to be satisfied that everything was in order for the show, and he walked quickly to the front of the little room.

"Thank you all for coming," he said. "Please bow your heads for a short prayer." The Major bowed his head and clasped his hands together, and everyone in the chapel bowed with him. "Dear Lord, thank you for this time together," he prayed. "Thank you for your many blessings. Keep us all safe from harm and show us the way. Amen." Then he began walking back down the center aisle toward the projector.

"Okay, the movie is *The Passion of the Christ*," he announced as he walked. "I think you will like it." He flipped the switch on the projector and the movie started rolling.

It was warm in the chapel. I unlaced my wet tennis shoes and slipped my feet out of them. It felt good.

We were probably about a third of the way through the movie, with the scenes flashing back and forth from love to hate and from tenderness to brutality, when I thought to myself, "Leave it to Mel Gibson to give us a bloody close-up of Jesus." When the Roman guards were lashing Jesus for the third time, I was looking for Danny Glover to come barging through the doors with guns blazing to drag Jesus to safety.

But the beatings went on and on.

I knew C could not take much more of this, and, sure enough, a few seconds later he got up from his seat and made his way slowly along the aisle by the wall; the flickering lights from the projector created a silhouette that preceded him. C saw me in the dim light and slid into the pew beside me. He leaned in close and cupped his hand over his mouth. "I give it one kernel," he whispered.

I was grateful for the comic relief. He leaned over again. "I liked the book much better," he whispered. I grinned again and nodded.

A few minutes passed as we watched the movie together. But I could tell by the way C was moving his feet and looking around the room (like a small child bored in church) that he would be leaving soon. Finally, he leaned in to me once again and whispered, "I've got to get out of here. I'll see you around." And off he went.

I stayed to watch Jesus be nailed to the cross, rise from the dead three days later, and leave this world a hero—lost, but not forgotten.

The credits were rolling when the Major turned on the lights. Five or six heads popped into sight, as men who had been lying down on the hard wooden pews were jarred from their sleep.

I could see the tears in the Major's eyes as he walked over to flip off the projector. He was, after all, a man of God—a believer. He had dedicated himself to this life—this serving and saving. I could picture him praying for us in the morning and before going to sleep at night.

I could only hope that his God was listening. It would be hard to refuse a man like the Major.

"Thank you for coming," said the Major in a loud voice. "Don't forget—we will show the movie again tomorrow; tell your friends!" He gazed at us with great depth and sincerity.

The crowd began to meander out of the chapel and into the wind and cold. We had no place to go, and it was a Tuesday, the only night of the week that no church in town served a free meal. I, too, made my way toward the exit. Just as I cracked open the big metal door to the outside, I heard a voice calling out, "Hey, mister! Hey, Richard!"

I let go of the door, and the howling wind shut it again quickly. I turned back to see a tall young man walking briskly toward me. He was a burly lad with red hair and a short red beard. He said, "Richard? C and a couple other guys here told me you have a car and might give me a ride."

"Where do you need to go? Which way?" I asked.

"Out that way," he said, pointing north. "Out by the edge of town. I've got a couple of bucks I can give you for gas," he offered.

"Sure," I said. "Come on." I pushed the door open again. The wind was whipping as we rushed to the van. Willow greeted me and hopped into my lap as the young man opened the passenger door and got in. Willow had waited patiently while I was gone, but now she was cold, so I opened my jacket and wrapped it around her so she could share my body heat.

The young man extended his right hand to me. "My name is Matthew; people call me Matt," he said. "That must be your dog, eh?"

"Yes, this is Willow," I said, reaching out to return his handshake. He had a strong grip.

A powerful gust of wind buffeted the van, and an old newspaper, a trash bag, and a cloud of city dust blew across the windshield.

"The people at my table at lunch were talking about you and Willow," Matt said. "You guys are famous."

"Famous?" I asked skeptically.

"Yeah! They told me you're writing a book," he said. "They're all excited about it. They said it's about homeless people; they all want to be in it."

"Well, I'm sorry to disappoint them," I replied, "but it's not much of a book, really. I've pretty much given up on it; it was just a dream. I've been writing at picnic tables in parks around town when it's not raining and when the wind isn't blowing like this. But winter's coming on. I'll probably end up throwing it in the dumpster."

"Hell, you can't give up now," the young man said. "All the people at Sally's are praying for you. They're expecting a book! The guy they call C—well, he told me about you. He said that you and your dog have been living in your car for about a year now."

"More than that, actually," I said, still clutching Willow tightly inside my coat to warm her up. But she knew better than I did when she was warm enough, and she wriggled free and hopped into Matt's lap.

"What a wonderful little dog," he said, smiling and stroking her head and back. "I used to have a golden retriever when I lived in Los Angeles."

I turned the ignition key and backed out of the parking space at Sally's. "So, we're heading north?" I asked as I headed down the alley to the main drag.

"Yep," Matt confirmed. He reached into his jeans pocket and handed me a couple of wadded-up dollar bills. "I'm heading up to the woods. There's a camp the guys call The Hilton. You know where that is?"

"I know exactly where it is," I said. We turned north onto the thoroughfare and sped up.

"I was sleeping in my car until a couple nights ago," Matt said. "I was parked on a side street that looked safe, but somebody stole my car. All my clothes were in it. I just got here a week ago from L.A."

EEEeeeEEEeeeEEEeeeEEEeee—the sound of sirens could be heard in the distance as we were crossing the Warren Avenue Bridge. I looked up to check the rearview mirror and saw two fire trucks coming on fast. The traffic in front of us began pulling over to let the trucks pass, and we did the same. One truck sped past, then the other.

"That's what I used to ride," Matt said, as I was pulling back into traffic and picking up speed.

"Really?" I was surprised—and a little incredulous.

"Yeah, I used to be a fireman in L.A.," he said. "Just a few years ago."

"What brought you up here?" I asked.

"Oh, it's a long story," he said, seeming reticent.

EEEeeeEEEeeeEEEeee—another siren. A fire engine was on our tail, with a medic unit close behind. The traffic again pulled over to let both vehicles rush by.

"Must be a big fire," said Matt.

"Ever been in a really big fire?" I asked.

"Oh, yes. Too many, really."

"Ever save anybody's life?"

"Yeah—people, cats, and dogs."

"So, you are a hero!"

"Maybe I was a hero, sort of," Matt replied, "but not anymore . . ."

I eased my foot off the gas pedal, checked my rearview mirror again, and then merged into the slow lane. "What happened to the hero?" I asked.

Matt was pensive for a moment. "You know, I just don't want to get into that," he said, turning his head and staring out the window.

We drove in silence for a mile or so and then saw the flashing lights of the fire trucks on a hill in the distance. Smoke filled the air above the fire scene.

"They must have water on it already," Matt said. "The smoke is white. I can't see any flames. They'll likely have it out pretty quick. I hope nobody got hurt."

"What was your last fire run like?"

"Not good, Richard. Not good. That was the beginning of the end for me." He sighed. "It was a warehouse fire in L.A. My truck had been on dozens of runs, and this should have been an easy one—well, as easy as any of them are, anyway. My pals on the truck were good: Luke and Bill. We were sharp. Never had a scratch on any of us, or on the truck. We covered each other's asses; we were a tight unit." He paused again, continuing to peer out the window at the lights in the distance. "It was a small fire; there wasn't any smoke or flames from the roof when we got there. It was all inside. We checked with the dispatcher by radio, and as far as everyone knew, there weren't any chemicals or combustibles stored inside that might explode. Still, we put on our masks before going inside.

"The fire was down at the end of a hallway on the first floor of a two-story. Some smoke, but not a lot. Luke took off his gloves to feel the metal door and told us through his mask that it wasn't even hot. But it was locked. Luke asked Bill if he thought he could knock it down, so Bill pulled out his axe and motioned us to step back. He took a big swing and dented the door. Then he swung again, making a hole in the metal. Then Luke sent me out to get the big crowbar from the truck.

"Just as I got outside, all hell broke loose. There was an explosion, and smoke came rolling out the front door. I raced back and saw the flames filling the hallway. Luke and Bill were still inside. I tried to get to them, but the heat and smoke were too much. The building totally went up in flames. Luke and Bill died that day. And most of me died with them."

He paused for a moment. "I tried to go on. People tried to help. The department sent me to support groups and counseling. My wife was understanding. I just couldn't forget, and I couldn't work. I sat around a lot. It took about two years to lose everything. The bank took the house and repossessed the car. My wife got tired of watching me do nothing, and she finally left with our son. My brother gave me some cash to buy a car, and I stayed in it for a while. But I couldn't handle being in L.A. anymore, so I worked my way north and ended up here. My guess is that all those people back home are glad I'm gone."

I searched for words to offer—something like "I bet they miss you" or "You'll always be a hero"—but nothing came. His story was too familiar. In silence, I drove him to his next home.

He was a hero trying to forget, and I had no heroic words to help him.

I would soon be dropping him off at what I knew to be a good place—The Hilton. There would be food there, at least, and I knew the women who helped Adam and the other young people living there would make sure he had clean clothes.

"How have you survived?" Matt asked me through the gulf of quiet. "You are—well, an older guy. It must be tougher."

"You know, I don't really know," I replied. "I ask myself that question at least once a day. I get a little help here, a little help there. People have helped me. They'll help you, too."

I made the final turn onto "Hilton Road." "The path to the camp is right over there," I said, pointing out the opening in the bushes. "Just follow the path back through the trees for about a quarter or half a mile. You'll see the clearing in the trees. Just yell out 'C sent me,' and they'll know you're okay. They'll make room for you, I'm sure. Tell Adam hello from Willow and me."

Matt stepped out into the wind. "Thanks, Richard," he said, closing the door behind him.

I watched as he walked across a wooden plank someone had placed over the drainage ditch beside the road and then disappeared into the thicket of cedars and pines swaying in the wind.

I put my foot on the gas pedal and pulled away.

As I headed back to the main highway, Willow whined to alert me that she needed to step out of the van. Wind or no wind, nature was calling.

We pulled into the parking lot of the local roller rink, Skateland; there was an undeveloped field right behind it. Willow jumped out as soon as I opened the door, and the wind tossed her ears and tail about. She braved the elements and the tall weeds to do her business and jumped back in the van. It was not a day for tarrying.

I reached to turn the ignition switch, but stopped. I thought of Matt.

I opened the glove compartment and pulled out the few pages of my book that were there, and a pen. I was out of clean paper, so I turned the pages over. I started to write, but nothing appeared. "Darn, it's out of ink," I said to myself. I scribbled on the corner of the page, just to check, and lo and behold, the ink began to flow again. The pen must have been cold.

I started recording my recollections of the afternoon and the way Matt had approached me. *He was a burly lad with red hair and a short, red beard . . .* I wrote. Then I lifted my pen from the paper. Matt reminded me of my son.

My son, too, had red hair, just like his mother. He was also a big, strong man with a powerful grip—much bigger than me. He was maybe thirty-four the last time I saw him; I couldn't quite remember. It had been almost two years now since I had seen him or talked with him on the phone.

I had done everything I could to forget our last conversation, but now it came back to me, almost word for word, as I sat there in the wind-buffeted van. I had asked him to lend me some money, and it made him very angry. The gist of it was something like: "Listen, you dumb son of a bitch. I am bigger and stronger than you, and I don't loan money to people like you. Don't ever call me again, or I will beat the hell out of you!"

I had lent him money—ten thousand when he needed to close on a house. And I had hired him to work for me when my business was steaming along. He had told me he'd make me proud. That he wanted to be just like me. But when the business failed, he not only lost his job, he lost faith in me. That is what hurt the most, probably for both of us—I had been his hero.

I had shared all I had with my son, but now when I needed help, he could not respond. And it was way beyond the money—he had rallied quite well financially and was selling real estate by that time.

His ugly words echoed in my brain.

"When did he learn to speak to anyone like that?" I wondered. I had never threatened or spoken that way to anyone in my life. Was it my fault? Had I failed him? The waves of self-doubt flooded my being.

I didn't want to think about that. I put the pen back to the paper. "The people at my table at lunch were talking about you and Willow. You guys are famous." Again, I lifted my pen from the crumpled paper and looked at the big, black clouds forming in the sky. "Famous?" I mused.

I thought once more about my son and remembered happier times when we had played "being famous."

I had mowed the big lawn and was pulling weeds in the garden when I heard the giggles of the neighborhood kids coming up the driveway of our home in Ohio. I was about thirty-eight at the time. Rich, my older son, called out to me to come play football. I watched him approach with Kyle, Kip, Shirley (the neighborhood tomboy), and Scott, my younger son, who was holding the football. They were all looking at me expectantly.

"Hey, guys. I'd like to, but I've got all these weeds to pull," I replied, getting a good grip on a thistle that was crowding out a tomato plant.

"Oh, come on, Dad. Please?" Scott pleaded.

As I unearthed the thistle from the ground, I traveled back across the years to when I would plead with my own father, who was sitting at his desk off the living room paying bills. "Hey, Dad, you want to play some pass?" I had asked, with baseball and glove at the ready. We went back and forth—he giving all the expected refusals and rationales, and I continuing to beg and plead—until I saw the twinkle in his eye that let me know I had won the contest. "Well, maybe I could take a break," he said, smiling as he pushed away from the desk. "Let me see that ball. I wonder where my glove might be?" And I had rushed for the hall closet, where I knew it would be.

How could I do any less for my sons? I tossed the handful of weeds off to the side of the garden. "Well, I guess I could take a break," I said, brushing the dirt off my hands. "Let me see that ball." Scott tossed it to me as I stood up. "Go deep, Scott," I said, and he was off and running as fast as his eight-year-old legs would carry him. I pulled my arm back and fired a pass that he caught over his shoulder.

We all headed for the middle of the yard. "How about the same teams as last time?" I suggested. That worked out well: Rich, Shirley, and Kip against Scott, me, and Kyle. At age eleven, Rich was obviously the group leader, and once he said "Okay," everyone else concurred.

"We're still the Buckeyes," freckle-faced Shirley announced.

"And we're still the Bengals," Scott chimed in.

"Okay then. The big elm tree is your goal line and that little pine tree is our goal," I said. "No arguing or fighting, and plays in question will get a do-over," I added. "I'm the referee, and I'll be fair."

Rich assured me that he trusted me.

We determined that the Bengals would kick off first, as we moved to our sides of "the field."

Rich yelled out that we were playing tackle, as we lined up for the kickoff.

"Oh, well, okay," I replied. "But not too rough. Remember Scott is just eight, and—"

"Don't worry about me," Scott interrupted, trying to sound big and strong. "I can play rough!"

I took the heel of my right foot and punched a hole in the ground to set the ball for the kickoff, turned, and took six steps back to get a run at the ball. "You ready?" I yelled.

"Ready," the Buckeyes yelled, and I ran forward and kicked the ball in the air. Shirley caught the ball and began running to the left, but when Kyle and Scott closed in, she wheeled and pitched the ball back to Rich, who turned and began galloping to the right. I headed toward Rich, but he changed direction and dashed to the middle of the field, toward Scott and Kyle. Scott reached out and wrapped his arms around Rich's waist, but slipped down until he had him only by one leg. It was enough to slow Rich down until I got there to help out. I grabbed Rich around the chest with one arm and then the other. I could feel the fragileness of his young body, but at the same time I could feel the strength of his heart and his determination to keep going toward the goal line.

As I gently pulled him down toward the ground, I did so with the unspoken trust between father and son. We both knew that I was twice as big and three times as strong as he was and that I could easily crush his body if I landed on it with my full weight, but we knew just as well that I would never do anything to harm him.

I placed the ball at about midfield, and the Buckeyes went into their huddle to dream up a play. They broke the huddle, with Shirley at center, Rich at quarterback, and Kip as wide receiver. Rich yelled "Hut, hut," and Shirley snapped the ball and did her best to block Scott. As Scott rushed in, Rich retreated and pulled back his arm to uncork a pass to the speeding Kip. But the ball was thrown just a little long and fell to the ground. I saw Scott rubbing the side of his face where Shirley's bony arm had bumped him in his rush to the quarterback. He brushed it off.

The Buckeyes huddled again, and this time Shirley was calling the plays. Kip centered the ball, and I could see Rich's eyes watching mine as he faked to the outside and then raced past me. Shirley launched a wobbly pass that just made it over my outstretched fingers and settled into Rich's arm for a touchdown.

The Buckeyes cheered as they headed for their end of the field.

And I smiled. For I was playing my role so well: to let them have fun; to score the touchdown; to let them win; to let them be heroes.

And, in turn, I was their hero.

The Bucks prepared to kick off to us. Just as I had done, Rich used the heel of his tennis shoe to make a hole in the ground for the kickoff. They lined up, and on Rich's signal, they charged forward, and Rich kicked the ball in the air.

"I got it!" Scott yelled, and he moved forward. The pigskin hit Scott in the chest and bounced to the ground. But he quickly picked it up, tucked it under his arm and began running, with his sandy-colored hair blowing in the breeze. Rich closed in on Scott and reached out to grab his shoulder, but the little man reversed field and Rich slipped on the grass. As Scott scampered to the left, he found himself corralled by Shirley and Kip.

"I got him!" Shirley growled, and Scott tossed the ball back over his head while yelling "*DAD!*" at the top of his lungs. The ball rolled on the ground and I reached down to pick it up. By then Kip had grabbed my right leg, and a second later Shirley was attached to my left. Rich then grabbed my waist and tugged with all his might to take me to the ground. I knew I was going to have to take a tumble, and I had to find a way to go down without falling on them and hurting them.

After I fell gracefully to the grass, I could feel three small bodies lying on top of me, their hearts pounding.

The sound of a car engine pulling into the Skateland parking lot ended my trip back in time. The doors of a station wagon flew open in the wind and five children scrambled out. A man stepped out from the driver's side.

"Dad, I forgot my knee pads," one of the children called out.

"Megan, that's the last thing I told you *not* to forget before we left," the father said. "We're not going back for them. Just make sure you don't fall down."

"Okay," the girl said as they slammed the car doors shut and headed for the rink.

The family I once knew was gone.

I was no different from millions of others—from the millions of teenagers on the street to the millions of aging heroes stored away like luggage in nursing homes across the country; I knew that I was in my family's way.

I finally understood that my son's outburst had come from the frustration that accompanies a problem that cannot be solved. My son was doing the same thing that I had done for over forty years—chasing the American Dream and trying to be somebody's hero. All I could do was hope that when he caught that dream, he would recognize it.

The homeless were my new family. They embraced me. They waved and smiled and treated me with dignity and respect. *We may be the most misunderstood and feared people in America,* I thought, *but we are still family to each other.*

Those who don't understand homelessness often share the groundless fear that we might rob them, or beat them up, or molest their children. They don't recognize that there's far more stealing going on at the gas pumps and in the boardrooms. Or that they are far more likely to be assaulted by a driver with road rage. Or that the real child molesters are more likely to be a next-door neighbor, a local priest or teacher, or someone surfing the Internet in a comfortable home.

I couldn't explain to my son what was happening to me—he had no frame of reference for my depression. I hardly understood it myself.

I knew he wanted me to be the hero I had been before, strong and confident. I was a stranger to him now. As I was to myself.

All I could do now was just *be.*

And the best thing I could do for my children was not to fall on them.

I put my pen back to the paper: *"Maybe I was a hero, sort of,"* Matt replied, *"but not anymore . . ."* His voice trailed off. I eased my foot off the gas pedal, checked my rearview mirror again, and then merged into the slow lane. "What happened to the hero?"*

Chapter 30

THE CHURCH MICE

What sounded like a nine-hundred-pound centipede on the move aroused Willow and me from our slumber on the flowered sofa in the long hallway on the lower level of the church.

It was a Monday morning, ending our fourth night of curling up in our old sleeping bag somewhere warm and dry, thanks to the kindness of the pastor, Earl.

Clomp, clomp, clomp, clomp—the centipede got louder as it made its way down the stairway.

I poked my head out from under its cover and peeked over the arm of the sofa to see a woman holding the end of a rope, followed by a dozen children, each holding on to the rope as they headed to a small playground just outside the church doorway.

I snuggled back down to savor the warmth and safety of this moment, feeling very lucky.

It had been a week of the worst weather most of the locals could remember. It had rained, and rained, and rained—the kind of rain that floods houses, washes out roads, makes streams overflow—the kind of rain that soaks you to the skin. It was the kind of weather that makes you want to tune out the world and curl up with a good book in front of a nice, blazing fire. But it was hard to keep a campfire blazing or even a book dry in a downpour like this (and a campfire was the best hope the homeless had for a fire of any kind).

Willow and I had managed pretty well up till now, burrowed down in the back of the van at night with our sleeping bags. Even when it was cold, we could usually warm each other up. And when my clothes got wet, I could usually crawl into something dry and make it through the night.

But the combination of being soaking wet *and* chilled to the bone was another thing entirely. I had no dry clothes left; everything I owned was wet. There was no way to warm up—and no way to take care of Willow. The pastor at the Methodist church where we usually parked the van at night finally suggested I see a friend of his on the other side of town, and off we went, begging again. The pastor at the new church, Pastor Earl, took pity on Willow and me, standing there shivering and dripping on his office carpet. He had just enough emergency money to put us up for a night in a motel.

So Willow and I spent that night at a motel, drying out and getting ready to face whatever was coming next. As usual, I had to smuggle her in and try to keep her quiet, and I worried the whole time that we would get caught and have to pay extra (which I didn't have) or be kicked out. Each of us had a good, hot, soapy shower and a rubdown with clean towels. It was heavenly to be dry after the days of heavy rain. I spread my clothes out to dry, and we watched some TV in the comfort of clean sheets. As we lay wrapped in this cocoon, I listened to the rain beating against the window, and I prayed that the next day would dawn clear, or at least dry.

Willow sighed in her sleep, and I wondered how much longer I could take care of her, living the way we did.

I awoke in the morning to the sound of the monotonous, continuous rain—again.

When it was time to leave the motel, I decided to go back to the church—First United Methodist Church—partly to say thank you for the gift of being warm and dry again, and partly to beg for some gas money. Pastor Earl invited me to sit and talk for a bit. After he had heard my story, he not only gave me twenty dollars for gas, he offered to let me sleep in the basement hallway of his church. We went downstairs to take a look. "I haven't got enough money to pay for a motel room again, but it's still raining really hard, and I am afraid you are going to get sick if you can't stay dry. You can sleep here," Pastor Earl said, pointing to a high-back couch pushed up against the wall of a long hallway, "at least for a few days, and maybe we can we figure something else out."

I had no idea what time it was. On Sunday I had sold my watch—a twenty-dollar Timex—for two dollars, which translated into another gallon of gas for the van. But I knew it was late enough for the "church people" (Pastor Earl, the secretaries, and others) to be in.

Somewhere in the back of my mind, I had been hoping that Willow and I could be "church mice," mostly out of sight during the day and free to roam the dark halls and large sanctuary at night. But I knew that this arrangement couldn't last long. In fact, it would probably end this morning when I climbed the stairs—rumpled, unshaven, and unbathed.

In my seemingly endless months of sleeping on the streets, I knew of only one other person who had slept in a church by himself overnight, and that was only because he had had pneumonia and someone had taken pity on him. I was the only one who had been invited to occupy the half-million square feet of empty church space in town.

Andy the Weed spent seventeen years out in the cold. C, Gentleman Jake, and a host of others never got inside. There were reasons, I knew, undoubtedly good reasons in someone's estimation. I was pretty sure the church's insurance company wouldn't approve of this, and I was darned sure some church members would be afraid I would steal something. The pastor had obviously made a mistake in a moment of weakness. He had actually given me a key to the front door, which I expected him to ask me to return when I climbed the stairs this morning.

I had nothing to give this man or his church. I certainly had no money. I had no fine voice to add to their choir. And with my faith in God gone, I had no inspirational story to tell the congregation. But maybe that was just as well. Andy had once told me as I drove him to the liquor store, "It is better to have no hope than just a little hope. A little hope just gets you thinking something good is about to happen. And when that little hope is taken away, you are worse off than before. *My* hope comes in a bottle."

I knew Willow was awake, but she just stretched and burrowed down deeper, enjoying the warmth of the dry bag and the comfort of the soft sofa.

I was reluctant to move myself. This little bit of comfort—or was it hope?—allowed just enough space to let some thoughts I tried to keep at bay come creeping back into my consciousness. While it had been almost a year since my trip to the bridge rail, my mind still flirted with thoughts of the peaceful rest that only death could bring. It would only take a few minutes—less time than drinking a cup of coffee—to drown all memories and end all worries about the future. Maybe I could go to the church service on Sunday and look for someone who would take good care of Willow, someone with a big yard and a big heart and lots of dog treats and bones and hamburgers.

Willow finally began making her way from under the covers, and her head popped out by my shoulder. She immediately began to lick my face. Again I was certain she could read my mind. I heard the big door at the end of the hall open. "A-marching we will go; a-marching we will go," the teacher and the children were singing as they entered, all still clinging to the rope. "Hi, ho, a-derry-o, a-marching we will go." As the teacher led them around the corner, one little boy at the very end of the rope spotted Willow and me and turned his head. "Hi," he said in a tiny voice, the rope pulling him forward.

It was time to get up; I couldn't avoid it any longer. I pushed the sleeping bag down and began to climb out. I stood up and stuffed my shirt back into my jeans. I found my shoes beside the sofa and sat back down to pull up my socks and lace my shoes. Ready at last, I hesitantly headed down the hall and began the ascent up the stairs. Willow followed right behind, hopping like a bunny rabbit up the stairs.

As I reached the top of the stairs, a line of pictures in gold-painted frames caught my eye. I walked over to take a closer look. A small brass nameplate was tacked to the bottom of each painting. The first was Matthew, then Mark, Luke, and John, and then Jesus—four of the disciples and their leader. They all wore their hair long and in tangles, and their faces were etched. Really, they looked like some of the men I had been eating with daily at Sally's. The likeness of Jesus reminded me of C.

I could hear the sound of laughter coming from the office down the hall. I held back, hesitant to see the people inside for fear of receiving an eviction notice, but Willow scooted past me and headed for the laughter. I had to pick up the pace to catch up with her.

The little dog rounded the corner and made a beeline for the office. "Well, look who's here," I heard a woman's voice say. "It's Willow."

There were two women in the office this morning: Mishara, the church secretary whom I had met the first day I stopped at the church, and another woman, standing by the desk with her hands full of papers. Mishara was bending down petting Willow as I entered. She stood up to greet me. "Good morning, Richard."

I smiled and sort of mumbled my greeting in return. Willow was now investigating the other woman, who said to her, "Well, aren't you just a cute little thing?"

"Richard, this is Charlene," said Mishara, as she reached over to pick up a bowl of salad from her desk.

"Good to meet you," Charlene said. "I'm another secretary around here." She lifted a coffee cup to her lips.

"It's good to meet you," I replied. I nodded to her, and then a plate sitting on the end of the counter caught my eye. It was laden with what looked like banana-nut bread—perhaps even homemade.

Charlene followed my glance. "I baked that last night," she said. "Help yourself." As I reached for a piece of the bread, she added, "There's fresh coffee in the pot in the kitchen, too. Come on; I'll show you."

She led the way out of the office and toward the kitchen. I could smell the coffee. "The mugs are right up here," she said, opening a cabinet door. She looked over the shelf, selecting the right one. "Here," she said. "Here's one with a Santa Claus on the side. Ho, ho, ho," she laughed as she handed the mug to me.

I accepted the mug and poured a cup of coffee. "Thank you so much," I said.

"You're welcome," Charlene said. "You can have all you want. I'm the only one who drinks it around here during the day. You can have more nut-bread, too. Mishara will eat maybe one piece. She eats salad all day. And Earl will only eat a piece or two." We moved back toward the office.

I gladly took Charlene up on her offer and picked up another piece of the delicious bread, all the while listening and watching for Pastor Earl. I thought I could hear him talking on the phone in his office, just adjacent to the main office. But I couldn't make out what he was saying.

"Did you see any mice downstairs last night?" Mishara asked.

I told her I hadn't.

"Well, there was one greeting me first thing this morning when I opened the office door," she said. "He ran across my desk, hopped down on the floor, and scurried out the door. He was kinda cute, but some people are afraid of them."

"I am," Charlene chimed in, shivering. "They give me the creeps."

I smiled at Charlene's shiver and thought that the mice were just like Willow and me, seeking someplace warm and dry while avoiding the predators outside.

"Good morning, Richard," Pastor Earl said as he rounded the corner from his office. He was a tall man with long arms, and he wrapped them around me in a brief, warm hug. Willow, who had been sitting on a chair by the office door, jumped down and scurried closer, rising up on her hind legs and using her front paws to get the big man's attention.

"Good morning to you, too, Willow," he said, bending down to pat the little dog on the head. "Come into the office," he said to me, turning and retracing his steps.

I followed behind, wondering how this kind man was going to phrase and rephrase the admission of his mistake in allowing me to sleep in the church and let me know when I must leave. Willow stepped past me and jumped into a comfy chair. "That must be her chair," laughed Earl, sitting down in his own swivel chair. "Hold on a second." He looked around on his old wooden desk covered with papers. "I've got to give this to Mishara to put into the computer." He picked up a piece of paper, studied it briefly, and made a correction. "I'll be right back," he said. He swiveled, got up, and walked out.

I surveyed the pastor's office. The back wall was full of books. There were Bibles of every kind, in large print and small, and writings of theologians, deciphering every phrase of the holy books and scrolls.

There were books on how to pray and when to pray. I saw a copy of *I've Got to Talk to Somebody, God.* There was also a copy of Spong's *A New Christianity for a New Millennium.*

Tacked to the wall with a pushpin was a child's crayon drawing of a brown violin and bow, and the words to "Twinkle, Twinkle, Little Star" written in blue. Below the child's drawing were two large Native American spirit-webs, with feathers and beads of red, white, blue and yellow.

As I turned around in my chair, a poster on the wall caught my eye:

> DO all the good you can
> by all the means you can
> in all the ways you can
> at all the times you can
> to all the people you can.
> As long as ever you live.

I got out of my chair and walked past the desk to look out the window. I saw a picture on the far wall of a yellow duck, its webbed feet on backwards, and at the bottom was printed: *Mallard Justed.*

Behind the old wooden desk was a print framed and under glass:

> Bach gave us God's Word.
> Mozart gave us God's Laughter.
> Beethoven gave us God's Fire.
> God gave us music, that we might pray without Words.

And leaning up against the side of the desk was a violin case.

I could hear Pastor Earl's footsteps coming down the hall, so I moved back to my chair. He bustled back into the office and sat down. "Sorry about that."

It was at that moment that I really looked into his face. He had a well-trimmed beard, short hair, and soft blue eyes. His face was lightly etched from some sixty-plus years of living. I thought then that whatever they call him—whether he was a minister, priest, reverend, or pastor—this soul was a man of God. This was not just a business to him, a way of making a living or passing the time for self-gratification. Here was a true believer.

"How are you doing on money?" he asked.

I reached in my back pocket and pulled out my wallet. "Not very good today," I said, showing him the empty folds of the worn leather.

I expected him to say, "How do you expect to live on nothing today, and the rest of the month?" But instead he reached into his back pocket and opened his own wallet. He took out all his cash—a five, then six ones—and he handed them to me. "Here, this might at least get you some gas."

I reached out, silently and humbly accepting the gift.

"How are you doing otherwise, Richard?" he asked.

I lowered my eyes to my lap and folded my hands. I felt I could trust this man. He seemed to be a true friend, maybe the first true friend I had ever known, except for C.

As I lifted my eyes to speak, I could feel the presence of others in the room. I turned my eyes to see Andy the Weed pulling a book from the shelf, and Karen (who had jumped from the Manette Bridge) looking out the window. Marcia (from the hospital waiting room) was beside me with a hand on my shoulder, and the Lady in Red who had emptied her purse and pockets for me so long ago was sitting on a chair, gently petting Willow.

Andy turned toward me. "Look, Richard, no walker anymore. And I don't need a ride to the liquor store."

The pastor sat silently and patiently, waiting for my answer to his question. I was sure that if I told him what I was seeing, he would think I was crazy.

"You are lucky to find a man like him," said Karen, still looking out the window.

"Why don't you let your subconscious—you know, your soul—talk to his soul?" asked the Lady in Red.

I turned my eyes to Pastor Earl, and it happened so easily. I let him see my soul. And in that second, he seemed to understand the mistakes I had made as well as the good I had done in life. I felt a sense of unconditional love. He reached out a hand to me, and I unfolded my hands to clasp his.

"I'm okay, I guess," I said, as I began to try to answer his question in the conscious world. "It's been kinda cold living in my car." I paused. "I think maybe I am ready to give up."

He looked at me with his heart in his eyes, searching for the word that would console me.

I asked my soul to talk to his.

"You know the song, Pastor: 'He Ain't Heavy, He's My Brother.' It's from the sixties. Well, I am heavy. I see all these sayings on your walls, all your books, the people who respect and love you, your thoughts, dreams, and plans, your violin in that case—that is your identity. I have no identity. I don't want one. I had one once, and, well, it's gone now. I have no hope."

"It sounds like you need hope," Pastor Earl's soul replied.

"I know you want to help me, but I am too heavy for you to carry. I am a smart man. In the past year and a half I have seen men who have been on the streets ten or fifteen years, just hoping death would come gracefully in the cold of the night. I have seen the fear in the eyes of young women and children, knowing there was just enough food, just enough cash, just enough begging to get by another day. Somehow they go on. They are stronger than me.

"So my soul asks your soul, in the future are you somehow going to let me stay and sleep in this church?"

"I will. This is your sanctuary."

"And when I fail to get a home, will you help me find one?"

"I'll do my best."

"And when my dog Willow gets ill, will you help me find a vet?"

"I will, and I'll hold your hand until Willow is well."

"And when I need someone to talk to in dark times, will you come listen to me and wipe the tears from my eyes?"

"I will, and I will cry with you."

"And if I ever begin dreaming again, will you dream with me?"

"Dreams do come true, Richard," his soul assured me.

"All my life I worked, loved, raised children, sang songs, danced, played games, and celebrated life," my soul said. "I gave to others. But now I have nothing to give you."

"Oh, yes you do," Earl's soul replied. "You have the greatest gift to give me: the chance to give to you."

"I pray for Richard when he goes to sleep at night," my soul said, whispering, somehow being inside and outside me at the same time. It was like I was now listening to another part of myself. "He catches me praying for him, for his children and grandchildren and loved ones, and he tells me it's a waste of time, but I wait until he falls back asleep. And I pray for C, Major Baker, and, well, all the people he has met on his journey.

"You know, every night before he climbs into the back of the van to go to sleep, he puts a note on the dashboard that says: 'If I die in my sleep and you find me, PLEASE find a good home for my dog. Her name is Willow.' And most of the time, just as sleep comes, he feels sad that no one would miss him—sad that no one would come to his funeral. Would you come to his funeral?"

"Only if he comes to mine first. Either way, I will be there," his soul said with a laugh.

My soul laughed, too.

"And I get the feeling that I won't be the only one there! There will be many," his soul said, with warm assurance.

Pastor Earl also assured me with real words, back in the room with the old desk and the sayings on the walls. "I've got to make a couple of telephone calls to get it totally approved, but I'm pretty sure that we can have you and Willow stay for as long as it is necessary for you to find a place," he said. "I can be pretty persuasive when I need to be." He laughed that pure-of-heart laugh that made everyone within hearing breathe more easily.

"You know, I just had an idea: Maybe you and Willow could be security guards for the church at night. We couldn't offer you any money for it, because we don't have any. But we can get some food in the fridge—some milk and cereal and stuff. Willow could be the church guard dog." I smiled at the picture of my little white dog with a SECURITY DOG badge hanging around her neck.

"That—well, that would be great," I said, when I was able to find words at all. "I have been writing a book; maybe I could work on it at night."

"Really? What kind of book?" Earl asked.

"It's about the homeless people I have met, mostly," I said. "I'm almost done with the writing, but it still needs a lot of work."

"You know, my wife has always wanted to edit a book," Earl said, his blue eyes dancing. "I'll run it by her tonight at dinner."

I could hardly believe how different this conversation was from the one I had imagined, and dreaded. "About staying here . . ." my voice trailed off. "I am just afraid that the people of your church may look at Willow and me as church mice. Some will see us as cute little pets, while others will be afraid of us."

"Not in this church," he replied. "Anyone who gets to know you and Willow will treat you with dignity, respect, and love. Have courage, my friend."

"Then I would like to thank you for being so kind to me, a stranger," I said.

"For some reason, you are not a stranger to me," the tall, gentle man said. "You seem more like the brother I never had."

Pastor Earl let go of my hand, sat back in his chair, and then stood up. "Have you had anything to eat yet today?" he asked.

"Just some of Charlene's delicious banana-nut bread," I said.

"Well, come on. I've got to stop at the bank to get a little cash, and then I'll buy you lunch," he said, smiling. "I'm hungry. Maybe we can talk about your book."

Earl reached over to get his coat from the back of a chair, and I slipped mine on. As we headed for the door, I looked back at Andy, Marcia, Karen, and the Lady in Red and nodded.

Andy put down the book he was reading and smoothed his hair back with his hand. He leaned toward the Lady in Red and said, "Anybody ever tell you that you look just like Vanna White?"

"No, they haven't," she blushed.

"Well, what are you doing today?" Andy asked.

"I have no plans," she replied.

Chapter 31

JUST ANOTHER HEADLINE

I was happy this Friday, December fifteenth morning when I pulled into Sally's parking lot for lunch. Being warm and dry most of the time for almost three weeks had done a lot for my spirits. There were still nights when I just couldn't quite trust my good fortune, and Willow and I would sleep in the van again, but it was never because we felt unwelcome at the church. I felt that if we should have to move on one morning, the loss might not be quite so devastating if we hadn't started to think of the church as "home."

I was a little late, and Sally's was packed. But because it was getting so close to Christmas, the Major had instructed the cooks to make extra, and there was plenty to eat—mashed potatoes, corn, and meatloaf. I grabbed my tray, and Chef Pat greeted me with a warning about being late, but her eyes were dancing all the while. There was only one seat left in the room, but it was a good one—right in the middle of a group of my friends: Mitty, John, and C.

John and Mitty were the sages of Sally's. John "the Mayor" was always a gentleman and Mitty a lady, and their collective personae often set the tone of the table. "What a bunch of characters," I thought as I moved toward the table. It occurred to me that I must be viewed as a character myself, and each diner could be thinking exactly the same thing.

I remember distinctly the first time I saw Mitty at Sally's. I was sitting at a table of young men on New Year's Eve when I eavesdropped on the conversation of two of my tablemates: "She's from L.A. She was an old film star, someone told me. She's been around here for a long time now. When no one else will help you, she will! All you have to do is ask. You got nothing to lose." After the men finished their lunch, one walked over to the lady sitting at the next table and whispered something in her ear. I watched as she reached into her pocket and handed a few dollars to the man. I would learn over the next year that Mitty practiced random acts of kindness, often providing survival cash and expecting nothing in return.

Mitty was seventy-plus, 4-foot-1, and skinny as a rail, with a deep masculine voice. She was from L.A., all right, and in fifteen years had still never acclimated to the Northwest's cool weather. She often wore a ski cap and a long-sleeve sweatshirt on a sunny, 70-degree day. The rumor that she was a black-and-white film star was just that: a rumor. But someone should have made a film about her!

She was a fairy godmother to many, not only doling out dollars from time to time, but also taking food to poor people when they were sick, arranging rides to the doctor for those with no car or bus pass, and encouraging those who were too ashamed to ask for help. More than once, she gently placed a ten in my hand, sensing my need. I learned that she wasn't a rich lady by any stretch of the imagination, but rather chose to deprive herself to help others. "We have to help each other out when we can," she would say in her deep voice.

Time after time, I saw the poor give to the poor. If you had twenty and someone asked you for ten, you *gave* it to them. It was difficult, but

I learned how to practice this kind of giving. When I got my hands on twenty bucks, it was as if some unseen force was telling someone in need to ask me for a five, and I would give up a ten. I discovered that the same force would somehow return the ten, plus ten more. I learned to give with joy.

Six teenagers were seated at the next table, directly behind the open spot I was heading toward: Josh, Ricky, Allen, Maria, and two boys I had never seen before. I noticed that Ricky looked like he had been crying. I nodded at him and he nodded back. I set my tray down and slid into my seat as John asked, "How's your book coming?"

"It's coming along," I said, picking up a napkin. "I'm almost done."

"That's what you said last month," John retorted.

Mitty came to my defense. "John, it takes a long time to write a book, you know," she said.

"I know. I'm just kidding him," John smiled.

Just as I was lifting the first bite of meatloaf to my mouth, I heard Ricky raise his voice. "Just leave me the fuck alone," he yelled, pounding his fists on the table.

"Hey, Ricky, you know there's no swearing in here," Chef Pat said sternly from behind the kitchen counter, shaking her serving spoon in the air.

"We're just trying to help, Ricky," I heard Maria whisper.

"You can't help," Ricky said, his voice trembling. "No one can fucking help! They killed him!" Ricky yelled. "Go ahead and throw me out! I don't care."

Major Baker came rushing in from his office. Either he had heard Ricky, or someone had gone and told him there was trouble in the hall. He weaved his way between the tables to Ricky, who had buried his head in his hands; only his stained red baseball cap with the big red "A" could be seen.

The young people scrambled from the table when they saw the Major motoring in their direction, fearing he was going to throw Ricky out of Sally's. The Major had strict rules: no alcohol, no fighting, no guns, and no swearing. But the Major also had a heart—a *big* heart.

He arrived at the table in all of his officialdom—dressed in black pants, black tie, and white shirt with the Salvation Army insignia on the shoulders—and sat down beside the tortured boy. He put his hand gently on Ricky's arm. "What's wrong, Ricky?" was all he said. He waited for a moment or two, then said, "We are not going to throw you out, Ricky. You're my friend."

It must have been the soothing voice, or maybe it was the touch of the Major's hand, that reached Ricky. He slowly lifted his head, revealing the tears running down his cheeks. "Oh, Major, my old teacher at school died . . . He *shot* himself. He was the only teacher who ever cared about me. The *only* one! The only person who ever gave me a second chance."

The Major put his arm around Ricky. "I'd like to hear about him, Ricky. He sounds like a wonderful man. Would you like to come into my office and tell me about him?"

Ricky hesitated, then said, "Sure."

"Let's go," the Major said. They both rose, and the Major put his arm around Ricky's shoulder, guiding him to the office.

The room was quiet as the Major closed the door—completely quiet.

Eventually, C broke the silence. "That display of compassion deserves a standing ovation—no, a twenty-one-gun salute," he said, looking at John.

"Well, since they don't allow guns in here, we can at least salute," John replied, rising to his feet.

C also stood up. Then Mitty and all the people at our table rose. John turned, lifting his hands to motion to the others in the room, and one by one everyone stood up. Then we all followed John's cue as he faced the door of the Major's office and raised his right hand to his forehead in a sharp salute to Major Baker.

"You know, these kids have it real tough on the street—*real* tough," Mitty said, after we had all settled back down. "It's good they have somebody like the Major."

"You know, Ricky was a baseball star at Aberdeen High School," John said. "He was a good pitcher, but I think he got kicked out when he was a junior. Or he quit; I'm not sure. And I don't know how he got here, but something sure happened. He's been living on the streets for quite a while. He had a great fastball. He had the stuff. You know, I think Aberdeen is a lot like Bremerton—it's not the type of town where people make their dreams come true.

"As far as I can recall, there has never been a famous ball player from Bremerton. They always end up working in the shipyard."

The crowd finished lunch, cleared the tables, and returned their trays. I noticed Ricky's tray was still sitting on the table, and I went over with the last of my coffee to clear for him.

There was a crumpled newspaper lying beside the tray, a four-day old copy of the *Kitsap Sun*. It was folded open to a story with the headline TEACHER OF THE YEAR COMMITS SUICIDE, so I sat down and began to read.

ABERDEEN: David McKay, the 2002 Teacher of the Year in Washington State from nearby Aberdeen, took his own life December 10. McKay, 42, was found in his pickup truck with self-inflicted wounds from his shotgun on a country road just south of Copalis Crossing, off the Ocean Beach Road.

McKay inspired his students to write books in his class, many of which were published. He met with President George Bush in 2002 and was recognized for his achievements in education.

McKay was facing possible discipline for viewing pornography on his computer at school, according to a Sheriff's Office investigation. Sheriff Mike Whelan said, "I've been thinking a lot about this. He was a very popular teacher, a man loved by hundreds of people. Like many of us, he had faults. But nothing he did was against the law, and there was nothing he did that warranted him taking his life."

I read on, trying to imagine how labels of "unprofessional conduct" and the threat of having his teaching certificate revoked would affect a gentle and sensitive man, a man who had devoted his life to teaching and caring about children, a man (it was also reported) who was suffering from depression. "Tragedy seems like such a hollow word to describe this situation," the sheriff was quoted as saying.

I set the paper down, took a sip of coffee, and pondered what those last thirty-odd days of Mr. McKay's life must have been like. They had seized his computer in early November, but he didn't, or couldn't, tell his wife what was happening—or call his mother, father, brother, or sisters.

Just a few months earlier, David had been the shining star in a small logging and whale-watching town, respected by hundreds, greeted with smiles and waves—a proud man who gave his family credit for his success. But when he needed help the most, he was all alone.

We had too much in common, this stranger from Aberdeen and I: we had it all, and we lost it all. He lost his way in the Internet; I lost mine in depression. He took his own life; I had attempted to take mine and still thought about trying again. In some ways, I felt just as dead as he was.

How frightening those final days must have been for him—hiding his fear, his shame, his depression while participating in the pre-Christmas rituals developed over fifteen years of family life—and what the terror of December 10th must have been for his wife and children.

Then the irony hit me: the irony of McKay living in Aberdeen. Just on the edge of town is a bridge millions of Americans have seen—the bridge in the film *Pay It Forward*. In the film, a young boy from Las Vegas develops a reverse pyramid scheme of goodness as a class project, and a homeless man is the recipient of one of boy's three good deeds, each recipient then being obligated to perform three good deeds himself. The man relapses into drug use after being helped by the boy, and the boy feels that his project has failed. But at this bridge, the homeless man saves the life of a weeping, shaking woman who has climbed on the rail, preparing to jump to her death. He stops her by begging her to save *his* life by having a cup of coffee and talking with him. She responds to his need, seeing the possibility that it might be more urgent even than her own.

I wondered why someone hadn't paid it forward for David McKay. He'd been supposedly seduced by the siren call of pornography on the Internet, but this was hardly unique. It's the number-one hit in the cyber world; gambling is second. His mistake was peering into that world on the school computer. I wondered why the principal or the superintendent hadn't just taken Mr. McKay out for a cup of coffee and a few words of advice. Had it really been necessary to confiscate his computer and call in the feds, to ruin his career, to destroy his fragile hold on life? Wouldn't a slap on the wrist and a warning have been enough? What happened to the concept of a second chance?

Sure, the principals in this scenario could hide behind the "legal ramifications" and the "liability factors," but for David McKay, the fall from Teacher of the Year to Internet Porn Addict was just too great. And now neither lawyers nor psychiatrists could save him.

All David McKay had needed was what we all need: someone to touch his life, just like he had touched Ricky's.

Big Bill, the tall, muscular man who cleaned the tables and mopped the floor at Sally's, was beginning to fold up the chairs and place them on top of the tables in the back of the room. I took another sip of coffee and looked at Bill. "You got fifteen minutes or so, son," he said. "I've still got to fill up the bucket and get the mop and stuff."

I picked up the newspaper one more time to check my horoscope. As I leafed through the pages, I stumbled on a familiar name. Right there at the top of the obituary section, just above Mr. McKay's notice, was this: MARCIA ULEP—my friend from the hospital waiting room months ago. Below her name was her picture, taken on a sunny day on a warm beach with sparkling water in the background. She had long dark hair, accentuated by a white orchid, and was wearing a print dress. She wore the same cross around her neck, the one with the ruby in the center. She looked big and strong, weighing maybe two hundred pounds. She had probably been in her late thirties when the picture was taken.

"Beloved wife, mother, grandmother, and friend, Marcia went to join Jesus after a long battle with cancer," the article read. "She will be in the thoughts each day of her loving husband Vonne, her seven children— Corazon of San Diego, Rafael of Denver, Christine of Dallas, Jaypee of Agana, Phillipines, Marcella of Los Angeles, Warren of Seattle, and Valerie of Pittsburgh—and her twelve grandchildren."

I smiled as I remembered my visit with Marcia in that waiting room. She died on the same day as Mr. McKay. I hoped that he was waiting in line to get into heaven with my friend Marcia. She would cheer him up, buy him a hot coffee and a hamburger, and show him her photo collection, all the way from Corazon through Angelee.

Chapter 32

THE HOLY GHOSTS

It was a week before Christmas when the ghosts of the church came to visit, or perhaps decided to reveal themselves to me.

I'd been staying in the sprawling building for almost a month now. Usually I slept in the sanctuary with Willow curled up beside me in my sleeping bag. It was the quietest place in the building, away from the noise of the busy road in front. And though it was peaceful, I could hear the old furnace firing up in the basement and the pump pounding as it routed hot water. When the furnace and pump stopped, I could hear the trickle of hot water cruising through the pipes.

It was a Wednesday night, and the church had been in a hubbub all day. The florist had delivered a truckload of poinsettias for the sanctuary; the organist (who was kind enough to bring me a shepherd's pie dinner) tuned up the organ for choir practice. Meanwhile there was an Alcoholics Anonymous meeting at one end of the church, where those in recovery got together in an effort to summon the courage not to imbibe during the holiday season; at the other end was a Boy Scouts' Christmas party. The choir members arrived in a festive mood, talking about how dizzy they were from shopping for their children and how busy they were preparing for their Christmas festivities. People were making plans to rush to the airport to pick up relatives flying into Seattle and lamenting that they just didn't have time to get everything done.

The choir director graciously asked if I wished to sing, but I begged off. "Maybe another time," I said. "I'd just like to listen, if that's okay." She gave me a warm smile and headed off for the director's stand with several copies of music tucked under her arm.

While the choir practiced, a group of young people moved a crèche into place to the right of the altar. They were carrying in small figurines of Mary, Joseph, the Three Wise Men, a lamb, a cow, and a horse, and a little girl carefully carried the figure of a baby. "I've got the Baby Jesus," she said proudly. An older boy lugged in a bale of hay to spread around the scene.

I sat in the back pew with Willow in my lap, watching from afar, wishing in some ways I had the desire to sing. But I was an anomaly—I was a homeless man living in a church who did not believe in God.

It was about nine thirty when the choir finished its last song and began to file out. Pastor Earl walked back to me. "Richard, would you make sure all the doors are locked and the lights are off before you turn in?" he asked. I assured him I would, and he reached down to pet Willow before heading for the door.

I made my way down to the ground floor to see if all the doors were locked. They were. I turned off all the lights and then climbed the stairs again to check the locks on the big double doors of the main entrance. They were secure. I returned to the sanctuary, slowly closing the large wood-and-glass doors of the massive room.

I was finally alone. Willow had curled up asleep under the pew where we had been sitting earlier.

A panel on the wall in the back of the church contained a dozen or more knobs and switches to control the lights that set the atmosphere in the sanctuary. I turned them all off except the one small spotlight that directed a narrow beam onto the altar, a good two hundred feet away.

The dim beam highlighted the cornucopia of flowers, the altar, and the crèche the children had made. I was tired, but I felt compelled to get a closer look. So I walked down the main aisle and peered at the baby doll that had been placed in the wooden crib and at the statues of Mary and Joseph.

I whispered to myself, "This is so beautiful." And I remembered doing this before, over fifty years ago, when my mother took me to a church for the first time. I was six years old and it was Christmas Eve.

I took a deep breath and closed my eyes. Oh, yes. I had done this many times before—walked in dim light slowly and softly to the side of a crib. I had done it in the hospital nursery the night each of my three children had come into the world; I had done it on the night we brought each one of them home and first placed them in their own cribs. I had done it whenever I heard them cry, or whimper, or cough. And each time I witnessed the miracle of their presence, I had whispered, "This is so beautiful."

I remembered walking my mother up the stairs of the old farmhouse we were renting in Ohio and into the room of our first child. She, too, had walked slowly to the side of the crib and stood there in silence, tears of joy rolling down her cheeks.

The sound of a bell ringing brought me abruptly back to the present. It was the doorbell at the front of the church. I figured one of the choir members must have forgotten something. Willow awoke and barked a couple of times as the bell rang again. I could see the shadow of a person pacing the walkway that ran along the side of the sanctuary to the front door. The figure turned back toward the door, and the bell rang a third time. "I'll be right there," I yelled through one of the windows. I walked the length of the sanctuary, flipped on the hall lights, and headed for the door.

A young girl I didn't recognize was standing at the door when I arrived.

"Can I help you?" I asked.

"I don't live far from here, and I came to church here once," she said. "I wondered if—if it would be all right if I came in and said a prayer." She was wearing just a T-shirt, jeans, and tennis shoes, and she was shivering.

"I don't know. It's kinda late," I said, though I found myself pushing the big door wide open.

"I won't take long, Father," she said. It appeared she'd been crying.

"Sure, sure. Come on in," I said, stepping back to let her in. The rush of cold air from outside filled my nostrils. "Where's your coat?" I asked.

"Oh, I forgot it," she said.

I let the door slam shut behind us and turned to see Willow jumping up on her leg to welcome her. "That's my dog, Willow," I said, as she reached down to pet her.

"I saw the light when I walked by, and I saw somebody was here," she said. "I hope I'm not bothering you, Father."

"No, you are not bothering us at all. But I'm not a Father or anything like that. Willow and I are . . . well . . . sorta like church mice. And they call them 'pastors' here. This is a Methodist church."

"Oh, I didn't know. My parents brought me here when I was little—just a couple times. It was before they split up. I haven't been in a church since."

"Come this way," I said.

She followed me silently down the hallway to the sanctuary, and I opened the door for her. "I'll leave you alone," I offered.

"Thank you so much," she said, stepping in. I let the door close.

Willow was at my feet giving me a quizzical look, trying to figure out what was next. "Let's go raid the fridge," I said to my furry friend.

As we entered the kitchen, I realized I'd forgotten to turn off the lights in there, and that was the light the girl had seen.

The four large refrigerators in the kitchen were frequently well stocked with treats for church functions, or at the very least contained milk, orange juice, cheese, peanut butter, jelly, and often some lunch meat that the staff or the preschool folks had left behind. Tonight I opened one of the refrigerator doors and knew I had hit the jackpot. Deviled-ham finger sandwiches were arranged on a platter covered with plastic wrap, and another tray held an array of chocolate cupcakes, probably awaiting a ladies' church meeting. I had often been encouraged to help myself, and I knew that if I just took a couple of the dainty sandwiches and rearranged the rest, they would not be missed at all. Along with a cupcake and a glass of milk, it made the perfect snack. I filled a small saucer with milk for Willow and placed it on the floor while I cleaned up the few dishes.

I thought it must be time to go check on the girl, so I turned off the kitchen lights and walked back to the sanctuary and opened the door. She was kneeling at the altar rail with her head buried in her hands, weeping. I started to close the door again, but Willow had scooted inside. So I stepped in after her and let the door close behind us, then leaned back against it, wondering what to do next.

Willow knew exactly what to do. She trotted quickly up the center aisle toward the girl. I had to follow. When she got to the front of the church, she jumped up on the girl, interrupting her crying. "Well, hello, Willow," she said in a broken and weary voice.

I stepped forward and knelt down beside her, putting my arm gently around her shoulders. "I'm sorry you are so sad," I offered. She buried her face in my shoulder and began weeping again.

I just let her cry, for what seemed like a very long time. No words; just crying.

Eventually the sobs subsided and she became quiet. I remembered the napkins in my pocket from the kitchen raid and pulled them out. When she looked up at me, the tears were still running down her cheeks, and I gently wiped them away. "Why are you so sad?" I asked.

She turned her face away from me then, as she struggled to find the words. "My dad kicked me out of the house tonight," she said. "He hates me. He ordered me to stay away from all my friends. He ordered me to stop seeing my boyfriend. He called all my girlfriends sluts and my boyfriend a pot-smoking bum." She struggled to hold back the tears. "He threw my clothes out in the yard and yelled at me to get the hell out and never come back."

I took one of her hands and just squeezed it tight.

"He was drunk again. Ever since my mom left and moved to California, he's gotten mean."

I was silent for a moment, trying to think of a solution. "Maybe you could go back home now? Maybe he has—well, settled down."

"Oh, no," she said. "He's raging drunk by now. I walked around for a couple of hours. I tried to find my boyfriend, but couldn't. I didn't know what to do. Then I walked past here and saw the lights on."

"I'm glad you rang the bell," I said.

"I have no place to go," she said, beginning to cry again. "I don't know what to do." She put her face against my shoulder as a fresh wave of sobs shook her body. Again, I just held her and let her cry. Again, I tried to think of what I could do to help her.

When she eventually became quiet, I said, "Well, it's already about midnight. And I don't think there is much we can do until morning. But I do think maybe this place has enough room for one more church mouse."

She pulled her head back off my shoulder. "You mean I could stay here?" she asked.

"You will even have your own room," I said. "The youth room downstairs has a big couch and some blankets and an afghan to keep you warm. Then you'll have to get up in the morning and talk to the pastor here. He comes in about eight thirty. I know he will help you."

"I don't want to cause you any trouble," she said. "I don't want to be a burden to anybody. It seems like I've always been a burden to my dad."

"You're no trouble," I said, giving her another quick hug and then helping her to her feet. "You are not a burden," I assured her. I asked her if she was hungry, and she admitted that she was.

"Well, come with me," I said. "I know where there are some delicious sandwiches and some cupcakes and milk!"

I escorted her to the kitchen, found her a towel and directed her to the sink, then pilfered four more sandwiches and two cupcakes and poured her a big glass of milk. I knew that I would be forgiven for my thievery. I set everything on the long kitchen table and pulled up a stool for her across the table from mine. "My name is Richard," I said, realizing that I hadn't told her that before.

"I'm Michelle," she said, accepting the place at the table. She took a bite of her sandwich and then looked at me more closely. "You know, I have seen you before. You came through the drive-thru at McDonald's one day and got a hamburger for your dog. I work there, at the one just up the street."

"Probably us," I said. "Willow loves McDonald's hamburgers."

"I'm trying to save up to get a car," she continued between bites. "Then I can get away from my father and leave this town. I'm eighteen." She took a drink of her milk. "Do you have any children?"

"No," I lied, looking away from her. I didn't want to think or talk about my children at the moment.

"That's too bad," the girl said. "You would be a good father. Not like my dad."

"Well, Michelle, I think fathers always love their children," I said. "Sometimes things go wrong—times can be tough—but deep down inside, love is there. He's probably out looking for you right now."

"Not my dad," she said, very firmly. "There is no love in him. He's just mad and drunk."

"Well, let's get some sleep. Things may be better in the morning," I replied. "You look tired."

"I am," she agreed. "And I've got to go to work early in the morning. I can't miss any more time or they'll fire me. I have to be there at six."

"Okay," I said, "but do try to come by and see the pastor after you get off. Maybe he can help you."

"Okay. I will," she said, finishing off her milk.

I could see that she was feeling better, as well as getting sleepy. "Follow me, and I'll show you your quarters for the night." I stood up and opened the kitchen door.

We walked downstairs. I turned on the light to the youth room and showed her the couch. She stretched out on it immediately. "I'm so tired," she said.

I took one of the blankets and gently placed it over her, and then placed the afghan over that. "That should keep you warm," I said. "And don't be afraid if you hear noises; it's just the furnace grumbling and the water running through the old pipes. I'll leave this light on for you," I added, flipping the wall switch for the lighted stained-glass display on the wall. Then I turned off the other lights.

"That's beautiful," she said.

"It is, isn't it?" I replied. "Well, I'll be upstairs sleeping in the sanctuary. Good night."

"Richard?" she called out as I began to close the door. "Would you pray for me?"

"Sure," I said, and closed the door gently.

As I climbed back up the stairs, I wondered if I had done the right thing. Would I face trouble in the morning and be kicked out of the church? I had no permission to do what I had done.

Well, I didn't care. I had done the only thing I could do, and it felt right.

I got my sleeping bag out from behind the pew, unrolled it on the scarlet carpet, and climbed in. Willow was right behind me.

The old church that had been filled earlier that evening with so many happy people—singing, partying, and sharing their stories—was now quiet.

I crossed my arms behind my head and replayed the sounds of the songs that the choir had been practicing. "Oh, holy night . . ." I started to sing. But I couldn't remember the words, so I lapsed into humming. Then I began softly singing a song that I did remember. "Silent night, holy night, all is calm, all is bright . . . Sleep in heavenly peace, sleep in heavenly peace."

Willow had fallen asleep. I rolled over, closed my eyes, and smiled to myself. I had learned that song when I was six years old.

Though I was tired, the building was not. It seemed to be creaking even more than usual. But it wasn't long before I accepted its sounds as natural—the furnace must be running a little more because it was cold outside. I was glad to be inside. I was happy Michelle was inside as well, rather than walking in the cold streets all alone. Then I remembered what she had asked me to do. "What good is it going to do for *me*—who does not believe—to pray for *her*?" I wondered. But I had said I would. So I closed my eyes and said a few words into the silence. *Dear God, please watch over Michelle and keep her safe. Thank you for having a place where she could come and have shelter for this night.*

"There. I did it. I said a prayer just as Michelle asked. Short, but not a bad prayer for a nonbeliever," I thought.

Then, lying there in the dim light, I began thinking of my own daughter. Her name was Michelle, too. I guess I really had two visitors this night—the girl downstairs and the daughter here in memory. How strange that they had the same name. I felt guilty for my deceit to the one downstairs, saying that I didn't have any children. I felt even worse knowing that I was denying the existence of my children.

My Michelle was about twenty-eight now, I thought. I wasn't exactly sure.

She had tried to help me when I had first lost everything. She let me sleep on her couch a few times and gave me what she could from her savings. Five dollars here, ten there. She even gave me two hundred dollars that she had received as a gift. But she had a small house, and her husband didn't want me sleeping there.

I remembered the last time I pulled into her driveway. She was feeding her two horses, and she looked up at the sound of my car. I could see a look in her eyes I had never seen there before. I knew in an instant that I had become a burden, an unwelcome guest. I was no longer wanted. I was a nuisance. It was three weeks before Christmas, and I had come to ask if I could sleep on her couch and borrow a few dollars—again. But I could tell from her body language that she would not help this time.

"Dad," she said. "If you have come here to ask for help again, I can't." Her voice was cracking. "I just don't have any money."

"I understand," I said. "I know this is hard for you. It's just that—well, I don't have any place to go."

"I'm sorry, Dad, but I can't have you here."

I walked over to her and hugged her tight. "I know," I said. "It's okay. I'll find somewhere else. I love you."

"Love you, too," Michelle said quietly, hugging me in return.

I walked back to the van. She looked at the ground. I got in and pulled away.

As I drove down the road, I felt a profound emptiness. I knew that I couldn't expect my daughter to understand my depression. I didn't understand it myself. If it was something that could be seen, like cancer, it might have been different for her. It must be hard for her to see me, her dad, like this. I had always been so strong, so confident, so full of life. Now her dad was a bum, looking for a handout and a couch to sleep on.

I promised myself that I would always love my daughter. But I knew I could not go back there. I never wanted to see that look in her eyes again. Not ever.

"Well, that is enough of that," I thought to myself, rolling over in my sleeping bag. I needed to get some sleep. I closed my eyes, began to make peace with my mind, and hoped for a silent night. I soon drifted off.

It was deep into the night when I heard a sound and felt a draft. I opened my eyes and saw a shadow move quickly across the wall.

It must be Michelle, I thought. She probably got scared downstairs. "Michelle?" I called out. There was no answer. It was quiet in the sanctuary. I closed my eyes again.

"Hello, sir," I heard a voice say. I opened my eyes quickly. But no one was there. I closed them again, thinking I must have been dreaming.

"Richard," the voice called out again. This time I kept my eyes shut tight. It had to be just a dream. Willow began to stir inside the sleeping bag, and she crawled to the opening. She climbed out and sat right by my side, but she didn't bark. I kept my eyes closed.

"We saw what you did for the girl," the voice said. "That was good of you."

"Will I get in trouble?" I asked.

"Oh, no; not at all. We will wake her up and get her off to her job in the morning," the voice replied. It was a powerful voice. It was the voice of a big, strong man.

"Who are 'we'?" I asked, eyes still tightly shut.

"I'm Horace," the voice replied. "I used to be the pastor here—oh, sixty or seventy years ago. I used to give 'em hell. I used to *scare* them to heaven!"

"You are scaring me now," I said.

"Nothing to be frightened of. I'm just here in spirit. We have been watching you."

"You said, 'we.' Are there others here?"

"Oh, yes. There are lots of us. We visit here. Long ago, after spending our days pounding metal at the navy base, selling real estate, working in the hospitals and restaurants, we did our best work here! We built the church, fed the poor, comforted the sick, and visited the lonely. It was here we were at our very best."

"Have you come to take me? I have prayed for that."

"Oh, no, no, no," the voice said. "You have much to do!"

"What am I to do?" I asked.

"It will come to you, and you will have much help," the voice replied. "In the meantime, somebody is here to talk to you."

There was a moment of utter silence, and then I felt the warmest feeling I had felt in many years. It was the warmth of my mother. "Richard?" her voice filled me.

"Mother?" I was stunned.

"Yes, son," the new voice said. "I want you to know I have been with you all the time during your journey. I was there when you were looking at the photos with Marcia in the hospital, there when you were helping Andy, and there at Lilly's. I am so proud of you."

"Mother, take me with you."

"No, you have things to do first. But I want you to know that I found your sister who was lost, and I am with your other sister and your brother and your father. We have been and will always be with you. I love you. And you, Willow the Wonder Dog, I want to thank you for taking such good care of my child. I love you, too."

Then the voices stopped. I listened intently in the silence, but I knew they were gone. I didn't need to open my eyes to be certain of that.

After a moment, Willow sighed, yawned, and wriggled back into the sleeping bag and settled into sleep.

I didn't understand what had just happened, and I doubted I would ever be able to ask anyone to help me figure it out. Were the voices real or imagined? Was I awake or dreaming? Somehow I wasn't worried about that. I had come to trust that not all things need to be understood or explained.

It didn't really seem to matter where or how truth came, or how we found the strength to continue sometimes.

At this moment, I wasn't even concerned about what I had to do.

The voices were gone. But the warmth I felt remained and covered me gently.

Chapter 33

SO MUCH TO WRITE

I awoke in the morning with Willow standing on my chest, licking my face. The sun was shining through a stained-glass window.

My little dog was doing her utmost to wipe the sleep from my eyes and clean away the remnants of the tears from the night before. I reached out and patted her on the head. "Is it time to get moving?" I asked.

I stretched my arms above my head, and she jumped off my chest onto the carpet. Now that I was conscious, I was eager to tell C of my nocturnal visitors and see what he thought. I wondered if I had reached a new level of craziness.

I quickly rolled up my sleeping bag, stowed it under a pew, and slipped on my shoes. Then I headed out to find C and the Armadillo. It was just after seven when we pulled into the lot of Allen's Mini-Mart. The Armadillo was gone.

My mind raced with speculations about the fate of my friend. Had the police finally caught up with him and put him in jail? Where were MyLynx and Calico? The only vestige of their existence was a pile of cat litter near the spot where the Armadillo had sat for so long.

I didn't know what to do except to ask Allen if he knew anything. I expected him to shake his head and grunt like he always did. I picked Willow up and carried her into the store.

"Hello, Richard." Allen greeted me, jumping off his stool. "This must be Willow the Wonder Dog. I have heard a lot about her." He reached across the counter and patted her gently.

The warm greeting left me at a loss for words. Overcoming my shock, I asked the obvious. "Where did C go?"

Allen reached below the counter and held up a stained and wrinkled brown paper bag. "He left this for you." Allen was smiling as he handed me the bag.

I opened it, and inside was a bottle of Dom Perignon champagne. I held it up and looked at the label. It was 1943, the year I was born.

"Very good," said Allen. "Very good year."

"Where is he?"—another obvious question.

Allen reached out and hit the round bell. It rang loudly. Then he extended his arms and waved them up and down like a bird in flight.

"You know C. He's an angel!" Allen exclaimed and smiled.

I was stunned. My mind was in turmoil for a moment, and then I understood.

God had, after all, sent me many angels. I had been blessed—blessed to meet C, blessed by the Lady in Red, blessed to be fed by Mrs. Peebles, to talk to Marcia at the hospital, to share time with Andy before he died, to look into the eyes of Karen before she took her life at the bridge. I was blessed to experience the Major's mystery pitch and Mary's miraculous hit, blessed to walk into the woods to visit Adam at The Hilton, to have Rodney share his lucky rocks with me, to be there for Lilly's dance for David, to share s'ghetti with Dorothea, Elijah, and Dustin. I was blessed to be watched over by the pastor as I slept in the parking lot of one church, and to be received as a beloved family member by a another pastor whose church had become my home.

Many were there to steady me if I began to fall—with a hot meal or a few dollars, with a caring glance or a touch of the hand, with kindness, understanding, and love. They treated me with respect, dignity, and grace, while so many others had snickered and scorned.

C was my Number One Angel.

He was a slovenly, half-blind, marijuana-smoking, drug-dealing, rum-drinking angel-in-training. He taught me the joy of rolling in the grass like a kid and helped me see the world through the eyes of others. He got me high by reading the works of the masters and got me flaming drunk on life.

C took me to windows where I could view the lives of others and opened up a chapter of the book of life—a chapter I had somehow missed. No one could have done it any better—not Joseph Campbell or Carlos Castaneda, not Steinbeck or Hemingway or Mann, not even Buddha or Jesus. He possessed knowledge beyond his years, and he had shared it with me, his fellow traveler.

C taught me you have to give half of what you have to help a fellow human being—and sometimes more. When the need is great enough, you must reach even deeper in your pocket and give all that you have to a stranger, with no hope of reward. And he taught me that this is the ultimate gift—not only to the receiver, but also to the one who gives.

Responding to a need is a leap of faith. *Life* is a leap of faith. And when you take that leap, you get the ultimate high, which no drug can supply and no amount of money can purchase—an irrepressible feeling that comes welling up from deep inside and causes every nerve to tingle. It makes you cry. It makes you trust that—somehow, somewhere, sometime—the things you need will come to you.

It's magic.

C had spread a roadmap before me with many paths to choose from. I could go on a bitter journey to a place of anger and hate, or head out on the highway of grace and kindness, though it may be the road less traveled and in greater need of repair.

I was going to choose the latter.

I had never told C of my journey to the bridge in the year I knew him. I had never learned his last name, or his real first name, for that matter. He had never told me. I had never asked.

"Thank you," I said, nodding to Allen and putting the gift back in the bag.

"You are a writer, right?" Allen asked.

"I'm trying to be."

"Well, you have a book to write. You must write now. I call you 'Peng-you'—that means 'Friend.'" Then Allen bowed to me from the waist, held up two fingers, and said, "Peace. Be safe!"

I bowed in return and then walked out of the mini-mart with my bottle of Dom Perignon.

After two years of wishing and waiting for the angel of death to take me in the night, I now wanted to live.

I had a reason and a passion to live. I had learned grace, found a new dignity—a real one, not based on what I owned—and a new identity, one that I loved. I was going to write a book.

Mark Twain's final chapter in *The Adventures of Huckleberry Finn* is entitled "Nothing More to Write." I, on the other hand, had *so much more* to write, and that would keep me alive for quite a while. I now had the wisdom of C, the knowledge of the street, and a new addiction, to the drug called Unconditional Love.

I was going to try to finish my book about people without a home. Would my writing open any hearts, minds, or doors so that other men, women, and children would not have to live in the street? Could it give a ray of hope to someone curled up under a blanket in a car or shivering in the cold in the woods? Would it help someone look twice and think twice when passing by a person in need?

I did not know. I had never been here before.

EPILOGUE
July 20, 2005

BE SELFISH: VOLUNTEER!

It was on July 20, 2002, that I became homeless.

I live in an apartment now, where Willow the Wonder Dog sits under the table as I write.

I was lucky. I am not sure I would have survived the last few years in Seattle or San Diego or Houston. The community in Bremerton, Washington, helped me out of homelessness. My miracle happened here.

Pastor Earl's soul provided everything my soul asked for that day in his office. Shelter in the church for nine months. Church members to cosign a rental agreement for an apartment. Others to fix my car when it broke down and to take Willow to the vet when she was sick. Still others to offer me friendship and family and the promise to be there when I die so that I don't have to fear dying alone. And Sandy to first edit this book. More importantly, by his own most gracious example, he put me in touch with God, so that we can have our own conversations now. Willow and I attend church every Sunday, where I sing in the choir; Willow sits beside me in the choir loft. She walks at my heel through the communion line, then eats the dropped crumbs of communion bread.

In the very act of writing this book, I have undergone healing. In 2003, I was diagnosed with depression-related memory loss; I could not recall the names of my grandchildren, friends or acquaintances throughout the years, streets I had lived on as a child, and many other details about my life. I didn't have a particular motive when I began writing; I just found my friend C very interesting to write about, and as I wrote I began to remember things and feel things and see things, and I wanted more. So I continued. Perhaps I am beginning to heal on many levels.

My daughter, Michelle, called me the other day and invited me to come to her house for Thanksgiving. We had turkey and dressing with all the trimmings and, best of all, I got to spend time with my eleven-year-old granddaughter, Sierra, who told me about her school, her friends, and the softball league she plays in each summer.

I gave a copy of my manuscript to Michelle and she read it. She then passed it on to my youngest son, Scott, in Ohio, who also read it. Scott then called me and flew out to buy me dinner the day after Christmas to tell me he loved the book. I had an exquisite salmon in a dill sauce with baby red potatoes and received an up-to-date photo of his family, including ten-year-old Makay, Kyler, now seven, and eleven-month-old Quiterie, which Scott tells me means "one who is in peace" in French. I still see my psychologist, Rodney, every two weeks, and he guides me down the river of life. I have learned to embrace my depression. I still go to the church dinners and play softball every Thursday on the Salvation Army "Field of Dreams" during the season. The Major is even talking about getting us some caps and T-shirts for the games.

Allen sold the mini-mart and went back to Hong Kong. It's now the newly remodeled Manette Mini-Mart and Deli. They even painted the inside of The Maple Leaf. But it still leans toward the road.

I love this town.

No, it's not perfect, but then a perfect town wouldn't be real, would it? The fact is there are more people living on the streets in this town and in towns across the country than there have been since the Great Depression. But there are also more people looking at the reality of homelessness and trying to do something about it. In Bremerton, several local churches have fought for and built a homeless shelter to house twenty men and one family. It has taken three years to wade through all the permit and construction complications. It seems so small compared to the four-story government center, the new and bigger jail, the convention center and parking facility, the new waterfront condo complex, and the new baseball field, but it is at least a start.

Many times, as I prepare to fall asleep with Willow beside me in my bed, I think about the hundreds of times we parked in a church parking lot and crawled into our sleeping bag in the damp and the cold, with no money in our pockets and no hope in our souls. We lived on daily miracles.

It was a journey I did not plan. But looking back, I would not change a day. Because I met and got to know so many wonderful people, including myself.

The homeless lost a dear friend when Mrs. Peebles passed away in February of 2006, at age seventy-four. Despite the repeated warnings from her doctor to slow down and let others do more of the work and the worrying at The Lord's Diner, she kept doing the things she loved and felt called to do. Her son, Michael, took over his mother's calling and, with a group of volunteers, still feeds hundreds of the hungry every Saturday and Sunday.

Gentleman Jake can be found at Sally's just about every day. He is now helping the guys coming back from Iraq. Many are homeless and lost.

C? He's off someplace helping some other souls, quoting Joseph Campbell, reading Shakespeare and Yeats from some bar stool and breaking bread with the poor and hopeless at a Sally's in Tulsa, Cincinnati, or Fargo. He's probably got the Armadillo parked next to some mini-mart and is reading *Hornblower* out loud to MyLynx.

Maybe he's in your town now.

IN APPRECIATION

"I get by with a little help from my friends."
—Lennon/McCartney

I have so many people to thank—people who made this book possible. Here are just a few:

Major James Baker of the Salvation Army in Bremerton, Washington, who helped me when I was down and out and gave me encouragement.

Pastor Earl Rice, First United Methodist Church, who got me off the streets and gave me a whole spacious church to live in. He renewed my faith in man and in God.

Michael Gordon, a talented and gifted young artist, who was able to capture personalities in his drawings that will help put a real face on homelessness.

Debbie Johnson, a friend who never gave up on me.

Sarah Murphy at Bainbridge Island Helpline, who would not allow me to stop writing in times of depression.

Rodney Hitchcock, my psychologist and mental-health guide, who, when I asked, "Is this book I'm writing some wild and crazy fantasy?" simply said, "No. You will be successful."

Robert Reinach, my psychiatrist.

Bill Hoke, a longtime friend and publishing advisor.

The poor and the homeless people of Bremerton, who treated me with respect, dignity, and kindness and offered me their friendship.

The women and men of the churches in Bremerton, Port Orchard, and Bainbridge Island, Washington, who provided free dinners.

Chuck Brewer, of the Perry Avenue Mall secondhand store, who gave me my Travelwriter, and Michael, who returned it to me.

Bill Sipple, Sharon Masters, Pastor Scott Huff, Reverend Randy Lord-Wilkinson, Dr. Thomas and Beatrice Burch, Bob Barnes, the YMCA staff who let me shower for free when I needed to, all the people at the First United Methodist Church, and the Baker family of Bremerton.

Roger Pike, for his literary advice.

Cindy Adams, who cashed my social security check and opened an account for me when no other bank would.

MaryLou Baille, who supported me emotionally and financially, and who was a veritable lifesaver for Willow.

Mildred "Mitty" Pratt, who was always there when I needed her most.

Lissa Jennings, known as the "clothes lady" for giving out free clothes at the Lord's Diner that kept me clean and stylish.

Ditto to Maryann and her helpers at God's Closet.

Lee Stiles, Director of Development at the Seattle headquarters of the Salvation Army North West, for his passion for the book and his desire to help the homeless.

Scott Sciuchetti, Donor Relations Director of the Salvation Army North West, for passing the word around about *Breakfast at Sally's,* and to Stacy Howard, Walt Mead, Captain Howard Bennett, and all the devoted people at the Salvation Army. James Knaggs, Commissioner of The Western Territory of the Salvation Army.

The kind people at TrueSense Marketing in Pittsburgh, Shawn Reed and his wife Karen, Nancy Shroads, and Matt Lorenz, who believed in my book.

Rachel Pritchett, Chris Henry, and Larry Steagall of the *Kitsap Sun*, and Danny Westneat of the *Seattle Times*.

For my editor Lilly Golden for her wonderful editing efforts.

For Tony Lyons at Skyhorse Publishing for taking a chance on a formerly homeless author with a story to tell.

Bill Block of the King County, Seattle Alliance to End Homelessness.

Sister Pat Millen of Catholic Community Services.

Bev Kincaid.

Gayle Smart who helped me and others have hope.

Leon and Christieann Martin.

Kristina Boewe, who as the church choir director invited me to sing joyfully again. Then, after reading the manuscript, she began singing for the homeless to give them a new wonderful voice. A gifted vocalist from hymns to rock and roll, she wrote a song from the book entitled "A Place Called Home," which she now sings with her daughter Madison and son Parker at events encouraging help for the homeless.

Mrs. Marcia Baker, Jim's wife.

Darla Quick, my friend and the administrative aide at the Salvation Army in Bremerton.

Guy and Christine Coe, and their son James and daughter Emily, who inspire me daily now.

This book has also led me back to my family.

My daughter, Michelle, gave me a notebook for my birthday. She wrote inside the cover: *Dad, here is to all your writings and thoughts. Keep working your magic.* I have been invited to many dinners at Michelle's and have had the thrill of seeing my granddaughter, Siena, play softball. She is a great second base player.

I have had a chance to visit my son Scott and his wife Sasha, and my four grandchildren: McKay, Quicarii, Vakai, and Kyler.

They think Grandpa is famous.

I have had the chance to see my granddaughter, Aimee.

And I am now a great grandpa.

All the readers of *Breakfast at Sally's* from around North America who have sent Willow and me hundreds of cards and letters—as you can see, this once lonely homeless man has got a lot of help, and I now have more friends offering to help others.

And last but not least, I must thank Willow the Wonder Dog, who accompanied me on this journey with nary a whine nor a whimper.

ABOUT THE AUTHOR

RICHARD LEMIEUX lived on the streets of Bremerton, Washington, with his dog, Willow, for a year and a half while writing *Breakfast at Sally's*. They lived and slept in his Oldsmobile van. Richard wrote on a secondhand manual typewriter at picnic tables in parks around the city. After eighteen months on the street, Richard and Willow were allowed by the pastor and the congregation of the First United Methodist Church to live inside the church. They were there for nine months. With the help of the church community, Richard moved into an apartment, where he finished his book a year later.

Richard was born in Urbana, Ohio, and attended Urbana College and Ohio State University. He was the sports director of WCOM Radio and a sportswriter and columnist for seventeen years at the *Springfield Sun* (Ohio), covering events ranging from Ohio State football and Cincinnati Reds baseball, to major professional golf and tennis tournaments, to basketball games and dog shows. He was known as "the Wizard" due to his uncanny knack for predicting the outcome of football and basketball games.

Richard has lived in Washington State since 1981. He worked as a fundraiser for the state Republican Party and also ran his own publishing company, The Source, producing medical and university directories for fourteen years. He became homeless when his business failed; he lost his livelihood, his home, his possessions, and his companion of seventeen years. Richard was diagnosed with severe depression in March 2003 after attempting to take his life by jumping off the Tacoma Narrows Bridge. His battle with depression continues.

Richard enjoyed taking Willow for long walks in the park. When he had money, he was an avid golfer and downhill skier, and he has traveled to Italy, France, Greece, Mexico, Panama, Costa Rica, the Bahamas, much of Canada, and forty states.

Willow was an avid grass-roller who found joy in meeting people and playing fetch with her ball, "Bounce."

Richard is now working on his second book, the story of a woman he met on his journey.

Richard has been the keynote speaker to large audiences at Microsoft, the Washington State Realtors and Indiana State Realtors conventions, and at a variety of companies across the United States and Canada. He has also spoke at many universities and colleges and his book is now required reading at Seattle University's "Poverty in America" course and at the University School of Nursing.

Breakfast at Sally's is more than just a book. It is a mission for Richard to try to help people understand homelessness and give hope to those that are homeless. If your company, university, or organization would like Richard to speak in your city, he can be reached by phone at 360-535-9591. Richard still uses his portable typewriter to write and does not have a computer. For more information or to contact Richard, visit his website at www.BreakfastatSallys.com.

WILLOW (August 1997–November 2009), Richard's constant and faithful companion, died on November the 21st, 2009, after an operation to remove cancer from her lung. At a memorial service for The Wonder Dog held in the Bremerton United Methodist Church, the mayor of Bremerton, Patty Lent, rose to say, "In the name of Willow and *Breakfast at Sally's* the city of Bremerton will make ending homelessness a top priority during my administration." Willow's spirit will live on. She is now rolling in heavenly grass.

Willow of 'Breakfast at Sally's' Fame Dies

By RACHEL PRITCHETT
RPRITCHETT@KITSAPSUN.COM

BREMERTON

Willow, the beloved dog and constant companion of Bremerton homelessness author Richard LeMieux, has died.

The 13-year-old bichon frise succumbed Saturday morning following cancer surgery Friday in a Lynnwood facility.

"There's so many people in this town that have loved that dog and cared about her," a tearful LeMieux said Saturday.

Maj. Jim Baker of the Bremerton Salvation Army was at LeMieux's side, offering what comfort he could.

LeMieux, author of "Breakfast at Sally's: One Homeless Man's Inspirational Journey," credits his dog with saving his life seven years ago when the thought of her caused him to pull back from jumping off the Tacoma Narrows Bridge. LeMieux was homeless and despondent then, and staying at the Bremerton Salvation Army, the inspiration for his book.

Since publication of the book last year, Willow has accompanied LeMieux on many presentations and book-signings across the nation.

"Her soul will live on," LeMieux said.

Willow died at the end of National Hunger and Homelessness Awareness Week.

BOOK CLUB OR CLASSROOM
DISCUSSION QUESTIONS

How would Richard's story have been different without the presence of Willow? Do you think that having the companionship of his dog affected Richard's outlook during his homelessness?

Richard notes that he had always asked for God to send him an angel, when instead he should have gone out looking for one. Do you agree with the idea that people must search to find goodness in the world? Why or why not?

Do you relate to any of the homeless people Richard encounters? Who, and why?

Do you think that Richard's journey to his faith is an important part of the story? Why or why not?

What do you think compelled Richard to write about his experiences with homelessness? In similar circumstances, would you share your story?

Throughout the book, Richard experiences a shift in his understanding of value. Having lost so much, he realizes the value of things he may have overlooked before he became homelessness. Where do you find true value in your own life?

Did Richard and Willow's story change your views about homelessness or cause to reevaluate them in any way? How so?

Think about your own encounters with homeless people and how you reacted. Did you exchange words with them? Give them money or food? Why or why not?

How did you feel knowing Richard's family would not help him in his time of need? What do you think could have caused them to act in this way?

Look up a local homeless shelter in your area and find out about volunteer opportunities. Take a trip with your book club, friends, or family and learn about Richard's experiences close up.

GETTING INVOLVED

"Nothing great was ever achieved without enthusiasm."
—Ralph Waldo Emerson

The making of *Breakfast at Sally's* is a tale of enthusiasm, persistence and dedication, and is a true example of the phrase, "It takes a village." After reading Richard's story, individuals and groups all over the country have been inspired to make a difference in their own communities. We are interconnected, and together we can make a difference. You personally can have a significant impact on the effort to end homelessness.

As you choose to get involved, keep these things in mind:
- Understand your individual strengths and talents, and use those gifts. We are most effective when we work from our strengths.
- Find out what existing organizations are doing in your area before starting something new. Consider how to help close the gaps in services.
- The solution is not *one* person doing *much*, but *many* doing *something*, and allowing compassion to spread.

Here's how to:

VOLUNTEER

Your time is invaluable. Dedicate your time and ideas to programs within your community and neighboring areas. We recommend:

- Organizing or participating in drives for local service agencies
- Examples include donating toiletries, toilet paper, socks, feminine hygiene products, diapers, wipes, sleeping bags, and bus passes. Consider a drive in your church or family, social or school group.
- Incorporating your skills to aid in efforts of housing first programs, supportive housing programs, and rapid re-housing initiatives
- Serving meals in your local soup kitchen
- Training homeless individuals for employment
- Working at a nearby housing organization
- Registering homeless persons to vote
- Recruiting others to join your efforts!
- Find a place to volunteer: www.hud.gov/volunteering/index.cfm

ADVOCATE

- Advocate for policies and programs that effectively serve homeless people at the local, state, and federal levels.
- Support plans that will create more affordable housing.
- Share your concerns with public officials and the media, and tell them that ending homelessness is important to you.
- The following resources are specially designed to aid in the advocacy for ending homelessness:
    - ◆ Visit the National Alliance to End Homelessness website: www.endhomelessness.org/section/policy/legislature
    - ◆ There, you'll find legislative updates and learn about bills Congress is currently considering that can have tremendous impact on how effectively and quickly communities across the nation are able to end homelessness.

The Advocacy section helps you choose the issues you wish to follow. It alerts you to important opportunities to join others who are making their voices heard in the critical struggle to end homelessness:
www.endhomelessness.org/section/policy/advocacy
Write a letter to your editor. Homelessness impacts every community. Give the homeless your voice by writing a letterabout your own opinions on the issue.
www.ehow.com/how_8921_write-letter-editor.html

STAY INVOLVED

We need people like you to keep this issue relevant and real. Stay connected to your local shelter, your community leaders, and national organizations to ultimately bring an end to homelessness. Also visit these worthy organizations online:

The National Alliance to End Homelessness
www.endhomelessness.org
The National Coalition for the Homeless
www.nationalhomeless.org
The National Policy and Advocacy Council on Homelessness
www.npach.org
The National Law Center on Homelessness & Poverty
www.nlchp.org
The Salvation Army
www.salvationarmy.org

There are many other worthy organizations nationwide and local meeting needs of those in your community. *Breakfast at Sally's* started in the heart of someone just like you. You too can make miracles happen.

The
WILLOW AND RICHARD
HOMELESS PROJECT

A foundation has been formed to help the homeless nationwide: The Willow and Richard Homeless Project.

Our work includes "actively cultivating a community of compassion" through homeless advocacy, sensitivity training, and targeted assistance projects. Presentations are given to school-age children, as well as to college, university, civic, and faith groups.

Richard has spoken to more than 400,000 people in the past four years alone, to groups such as the Long Island Coalition for the Homeless; The Microsoft Corporation Employee's Forum; The Indiana Realtor's Association, and many, many more from Portland, Maine to San Francisco, California.

If you would like to support the project, please send a check to:

The Willow and Richard Homeless Project
7653 Merastone Lane, Apt. F-102
Bremerton, WA 98311

For additional information, write to the address above, or visit **www.breakfastatsallys.com**.

If you wish to book Richard as an inspirational speaker, use the number listed on the website: (360) 535-9591.

44905600R00265